Residential Design
Using Autodesk Revit 2016

Daniel John Stine

SDC
Publications

SDC Publications
P.O. Box 1334
Mission, KS 66222
913-262-2664
www.SDCpublications.com
Publisher: Stephen Schroff

ISBN-13: 978-1-58503-977-7
ISBN-10: 1-58503-977-2

Printed and bound in the United States of America.

FOREWORD

To the Student:

This book has been written with the assumption that the reader has no prior experience using Autodesk® Revit®. The intent of this book is to provide the student with a well-rounded knowledge of the architectural tools and techniques for use in both school and industry.

The book consists of a series of tutorials which primarily focus on the development of a single project. When you finish the book you will have learned how to document and model all of the major architectural aspects of a residential project. This includes floor plans, interior and exterior elevations, wall and building sections, door and room finish schedules and organizing drawings on sheets for printing.

The disc has several videos that supplement the book. Studying these videos along with the book will help the reader to better understand Autodesk Revit features. The book and videos will also help you prepare for the Autodesk Revit Architecture Certification Exam; see Appendix B for more information.

Be sure to check out the additional material on the disc.

To the Instructor:

This book was designed for the architectural student using *Autodesk Revit 2016*. Note: a student can successfully work through this book using *Autodesk Revit Architecture 2016* as well. Throughout the book, the student develops a single family residence. The drawings start with the floor plans and develop all the way to photo-realistic renderings similar to the one on the cover of this book.

Throughout the book many Autodesk Revit architectural tools and techniques are covered while creating the house model. Also, in a way that is applicable to the current exercise, industry standards and conventions are covered. Access to the internet is required for some exercises.

Each chapter concludes with a self-exam and review questions. The answers to the self-exam questions are provided, but review question answers are not (they can only be found in the Instructor's Guide available from the publisher).

Since its initial release in 2005, this book has been updated every year for the latest version of Autodesk Revit. The printed text has always been available for the fall term.

An Instructor's Resource Guide is available for this book. It contains:
- Answers to the questions at the end of each chapter
- Example images of each exercise to be turned in (can be used to grade students' work)
- Outline of tools and topics to be covered in each lesson's lecture
- Suggestions for additional student work (for each lesson)
- Author's direct contact information

Errata:

Please check the publisher's website from time to time for any errors or typos found in this book after it went to the printer. Simply browse to www.SDCpublications.com, and then navigate to the page for this book. Click the **View/Submit errata** link in the upper right corner of the page. If you find an error, please submit it so we can correct it in the next edition.

You may contact the publisher with comments or suggestions at **service@SDCpublications.com**.

About the Author:

Dan Stine is a registered Architect with twenty-three years of experience in the architectural field. He currently works at LHB (a 250 person multidiscipline firm; www.LHBcorp.com) in Duluth, Minnesota as the BIM Administrator, providing training, customization and support for two regional offices. Dan has worked in a total of four firms. While at these firms, he has participated in collaborative projects with several other firms on various projects (including Cesar Pelli, Weber Music Hall – University of Minnesota - Duluth). Dan is a member of the Construction Specification Institute (CSI) and has taught AutoCAD and Revit Architecture classes for 12 years at Lake Superior College, and currently teaches Revit to Interior Design and Architecture students at North Dakota State University (NDSU); additionally, he is a Certified Construction Document Technician (CDT). He has presented at Autodesk University in Las Vegas (http://au.autodesk.com) and internationally via the Revit Technology Conference (http://www.revitconference.com). Mr. Stine has written the following textbooks (published by SDC Publications):

- *Residential Design Using Autodesk Revit 2016*
- *Architectural Commercial Design Using Autodesk Revit 2016*
- *Design Integration Using Autodesk Revit 2016 (Architecture, Structure and MEP)*
- *Interior Design Using Autodesk Revit 2016 (with co-author Aaron Hansen)*
- *Residential Design Using AutoCAD 2016*
- *Commercial Design Using AutoCAD 2013*
- *Chapters in Architectural Drawing (with co-author Steven H. McNeill, AIA, LEED AP)*
- *Interior Design Using Hand Sketching, SketchUp and Photoshop (also with Steven H. McNeill)*
- *Google SketchUp 2013 for Interior Designers; Just the Basics*

Thanks:

I could not have done this without the support from my family: Cheri, Kayla and Carter.

Many thanks go out to SDC Publications for making this book possible!

TABLE OF CONTENTS

Page

1. Getting Started with Autodesk® Revit® 2016
1-1	What is Revit Architecture 2016?	1-1
1-2	Overview of the Revit User Interface	1-11
1-3	Open, Save and Close a Revit Project	1-26
1-4	Creating a New Project	1-31
1-5	Using Pan and Zoom to View Your Drawings	1-33
1-6	Using Revit's Help System	1-38
1-7	Introduction to Autodesk 360	1-41
	Self-Exam and Review Questions	

2. Lake Cabin: FLOOR PLAN (The Basics)
2-1	Walls	2-1
2-2	Doors	2-5
2-3	Windows	2-7
2-4	Roof	2-9
2-5	Annotation and Dimensions	2-11
2-6	Printing	2-15
	Self-Exam and Review Questions	

3. Overview of Linework and Modify Tools
3-1	Lines and Shapes	3-1
3-2	Snaps	3-15
3-3	Edit Tools	3-20
3-4	Annotations	3-33
	Self-Exam and Review Questions	

4. Drawing 2D Architectural Objects
4-1	Sketching Rectilinear Objects	4-1
4-2	Sketching Objects with Curves	4-11
	Self-Exam and Review Questions	

5. Residence: FLOOR PLAN (First Floor)
5-1	Project Setup	5-1
5-2	Exterior Walls	5-7
5-3	Interior Walls	5-23
5-4	Doors, Openings and Windows	5-35
5-5	Adding a Fireplace	5-54
	Self-Exam and Review Questions	

6. Residence: FLOOR PLANS (Second Floor and Basement Plans)
6-1	View Setup and Enclosing the Shell	6-1
6-2	Adding the Interior Walls	6-6
6-3	Adding Doors, Openings and Windows	6-10
6-4	Basement Floor Plan	6-15
6-5	Stairs	6-22
6-6	Dimensions	6-35
	Self-Exam and Review Questions	

7. Residence: ROOF
7-1	Roof Design Options	7-1
7-2	Gable Roof	7-11
7-3	Low Roof Elements	7-19
7-4	Skylights	7-30
	Self-Exam and Review Questions	

8. Residence: FLOOR SYSTEMS AND REFLECTED CEILING PLANS

8-1	Floor Systems	8-1
8-2	Ceiling Systems (Susp. ACT and Gypsum Board)	8-16
8-3	Placing Light Fixtures	8-31
8-4	Annotations	8-36
	Self-Exam and Review Questions	

9. Residence: ELEVATIONS

9-1	Creating and Viewing Exterior Elevations	9-1
9-2	Modifying the Project Model: Exterior Elevations	9-9
9-3	Creating and Viewing Interior Elevations	9-16
9-4	Modifying the Project Model: Interior Elevations	9-22
9-5	Design Options	9-25
	Self-Exam and Review Questions	

10. Residence: SECTIONS

10-1	Specify Section Cutting Plane in Plan View	10-1
10-2	Modifying the Project Model in Section View	10-7
10-3	Wall Sections	10-15
10-4	Annotation and Detail Components	10-25
	Self-Exam and Review Questions	

11. Residence: INTERIOR DESIGN

11-1	Bathroom Layouts	11-1
11-2	Kitchen Layout	11-7
11-3	Furniture	11-20
11-4	Adding Guardrails	11-25
	Self-Exam and Review Questions	

12. Residence: SCHEDULES

12-1	Room and Door Tags	12-1
12-2	Generate a Door Schedule	12-6
12-3	Generate a Room Finish Schedule	12-10
	Self-Exam and Review Questions	

13. Residence: SITE TOOLS & PHOTO-REALISTIC RENDERING

13-1	Site Tools	13-1
13-2	Creating an Exterior Rendering	13-15
13-3	Rendering an Isometric in Section	13-28
13-4	Creating an Interior Rendering	13-35
13-5	Adding People to the Rendering	13-42
	Self-Exam and Review Questions	

14. Residence: CONSTRUCTION DOCUMENTS SET

14-1	Setting Up a Sheet	14-1
14-2	Sheet Index	14-10
14-3	Printing a Set of Drawings	14-17
	Self-Exam and Review Questions	

15. INTRODUCTION TO PHASING AND WORKSHARING

15-1	Introduction to Phasing	15-1
15-2	Introduction to Worksharing	15-10
15-3	Phasing Exercise	15-23
15-4	Worksharing Exercises	15-35
	Self-Exam and Review Questions	

16. INTRODUCTION TO REVIT CONTENT CREATION

16-1	Basic Family Concepts	16-1
16-2	The Box: Creating the Geometry	16-13
16-3	The Box: Adding Parameters	16-29
16-4	The Box: Formulas and Materials	16-45
16-5	The Box: Family Types and Categories	16-59
	Self-Exam & Review Questions	

DISC CONTENT

17. **INTRODUCTION TO COMPUTERS** - 46 pages
    17-1   Computer Basics: Terms and Functions
    17-2   Overview of the Windows User Interface
    17-3   File Management Introduction
              Self-Exam & Review Questions

Appendix A – ENGINEERING GRAPHICS - 38 pages

Appendix B – AUTODESK REVIT CERTIFICATION EXAM - 10 pages

Appendix C – ROOF STUDY WORKBOOK – DRAFT EDITION - 90 pages

Appendix D – FINDING MISSING ELEMENTS IN REVIT - 24 pages

Appendix E – INTRODUCTION TO HAND SKETCHING - 42 pages

Appendix S – INTRODUCTION TO AUTODESK SHOWCASE - 80 pages

Videos

1. **User Interface**
2. **Walls**
3. **Doors and Windows**
4. **Stairs**
5. **Roofs**
6. **Floors**
7. **Ceilings**
8. **Elevations**
9. **Sections**
10. **Schedules**
11. **Rendering**
12. **Design Options**
13. **Sheets and Sheet Lists**
14. **Worksharing Introduction**
15. **Phases**
16. **Sweeps and Reveals**

Notes:

Lesson 1
Getting Started with Autodesk Revit 2016:

This chapter will introduce you to Autodesk® Revit® 2016. You will study the User Interface and learn how to open and exit a project and adjust the view of the drawing on the screen. It is recommended that you spend an ample amount of time learning this material, as it will greatly enhance your ability to progress smoothly through subsequent chapters.

Exercise 1-1:
What is Revit Architecture 2016?

What is Autodesk Revit used for?

Autodesk Revit (Architecture, Structure and MEP) is the world's first fully parametric building design software. This revolutionary software, for the first time, truly takes architectural computer aided design beyond simply being a high tech pencil. Revit is a product of Autodesk, makers of AutoCAD, Civil 3D, Inventor, 3DS Max, Maya and many other popular design programs.

Revit can be thought of as the foundation of a larger process called **Building Information Modeling** (BIM). The BIM process revolves around a virtual, information rich 3D model. In this model all the major building elements are represented and contain information such as manufacturer, model, cost, phase and much more. Once a model has been developed in Revit, third-party add-ins and applications can be used to further leverage the data. Some examples are Facilities Management, Analysis (Energy, Structural, Lighting), Construction Sequencing, Cost Estimating, Code Compliance and much more!

Revit can be an invaluable tool to designers when leveraged to its full potential. The iterative design process can be accomplished using special Revit features such as *Phasing* and *Design Options*. Material selections can be developed and attached to various elements in the model, where one simple change adjusts the wood from oak to maple throughout the project. The power of schedules may be used to determine quantities and document various parameters contained within content (this is the "I" in BIM, which stands for Information). Finally, the three-dimensional nature of a Revit-based model allows the designer to present compelling still images and animations. These graphics help to more clearly communicate the design intent to clients and other interested parties. This book will cover many of these tools and techniques to **assist** in the creative process.

What is a parametric building modeler?

Revit is a program designed from the ground up using state-of-the-art technology. The term parametric describes a process by which an element is modified and an adjacent element(s) is automatically modified to maintain a previously established relationship. For example, if a wall is moved, perpendicular walls will grow, or shrink, in length to remain attached to the related wall. Additionally, elements attached to the wall will move, such as wall cabinets, doors, windows, air grilles, etc.

Revit stands for **Rev**ise **I**nstantly; a change made in one view is automatically updated in all other views and schedules. For example, if you move a door in an interior elevation view, the floor plan will automatically update. Or, if you delete a door, it will be deleted from all other views and schedules.

A major goal of Revit is to eliminate much of the repetitive and mundane tasks traditionally associated with CAD programs allowing more time for design, coordination and visualization. For example, all sheet numbers, elevation tags and reference bubbles are updated automatically when changed anywhere in the project. Therefore it is difficult to find a mis-referenced detail tag.

The best way to understand how a parametric model works is to describe the Revit project file. A single Revit file contains your entire building project. Even though you mostly draw in 2D views, you are actually drawing in 3D. In fact, the entire building project is a 3D model. From this 3D model you can generate 2D elevations, 2D sections and perspective views. Therefore, when you delete a door in an elevation view you are actually deleting the door from the 3D model from which all 2D views are generated and automatically updated.

Window model size controlled by parameters *Width* and *Height*

Another way in which Revit is a parametric building modeler is that **parameters** can be used to control the size and shape of geometry. For example, a window model can have two *parameters* set up which control the size of the window. Thus, from a window's properties it is possible to control the size of the window without using any of the drawing modify tools such as *Scale* or *Move*. Furthermore, the *parameter* settings (i.e., width and height in this example) can be saved within the window model (called a *Family*). You could have the 2′ x 4′ settings saved as "Type A" and the 2′ x 6′ as "Type B." Each saved list of values is called a *Type* within the *Family*. Thus, this one double-hung window *Family* could represent an unlimited number of window sizes! You will learn more about this later in the book.

What about the different "flavors" of Revit?

Revit comes in three different "flavors": **Revit Architecture**, **Revit Structure** and **Revit MEP** (which stands for Mechanical, Electrical and Plumbing). There is also a fourth option in which all disciplines are available in one application; this is just called **Revit**. The all-in-one version only comes with the *Autodesk Building Design Suite* Premium or Ultimate. Any "flavor" of Revit can open and edit the same Revit project file or content (aka, *Families*). The only requirement is that each "flavor" of Revit be the same version, for example, Autodesk Revit Architecture 2016, Autodesk Revit Structure 2016 and Autodesk Revit MEP 2016.

The tutorials in this textbook are based on Revit; you can also use Revit Architecture. You can download the free 30 day trial from autodesk.com. Students may download a free 3 year version of Revit, the all-in-one version, at www.autodesk.com/education.

Revit model of an existing building, with architecture, structural, mechanical, plumbing and electrical all modeled.

Image courteous of LHB, Inc.   www.LHBcorp.com

Now is as good a time as any to make sure the reader understands that Revit is not, nor has it ever been, backwards compatible. This means there is no *Save-As* back to a previous version of Revit. Also, an older version of Revit cannot open a file, project or content, saved in a newer format. So make sure you consider what version your school or employer is currently standardized on before upgrading any projects or content. Revit will automatically upgrade an older format when opened in a newer version of the software. This is a onetime process which can take several minutes.

3D model of lunch room created in *Interior Design using Autodesk Revit 2016*

Lobby rendering from *Interior Design using Autodesk Revit 2016*

Why use Revit?

Many people ask the question, why use Revit versus other programs? The answer can certainly vary depending on the situation and particular needs of an individual or organization.

Generally speaking, this is why most companies use Revit:

- Many designers and drafters are using Revit to streamline repetitive drafting tasks and focus more on designing and detailing a project.
- Revit is a very progressive program and offers many features for designing buildings. Revit is constantly being developed and Autodesk provides incremental upgrades and patches on a regular basis; Revit 2016 was released about a year after the previous version.
- Revit was designed specifically for architectural design and includes features like:
  - *Mental Ray* and *Autodesk Renderer* Photo Realistic Rendering
  - Phasing; model changes over time
  - Design Options; model changes during the same time
  - Live schedules
  - Cloud Rendering via *Autodesk A360*
  - Conceptual Energy Analysis via *Autodesk A360*
  - Daylighting Analysis via *Autodesk A360*

A few basic Revit concepts:

The following is meant to be a brief overview of the basic organization of Revit as a software application. You should not get too hung up on these concepts and terms as they will make more sense as you work through the tutorials in this book. This discussion is simply laying the groundwork so you have a general frame of reference on how Revit works.

The Revit platform has three fundamental types of elements:
- Model Elements
- Datum Elements
- View-Specific Elements

Model Elements

Think of *Model Elements* as things you can put your hands on once the building has been constructed. They are typically 3D but can sometimes be 2D. There are two types of *Model Elements*:

- **Host Elements**: walls, floors, slabs, roofs, ceilings – Tools are the same for each "flavor" of Revit.

- **Model Components**: Stairs, Doors, Furniture, Beams, Columns, Pipes, Ducts, Light Fixtures, Model Lines – Options vary depending on the "flavor" of Revit, e.g., Revit MEP has a Duct tool whereas Revit Architecture and Revit Structure do not.

  o Some *Model Components* require a host before they can be placed within a project. For example, a window can only be placed in a host, which could be a wall, roof or floor depending on how the element was created. If the host is deleted, all hosted or dependent elements are automatically deleted.

Model Elements
Windows & Doors; require a host

Host Elements
Roof, Wall & Floor

Model Elements
Stair & Washer/Dryer; do not require a host

Datum Elements

Datum Elements are reference planes within the building that graphically and parametrically define the location of various elements within the model. These features are available in all "flavors" of Revit. These are the three types of *Datum Elements*:

- **Grids**
  - Typically laid out in a plan view to locate structural elements such as columns and beams, as well as walls. Grids show up in plan, elevation and section views. Moving a grid in one view moves it in all other views as it is the same element. (See the next page for an example of a grid in plan view.)

- **Levels**
  - Used to define vertical relationships, mainly surfaces that you walk on. They only show up in elevation and section views. Many elements are placed relative to a *Level*; when the *Level* is moved those elements move with it (e.g., doors, windows, casework, ceilings). **WARNING:** *If a* Level *is deleted, those same "dependent" elements will also be deleted from the project!*

- **Reference Planes**
  - These are similar to grids in that they show up in plan and elevation or sections. They do not have reference bubbles at the end like grids. Revit breaks many tasks down into simple 2D tasks which result in 3D geometry. *Reference Planes* are used to define 2D surfaces on which to work within the 3D model. They can be placed in any view, either horizontally or vertically.

View-Specific Elements

As the name implies, the items about to be discussed only show up in the specific view in which they are created. For example, notes and dimensions added in the architectural floor plans will not show up in the structural floor plans. These elements are all 2D and are mainly communication tools used to accurately document the building for construction or presentations.

- **Annotation elements** (text, tags, symbols, dimensions)
  - Size automatically set and changed based on selected drawing scale

- **Details** (detail lines, filled regions, 2D detail components)

Grids

Dimensions

Text

Tags
(Door & Room)

Symbol
(North Arrow)

Filled
Region
(Cross Hatch)

File Types (and extensions):

Revit has four primary types of files that you will work with as a Revit user. Each file type, as with any Microsoft Windows based program, has a specific three letter file name extension, that is, after the name of the file on your hard drive you will see a period and three letters. They are:

.RVT	Revit project files; the file most used (also for backup files)
.RFA	Revit family file; loadable content for your project
.RTE	Revit template; a project starter file with office standards preset
.RFT	Revit family template; a family starter file with parameters

The Revit platform has three fundamental ways in which to work with the elements (for display and manipulation):

- Views
- Schedules
- Sheets

The following is a cursory overview of the main ideas you need to know. This is not an exhaustive study on views, schedules and sheets.

Views

Views, accessible from the *Project Browser* (see Page 5-4), is where most of the work is done while using Revit. Think of views as slices through the building, both horizontal (plans) and vertical (elevations and sections).

- **Plans**
  - A *Plan View* is a horizontal slice through the building. You can specify the location of the **cut plane** which determines if certain windows show up or how much of the stair is seen. A few examples are architectural floor plan, reflected ceiling plan, site plan, structural framing plan, HVAC floor plan, electrical floor plan, lighting [ceiling] plan, etc. The images below show this concept; the image on the left is the 3D BIM. The middle image shows the portion of building above the cut plane removed. Finally, the last image on the right shows the plan view in which you work and place on a sheet.

- **Elevations**
  - Elevations are vertical slices but where the slice lies outside the floor plan as in the middle image below. Each elevation created is listed in the *Project Browser*. The image on the right is an example of a South exterior elevation view, which is a "live" view of the 3D model. If you select a window here and delete it, the floor plans will update instantly.

- **Sections**
  - Similar to elevations, sections are also vertical slices. However, these slices cut through the building. A section view can be cropped down to become a wall section or even look just like an elevation. The images below show the slice, the portion of building in the foreground removed, and then the actual view created by the slice. A setting exists, for each section view, to control how far into that view you can see. The example on the right is "seeing" deep enough to show the doors on the interior walls.

- **3D and Camera**
  - In addition to the traditional "flattened" 2D views that you will typically work in, you are able to see your designs more naturally via 3D and Camera views. A 3D view is simply a non-perspective 3D view of the project viewed from the exterior. A Camera view is a true perspective view; cameras can be created both in and outside of the building. Like the 2D views, these 3D/Camera views can be placed on a sheet to be printed. Revit provides a number of tools to help explore the 3D view, such as Section Box, Steering Wheel, Temporary Hide and Isolate, and Render.

    The image on the left is a 3D view set to "shade mode" and has shadows turned on. The image on the right is a camera view set up inside the building; the view is set to "hidden line" rather than shaded, and the camera is at eyelevel.

Schedules

Schedules are lists of information generated based on content that has been placed, or modeled, within the project. A schedule can be created, such as the door schedule example shown below, that lists any of the data associated with each door that exists in the project. Revit allows you to work directly in the schedule views. Any change within a schedule view is a change directly to the element being scheduled. Again, if a door were to be deleted from this schedule, that door would be instantly deleted from the project.

	DOOR AND FRAME SCHEDULE											
DOOR NUMBER	DOOR				FRAME		DETAIL				FIRE RATING	HDWR GROUP
	WIDTH	HEIGHT	MATL	TYPE	MATL	TYPE	HEAD	JAMB	SILL	GLAZING		
1000A	3' - 8"	7' - 2"	WD		HM		11/A8.01	11/A8.01				
1046	3' - 0"	7' - 2"	WD	D10	HM	F10	11/A8.01	11/A8.01 SIM				34
1047A	6' - 0"	7' - 10"	ALUM	D15	ALUM	SF4	6/A8.01	6/A8.01	1/A8.01 SIM	1" INSUL		2	CARD READER N. LEAF
1047B	6' - 0"	7' - 2"	WD	D10	HM	F13	12/A8.01	11/A8.01 SIM			60 MIN	85	MAG HOLD OPENS
1050	3' - 0"	7' - 2"	WD	D10	HM	F21	8/A8.01	11/A8.01		1/4" TEMP		33
1051	3' - 0"	7' - 2"	WD	D10	HM	F21	8/A8.01	11/A8.01		1/4" TEMP		33
1052	3' - 0"	7' - 2"	WD	D10	HM	F21	8/A8.01	11/A8.01		1/4" TEMP		33
1053	3' - 0"	7' - 2"	WD	D10	HM	F21	8/A8.01	11/A8.01		1/4" TEMP		33
1054A	3' - 0"	7' - 2"	WD	D10	HM	F10	8/A8.01	11/A8.01		1/4" TEMP	-	34
1054B	3' - 0"	7' - 2"	WD	D10	HM	F21	8/A8.01	11/A8.01		1/4" TEMP	-	33
1055	3' - 0"	7' - 2"	WD	D10	HM	F21	8/A8.01	11/A8.01		1/4" TEMP		33
1056A	3' - 0"	7' - 2"	WD	D10	HM	F10	9/A8.01	9/A8.01			20 MIN	33
1056B	3' - 0"	7' - 2"	WD	D10	HM	F10	11/A8.01	11/A8.01			20 MIN	34
1056C	3' - 0"	7' - 2"	WD	D10	HM	F10	20/A8.01	20/A8.01			20 MIN	33
1057A	3' - 0"	7' - 2"	WD	D10	HM	F10	8/A8.01	11/A8.01			20 MIN	34
1057B	3' - 0"	7' - 2"	WD	D10	HM	F30	9/A8.01	9/A8.01		1/4" TEMP	20 MIN	33
1058A	3' - 0"	7' - 2"	WD	D10	HM	F10	9/A8.01	9/A8.01			-	33

Sheets

You can think of sheets as the pieces of paper on which your views and schedules will be printed. Views and schedules are placed on sheets and then arranged. Once a view has been placed on a sheet, its reference bubble is automatically filled out and that view cannot be placed on any other sheet. The setting for each view, called "view scale," controls the size of the drawing on each sheet; view scale also controls the size of the text and dimensions.

Exercise 1-2:
Overview of the Revit User Interface

Revit is a powerful and sophisticated program. Because of its powerful feature set, it has a measurable learning curve, though its intuitive design makes it easier to learn than other CAD or BIM based programs. However, like anything, when broken down into smaller pieces, we can easily learn to harness the power of Revit. That is the goal of this book.

This section will walk through the different aspects of the User Interface (UI). As with any program, understanding the user interface is the key to using the program's features. Note that the image below shows the all-in-one Revit user interface. However, the UI is virtually identical between discipline versions with the exception of the total number of tabs available.

FIGURE 1-2.1 Revit User Interface

The Revit User Interface:

TIP: See the disc for a more in-depth look at the User Interface.

Application Title Bar:

In addition to the *Application Menu, Quick Access Toolbar* and *Info Center*, which are all covered in the next few sections, you are also presented with the product name, version and the current file-view, in the center. The product name shown (Figure 1-2.1) indicates the all-in-one version simply called *Revit*; depending on the software installed, you might also see *Revit Architecture, Revit Structure* and/or *Revit MEP* listed. As previously noted already, the version is important as you do not want to upgrade unless you have coordinated with other staff and/or consultants; everyone must be using the same version of Revit.

Application Menu:

Access to *File* tools such as *Save, Plot, Export* and *Print* (both hardcopy and electronic printing). You also have access to tools which control the Revit application as a whole, not just the current project, such as *Licensing* and *Options* (see the end of this section for more on *Options*).

Recent and Open Documents:

These two icons (from the *Application* menu) toggle the entire area on the right to show either the recent documents you have been in (icon on the left) or a list of the documents you currently have open.

In the *Recent Documents* list you click a listed document to open it. This saves time as you do not have to click *Open* → *Project* and browse for the document (*Document* and *Project* mean the same thing here). Finally, clicking the "Pin" keeps that project from getting bumped off the list as additional projects are opened.

In the *Open Documents* list the "active" project you are working in is listed first; clicking another project switches you to that open project.

The list on the left, in the *Application Menu* shown above, represents three different types of buttons: *button, drop-down button* and *split button*. Save and Close are simply **buttons**. Save-As and Export are **drop-down buttons**, which means to reveal a group of related tools. If you click or hover your cursor over one of these buttons, you will get a list of tools on the right. Finally, **split buttons** have two actions depending on what part of the button you click on; hovering over the button reveals the two parts (see bottom image to the right). The main area is the most used tool; the arrow reveals additional related options.

Button

Drop-down Button

Split Button

Quick Access Toolbar:

Referred to as *QAT* in this book, this single toolbar provides access to often used tools (*Open, Save, Undo, Redo, Measure, Tag,* etc.). It is always visible regardless of what part of the *Ribbon* is active.

The *QAT* can be positioned above or below the *Ribbon* and any command from the *Ribbon* can be placed on it; simply right-click on any tool on the *Ribbon* and select *Add to Quick Access Toolbar.* Moving the *QAT* below the *Ribbon* gives you a lot more room for your favorite commands to be added from the *Ribbon.* Clicking the larger down-arrow to the far right reveals a list of common tools which can be toggled on and off.

Some of the icons on the *QAT* have a down-arrow on the right. Clicking this arrow reveals a list of related tools. In the case of *Undo* and *Redo,* you have the ability to undo (or redo) several actions at once.

Ribbon – Architecture Tab:

The *Architecture* tab on the *Ribbon* contains most of the tools the architect needs to model a building, essentially the things you can put your hands on when the building is done. The specific discipline versions of Revit omit some of the other discipline tabs.

Each tab starts with the *Modify* tool, i.e., the first button on the left. This tool puts you into "selection mode" so you can select elements to modify. Clicking this tool cancels the current tool and unselects elements. With the *Modify* tool selected you may select elements to view their properties or edit them. Note that the *Modify* tool, which is a button, is different than the *Modify* tab on the *Ribbon*.

The *Ribbon* has three types of buttons, *button*, *drop-down button* and *split*, as covered on the previous page. In the image above you can see the *Wall* tool is a **split button**. Most of the time you would simply click the top part of the button to draw a wall. Clicking the down-arrow part of the button, for the *Wall* tool example, gives you the option to draw a *Wall*, *Structural Wall*, *Wall by Face*, *Wall Sweep*, and a *Reveal*.

TIP: The Model Text tool is only for placing 3D text in your model, not for adding notes!

Ribbon – Annotate Tab:

To view this tab, simply click the label "Annotate" near the top of the *Ribbon*. This tab presents a series of tools which allow you to add notes, dimensions and 2D "embellishments" to your model in a specific view, such as a floor plan, elevation, or section. All of these tools are **view specific**, meaning a note added in the first floor plan will not show up anywhere else, not even another first floor plan: for instance, a first floor electrical plan.

Notice, in the image above, that the *Dimension* panel label has a down-arrow next to it. Clicking the down-arrow will reveal an **extended panel** with additional related tools.

Finally, notice the *Component* tool in the image above; it is a **split button** rather than a *drop-down button*. Clicking the top part of this button will initiate the *Detail Component* tool. Clicking the bottom part of the button opens the fly-out menu revealing related tools. Once you select an option from the fly-out, that tool becomes the default for the top part of the split button for the current session of Revit (see image to right).

Ribbon – Modify Tab:

Several tools which manipulate and derive information from the current model are available on the *Modify* tab. Additional *Modify* tools are automatically appended to this tab when elements are selected in the model (see *Modify Contextual Tab* on the next page).

> *TIP: Do not confuse the Modify tab with the Modify tool when following instructions in this book.*

Ribbon – View Tab:

The tools on the *View* tab allow you to create new views of your 3D model; this includes views that look 2D (e.g., floor plans, elevations and sections) as well as 3D views (e.g., isometric and perspective views).

The *View* tab also gives you tools to control how views look, everything from what types of elements are seen (e.g., Plumbing Fixture, Furniture or Section Marks) as well as line weights.

> *NOTE: Line weights are controlled at a project wide level but may be overridden on a view by view basis.*

Finally, notice the little arrow in the lower-right corner of the *Graphics* panel. When you see an arrow like this you can click on it to open a dialog box with settings that relate to the panel's tool set (*Graphics* in this example). Hovering over the arrow reveals a tooltip which will tell you what dialog box will be opened.

Ribbon – Modify Contextual Tab:

The *Modify* tab is appended when certain tools are active or elements are selected in the model; this is referred to as a *contextual tab*. The first image below shows the *Place Wall* tab which presents various options while adding walls. The next example shows the *Modify Walls* contextual tab which is accessible when one or more walls are selected.

Place Wall contextual tab – visible when the Wall tool is active.

Modify Walls contextual tab – visible when a wall is selected.

Ribbon – Customization:

There is not too much customization that can be done to the *Ribbon*. One of the only things you can do is pull a panel off the *Ribbon* by clicking and holding down the left mouse button on the titles listed across the bottom. This panel can be placed within the *drawing window* or on another screen if you have a dual monitor setup.

The image above shows the *Build* panel, from the *Architecture* tab, detached from the *Ribbon* and floating within the drawing window. Notice that the *Insert* tab is active. Thus, you have constant access to the *Build* tools while accessing other tools. Note that the *Build* panel is not available on the *Architecture* tab as it is literally moved, not just copied.

When you need to move a detached panel back to the *Ribbon* you do the following: hover over the detached panel until the sidebars show up and then click the "Return panels to ribbon" icon in the upper right (identified in the image above).

FYI: Whenever the resolution of your monitor is too low or you don't have the Revit application maximized on the screen the buttons may be modified to take up less room on the Ribbon; typically the words are removed. Compare the image to the right with the Build panel above.

If you install an **add-in** for Revit on your computer, you will likely see a new tab appear on the Ribbon. Some add-ins are free while others require a fee. If an add-in only has one tool, it will likely be added to the catch-all tab called Add-Ins (shown in the image below).

Ribbon – States:

The *Ribbon* can be displayed in one of four states:

- Full Ribbon (default)
- Minimize to Tabs
- Minimize to Panel Tiles
- Minimize to Panel Buttons

The intent of this feature is to increase the size of the available drawing window. It is recommended, however, that you leave the *Ribbon* fully expanded while learning to use the program. The images in this book show the fully expanded state. The images below show the other three options. When using one of the minimized options you simply hover (or click) your cursor over the Tab or Panel to temporarily reveal the tools.

FYI: Double-clicking on a Ribbon tab will also toggle the states.

Minimize to Tabs

Minimize to Panel Tiles

Minimize to Panel Buttons

Ribbon – References in this Book:

When the exercises make reference to the tools in the *Ribbon* a consistent method is used to eliminate excessive wording and save space. Take a moment to understand this so that things go smoothly for you later.

Throughout the textbook you will see an instruction similar to the following:

23. Select **Architecture** → **Build** → **Wall**

This means click the ***Architecture*** tab, and within the ***Build*** panel, select the ***Wall*** tool. Note that the *Wall* tool is actually a split button, but a subsequent tool was not listed so you are to click on the primary part of the button. Compare the above example to the one below:

23. Select **Architecture** → **Build** → **Wall** → **Structural Wall**

The above example indicates that you should click the down-arrow part of the *Wall* tool in order to select the *Structural Wall* option.

Thus the general pattern is this:

Tab → Panel → Tool → drop-down list item

#1 *Tab:* This will get you to the correct area within the *Ribbon*.

#2 *Panel:* This will narrow down your search for the desired tool.

#3 *Tool:* Specific tool to select and use.

Drop-down list item: This will only be specified for drop-down buttons and sometimes for split buttons.

The image below shows the order in which the instructions are given to select a tool; note that you do not actually click the panel title.

Options Bar:

This area dynamically changes to show options that complement the current operation. The *Options Bar* is located directly below the *Ribbon*. When you are learning to use Revit you should keep your eye on this area and watch for features and options appearing at specific times. The image below shows the *Options Bar* example with the *Wall* tool active.

| Modify | Place Wall | Height ▼ | Unconn ▼ | 20' 0" | Location Line: Wall Centerline ▼ | ☑ C |

Properties Palette – Element Type Selector:

The *Properties Palette* provides instant access to settings related to the element selected or about to be created. When nothing is selected, it shows information about the current view. When multiple elements are selected, the common parameters are displayed.

The *Element Type Selector* is an important part of the *Properties Palette*. Whenever you are adding elements or have them selected, you can select from this list to determine how a wall to be drawn will look, or how a wall previously drawn should look (see image to right). If a wall type needs to change, you never delete it and redraw it; you simply select it and pick a new type from the *Type Selector*.

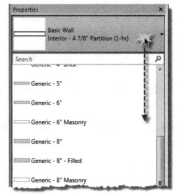

Type Selector; Wall tool active or a Wall is selected

The **Selection Filter** drop-down list below the *Type Selector* lets you know the type and quantity of the elements currently selected. When multiple elements are selected you can narrow down the properties for just one element type, such as *wall*. Notice the image to the right shows four walls are in the current selection set. Selecting **Walls (4)** will cause the *Palette* to only show *Wall* properties even though many other elements are selected (and remain selected).

The width of the *Properties Palette* and the center column position can be adjusted by dragging the cursor over that area. You may need to do this at times to see all the information. However, making the *Palette* too wide will reduce the useable drawing area.

Selection Filter; multiple elements selected

The *Properties Palette* should be left open; if you accidentally close it you can reopen it by **View → Window → User Interface → Properties** or by typing **PP** on the keyboard.

Project Browser:

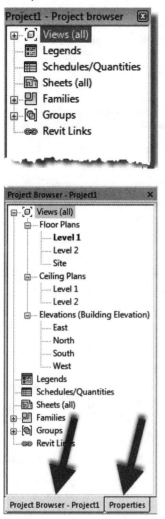

The *Project Browser* is the "Grand Central Station" of the Revit project database. All the views, schedules, sheets and content are accessible through this hierarchical list. The first image to the left shows the seven major categories; any item with a "plus" next to it contains sub-categories or items.

Double-clicking on a View, Legend, Schedule or Sheet will open it for editing; the current item open for editing is bold (**Level 1** in the example to the left). Right-clicking will display a pop-up menu with a few options such as *Delete* and *Copy*.

Right-click on *Views (all)*, at the top of the *Project Browser*, and you will find a **Search** option in the pop-up menu. This can be used to search for a *View*, *Family*, etc., a very useful tool when working on a large project with 100s of items to sift through.

Like the *Properties Palette*, the width of the *Project Browser* can be adjusted. When the two are stacked above each other, they both move together. You can also stack the two directly on top of each other; in this case you will see a tab for each at the bottom as shown in the second image to the left.

The *Project Browser* should be left open; if you accidentally close it, by clicking the "X" in the upper right, you can reopen it by **View → Window → User Interface → Project Browser**.

The *Project Browser* and *Properties Palette* can be repositioned on a second monitor, if you have one, when you want more room to work in the drawing window.

Status Bar:

This area will display information, on the far left, about the current command or list information about a selected element. The right hand side of the *Status Bar* shows the number of elements selected. The small funnel icon to the left of the selection number can be clicked to open the *Filter* dialog box, which allows you to reduce your current selection to a specific category; for example, you could select the entire floor plan, and then filter it down to just the doors. This is different than the *Selection Filter* in the *Properties Palette* which keeps everything selected.

On the *Status Bar*, the five icons on the right, shown in the image below, control how elements are selected. From left to right these are:

- Select Links
- Select Underlay Elements
- Select Pinned Elements
- Select Elements by Face
- Drag Elements on Selection

Hover your cursor over an icon for the name and for a brief description of what it does. These are toggles that are on or off; **the red 'X' in the upper right of each icon means you cannot select that type of element within the model.** These controls help prevent accidentally moving or deleting things. Keep these toggles in mind if you are having trouble selecting something; you may have accidentally toggled one of these on.

Finally, the two drop-down lists towards the center of the *Status Bar* control **Design Options** and **Worksets** (see image on previous page). The latter is not covered in this book but *Design Options* are. *Worksets* relate to the ability for more than one designer to be in the model at a time.

View Control Bar:

This is a feature which gives you convenient access to tools which control each view's display settings (i.e., scale, shadows, detail level, graphics style, etc.). The options vary slightly between view types: 2D View, 3D view, Sheet and Schedule. The important thing to know is that these settings only affect the current view, the one listed on the *Application Title Bar*. All of these settings are available in the *Properties Palette*, but this toolbar cannot be turned off like the *Properties Palette* can.

Context Menu:

The *context menu* appears near the cursor whenever you right-click on the mouse (see image at right). The options on that menu will vary depending on what tool is active or what element is selected.

Drawing Window:

This is where you manipulate the Building Information Model (BIM). Here you will see the current view (plan, elevation or section), schedule or sheet. Any changes made are instantly propagated to the entire database.

Context menu example with a wall selected

Elevation Marker:

This item is not really part of the Revit UI but is visible in the drawing window by default via the various templates you can start with, so it is worth mentioning at this point. The four elevation markers point at each side of your project and ultimately indicate the drawing sheet on which you would find an elevation drawing of each side of the building. All you need to know right now is that you should draw your floor plan generally in the middle of the four elevation markers that you will see in each plan view; DO NOT delete them as this will remove the related view from the *Project Browser*.

Revit Options:

There are several settings, related to the *User Interface*, which are not tied to the current model. That is, these settings apply to the installation of Revit on your computer, rather than applying to just one model or file on your computer. A few of these settings will be briefly discussed here. It is recommended that you don't make any changes here right now.

Click on **Options** in the *Application Menu* (the purple "R"). The options in the <u>User Interface</u> section are fairly self-explanatory. In the <u>Graphics</u> section you can verify your display driver is approved (i.e., tested) by Autodesk. If Revit is crashing or exhibits strange behavior, it likely relates to your graphics driver. You can bypass this problem by turning off *Use Hardware Acceleration*, but this will make Revit run slower.

This concludes your brief overview of the Revit user interface. Many of these tools and operations will be covered in more detail throughout the book.

Efficient Practices

The *Ribbon* and menus are really helpful when learning a program like Revit; however, most experienced users rarely use them! The process of moving the mouse to the edge of the screen to select a command and then back to where you were is very inefficient, especially for those who do this all day long, five days a week. Here are a few ways experienced BIM operators work:

- Use the wheel on the mouse to Zoom (spin the wheel), Pan (press and hold the wheel button while moving the mouse) and Zoom Extents (double-clicking the wheel button). All this can be done while in another command; so, if you are in the middle of drawing walls and need to zoom in to see which point you are about to Snap to, you can do it without canceling the Line command and without losing focus on the area you are designing by having to click an icon near the edge of the screen.

- Revit conforms to many of the Microsoft Windows operating system standards. Most programs, including Revit, have several standard commands that can be accessed via keyboard shortcuts. Here are a few examples (press both keys at the same time):

  - Ctrl + S   Save   *(saves the current model)*
  - Ctrl + A   Select All   *(selects everything in text editor)*
  - Ctrl + Z   Undo   *(undoes the previous action)*
  - Ctrl + X   Cut   *(Cut to Windows clipboard)*
  - Ctrl + C   Copy   *(does not replace Revit's Copy tool)*
  - Ctrl + V   Paste   *(used to copy between models/views/levels)*
  - Ctrl + Tab   Change View   *(toggles between open views)*
  - Ctrl + P   Print   *(opens print dialog)*
  - Ctrl + N   New   *(create new project file)*
  - F7   Spelling   *(launch spell check feature)*
  - ENTER   Previous Command   *(repeat previous command)*

- If you recall, the *Open Documents* area in the *Application* menu lists all the views that are currently open on your computer. By clicking one of the names in the list you "switch" to that view. A shortcut is to press **Ctrl + Tab** to quickly cycle through the open drawings.

- Many Revit commands also have keyboard shortcuts. So, with your right hand on the mouse (and not moving from the "design" area), your left hand can type **WA** when you want to draw a Wall for example. You can see all the preloaded shortcuts and add new ones by clicking *View (tab)* → *User Interface (drop-down)* → *Keyboard Shortcuts*.

It should be noted that any customized keyboard shortcuts are specific to the computer you are working on, not the project. You can use the *Export* button (see image to right) to save the entire keyboard shortcuts list to a file, and then *Import* it into another computer's copy of Revit.

This concludes your brief overview of the Revit user interface. Many of these tools and operations will be covered in more detail throughout the book.

Keyboard shortcuts dialog

Exterior rendering from Design Integration using Autodesk Revit 2016

Exercise 1-3:
Open, Save and Close a Revit Project

To *Open* **Revit 2016**:

Start → All Programs → Autodesk → Autodesk Revit 2016

Revit 2016

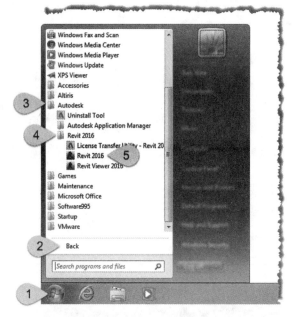

Or double-click the Revit icon from your desktop.

This may vary slightly on your computer; see your instructor or system administrator if you need help.

TIP: If you are using a discipline-specific version of Revit you will see one of the following options:
- Revit Architecture 2016
- Revit MEP 2016
- Revit Structure 2016

FIGURE 1-3.1 Starting Revit

How to Open a Revit Project:

By default, Revit will open in the *Recent Files* window, which will display thumbnails of recent projects you have worked on. Clicking on the preview will open the project.

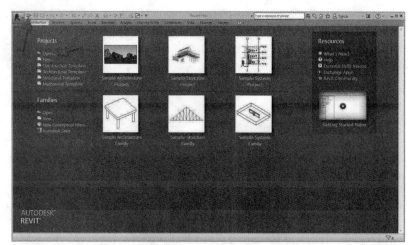

1. Click the **Open** link (see the image to the right).

FIGURE 1-3.2 Recent Files startup screen

You may click open under *Project* or on the *Quick Access Toolbar*.

Next you will open an existing Revit project file. You will select a sample file provided on the disc that came with this book.

2. Click the drop-down box at the top of the *Open* dialog (Figure 1-3.3). Browse to your disc drive; the drive letter will vary from computer to computer.

    TIP: If you cannot locate the disc that came with this textbook, you can substitute any Revit file you can find. Some sample files may be found here on your computer's hard drive:
    C:\Program Files\Autodesk\Revit 2016\Samples

FIGURE 1-3.3 Open dialog; disc contents shown

3. Select the file named **Office Building.rvt** and click **Open**.

FYI: Notice the preview of the selected file. This will help you select the correct file before taking the time to open it.

The *Office Building.rvt* file is now open and the last saved view is displayed in the drawing window (Figure 1-3.4).

FIGURE 1-3.4 Sample file "Office Building.rvt"

The *Application Menu* lists the projects and views currently open on your computer (Figure 1-3.4).

4. Click **Application Menu →
    Open Documents (icon)**
    (Figure 1-3.5).

Notice that the *Office Building.rvt*
project file is listed. Next to the
project name is the name of a view
open on your computer (e.g., floor
plan, elevation).

Figure 1-3.5 Application Menu: Open Documents view

Additional views will be added to the list as you open them. Each view has the project name as a prefix. The current view, the view you are working in, is always at the top of the list. You can quickly toggle between opened views from this menu by clicking on them.

You can also use the *Switch Windows* tool on the *View* tab; both do essentially the same thing.

Switch
Windows

Opening Another Revit Project:

Revit allows you to have more than one project open at a time.

5. Click **Open** from the *Quick Access Toolbar*.

6. Per the instructions previously covered, browse to the **disc**.

7. Select the file named **Church Building.rvt** and click **Open** (Figure 1-3.6).

TIP: If you cannot locate the disc that came with this textbook, substitute one of the sample files.

FIGURE 1-3.6 Sample file "Church Building.rvt"

8. Click **Open Documents** from the *Application* menu (Figure 1-3.7).

Notice that the *Church Building.rvt* project is now listed along with a view: Floor Plan: Level 1.

Try toggling between projects by clicking on *Office Building.rvt – 3D View: 3D View 1.*

FIGURE 1-3.7 Open Documents

Close a Revit Project:

9. Select **Application menu → Close**; click **No** if prompted to save.

This will close the current project/view. If more than one view is open for a project, only the current view will close. The project and the other opened views will not close until you get to the last open view.

10. Repeat the previous step to close the other project file.

If you made changes and have not saved your project yet, you will be prompted to do so before Revit closes the view. **Do not save at this time.** When all open project files are closed, you find yourself back in the *Recent Files* screen – which is where you started.

Saving a Revit Project:

At this time we will not actually save a project.

To save a project file, simply select *Save* from the *Quick Access Toolbar.* You can also select *Save* from the *Application* menu or press *Ctrl + S* on the keyboard.

You should get in the habit of saving often to avoid losing work due to a power outage or program crash.

You can also save a copy of the current project by selecting **Save As** from the Application Menu. Once you have used the *Save As* command you are in the new project file and the file you started in is then closed.

Closing the Revit Program:

Finally, from the *Application* menu select **Exit Revit**. This will close any open projects/views and shut down Revit. Again you will be prompted to save, if needed, before Revit closes the view. **Do not save at this time**.

You can also click the "X" in the upper right corner of the *Revit Application* window.

| Exercise 1-4: |
| Creating a New Project |

Open **Autodesk Revit Architecture**.

Creating a New Project File:

The steps required to set up a new Revit Architecture model project file are very simple. As mentioned earlier, simply opening the Revit program starts you in the *Recent Files* window.

To manually create a new project (maybe you just finished working on a previous assignment and want to start the next one):

1. Select **Application menu → New → Project**.

   FYI: You can also select the New *link in the* Recent Files *startup screen.*

After clicking *New → Project* you will get the **New Project** dialog box (Figure 1-4.1).

FIGURE 1-4.1 New Project dialog box

The *New Project* dialog box lets you specify the template file you want to use, or not use a template at all. You can also specify whether you want to create a new project or template file.

2. Select the **Architectural Template** *template file*. Leave *Create new* set to **Project** (Figure 1-4.1).

3. Click **OK**. You now have a new unnamed/unsaved project file.

To name an unnamed project file you simply *Save*. The first time an unnamed project file is saved you will be prompted to specify the name and location for the project file.

4. Select **Application menu → Save** from the *Menu Bar*.

5. Specify a **name** and **location** for your new project file.
    Your instructor may specify a location or folder for your files if in a classroom setting.

What is a Template File?

A template file allows you to start your project with specific content and certain settings preset the way you like or need them.

For example, you can have the units set to *Imperial* or *Metric*. You can have the door, window and wall families you use most loaded and eliminate other less often used content. Also, you can have your company's title block preloaded and even have all the sheets for a project set up.

A custom template is a must for design firms using Revit and will prove useful to the student as he or she becomes more proficient with the program.

Be Aware:
It will be assumed from this point forward that the reader understands how to create, open and save project files. Please refer back to this section as needed. If you still need further assistance, ask your instructor for help.

Exercise 1-5:
Using Zoom and Pan to View Your Drawings

Learning to *Pan* and *Zoom* in and out of a drawing is essential for accurate and efficient drafting and visualization. We will review these commands now so you are ready to use them with the first design exercise.

Open **Revit Architecture**.

You will select a sample file from the disc that came with this textbook.

1. Select **Open** from the *Quick Access Toolbar.*

2. Browse to the **disc** (usually the D drive, but this can vary).

3. Select the file named **Church Building.rvt** and click **Open** (Figure 1-5.1).

> *TIP: If you cannot locate the disc that came with this textbook, substitute any of the training files that come with Revit, found at C:\Program Files\Autodesk\Revit 2016\Samples.*

FIGURE 1-5.1 Church Building.rvt project

If the default view that is loaded is not **Floor Plan: Level 1**, double-click on **Level 1** under **Views\Floor Plans** in the *Project Browser*. Level 1 will be bold when it is the active or current view in the drawing window.

Using Zoom and Pan Tools:

You can access the zoom tools from the *Navigation Bar*, or the *scroll wheel* on your mouse.

The *Zoom* icon contains several *Zoom* related tools:
- The default (i.e., visible) icon is *Zoom in Region*, which allows you to window an area to zoom into.
- The *Zoom* icon is a **split button**.
- Clicking the down-arrow part of the button reveals a list of related *Zoom* tools.
- You will see the drop-down list on the next page.

Zoom In

4. Select the top portion of the *Zoom* icon (see image to right).

5. Drag a window over your plan view (Figure 1-5.2).

Selection window: Pick two diagonal points, that is, two opposite corners to define the window.

FIGURE 1-5.2 Zoom In window

You should now be zoomed in to the specified area (Figure 1-5.3).

FIGURE 1-5.3 Zoom In results

Zoom Out

6. Click the down-arrow next to the zoom icon (Figure 1-5.4). Select **Previous Pan/Zoom**.

You should now be back where you started. Each time you select this icon you are resorting to a previous view state. Sometimes you have to select this option multiple times if you did some panning and multiple zooms.

7. **Zoom** into a smaller area, and then **Pan**, i.e., adjust the portion of the view seen by holding down the scroll wheel button.

FIGURE 1-5.4 Zoom Icon drop-down

The Pan tool just changes the portion of the view you see on the screen, it does not actually move the model.

Take a minute and try the other *Zoom* tools to see how they work. When finished, click **Zoom to Fit** before moving on.

TIP: You can double-click the wheel button on your mouse to Zoom Extents *in the current view.*

Default 3D View

Clicking on the *Default 3D View* icon, on the *QAT*, loads a 3D View. This allows you to quickly switch to a 3D view.

8. Click on the **Default 3D View** icon.

9. Go to the **Open Documents** listing in the *Application Menu* and notice the *3D View* and the *Floor Plan* view are both listed at the bottom.

    📂 Open Documents

    Church Building.rvt - 3D View: {3D}

    Church Building.rvt - Floor Plan: Level 1

    REMEMBER: You can toggle between views here.

10. Click the **Esc** key to close the *Application* menu.

ViewCube

The *ViewCube* gives you convenient view control over the 3D view. This technology has been implemented in many of Autodesk's programs to make the process seamless for the user.

11. You should notice the ***ViewCube*** in the upper right corner of the drawing window (Figure 1-5.5). If not, you can turn it on by clicking *View* → *Windows* → *User Interface* → *ViewCube*.

    TIP: The ViewCube only shows up in 3D views.

Hovering your cursor over the *ViewCube* activates it. As you move about the *Cube* you see various areas highlight. If you click, you will be taken to that highlighted area in the drawing window. You can also click and drag your cursor on the *Cube* to "roll" the model in an unconstrained fashion. Clicking and dragging the mouse on the disk below the *Cube* allows you to spin the model without rolling. Finally, you have a few options in a right-click menu, and the **Home** icon, just above the *Cube*, gets you back to where you started if things get disoriented!

Home icon

FIGURE 1-5.5 ViewCube

12. Give the *ViewCube* a try, then click the **Home** icon when you are done.

    REMEMBER: The Home icon only shows up when your cursor is over the ViewCube.

Navigation Wheel

Similar to the *ViewCube*, the *Navigation Wheel* aids in navigating your model. With the *Navigation Wheel* you can walk through your model, going down hallways and turning into rooms. Revit has not advanced to the point where the doors will open for you; thus, you walk through closed doors or walls as if you were a ghost!

The *Navigation Wheel* is activated by clicking the upper icon on the *Navigation Bar*.

Unfortunately, it is way too early in your Revit endeavors to learn to use the *Navigation Wheel*. You can try this in the chapter on creating photorealistic renderings and camera views. You would typically use this tool in a camera view.

Figure 1-5.6 Navigation Wheel

13. **Close** the *Church Building* project **without** saving.

Using the Scroll Wheel on the Mouse

The scroll wheel on the mouse is a must for those using BIM software. In Revit you can *Pan* and *Zoom* without even clicking a zoom icon. You simply **scroll the wheel to zoom** and **hold the wheel button down to pan**. This can be done while in another command (e.g., while drawing walls). Another nice feature is that the drawing zooms into the area near your cursor, rather than zooming only at the center of the drawing window. Give this a try before moving on. Once you get the hang of it, you will not want to use the icons. Also, double-clicking the wheel button does a *Zoom to Fit* so everything is visible on the screen.

Exercise 1-6:
Using Revit's Help System

This section of your introductory chapter will provide a quick overview of Revit's *Help System*. This will allow you to study topics in more detail if you want to know how something works beyond the introductory scope of this textbook.

1. Click the **round question mark** icon in the upper-right corner of the screen.

You are now in Revit's Help site (Figure 1-6.1). This is a website which opened in your web browser. The window can be positioned side by side with Revit, which is especially nice if you have a dual-screen computer system. This interface requires a connection to the internet. As a website, Autodesk has the ability to add and revise information at any time, unlike files stored on your hard drive. This also means that the site can change quite a bit, potentially making the following overview out of date. If the site has changed, just follow along as best you can for the next three pages.

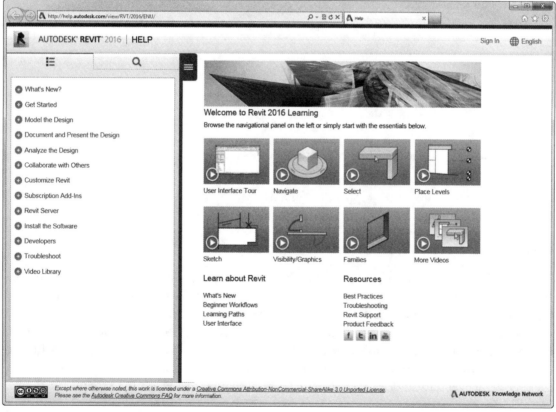

FIGURE 1-6.1 Autodesk Help site

In the upper left you can click the magnifying glass and search the *Help System* for a word or phrase. You may also click any one of the links to learn more about the topic listed. The next few steps will show you how to access the *Help System's* content on the Revit user interface, a topic you have just studied.

2. On the left, click the **plus symbol** next to **Get Started**.

3. Now, click the **plus symbol** next to **User Interface** (Figure 1-6.2).

Notice the tree structure on the left. You can use this to quickly navigate the help site.

4. Finally, click directly on **Ribbon**.

You now see information about the *Ribbon* as shown in the image below. Notice additional links are provided below on the current topic. You can use the browser's *Back* and *Forward* buttons to move around in the *Help System*.

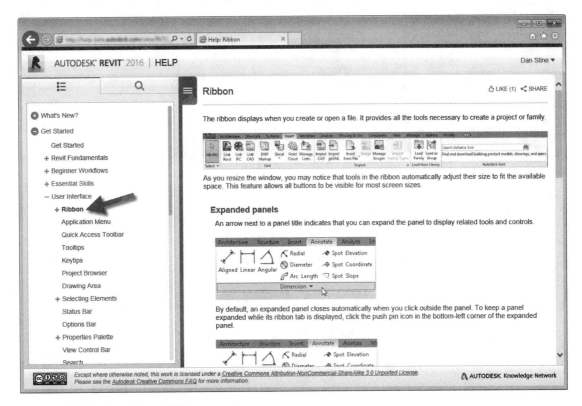

FIGURE 1-6.2 Help window; Ribbon overview

Next, you will try searching the Revit *Help System* for a specific Revit feature. This is a quick way to find information if you have an idea of what it is you are looking for.

5. In the upper-left corner of the current *Help System* web page, click the magnifying glass and then click in the *Search* textbox and enter **gutter**.

6. Press **Enter** on the keyboard.

The search results are shown in Figure 1-6.3. Each item, in the list on the left, is a link which will take you to information on that topic.

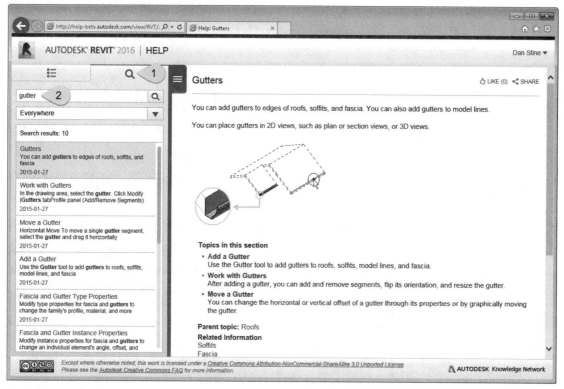

FIGURE 1-6.3 Help search results

The *Help System* can be used to complement this textbook. It is a reference resource, not a tutorial. As you are working though the tutorials in this book, you may want to use the *Help System* to fill in the blanks if you are having trouble or want more information on a topic.

Exercise 1-7:
Introduction to Autodesk 360

We will finish this chapter with a look at Autodesk 360, which is "ground zero" for all of Autodesk's **Cloud Services**. It is important that the student read this information in order to follow along in the book when specific steps related to using these cloud services are covered. The reader does not necessarily need to use Autodesk's cloud services to successfully complete this book.

The main features employed in the book are:

- Saving your work to *Autodesk 360* so you can access the data anywhere and know that the files are in a secure, backed up location. This feature is free to anyone, with some limitations to be discussed later.
- Sending your photorealistic rendering project to the *Cloud* to dramatically reduce the overall processing time. This feature is free to students and a free trial is available to everyone else.

Here is how Autodesk describes *Autodesk 360* on their website:

> The Autodesk® 360 cloud-based framework provides tools and services to extend design beyond the desktop. Streamline your workflows, effectively collaborate, and quickly access and share your work anytime, from anywhere. With virtually infinite computing power in the cloud, Autodesk 360 scales up or down to meet business needs without the infrastructure or upfront investment required for traditional desktop software.

Before we discuss *Autodesk 360* with more specificity, let's define what the *Cloud* is. **The Cloud is a service, or collection of services, which exists partially or completely online.** This is different from the *Internet*, which mostly involves downloading static information, in that you are creating and manipulating data. Most of this happens outside of your laptop or desktop computer. This gives the average user access to massive amounts of storage space, computing power and software they could not otherwise afford if they had to actually own, install and maintain these resources in their office, school or home. In one sense, this is similar to a *Tool Rental Center*, in that the average person could not afford, nor would it be cost-effective to own, a jackhammer. However, for a fraction of the cost of ownership and maintenance, we can rent it for a few hours. In this case, everyone wins!

Creating a Free Autodesk 360 Account

The first thing an individual needs to do in order to gain access to *Autodesk 360* is create a free account at https://360.autodesk.com (students: see tip below); the specific steps will be covered later in this section, so you don't need to do this now. This account is for an individual person, not a computer, not an installation of Revit or AutoCAD, nor does it come from your employer or school. Each person who wishes to access *Autodesk 360* services must create an account, which will give them a unique username and password.

> *TIP:* Students should first create an account at http://students.autodesk.com. This is the same place you go to download free Autodesk software. Be sure to use your school email address as this is what identifies you as a qualifying student. Once you create an account there, you can use this same user name and password to access *Autodesk 360*. Following these steps will give you access to more storage space and unlimited cloud rendering!

Generally speaking, there are three ways you can access *Autodesk 360* cloud services:
- Autodesk 360 website
- Within Revit or AutoCAD; local computer
- Mobile device; smart phone or tablet

Autodesk 360 Website

When you have documents stored in the *Cloud* you may access them via your web browser. Here you can manage your files, view them without the full application (some file formats not supported) and share them. These features use some advanced browser technology, so you need to make sure your browser is up to date; specifically:

To view most 2D documents, use these browsers:

- Mozilla® Firefox® 10 and later

- Google Chrome™ 16 and later

- Microsoft® Internet Explorer® 8 and later

- Apple® Safari® 5.1 and later

To view both 2D and 3D documents, use these browsers:

- Mozilla® Firefox® 10 and later

- Google Chrome™ 16 and later

Important: Depending on your browser, the Adobe® Flash® Player may be required to upload files and view video.

Using the website, you can upload files from your computer to store in the *Cloud*. To do this, you switch to the **Folders and Categories** section and click the **Upload** option (Figure 1-7.1). **Tip:** If using Firefox or Chrome, you can drag and drop documents into the *Upload Documents* window. This is a great way to create a secure backup of your documents.

FIGURE 1-7.1 Viewing files stored in the cloud

You can share files stored in the *Cloud* with others. <u>Private sharing</u> with others who have an *Autodesk 360* account is very easy. Another option is <u>public sharing</u>, which allows you to send someone a link and they can access the file, even if they don't have a 360 account. Simply right-click on a file within *Autodesk 360* to see the sharing options (Figure 1-7.2).

FIGURE 1-7.2 Sharing files stored in the cloud

Autodesk 360 within Revit or AutoCAD; local computer

Another way in which you can access your data stored in the cloud, is from within your Autodesk application; for example, Revit or AutoCAD. This is typically the most convenient as you can open, view and modify your drawings. Once logged in, you will also have access to any *Cloud Services* available to you from within the application, such as rendering or *Green Building Studio*.

To sign in to *Autodesk 360* within your application, simply click the **Sign In** option in the notification area in the upper right corner of the window. You will need to enter your student email address and password (or personal email if you are not a student) as discussed in the previous section. When properly logged in, you will see your username or email address listed as shown in Figure 1-7.3 below. You will try this later in this section.

FIGURE 1-7.3 Example of user logged into Autodesk 360

Once you are logged in, and if *Autodesk 360* is installed on your computer, you will also see an *Autodesk 360* option in the drop-down list of the *Open* dialog box, as shown in Figure 1-7.4.

FIGURE 1-7.4 Autodesk 360 accessed from the open dialog

Keep in mind that ALL files stored in Autodesk 360 are saved on the hard drive of ANY computer you are using; this is ONLY true if you log into *Autodesk 360*. The files are not easy to find manually, but a search could reveal them rather quickly. The files are NOT deleted off of the local computer when you log out either. This should not be a problem for working through this book, but you will want to be careful when working with design files from your firm or office (if you work in one).

When you are logged into *Autodesk 360* from within your application, you can also view your files using *Windows Explorer*. Notice in the image below (Figure 1-7.5) that *Autodesk 360* is listed as a *Favorite*. When you click the Autodesk 360 link, your files and folders are shown to the right. Using this view, you can more easily add folders and copy files.

FIGURE 1-7.5 Autodesk 360 files accessed from windows explorer

Using Revit or AutoCAD on your computer, it is possible to work on files directly in the cloud – kind of. You actually work on the local version of your files, which are automatically synced with the online version anytime they change. Keep in mind this does not work for the multi-user environment, called work-sharing, which Revit is capable of.

When *Autodesk 360* is installed on your local computer system, you will have an icon for it in the *Windows 7* system tray as shown in Figure 1-7.6. If you right-click on this icon you will be presented with a few options such as open the local folder, open the website view, Sync now, pause sync and preferences.

FIGURE 1-7.6 Autodesk 360 in the system tray

Clicking preferences presents the dialog box shown in Figure 1-7.7. Here you can see how much space you have available, enable automatic log-in upon system start up and what to do with linked files. You can also force a *Sign Out* to manually break the connection to the *Cloud*. Your local version of the files will still be on your computer, but the Autodesk 360 links will not reveal them.

FIGURE 1-7.7 Autodesk 360 preferences for your computer

When using the **Render in Cloud** feature, you must be logged into *Autodesk 360* within the application. This is how the *Cloud Service* validates your job request. You either need to be a student, have an account associated with Autodesk Subscription, or have pre-paid for Autodesk Cloud credits.

Render   Render
in Cloud Gallery

On the **Autodesk 360** tab (Figure 1-7.8) you have several tools and settings related to *Autodesk 360* close services. One option is to back up any customization you have made to your AutoCAD software. These settings will then follow you to each computer you work on, as long as you are logged into Autodesk 360. You should not need to do this while working through this book. You can also share a document; this might be an option for turning in your assignments for class.

FIGURE 1-7.8 Cloud-based tools within the AutoCAD application

The first time you log into Autodesk 360 you are presented with a dialog box to set a default option related to syncing data (Similar to Figure 1-7.9).

This option is to sync your customization setting in AutoCAD. As previously mentioned, you may not want to do this until you are more experienced; if you mess something up, you don't want those settings following you to another computer.

FIGURE 1-7.9 Initial settings dialog

You can access these settings later by typing **Options** in the *Command Window*. Within the *Online* tab you will see these options, plus additional information (Figure 1-7.10). Notice the amount of *Cloud Storage* space is listed.

FIGURE 1-7.10 Online settings via AutoCAD options dialog

Autodesk 360 Mobile

Once you have your files stored in the *Cloud* via Autodesk 360, you will also be able to access them on your tablet or smart phone if you have one. Autodesk has a free app called *Autodesk 360 Mobile* for both the Apple or Android phones and tablets.

Some of the mobile features include:
- Open and view files stored in your Autodesk 360 account
- 2D and 3D DWG™ and DWF™ files
- Revit® and Navisworks® files
- Use multi-touch to zoom, pan, and rotate drawings
- View meta data and other details about elements within your drawing
- Find tools that help you communicate changes with your collaborators

The Android app is installed via *Google Play* and the Apple app comes from *iTunes*.

FIGURE 1-7.11
Viewing files on a smart phone

Setting up your Autodesk 360 account

The next few steps will walk you through the process of setting up your free online account at *Autodesk 360*. These steps are not absolutely critical to completing this book, so if you have any reservations about creating an *Autodesk 360* account – don't do it.

1. To create a free Autodesk 360 account, do one of the following:

   a. If you are a **student**, create an account at http://students.autodesk.com.

   b. If you work for a company who has their Autodesk software on **subscription**, ask your *Contract Administrator* (this is a person in your office) to create an account for you and send you an invitation via http://subscription.autodesk.com.

   c. **Everyone else** create an account at https://360.autodesk.com

   FYI: The "s" at the end of "http" in the *Autodesk 360* URL means this is a secure website.

2. Open your application; AutoCAD or Revit.

3. Click the **Sign In** option in the upper-right corner of the application window (Figure 1-7.12).

FIGURE 1-7.12 Signing in to Autodesk 360

It is recommended, as you work through this book, that you save all of your work in the *Cloud*, via Autodesk 360, so you will have a safe and secure location for your files. These files can then be accessed from several locations via the three methods discussed here. It is still important to maintain a separate copy of your files on a flash drive, portable hard drive or in another *Cloud*-type location such as *Dropbox*. This will be important if your main files ever become corrupt. You should manually back up your files to your backup location so a corrupt file does not automatically corrupt your backup files.

TIP: If you have a file that will not open try one of the following:

- In AutoCAD: Open AutoCAD and then, from the *Application Menu*, select Drawing Utilities → Recover → Recover. Then browse to your file and open it. AutoCAD will try and recover the drawing file. This may require some things to be deleted but is better than losing the entire file.

- In Revit: Open Revit and then, from the *Application Menu*, select Open, browse to your file, and select it. Click the Audit check box, and then click Open. Revit will attempt to repair any problems with the project database. Some elements may need to be deleted, but this is better than losing the entire file.

Be sure to check out the Autodesk website to learn more about Autodesk 360 and the growing number of cloud services Autodesk is offering.

Self-Exam:

The following questions can be used as a way to check your knowledge of this lesson. The answers can be found at the bottom of this page.

1. The *View* tab allows you to save your project file. (T/F)

2. You can zoom in and out using the wheel on a wheel mouse. (T/F)

3. Revit is a parametric architectural design program. (T/F)

4. A _____ file allows you to start your project with specific content and certain settings preset the way you like or need them.

5. Autodesk 360 allows you to save your files safely in the _____.

Review Questions:

The following questions may be assigned by your instructor as a way to assess your knowledge of this section. Your instructor has the answers to the review questions.

1. The *Options Bar* dynamically changes to show options that complement the current operation. (T/F)

2. Revit is strictly a 2D drafting program. (T/F)

3. The Projects/Views listed in the *Open Documents* list allow you to see which Projects/Views are currently open. (T/F)

4. When you use the *Pan* tool you are actually moving the drawing, not just changing what part of the drawing you can see on the screen. (T/F)

5. Revit was not originally created for architecture. (T/F)

6. The icon with the floppy disk picture (💾) allows you to _____ a project file.

7. Clicking on the _____ next to the *Zoom* icon will list additional zoom tools not currently shown in the *View* toolbar.

8. You do not see the *ViewCube* unless you are in a _____ view.

9. Creating an *Autodesk 360* account is free. (T/F)

10. Synched files are deleted from your hard drive when you log out of *Autodesk 360*. (T/F)

Lesson 2
Lake Cabin: FLOOR PLAN:

In this lesson you will get a down and dirty overview of the functionality of Autodesk® Revit® for architectural design. We will cover the very basics of creating the primary components of a floor plan: Walls, Doors, Windows, Roof, Annotation and Dimensioning. This lesson will show you the amazing "out-of-the-box" powerful, yet easy to use, features in Autodesk Revit. It should get you very excited about learning this software program. Future lessons will cover these features in more detail while learning other editing tools and such along the way.

Exercise 2-1:
Walls

In this exercise we will draw the walls, starting with the exterior. Read the directions carefully; everything you need to do is clearly listed.

Rough Sketch of Lake Cabin Plan:

This sketch is just to give you an idea of what you will be creating in this chapter (Figure 2-1.1).

FIGURE 2-1.1 Lake Cabin Sketch

Exterior Walls:

1. Start a new project named **Lake Cabin**. *See Lesson 1 on creating a new project.*

2. Click **Architecture → Build → Wall** (i.e., the upper part of the icon, not the down-arrow part). See Figure 2-1.2.

Notice that the *Ribbon*, *Options Bar* and *Properties Palette* have changed to show options related to drawing walls. Next you will modify those settings.

FIGURE 2-1.2 Wall tool

3. Modify the *Ribbon* and *Options Bar* to the following (Figure 2-1.3):
   a. *Change Element Type (via the Type Selector):* Click the down-arrow and select **Generic – 12″**.
   b. *Height:* Change the height from 20′-0″ to **9′-0″**.
   c. *Location Line:* Set this to **Finish Face: Exterior**.

FIGURE 2-1.3 Ribbon, Options Bar and Type Selector

You are now ready to draw the exterior walls in the *Level 1* view.

4. In the drawing window, **click** in the upper left corner.

   TIP: Remember to draw within the four elevation marks (see the image to right).

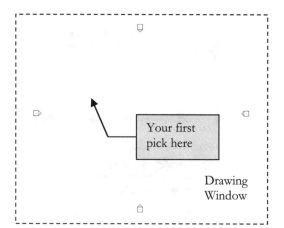

FIGURE 2-1.4 First pick point

5. Start moving the mouse to the right. **Click** when the wall is **48′-0″** long and horizontal.

Notice as you move the mouse Revit dynamically displays a length and an angle. If you want a horizontal line you move the mouse straight across the screen. A dashed line and a tooltip will appear when the line is snapped to the horizontal (Figure 2-1.4).

FIGURE 2-1.5 Horizontal tooltip displayed

> *TIP: If your mouse moved a little when you clicked and the wall is not exactly 48′-0″, simply click on the dimension and type 48 and press Enter. You do not need to type the foot symbol.*

You are now ready for your second wall.

6. Start moving your mouse straight down, or South, until the dashed line and tooltip appear (indicating a vertical line); type **26** and press **Enter**.

> *TIP: Once the wall is drawn the temporary dimension will say 25′-6″ as it is to the wall centerline on the north corner.*

Typing the length allows you to accurately input a length without having to spend a lot of time setting the mouse in just the right position. However, you can still adjust the dimension after the wall is drawn.

7. Draw the other two exterior walls.

Interior Walls:

The same tool is used to draw both interior and exterior walls.

8. Select the *Wall* tool and modify the ***Ribbon, Options Bar*** and ***Properties Palette*** to the following:
   a. *Type Selector:* Click the down-arrow and select **Generic – 5″**.
   b. *Location Line:* Set this to **Wall Centerline**.

9. Drawing a wall between bedrooms: *Snap* (you will see a triangle symbol appear before clicking) to the midpoint of the east wall (Figure 2-1.6). Do not click the second point yet; see the next step to finish the wall.

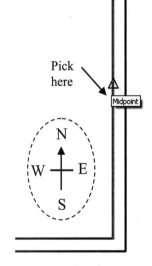

FIGURE 2-1.6 Interior wall start point

10. While moving the mouse to the West (left) and snapped to the horizontal plane, type **20 2 1/2**.

   TIP: Type the length as shown; you don't need a dash, the foot or the inch symbol as they are assumed here. You do need two spaces – after the feet and before the fraction.

11. Draw the vertical wall to close off the bedrooms. Revit allows you to do this with one wall segment by selecting your points in a particular way. See **Figure 2-1.7** for a graphical description of this process; press **Esc** twice to unselect the new wall (first Esc pressed) and cancel the *Wall* command (second Esc pressed).

FIGURE 2-1.7 Draw wall with object tracking

12. **One More Step:** Draw the two interior walls for the bathroom to complete the interior walls; dimensions are to center of walls (Figure 2-1.1).

13. **Save** your project (*Lake Cabin.rvt*) via the *QAT*.

Exercise 2-2:
Doors

In this exercise you will add doors to your cabin floor plan.

    1.   Open **Lake Cabin.rvt** created in Exercise 2-1.

FIGURE 2-2.1 Door tool

Placing Doors:

    2.   Click **Architecture → Build → Door** (Figure 2-2.1).

Notice that the *Ribbon*, *Options Bar* and *Properties Palette* has changed to show options related to doors. Next you will modify those settings.

The *Type Selector* indicates the door style, width and height. Clicking it lists all the doors loaded into the current project.

FIGURE 2-2.2 Door type selected

The default template project that you started from has several sizes for a single flush door. Notice that there are two standard heights in the list. The 80″ (6′-8″) doors are the standard residential height and the 84″ (7′-0″) doors are the standard commercial door height.

    3.   Change the *Type Selector* to **36″ x 80″**; see Figure 2-2.2.

    4.   Move your cursor over a wall and position the door as shown in **Figure 2-2.4**. Notice that the swing of the door changes depending on what side of the wall your cursor is favoring (Figure 2-2.4).

    5.   Click to place the door and Revit will automatically trim the wall.

    6.   While the door is still selected, click on the *change swing (control arrows)* symbol to make the door swing against the wall (Figure 2-2.3).

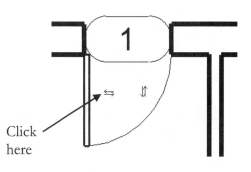

Click here

FIGURE 2-2.3 Changing door swing

FIGURE 2-2.4 Dynamic graphical info during door insertion

Revit allows you to continue inserting doors until you select a different tool from the *Ribbon* or press *Esc*.

7. Insert the doors into the bedrooms as shown in **Figure 2-1.1**. The exact position is not important in this exercise.

8. Change the *Type Selector* to **30″ x 80″**.

9. Insert a door into the bathroom.

Notice that door types recently used are listed at the bottom of the list (Figure 2-2.5). Also, notice the **Search** box near the top—this allows the list to be shortened on large projects with several doors and door types from which to choose.

FIGURE 2-2.5
Door Element Types

Deleting Doors:

Next you will learn how to delete a door. This process will work for most objects (i.e., walls, windows, text, etc.) in Revit.

10. Insert a door between the two bedrooms, any size.

11. Press the **Esc** key twice.

TIP: You can also click the Modify icon located on the left of every tab on the Ribbon.

Modify

12. Click on the door you just inserted, between bedrooms, and press the **Delete** key on your keyboard.

13. **Save** your project (*Lake Cabin.rvt*).

Exercise 2-3:
Windows

In this exercise you will add windows to your cabin floor plan.

1. Open **Lake Cabin.rvt** created in Exercise 2-2.

Placing *Windows*:

2. Click **Architecture → Build → Window** (Figure 2-3.1).

FIGURE 2-3.1 Window tool

Again, notice that the *Ribbon, Options Bar* and *Properties Palette* have changed to show options related to windows. Next you will modify those settings.

The *Type Selector* indicates the window style, width and height. Clicking the *Type Selector* lists all the windows loaded in the current project.

3. Change the *Type Selector* to **36″ x 72″** (Figure 2-3.2).

4. Move your cursor over a wall and place two windows as shown in **Figure 2-3.3**. Notice, as you move your cursor near a wall, that the position of the window changes depending on what side of the wall your cursor is favoring.

FIGURE 2-3.2 Window options

5. With the Window tool still active, change the *Type Selector* to **24″ x 72″**.

6. Place the other four windows in the living room area as shown in **Figure 2-1.1**. Again, in this exercise we are not concerned with the exact placement of the windows.

7. Change the *Type Selector* to **24″ x 48″**.

8. Place the remaining five windows: two in each bedroom and one in the bathroom, as shown in **Figure 2-1.1**.

9. **Save** your project (*Lake Cabin.rvt*).

FIGURE 2-3.3 Two large windows

Object Snap Symbols:

By now you should be well aware of the snaps that Revit suggests as you move your cursor about the drawing window.

If you hold your cursor still for a moment while a snap symbol is displayed, a tooltip will appear on the screen. However, when you become familiar with the snap symbols you can pick sooner (Figure 2-3.4).

The TAB key cycles through the available snaps near your cursor.

The keyboard shortcut turns off the other snaps for one pick. For example, if you type SE (snap endpoint) on the keyboard while in the Wall command, Revit will only look for an endpoint for the next pick.

Finally, typing SO (snaps off) turns all snaps off for one pick.

See Exercise 3-2 for more information.

Symbol	Position	Keyboard Shortcut
✕	Intersection	SI
□	Endpoint	SE
△	Midpoint	SM
○	Center	SC
✕	Nearest	SN
⌐	Perpendicular	SP
○	Tangent	ST

FIGURE 2-3.4 Snap Reference Chart

Exercise 2-4:
Roof

You will now add a simple roof to your lake cabin.

1. Open **Lake Cabin.rvt** created in Exercise 2-3 (if necessary).

Sketching a Roof:

2. Click **Architecture → Build → Roof** (click the bottom part of the button); a fly-out menu will appear (Figure 2-4.1).

FIGURE 2-4.1 Roof tool

The fly-out prompts you for the method you want to use to create the roof.

3. Click **Roof by footprint**.

When Revit detects an issue that might not be appropriate, a warning is displayed. In this case you see *Roof is on the Lowest Level* warning.

Revit notices that you are on Level 1 and asks you if you want to move the roof to another level. In our case we want to move it to Level 2 (Figure 2-4.2).

FIGURE 2-4.2 Roof is on the Lowest Level prompt

4. Make sure **Level 2** is selected and click **Yes** (Figure 2-4.2).

You are still on Level 1, but Revit will move the roof to Level 2 once you are finished drawing it. The entire model is grayed out at the moment because you are in "Sketch Mode"; when finished sketching, the roof and everything will return to normal. You will not see the roof as it will be above the current view (i.e., Level 1); you will learn more about this on the next page.

Also notice the *contextual tab* **Create Roof Footprint** has temporarily been added to the *Ribbon*, which has design options relative to the roof (Figure 2-4.3) as with the *Options Bar* directly below the *Ribbon*.

FIGURE 2-4.3 Roof sketch options on the *Ribbon* and *Options Bar*

5. Pick each of the exterior walls to specify the roof footprint.
    Be sure to pick the exterior side of the wall.

6. Click **Finish Edit Mode** via the green checkmark on the *Ribbon*.

You should be on Level 1. You can see this in the *Project Browser*, as Level 1 is bold.

7. To see the roof click the **Default 3D View** icon on the *QAT* (Figure 2-4.4).

The roof has no overhang and is hovering above the exterior walls about 1'-0". We will save these types of modifications for future lessons.

FIGURE 2-4.4 Default 3D View

8. Click the **X** in the upper right corner of the drawing window to close the current view (3D). This will close the 3D view but not the project or the Level 1 view.

    NOTE: *Clicking the red X on the Title Bar closes Revit.*

Closing a View

Exercise 2-5:
Annotation and Dimensions

Adding text is very simple in Revit. In this exercise we will add labels to each room in our lake cabin floor plan. We will also place two dimensions.

Placing Text:

1. Open **Lake Cabin.rvt** created in Exercise 2-4, if not already open.

2. Make sure your current view is **Level 1**. The word "Level 1" will be bold under the heading *Floor Plans* in your *Project Browser*. If Level 1 is not current, simply double-click on the "Level 1" text in the *Project Browser* (Figure 2-5.1).

3. Select **Annotate → Text → Text**; do not select *Model Text* from the *Architecture* tab of the *Ribbon*.

   TIP: You can also select the Text *tool from the Quick Access Toolbar (QAT).*

FIGURE 2-5.1 Project Browser

Once again, notice the *Ribbon* has changed to display some text options; all of this falls under a *contextual tab* named *Modify | Place Text* (Figure 2-5.2).

FIGURE 2-5.2 Ribbon: contextual tab for Text tool

The *Type Selector* indicates the text size. From this *Contextual Ribbon* you can also place text with arrow lines, or leaders, and set the text alignment, Left justified, Centered or Right justified. We will not adjust these settings at this time.

4. You will now place the words "Living Room." **Click** within the living room area to place the text (Figure 2-5.3).

5. Type **Living Room**, then click somewhere in the plan view to finish the text.

You may notice that the text seems too large. This is a good time to explain what the text height is referring to in the *Type Selector (i.e., ¼″ Arial)*. The text height, in the *Properties Palette*, refers to the size of the text on a printed piece of paper. For example, if you print your plan you should be able to place a ruler on the text and measure ¼″ in height when the text is set to ¼″ in the *Type Selector.*

This can be a complicated process in other CAD programs; Revit makes it very simple. All you need to do is change the *View Scale* for **Level 1** and Revit automatically adjusts the text and annotation to match that scale. Currently our *View Scale* is set to ⅛″ = 1′-0″; we want the *View Scale* to be ¼″ = 1′-0″. With the *View Scale* set to ⅛″ = 1′-0″ our text is twice as big as it should be. Next you will change the *View Scale* for Level 1.

FIGURE 2-5.3 Placing text

In the lower-left corner of the drawing window, on the *View Control Bar*, click on the text of the listed scale (i.e., ⅛″ = 1′-0″).

6. In the pop-up menu, which lists several standard scales, select **¼″ = 1′-0″** (Figure 2-5.4).

You should now notice that your text and even your door and window tags are half the size they used to be (Figure 2-5.5).

You should understand that this scale adjustment only affected the current view (i.e., Level 1). If you switched to Level 2 you would notice it is still set to ⅛″ = 1′-0″. This is nice because you may, on occasion, want one plan at a larger scale to show more detail.

7. Finally, using the *Text* tool, place a room name label in each room as shown in **Figure 2-1.1** and **Figure 2-5.5** below.

8. **Save** your project.

FIGURE 2-5.4 Changing View Scale

FIGURE 2-5.5 Floor Plan with text at ¼″ = 1′-0″

Place Dimensions:

To finish this exercise you will place two overall plan dimensions.

Aligned

9. Select **Annotate** → **Dimension** → **Aligned** (see icon to right).

10. On the *Options Bar*, change the drop-down list that says *Wall centerlines* to **Wall faces**. This option will allow you to dimension to the outside face of your building, as you would normally do when dimensioning the overall footprint of your building.

Modify | Place Dimensions   Wall faces   ▼   Pick: Individual Reference ▼ Options

11. Place a dimension by selecting two walls and then clicking a third point to specify where the dimension line should be located relative to the walls (Figure 2-5.6).

FIGURE 2-5.6 Placing Dimensions

12. Place one more dimension indicating the depth of the building.

The *Dimension* tool, as just used, places permanent dimensions; they can be deleted, however. Revit also provides a tool to list a distance but not actually place a permanent dimension; this is called the **Measure** tool. The *Measure* tool is convenient when you simply want to know what a dimension is but do not need to document it for the construction drawings.

13. **Save** your project.

Exercise 2-6:
Printing

The last thing you need to know to round off your basic knowledge of Revit is how to print the current view. Printing will be covered in more detail later in the text; this section will just brush over the surface of the process.

Printing the Current View:

1. Select **Application Menu** → **Print** (hover) → **Print**.

2. Adjust your settings to match those shown in **Figure 2-6.1**.

   - Select a printer from the list that you have access to.
   - Set *Print Range* to **Visible portion of current window**

FIGURE 2-6.1 Print dialog

3. Click on the **Setup** button to adjust additional print settings.

4. Adjust your settings to match those shown in **Figure 2-6.2**.

   - Set Zoom to **Fit to page**.

FIGURE 2-6.2 Print Settings dialog

5. Click **OK** to close the *Print Setup* dialog and return to *Print*.

6. Click **No** if you get the following prompt (Figure 2-6.3).

FIGURE 2-6.3 Save Print Settings prompt

7. Click the **Preview** button in the lower left corner. This will save paper and time by verifying the drawing will be correctly positioned on the page (Figure 2-6.4).

8. Click the **Print** button at the top of the preview window.

9. Click **OK** to print to the selected printer.

FYI:

Notice you do not have the option to set the scale (i.e., ⅛″ = 1'-0″). If you recall from our previous exercise the scale is set in the properties for each view.

If you want a quick half-scale print you can change the zoom factor to 50%. You could also select **Fit to Page** to get the largest image possible but not to scale – which is selected above as this plan will not fit on 8½″ x 11″ (letter) sized paper at ¼″ = 1'-0″.

Printer versus Plotter?

Revit can print to any printer or plotter installed on your computer.

A **Printer** is an output device that uses smaller paper (e.g., 8½″x11″ or 11″x17″). A **Plotter** is an output device that uses larger paper; plotters typically have one or more rolls of paper ranging in size from 18″ wide to 42″ wide. A roll feed plotter has a built-in cutter that can, for example, cut paper from a 36″ wide roll to make a 24″x36″ sheet.

FIGURE 2-6.4 Print Preview

Plotter with three paper rolls

Color **printer**/copier

Self-Exam:

The following questions can be used as a way to check your knowledge of this lesson. The answers can be found at the bottom of the page.

1. The *Measure* tool is used to dimension drawings. (T/F)

2. Revit will automatically trim the wall lines when you place a door. (T/F)

3. Snap will help you draw faster and more accurately. (T/F)

4. A 6'-8" door is a standard door height in _____ construction.

5. While using the *Wall* tool, the height can be quickly adjusted on the

    _____ bar.

Review Questions:

The following questions may be assigned by your instructor as a way to assess your knowledge of this section. Your instructor has the answers to the review questions.

1. The *View Scale* for a drawing/view is set by clicking the scale listed on the *View Control Bar*. (T/F)

2. Dimensions are placed with only two clicks of the mouse. (T/F)

3. The relative size of text in a drawing is controlled by the *View Scale*. (T/F)

4. You can quickly switch to a different view by double-clicking on that view's label in the *Project Browser*. (T/F)

5. You cannot select which side of the wall a window is offset to. (T/F)

6. The _____ key cycles through the available snaps near your cursor.

7. Which specific *Roof* tool did you use in this chapter? _____

8. While in the *Door* tool you can change the door style and size via the

    _____ within the *Properties Palette*.

9. When plotting, you must tell Revit the desired scale (i.e., ⅛" = 1'-0", ¼" = 1'-0", etc.), while in the *Plot* dialog box. (T/F)

10. The *Quick Access Toolbar* has a tool which gives you quick access to a 3D view of your model. (T/F)

Lesson 3
Overview of Linework and Modify Tools:

It may seem odd to you that, in a revolutionary 3D design program, you will begin by learning to draw and edit 2D lines and shapes. However, any 3D object requires, at a minimum, detailed information in at least two of the three dimensions. Once two dimensions are defined, Autodesk® Revit® can begin to automate much of the third dimension for you. Many building components and features will require you to draw the perimeter using 2D lines.

Many of the edit tools that are covered in this lesson are the same tools that are used to edit the 3D building components.

Exercise 3-1:
Lines and Shapes

Drawing Lines

You will draw many 2D lines in Autodesk Revit, typically in what is called *Sketch* mode. Two dimensional lines in Autodesk Revit are extremely precise drawing elements. This means you can create very accurate drawings. Lines, or any drawn object, can be as precise as 8 decimal places (i.e., 24.999999999) or 1/256.

Autodesk Revit is a vector based program. That means each drawn object is stored in a numerical database. When geometry needs to be displayed on the screen, Autodesk Revit reads from the project database to determine what to display on the screen. This ensures that the line will be very accurate at any scale or zoom magnification.

A raster based program, in contrast to vector based, is comprised of dots that infill a grid. The grid can vary in density and is typically referred to as resolution (e.g., 600x800, 1600x1200, etc.). This file type is used by graphics programs that typically deal with photographs, such as Adobe Photoshop. There are two reasons this type of file is not appropriate for Computer Aided Design (CAD) programs:

- A raster based line, for example, is composed of many dots on a grid, representing the line's width. When you zoom in, magnifying the line, it starts to become pixilated, meaning you actually start to see each dot on the grid. In a vector file you can "infinitely" zoom in on a line and it will never become pixilated because the program recalculates the line each time you zoom in.

- A CAD program, such as Revit, only needs to store the starting point and end point coordinates for each wall, for example, the dots needed to draw the wall are calculated on-the-fly for the current screen resolution. Whereas a raster file has to store each dot that represents the full length and width of the line, or lines in the wall example. This can vary from a few hundred dots to several thousand dots, depending on the resolution, for the same line.

The following graphic illustrates this point:

Vector vs. Raster Lines

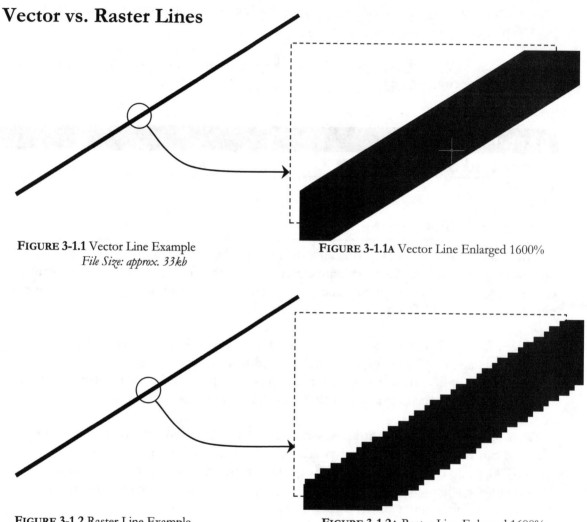

FIGURE 3-1.1 Vector Line Example
File Size: approx. 33kb

FIGURE 3-1.1A Vector Line Enlarged 1600%

FIGURE 3-1.2 Raster Line Example
File Size: approx. 4.4MB

FIGURE 3-1.2A Raster Line Enlarged 1600%

The Detail Lines Tool:

You will now study the *Detail Lines* tool.

1. **Open** Revit.

Each time you start Revit, you are in the *Recent Files* view. This view is closed automatically when a new or existing project is opened.

2. Start a new project: select **Application Menu → New → Project** and then click **Browse**, select **default.rte**, click **Open** and then **OK**.

The drawing window is set to the *Level 1 Floor Plan* view. The 2D drafting will be done in a drafting view. Next you will learn how to create one of these views.

3. Select **View → Create → Drafting View**.
   (Remember: this means *Tab → Panel → Icon* on the *Ribbon*.)

Drafting
View

4. In the *New Drafting View* dialog box, type **Ex 3-1** for the *Name* and set the *Scale* to **3/4″ = 1′-0″** by clicking the down-arrow at the right (Figure 3-1.3).

New Drafting View		X
Name:	Ex 3-1	
Scale:	3/4" = 1'-0" ▼	
Scale value 1:	16	
	OK	Cancel

FIGURE 3-1.3 New Drafting View dialog

You are now in the new view and the *Project Browser* will contain a category labeled *Drafting Views (Detail)*. Here, each *Drafting View* created will be listed.

5. In the *Project Browser*, click the plus symbol next to the label **Drafting Views (Detail)**; this will display the *Drafting Views* that exist in the current project (Figure 3-1.4).

You are now ready to start looking at the *Detail Lines* tool:

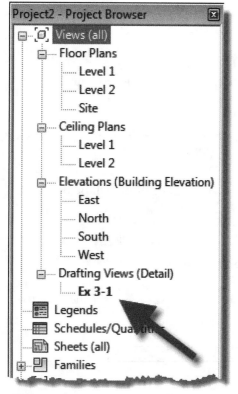

FIGURE 3-1.4 Project Browser: Drafting Views

6. Select the ***Annotate*** tab on the *Ribbon*.

7. On the *Detail* panel, select **Detail Line** (Figure 3-1.5).

   TIP: *Do not use the "Model Line" tool on the Architecture tab.*

   Detail Line

8. **Draw a line** from the lower left corner of the screen to the upper right corner of the screen, by simply clicking two points on the screen within the drawing window (Figure 3-1.6).

   NOTE: *Do not drag or hold your mouse button down; just click.*

After clicking your second point, you should notice the length and the angle of the line are graphically displayed; this information is temporary and will disappear when you move your cursor.

FIGURE 3-1.5 Annotate tab

You should also notice that the *Detail Line* tool is still active, which means you could continue to draw additional lines on the screen.

9. After clicking your second point, select the **Modify** tool from the left side of the *Ribbon*.

Modify

Selecting *Modify* cancels the current tool and allows you to select portions of your drawing for information or editing. Revit conveniently places the *Modify* tool in the same location on each tab so it is always available no matter which tab on the *Ribbon* is active.

TIP: Pressing the Esc key twice reverts Revit back to Modify mode.

Did You Make a Mistake?

Whenever you make a mistake in Revit you can use the **UNDO** command, via the *QAT*, to revert to a previous drawing state. You can perform multiple UNDOs all the way to your previous *Save*.

Similarly, if you press Undo a few too many times, you can use **REDO**.

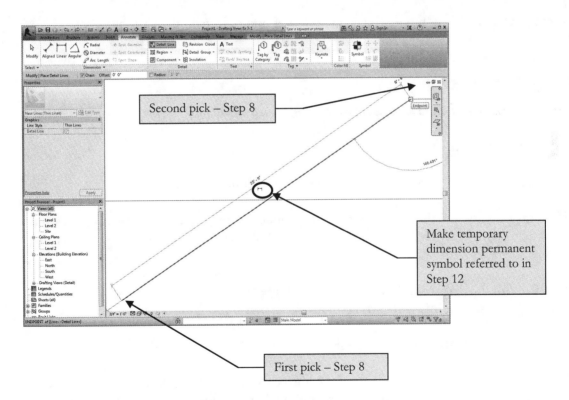

Second pick – Step 8

Make temporary dimension permanent symbol referred to in Step 12

First pick – Step 8

FIGURE 3-1.6 Your first detail line; exact dimensions are not important at this point.

Notice in the image above, that while the *Detail Line* tool is active, the *Modify | Place Detail Line* contextual tab is shown. As soon as you click the *Modify* button or press Esc, the tab reverts back to the basic *Modify* tab.

This constitutes your first line! However, as you are probably aware, it is not a very accurate line as far as length and angle are concerned. Your line will likely be a different length due to where you picked your points and the size and resolution of your monitor.

Typically you need to provide information such as length and angle when drawing a line; you rarely pick arbitrary points on the screen as you did in the previous steps. Revit allows you to get close with the on-screen dimension and angle information. Most of the time you also need to accurately pick your starting point. For example, how far one line is from another or picking the exact middle point on another line.

Having said that, however, the line you just drew still has precise numbers associated with its length and angle; this information is displayed after the line is drawn. The dimension and angle information is displayed until you begin to draw another line or select another tool. You can also select the line. While the dimensions are still visible, they can be used to modify the length and angle of the line; you will try that later.

10. If not already selected, click the **Modify** tool from the *Ribbon*.

Notice that the temporary dimensions have disappeared.

While you are in *Modify* mode, you can select lines and objects in the current view.

11. Now **select the line** by clicking the mouse button with the cursor directly over the line.

FYI: Always use the left button unless the right button is specifically mentioned.

Notice that the temporary dimensions have returned.

The following step shows how to make a temporary dimension permanent:

If, at any point, you want to make a temporary dimension permanent, you simply click the "make this temporary dimension permanent" symbol near the dimension. You will try this now.

12. With the diagonal line still selected, click the "make this temporary dimension permanent" symbol near the dimension (Figure 3-1.6).

13. Select **Modify** to unselect the line.

The dimension indicating the length of the line is now permanent (Figure 3-1.7). The value of your dimension will not be the same as the one in this book as the size of your monitor and the exact points picked can vary greatly.

FIGURE 3-1.7 Temp dimension converted to permanent dimension

The following shows how to change the length of the line:

Currently, the line is approximately 20 - 30′ long (27′-6″ in Figure 3-1.7). If you want to change the length of the line to 22′-6″, you select the line and then change the dimension text, which in turn changes the line length. This can also be done with the temporary dimensions; the key is that the line has to be selected. You will try this next.

FYI: Your detail line length will vary slightly depending on the size and resolution of your computer monitor, as you will be seeing more or less of the drawing area. This also assumes you have not performed any zooming, including spinning the wheel button on your mouse. If your line is way off you should Undo or start over so the next several steps work out as intended.

14. In *Modify* mode, select the diagonal line.

15. With the line currently selected, click on the dimension-text.

A dimension-text edit box appears directly over the dimension, within the drawing window. Whatever you type as a dimension changes the line to match.

16. Type **22 6** (i.e., 22 *space* 6) and press **Enter** (Figure 3-1.8).

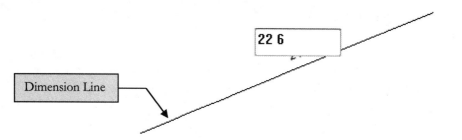

FIGURE 3-1.8 Editing dimension to change line length

You should have noticed the line changed length. Revit assumes that you want the line to change length equally at each end, so the midpoint does not move. Try changing the dimension to 100′ and then Undo.

Locking Dimensions:

Revit allows you to *Lock* a dimension, which prevents the dimension and line length from changing. You will investigate this now to help avoid problems later.

17. Make sure the line is *not* selected; to do this press Esc or click *Modify*.

18. Select the dimension, not the line, and note the following about the selected dimension (Figure 3-1.9).

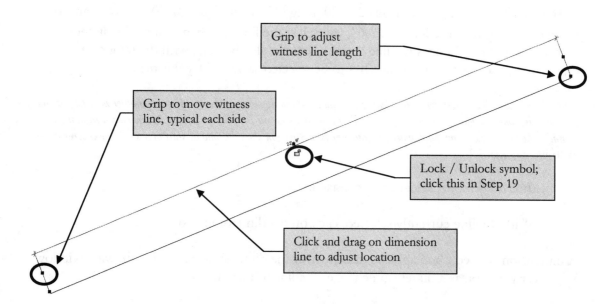

Grip to adjust witness line length

Grip to move witness line, typical each side

Lock / Unlock symbol; click this in Step 19

Click and drag on dimension line to adjust location

FIGURE 3-1.9 Selected dimension

19. Click on the **Lock/Unlock** padlock symbol to lock the dimension (Figure 3-1.9).

The dimension is now locked. Again, this means that you cannot change the dimension OR the line, though you can move it. The dimension is attached to the line in such a way that changing one affects the other. Next you will see what happens when you try to modify the dimension while it is locked.

Any time the line or dimension are selected you will see the lock or unlock symbol in the locked position.

FYI: Clicking the dimension's padlock icon anytime it is visible will toggle the setting between locked and unlocked.

20. Select **Modify** to unselect the *Dimension*.

21. Select the line (not the dimension).

22. Click on the dimension text and attempt to modify the line length to **21′**.

As you can see, Revit will not let you edit the text.

Even though your current view is showing a relatively small area, i.e., your *Drafting View,* it is actually an infinite drawing board.

In architectural CAD drafting, everything is drawn true to life size, or full-scale, ALWAYS! If you are drawing a building, you might draw an exterior wall that is 600′-0″ long. If you are drawing a window detail, you might draw a line that is 8″ long. In either case you are entering that line's actual length.

You could, of course, have an 8″ line and a 600′-0″ line in the same *Drafting View.* Either line would be difficult to see at the current drawing magnification (i.e., approximately 22′ x 16′ area; also recall that your diagonal line is 22′-6″ long). So, you would have to zoom in to see the 8″ line and zoom out to see the 600′-0″ line. Next you will get to try this.

When the diagonal line is selected, notice the *Properties Palette* lists the type of entity selected (i.e., Lines), the *Style* (i.e., Thin Lines) and the *Length* (i.e., 22′-6″). See Chapter 1 for more information on the *Properties Palette* and how to open it if you accidentally closed it.

FIGURE 3-1.10 Properties Palette with diagonal line selected

Draw an 8″ Line:

The next steps will walk you through drawing an 8″ horizontal line. Revit provides more than one way to do this. You will try one of them now.

23. Select **Annotate → Detail → Detail Line**.

24. Pick a point somewhere in the upper left corner of the drawing window.

25. Start moving the mouse towards the right and generally horizontal until you see a dashed reference line extending in each direction of your line appear on the screen, as in Figure 3-1.11.

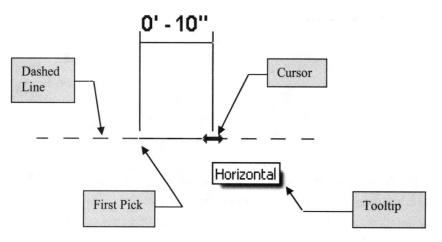

FIGURE 3-1.11 Drawing a line with the help of Revit

TIP: You will see a dashed horizontal line and a tooltip when the line is horizontal.

As you move the mouse left and right, you will notice Revit displays various dimensions that allow you to quickly draw your line at these often used increments. See the next exercise to learn more about how to control the increments shown.

26. With the dashed line and *tooltip* visible on the screen, take your hand off the mouse, so you do not accidentally move it, and type **8″** and then press **Enter**.

TIP: Remember, you have to type the inch symbol; Revit always assumes you mean feet unless you specify otherwise. A future lesson will review the input options in more detail.

You have just drawn a line with a precise length and angle!

27. Use the **Measure** tool to verify it was drawn correctly. Click *Modify* →
    Measure → *Measure (down arrow)* → *Measure Between Two References*

28. Use the **Zoom In Region** tool to enlarge the view of the 8″ line via the
    Navigation Bar (image to right).

29. Now use the **Zoom to Fit** or **Previous Pan/Zoom** tools so that both lines are
    visible again.

Draw a 600′ Line:

30. Select the **Detail Line** tool and pick a point in the
    lower right corner of the drawing window.

31. Move the cursor straight up from your first point
    so that the line snaps to the vertical and the dashed
    line appears (Figure 3-1.12).

32. With the dashed line and *tooltip* visible on the
    screen, take your hand off the mouse so you do
    not accidentally move it; type **600** and then press
    Enter.

    *TIP #1: Notice this time you did not have to type the foot
    symbol (′).*

    *TIP #2: You do not need to get the temporary dimension close to reading 600′; the temporary dimension
    is ignored when you type in a value.*

FIGURE 3-1.12 Drawing another
Detail Line; 600′-0″ vertical line
– lower right

33. Press the **Esc** key twice to exit the *Detail Line* tool and return to the *Modify* mode.

Because the visible portion of
the drawing area is only about
16′ tall, you obviously would
not expect to see a 600′ line.
You need to change the
drawing's magnification by
zooming out to see it.

34. Use **Zoom to Fit** to see
    the entire drawing (Fig. 3-
    1.13).

    *TIP: Double-click your wheel
    button to Zoom Extents.*

600′ line visible
after Zoom to Fit

First two lines
barely visible

FIGURE 3-1.13 Detail view with three lines

Drawing Shapes:

Revit provides several tools to draw common shapes like squares, rectangles, circles and ellipses. These tools can be found on the *Ribbon* while the *Detail Line* tool is active. You will take a look at *Rectangle* and *Circle* now.

Creating a Rectangle:

35. Use **Previous Pan/Zoom**, or *Zoom Region*, to get back to the original view where the diagonal line spans the screen.

36. Select the **Detail Line** tool.

Notice the *Ribbon*, *Options Bar* and *Properties Palette* have changed to show various options related to *Detail Lines* (Figure 3-1.14).

FIGURE 3-1.14 Place Detail Lines contextual Tab on Ribbon

37. Select the **Rectangle** tool from the *Ribbon*.

    TIP: Hover your cursor over the icon to see tooltip until you learn what tools the icons represent.

38. Pick the "**first corner point**" somewhere near the lower center of the drawing window (Figure 3-1.15).

Notice the temporary dimensions are displaying a dimension for both the width and height. At this point you can pick a point on the screen, trying to get the dimensions correct before clicking the mouse button. If you do not get the rectangle drawn correctly, you can click on each dimension-text and change the dimension while the temporary dimensions are displayed; see the next two steps for the rectangle dimensions.

39. Draw a 2'-8" x 4'-4" rectangle using the temporary dimensions displayed on the screen; if you do not draw it correctly do the following:

    a. Click the dimension-text for the horizontal line, then type **2'-8"** and then press **Enter**.

    b. Type **4'-4"** and then press **Enter** for the vertical dimension.

FIGURE 3-1.15 Drawing with Rectangle and Circle to be added (shown dashed for clarity)

Creating a Circle:

40. With the *Detail Line* tool active, select **Circle** from the *Ribbon* (Figure 3-1.16).

41. You are now prompted to pick the center point for the circle; pick a point approximately as shown in (Figure 3-1.15).

FIGURE 3-1.16 Detail Line shapes

You should now see a dynamic circle and a temporary dimension attached to your cursor, which allows you to visually specify the circle's size. Move your mouse around to see that you could arbitrarily pick a point on the screen to create a quick circle if needed, then proceed to Step 42 where you will draw a circle with a radius of 1'-6⅝".

42. Type **1 6 5/8** and then press **Enter** (Figure 3-1.17).

FIGURE 3-1.17 Drawing with Rectangle and Circle added

Notice in the image above, the *Detail Line* is still active because the *contextual tab*, **Modify | Place Detail Lines**, is visible and the *Status Bar* is prompting to "Click to enter circle center." You need to press **Esc** or click *Modify* to cancel the command; clicking another command will also cancel the current command.

43. **Select the circle** and notice a temporary dimension appears indicating the circle's radius. Press **Esc** to unselect it (Figure 3-1.18).

    TIP: This temporary dimension can be used to change the radius of the circle while the circle is selected.

44. **Save** your project as "**ex3-1.rvt**".

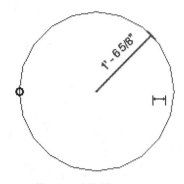

FIGURE 3-1.18
Circle selected

Exercise 3-2:
Snaps

Snaps are tools that allow you to accurately pick a point on an element. For example, when drawing a line you can use *Object Snap* to select, as the start-point, the endpoint or midpoint of another line or wall.

This feature is absolutely critical to drawing accurate technical drawings. Using this feature allows you to be confident you are creating perfect intersections, corners, etc. (Figure 3-2.1).

Object Snaps Options:

You can use *Object Snaps* in one of two ways.

o "Normal" mode
o "Temporary Override" mode

FIGURE 3-2.1 Typical problem when *Snaps* are not used

"Normal" *SNAP* mode is a feature that constantly scans the area near your cursor when Revit is looking for user input. You can configure which types of points to look for.

NOTE: The term "normal" is not a Revit term, rather it is simply a description used in this book to differentiate this portion of the Snaps feature from the Temporary Override portion discussed next.

Using a "Temporary Override" *Object Snap* for individual pick-points allows you to quickly select a particular point on an element. This option will temporarily disable the other *Object Snap* settings, which means you tell Revit to just look for the endpoint on an object, for the next pick-point only, rather than the three or four types being scanned for by the "normal" *Object Snaps* feature.

Overview of the Snaps Dialog Box:

Revit provides a *Snaps* dialog box where you specify which *Object Snaps* you want enabled. Next you will take a look at it.

1. Open project **Ex3-1** and select **Manage → Settings → Snaps**.

Snaps

You should now see the *Snaps* dialog box (Figure 3-2.2). Take a minute to study the various settings that you can control with this dialog box. Notice the check box at the top that allows you to turn this feature off completely.

Dimension Snaps
This controls the automatic dimensions that Revit suggests when you are drawing. Following the given format you could add or remove increments. If you are zoomed in close, only the smaller increments are used.

Object Snaps
This controls the "normal" *Object Snaps* that Revit scans for while you are drawing. Unchecking an item tells Revit not to scan for it anymore. Currently, all *Object Snaps* are enabled (Figure 3-2.2).

Temporary Overrides
This area is really just information on how to use Temporary Overrides.

FIGURE 3-2.2 Snaps dialog box; default settings

While drawing you will occasionally want to tell Revit you only want to *Snap* to an Endpoint for the next pick. Instead of opening the *Snaps* dialog and un-checking every *Object Snap* except for Endpoint, you can specify a *Temporary Override* for the next pick. You do this by typing the two letters, in parentheses, in the *Object Snaps* area of the *Snaps* dialog (Figure 3-2.2).

2. Make sure the *Snaps Off* option is unchecked in the upper-left corner of the dialog box; this turns Snaps completely off.

3. Click on the **Check All** button to make sure all *Snaps* are checked.

4. Click **OK** to close the *Snaps* dialog box.

Understanding Snap Symbols:

Again, you should be well aware of the *Object Snap* symbols that Revit displays as you move your cursor about the drawing window while you are in a tool like *Wall* and Revit is awaiting your input or pick-point.

If you hold your cursor still for a moment, while a snap symbol is displayed, a tooltip will appear on the screen. However, when you become familiar with the snap symbols you can pick sooner, rather than waiting for the tooltip to display (Figure 3-2.3).

The TAB key cycles through the available snaps near your cursor.

Symbol	Position	Keyboard Shortcut
✕	Intersection	SI
☐	Endpoint	SE
△	Midpoint	SM
○	Center	SC
✕	Nearest	SN
ㄴ	Perpendicular	SP
○	Tangent	ST

FIGURE 3-2.3 Snap symbols

Finally, typing **SO** turns all snaps off for one pick.

FYI: The Snaps shown in Figure 3-2.2 are for Revit in general, not just the current project. This is convenient; you don't have to adjust to your favorite settings for each Project or View, existing or new.

Setting Object Snaps:

You can set Revit to have just one or all Snaps running at the same time. Let us say you have Endpoint and Midpoint set to be running. While using the *Wall* tool, you move your cursor near an existing wall. When the cursor is near the end of the wall you will see the Endpoint symbol show up; when you move the cursor towards the middle of the line you will see the Midpoint symbol show up.

The next step shows you how to tell Revit which Object Snaps you want it to look for. First you will save a new copy of your project.

5. Select **Application Menu → Save-As → Project**.

6. Name the project **ex3-2.rvt**.

7. As discussed previously, open the ***Snaps*** dialog box.

8. Make sure only the following *Snaps* are checked:
    a. Endpoints
    b. Midpoints
    c. Centers
    d. Intersections
    e. Perpendicular

9. Click **OK** to close the dialog box.

For More Information:

For more on using Snaps, search Revit's *Help System* for **Snaps**. Then double-click **Snap Points** or any other items found by the search.

Now that you have the *Snaps* adjusted, you will give this feature a try.

10. Using the ***Detail Line*** tool, move your cursor to the lower-left portion of the diagonal line (Figure 3-2.4).

11. Hover the cursor over the line's endpoint (without picking); when you see the *Endpoint* symbol you can click to select that point.

Just So You Know

It is important that you see the *SNAP* symbol before clicking. Also, once you see the symbol you should be careful not to move the mouse too much.

These steps will help to ensure accurate selections.

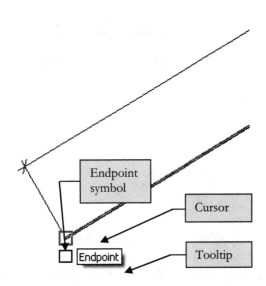

FIGURE 3-2.4 Endpoint SNAP symbol visible

While still in the Detail Line tool you will draw lines using *Snaps* to sketch accurately.

12. Draw the additional lines shown in **Figure 3-2.5** using the appropriate *Object Snap*, changing the selected Snaps as required to select the required points.

   TIP #1: At any point while the Line tool is active, you can open the SNAP dialog box and adjust its settings. This will not cancel the Line command.

   TIP #2: Also, remember you can press Tab to cycle through the various snap options below or near your cursor.

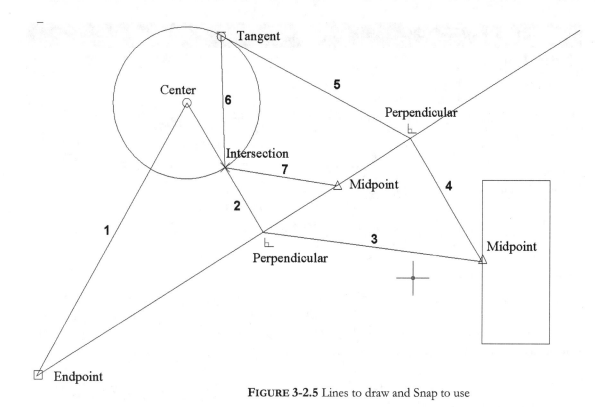

FIGURE 3-2.5 Lines to draw and Snap to use

13. **Save** your project.

Your drawing might look slightly different depending on where you drew the rectangle and circle in the previous steps.

This is a Residential Example?

OK, this is not really an architectural example yet. However, the point here is to focus on the fundamental concepts and not architecture just yet.

Save Reminders:

Revit is configured to remind you to save every 30 minutes so you do not lose any work (Figure 3-2.6).

It is recommended that you do not simply click *Cancel*, but do click the **Save the project** option.

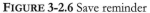

FIGURE 3-2.6 Save reminder

Exercise 3-3:
Edit Tools

The *edit tools* are used often in Revit. A lot of time is spent tweaking designs and making code and client related revisions.

Example: you use the *design tools* (e.g., Walls, Doors, Windows) to initially draw the project. Then you use the *edit tools* to *Move* a wall so a room becomes larger, *Mirror* a cabinet so it faces in a different direction, or *Rotate* the furniture per the owner's instructions.

FIGURE 3-3.1 Modify panel

You will usually access the various edit tools from the Modify tab on the *Ribbon*. You can probably visualize what most of the commands do by the graphics on the icons; see Figure 3-3.1. When you hover over an icon, the tool name will appear. The two letters shown to the right is its keyboard shortcut; pressing those two keys, one at a time, activates that tool.

In this exercise you will get a brief overview of a few of the edit tools by manipulating the tangled web of lines you have previously drawn.

1. **Open** project **ex3-2.rvt** from the previous lesson.

2. **Save-As** "**ex3-3.rvt**".

FYI: You will notice that instructions or tools that have already been covered in this book will have less "step-by-step" instruction.

Delete Tool:

It is no surprise that the *Delete* tool is a necessity; things change and mistakes are made. You can *Delete* one element at a time or several. Deleting elements is very easy: you select the elements, and then pick the *Delete* icon. You will try this on two lines in your drawing.

3. While holding the **Ctrl** key, select the lines identified in **Figure 3-3.2**.

   TIP: See the section below Figure 3-3.2 on Selecting Entities.

4. Select **Delete** from the *Ribbon* (or press the **Delete** key on the keyboard).

The lines are now deleted from the project.

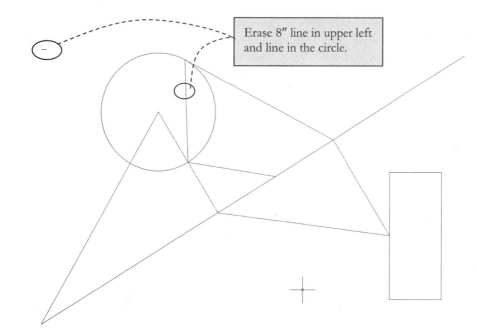

Erase 8″ line in upper left and line in the circle.

FIGURE 3-3.2 Lines to be erased

Selecting Objects:

At this time we will digress and take a quick look at the various techniques for selecting entities in Revit. Most tools work the same when it comes to selecting elements.

When selecting entities, you have two primary ways to select them:
- o   Individually select entities one at a time
- o   Select several entities at a time with a window

You can use one or a combination of both methods to select elements when using the *Copy* tool.

Individual Selections:
When prompted to select entities to copy or delete, for example, you simple move the cursor over the element and click; holding the **Ctrl** key you can select multiple objects. Then you typically click the tool you wish to use on the selected items. Press **Shift** and click on an item to subtract it from the current selection set.

Continued on next page

<u>Window Selections:</u>

Similarly, you can pick a *window* around several elements to select them all at once. To select a *window*, rather than selecting an object as previously described, you select one corner of the *window* you wish to define. That is, you pick a point in "space" and hold the mouse button down. Now, as you move the mouse you will see a rectangle on the screen that represents the windowed area you are selecting; when the *window* encompasses the elements you wish to select, release the mouse.

You actually have two types of windows you can select. One is called a **window** and the other is called a **crossing window**.

Window:

This option allows you to select only the objects that are completely within the *window*. Any lines that extend out of the *window* are not selected.

Crossing Window:

This option allows you to select all the entities that are completely within the *window* and any that extend outside the *window*.

Using Window versus Crossing Window:

To select a *window* you simply pick and drag from left to right to form a rectangle (Figure 3-3.3a).

Conversely, to select a *crossing window*, you pick and drag from right to left to define the two diagonal points of the window (Figure 3-3.3b).

Selecting a chain of lines (hover, tab, click):

Revit provides a quick and easy way to select a chain of lines, that is, a series of lines (or walls) whose endpoints are perfectly connected. You simply hover your cursor over one line so it highlights, then press the Tab key once, and then click the mouse button. This trick can be used to quickly select all the exterior walls on a building, for example.

Turning off **Drag Element on Selection** on the *Status Bar* helps to avoid accidentally clicking directly on an element and moving it rather than starting the intended first corner of a selection window.

Remember, all these draw, modify and select tools have direct application to working with Revit's 3D building components, not just the 2D geometry being covered in this chapter.

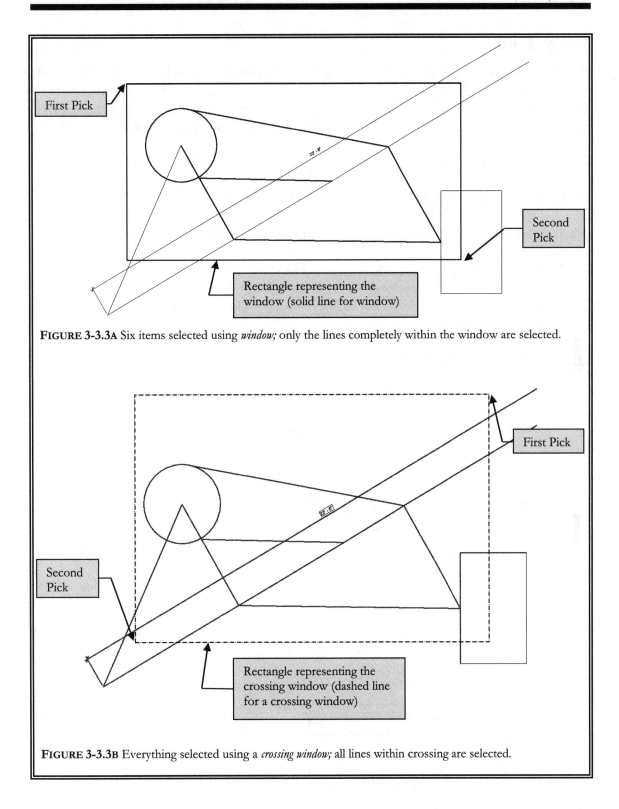

First Pick

Second Pick

Rectangle representing the window (solid line for window)

FIGURE 3-3.3A Six items selected using *window;* only the lines completely within the window are selected.

First Pick

Second Pick

Rectangle representing the crossing window (dashed line for a crossing window)

FIGURE 3-3.3B Everything selected using a *crossing window;* all lines within crossing are selected.

Copy Tool:

The *Copy* tool allows you to accurately duplicate an element(s). You select the items you want to copy and then pick two points that represent an imaginary vector, which provides both length and angle, defining the path used to copy the object. You can also type in the length if there are no convenient points to pick in the drawing. You will try both methods next.

5. **Select the circle.**

6. Select **Copy** from the *Ribbon*.

Notice the prompt on the Status Bar: Click to enter move start point.

7. Pick the **center** of the **circle** (Figure 3-3.4).

   > *FYI: You actually have three different Snaps you can use here: Center, Endpoint and Intersection. All occur at the exact same point.*

Notice the prompt on the Status Bar: Click to enter move end point.

8. Pick the **endpoint** of the angled line in the lower left corner (Figure 3-3.4).

   > *FYI: If you want to make several copies of the circle, select* Multiple *on the* Options Bar.

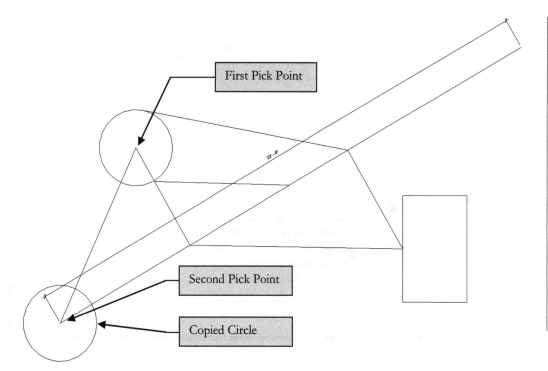

FIGURE 3-3.4 Copied circle; also indicates points selected

9. **Select the rectangle** *(all four lines).*

   TIP: Try the "hover, tab, click" method discussed on page 3-22.

10. Select **Copy**.

11. Pick an arbitrary point on the screen. In this scenario it makes no difference where you pick; you will see why in a moment.

At this point you will move the mouse in the direction you want to copy the rectangle, until the correct angle is displayed, and then type in the distance rather than picking a second point on the screen.

12. Move the mouse towards the upper right until 45 degrees displays, then type **6′** and then press **Enter** (Figure 3-3.5).

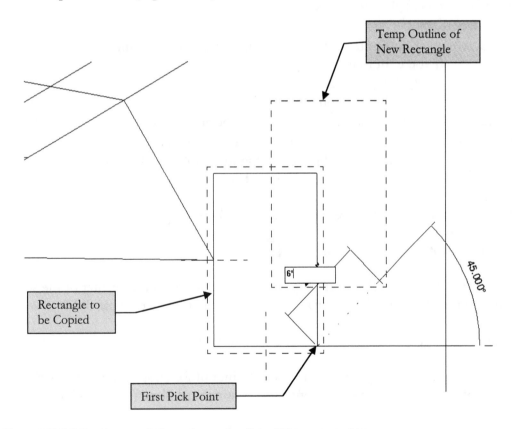

FIGURE 3-3.5 Copying rectangle; angle set visually and distance typed in

NOTE: Your drawing may look a little different than this one because your drawing is not completely to scale.

Move Tool:

The *Move* tool works exactly like the *Copy* tool except, of course, you move the element(s) rather than copy it. Given the similarity to the previous tool covered, the *Move* tool will not be covered now. You are encouraged to try it yourself; just Undo your experiments before proceeding.

Rotate Tool:

With the *Rotate* tool, you can arbitrarily or accurately rotate one or more objects in your drawing. When you need to rotate accurately, you can pick points that define the angle, assuming points exist in the drawing to pick, or you can type a specific angle.

Rotate involves the following steps:
- Select element(s) to be rotated
- Select *Rotate*
- Determine if the Center of Rotation symbol is where you want it.
    - If you want to move it:
        - Simply drag it, or
        - Click *Place* on the *Options Bar*
- Select a point to define a reference line and begin rotation.
- Pick a second point using one of the following methods:
    - By selecting other objects or using the graphic angle display *or*
    - You can type an angle and press **Enter**.

13. **Select the new rectangle** you just copied *(all four lines)*.

14. Select **Rotate** on the *Ribbon*.

Notice that the "Center of Rotation" grip, by default, is located in the center of the selected elements. This is the point about which the rotation will occur. See Figure 3-3.6.

You will not change the "Center of Rotation" at this time.

15. Pick a point directly to the right of the "Center of Rotation" grip; this tells Revit you want to rotate the rectangle relative to the horizontal plane (Figure 3-3.6).

Now, as you move your mouse up or down, you will see the temporary angle dimension displayed. You can move the mouse until the desired angle is displayed and then click to complete the rotation, or you can type the desired angle and then press **Enter**. If you recall, the *Snaps* dialog box controls the increments of the angles that Revit displays; they are all whole numbers. So if you need to rotate something 22.45 degrees, you must type it as Revit will never display that number as an option.

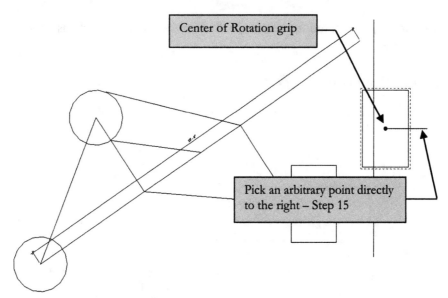

Center of Rotation grip

Pick an arbitrary point directly to the right – Step 15

FIGURE 3-3.6 Rotate tool; first step – select lines and then click Rotate

16. Move the mouse up and to the left until 90 degrees is displayed and then click to complete the rotation (Figure 3-3.7).

90.000°

FIGURE 3-3.7 Rotate tool; last step – select angle visually or type angle

The previous steps just rotated the rectangle 90 degrees counter-clockwise about its center point (Figure 3-3.8).

17. Select the **Undo** icon.

FIGURE 3-3.8 Rotate tool; rectangle rotated about its center point

Now you will do the same thing, except with a different angle and "Center of Rotation."

18. **Select the rectangle** and then pick **Rotate**.

19. Click and drag the "Center of Rotation" grip to the left and *Snap* to the midpoint of the vertical line (Figure 3-3.9).

> *TIP: You can also click the **Place** button on the Options Bar.*

20. Pick a point to the right, creating a horizontal reference line.

21. Start moving your mouse downward, then type **22.5** and then press **Enter** (Figure 3-3.10).

The rectangle is now rotated 22.5 degrees in the clockwise direction (Figure 3-3.11).

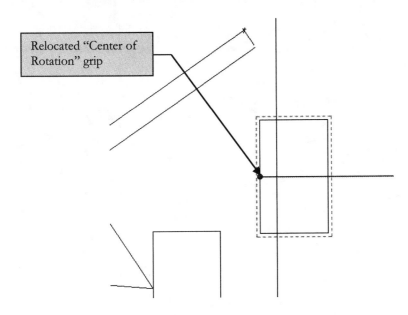

Relocated "Center of Rotation" grip

FIGURE 3-3.9 Rotate tool; relocated Center of Rotation grip

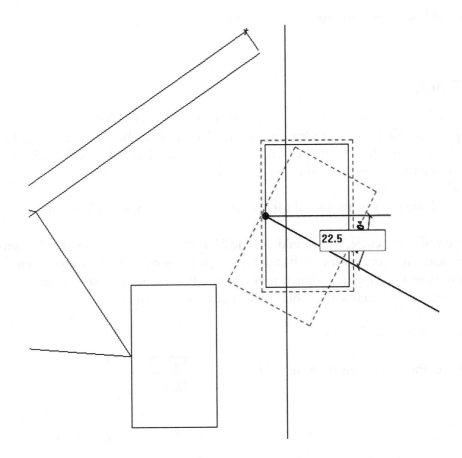

22.5

FIGURE 3-3.10 Rotate tool; typing in exact angle

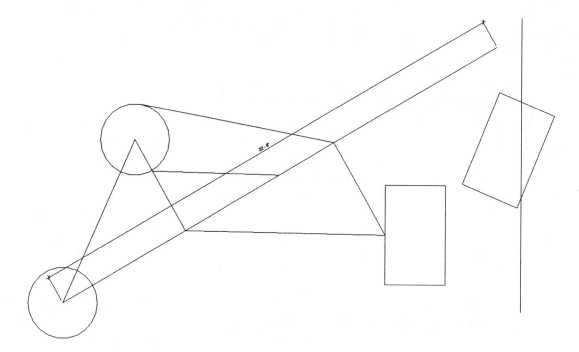

FIGURE 3-3.11 Rotate tool; rectangle rotated 22.5 degrees

Scale Tool:

The *Scale* tool has steps similar to the *Rotate* tool. First you select what you want to scale or resize, specify a scale factor and then you pick the base point. The scale factor can be provided by picks on the screen or entering a numerical scale factor (e.g., 2 or .5, where 2 would be twice the original size and .5 would be half the original size).

Next you will use the *Scale* tool to adjust the size of the circle near the bottom.

Before you resize the circle, you should use the *Modify* tool/mode to note the **diameter** of the circle. Select the circle and view its temporary dimensions. After resizing the circle, you will refer back to the temporary dimensions to note the change. This step is meant to teach you how to verify the accuracy and dimensions of entities in Revit.

22. Select the bottom circle.

23. Select the **Scale** icon from the *Ribbon*.

On the *Options Bar* you will specify a numeric scale factor of .5 to resize the circle to half its original size.

| Modify | Lines | ◯ Graphical ⦿ Numerical Scale: 0.5 |

24. Click **Numerical** and then type **.5** in the textbox *(see the Options Bar above)*.

You are now prompted **Click to enter origin** on the *Status Bar*. This is the base point about which the circle will be scaled; see examples in Figure 3-3.13 on the next page.

25. Click the center of the circle.

You just used the *Scale* tool to change the size of the circle from 1'-6 5/8″ to 9 5/16″ radius. A scale factor of .5 reduces the entities to half their original scale (Figure 3-3.12).

Selecting the Correct Center of Rotation *(Base Point)*:

You need to select the appropriate *Center of Rotation*, or Base Point, for both the *Scale* and *Rotate* commands to get the results desired. A few examples are shown in Figure 3-3.13. The dashed line indicates the original position of the entity being modified. The black dot indicates the base point selected.

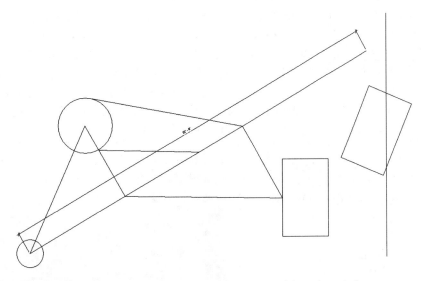

FIGURE 3-3.12 Resize circle; notice it is half the size of the other circle

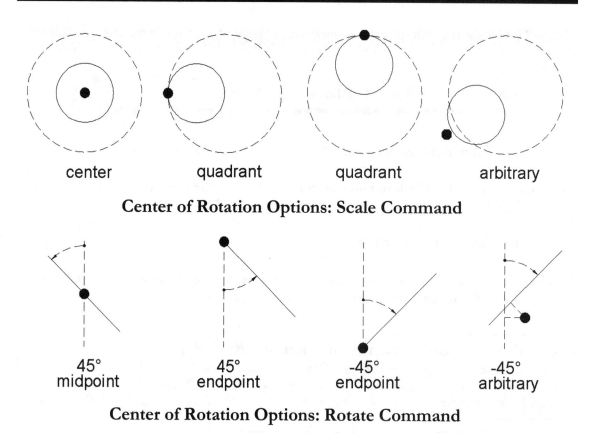

Center of Rotation Options: Scale Command

Center of Rotation Options: Rotate Command

FIGURE 3-3.13 Center of Rotation Options and the various results

This will conclude the brief tour of the *Edit* tools. Do not forget, even though you are editing 2D lines, the edit tools work the same way on 3D elements such as walls, floors, roofs, etc. Exception: you cannot *Scale* walls, doors, etc.; these objects have to be modified by other methods. You would not typically change the door thickness when changing its width and height as would happen if you could use the *Scale* tool on it.

As you surely noticed, the *Modify* panel on the *Ribbon* has a few other tools that have not been investigated yet. Many of these will be covered later in this book.

26. **Save** the project. Your project should already be named "ex3-3.rvt" per Step 2 above.

Carter Residence

Exercise 3-4:
Annotations

Annotations, or text and notes, allow the designer and technician to accurately describe the drawing. Here you will take a quick look at this feature set.

Annotations:

Adding annotations to a drawing can be as essential as the drawing itself. Often the notes describe a part of the drawing that would be difficult to discern from the drawing alone.

For example, a wall framing drawing showing a bolt may not indicate, graphically, how many bolts are needed or at what spacing. The note might say *"5/8" anchor bolt at 24" O.C."*

Next you will add text to your drawing.

1. **Open** project **ex3-3.rvt** from the previous lesson.

2. **Save-As** "**ex3-4.rvt**".

3. Use **Zoom** if required to see the entire drawing, except for the 600' line which can run off the screen.

4. Select **Annotate → Text → Text**.

   Note that the *Model Text* tool on the *Architecture* tab is only for drawing 3D text; *Drafting Views* are only 2D so that command is not even an option currently.

From the *Text* icon tooltip (see image to the right) you can see that the keyboard shortcut for the *Text* tool is **TX**. Thus, at any time you can type T and then X to activate the *Text* tool; if you have another command active, Revit will cancel it.

Text icon's tooltip (hover cursor over icon)

Experienced and efficient designers use a combination of keyboard shortcuts and mouse clicks to save time. For example, while your left hand is typing TX, your right hand can be moving toward the location where you want to insert the text. This process is generally more efficient than switching between tabs on the *Ribbon* and clicking icons, or fly-out icons which require yet another click of the mouse.

Notice the current *prompt* on the *Status Bar* at the bottom of the screen; you are asked to "Click to start text or click and drag rectangle to create text wrapping text." By clicking on the screen you create one line of text, starting at the point picked, and press **Enter** to create additional lines. By clicking and dragging a rectangle you specify a window, primarily for the width, which causes Revit to automatically move text to the next line. When the text no longer fits within the window it is pushed below, or what is called "text wrapping" (Figure 3-4.1).

FIGURE 3-4.1 Status Bar while Text tool is active

You should also notice the various text options available on the *Ribbon* while the *Text* tool is active (Figure 3-4.2). You have two text heights loaded from the template file you started with, text justification icons (Left, Center, Right) and the option to attach leaders, or pointing arrows, to your drawings. The *Text* tool will be covered in more detail later in this book.

FYI: The text heights shown (i.e., ¼", 3/32" via Type Selector) are heights the text will be when printed on paper, regardless of the view scale.

FIGURE 3-4.2 Ribbon and Properties Palette with the Text tool active

5. Pick a point in the upper left portion of the view as shown in Figure 3-4.3.

6. Type "**Learning Revit Architecture is fun!**"

7. Click anywhere in the view, except on the active text, to finish the *Text* command; pressing **Enter** will only add new lines.

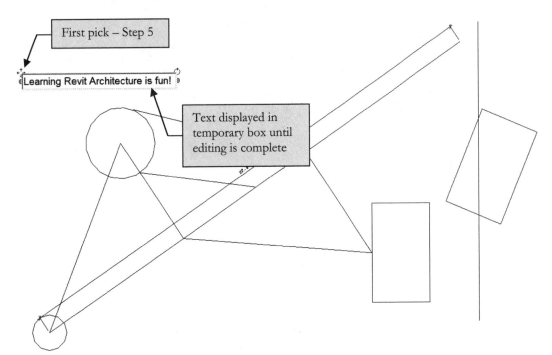

FIGURE 3-4.3 Text tool; picking first point and typing text.

As soon as you complete the text edit, the text will still be selected and the *Move* and *Rotate* symbols will be displayed near the text; this allows you to more quickly *Move* or *Rotate* the text after it is typed (Figure 3-4.4).

FIGURE 3-4.4 Text tool; text typed with Move and Rotate symbols showing.

8. Finish the *Text* tool completely by pressing *Modify* or clicking in the drawing.

TIP: Notice that the text is no longer selected and the symbols are gone; the contextual tab also disappears on the Ribbon.

Your text should generally look similar to Figure 3-4.5.

9. Print your drawing; refer back to page 2-15 for basic printing information. Your print should fit the page and look similar to Figure 3-4.5.

10. **Save** your project.

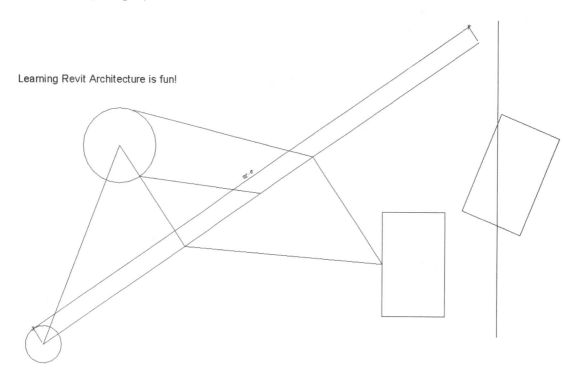

Learning Revit Architecture is fun!

FIGURE 3-4.5 Text tool; text added to current view

Carter Residence

Images courtesy of LHB
www.LHBcorp.com

Self-Exam:

The following questions can be used as a way to check your knowledge of this lesson. The answers can be found at the bottom of the page.

1.   Revit is only accurate to three decimal places. (T/F)

2.   The triangular shaped Snap symbol represents the Midpoint snap. (T/F)

3.   You can move or rotate text via its modify symbols when text is selected. (T/F)

4.   Use the _____ tool to duplicate objects.

5.   When selecting objects, use the _____ to select all the objects in the selection window and all objects that extend through it.

Review Questions:

The following questions may be assigned by your instructor as a way to assess your knowledge of this section. Your instructor has the answers to the review questions.

1.   Revit is a raster based program. (T/F)

2.   The "Center of Rotation" you select for the *Rotate* and *Scale* commands is not important. (T/F)

3.   Entering 16 for a distance actually means 16'-0" to Revit. (T/F)

4.   Use the *Detail Line* tool, with _____ selected on the *Ribbon*, to create squares.

5.   You can change the height of the text from the *Type Selector.* (T/F)

6.   Pressing the _____ key cycles you through the snap options.

7.   Where do the two predefined text heights come from? _____

8.   Specifying degrees with the *Rotate* tool, you must type the number when Revit does not display the number you want; the increments shown on-screen are set in the

     _____ dialog box.

9.   List all the Snap points available on a circle (ex. Line: endpoint, midpoint,

     nearest) _____.

10.   The Snaps Off option must not be checked in the Snaps dialog box to automatically and accurately select snap points while drawing. (T/F)

Notes:

Lesson 4
Drawing 2D Architectural Objects:

This lesson is intended to give you practice drawing in Autodesk® Revit®; while doing so you will become familiar with the various shapes and sizes of the more common symbols used in a residential design.

Do not forget that learning to draw 2D is important in Autodesk Revit. You often define 3D items, like walls, in 2D floor plans, while Autodesk Revit takes care of the third dimension automatically. Additionally, you will often want to embellish a view with 2D lines; for example, the exterior elevation, which is a 2D projection of a 3D model.

If you have used other design programs, like AutoCAD or AutoCAD Architecture, these lessons will help you understand the different ways to draw using Autodesk Revit, a more visual or graphic based input system.

Each drawing will be created in its own *Drafting View*.

For some of the symbols to be drawn, you will have step-by-step instruction and a study on a particular tool that would be useful in the creation of that object. Other symbols to be drawn are for practice by way of repetition and do not provide step by step instruction.

Do NOT draw the dimensions provided; they are for reference only.

Exercise 4-1:
Sketching Rectilinear Objects

Overview:

All the objects you will draw in this exercise consist entirely of straight lines, either orthogonal or angular.

As previously mentioned, all the objects MUST BE drawn in SEPARATE *Drafting Views*. Each object will have a specific name provided, which is to be used to name the *Drafting View*. All views will be created in one Revit project file which should be saved in your personal folder created for this course.

view name: **Bookcase**

3'-0"

1'-0"

This is a simple rectangle that represents the size of a bookcase.

1. **Open** a new project; **Save** the project as **Ex4-1.rvt**.

2. Create a new *Drafting View* named **Bookcase** (Figure 4-1.1) *(from the View tab)*.

3. Select **Detail Line** from the *Annotate* tab.

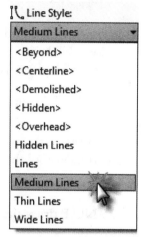

By default, the current line thickness is set to *Thin Lines*. You can see this on the *Ribbon* when the *Detail Line* tool is active. You will change this to *Medium* next.

4. Set the line thickness to **Medium Lines** (Figure 4-1.2; also see image to the right).

> *NOTE: Use this setting for all the drawings in this chapter.*

5. Click the **Rectangle** button on the *Ribbon* (Figure 4-1.2).

6. **Draw a rectangle**, per the dimensions shown above, generally in the center of the drawing window.

> *TIP: You should be able to accurately draw the rectangle using the temporary dimensions; if not, click on the dimension text to change it.*

New Drafting View

Name:	Bookcase
Scale:	1 1/2" = 1'-0"
Scale value 1:	8

OK   Cancel

FIGURE 4-1.1 New Drafting View dialog

Modify | Place Detail Lines

Line Style:
Medium Lines

Create   Draw   Line Style

FIGURE 4-1.2 Ribbon; Medium Lines and Rectangle selected

view name: **Coffee Table**

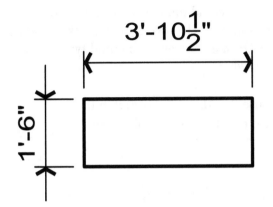

7. Create a new *Drafting View*.

   NOTE: This step will be assumed for the rest of the drawings in this exercise.

8. Similar to the steps listed above, plus the suggestions mentioned below, create the coffee table shown to the left.

Draw the rectangle as closely as possible using the visual aids; you should be able to get the 1'-6" dimension correct. Then click on the text for the temporary horizontal dimension and type in 3'-10 1/2".

Entering fractions: the 3'-10½" can be entered in one of four ways.

o	3 10.5	*Notice there is a space between the feet and inches.*
o	3 10 1/2	*Two spaces separate the feet, inches and fractions.*
o	0 46.5	*This is all in inches; that is 3'-10½" = 46.5".*
o	46.5"	*Omit the feet and use the inches symbol.*

view name: **Desk-1**

9. Draw the *Desk* in its own view, similar to the steps outlined above.

TIP: You should double-check your drawing's dimensions using the Measure *tool. Pick the icon from the* Modify *tab and then pick two points. A temporary dimension will display.*

view name: **Night Table**

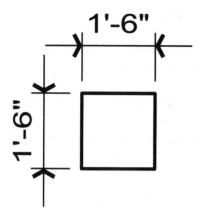

Obviously you could draw this quickly per the previous examples. However, you will take a look at copying a *Drafting View* and then modifying an existing drawing.

You will use the *Move* tool to stretch the 3'-0" wide desk down to a 1'-6" wide night table.

First you will look at *Drafting Views* and how they are organized in the *Project Browser*, and then you will copy the *Desk-1 Drafting View* to start the *Night Table* drawing/view.

10. Locate the **Drafting Views** section in the *Project Browser* and expand it by clicking on the "plus" symbol.

Notice that the three views you previously created are listed (Figure 4-1.3). The *Desk-1* view is shown with bold text because it is the current view. All *Drafting Views* are listed here and can be renamed, copied or deleted at anytime by right-clicking on the item in the list. You will copy the *Desk-1* view next.

FIGURE 4-1.3 Project Browser: Drafting Views section expanded

11. Right-click on the *Desk-1* view (Figure 4-1.4).

Next you will select *Duplicate with Detailing* which will copy the *View* and the *View's* contents, whereas the *Duplicate* option will only copy the *View* and its settings but without any line work.

12. Select **Duplicate View → Duplicate with Detailing** from the pop-up menu (Figure 4-1.4).

You now have a new View named *Copy of Desk-1* in the *Drafting Views* list. This *View* is open and current.

Figure 4-1.4 Drafting Views list – Right click on Desk-1 view for menu

13. Right-click on the new view name, *Copy of Desk-1*, and select **Rename** from the pop-up menu.

14. Type **Night Table** and then click **OK** (Figure 4-1.5).

FIGURE 4-1.5 Rename View dialog – Night Table entered

You are now ready to modify the copy of the *Desk-1* linework. You will use the *Move* tool to change the location of one of the vertical lines, which will cause the two horizontal lines to stretch with it. Autodesk Revit *Detail Lines* automatically have a parametric relationship to adjacent lines when their endpoints touch them.

15. Select the vertical line on the right and then click the **Move** icon on the *Ribbon*.

16. Pick the midpoint of the vertical line, then move the mouse 1'-6" to the left and click again (Figure 4-1.6).

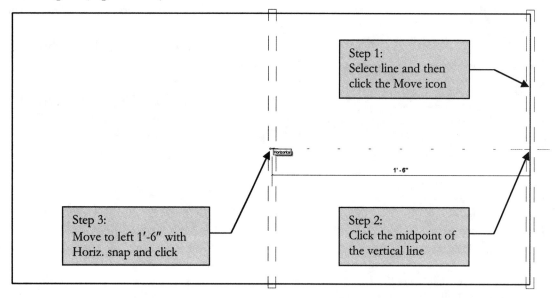

Step 1:
Select line and then click the Move icon

Horizontal

1'-6"

Step 3:
Move to left 1'-6" with Horiz. snap and click

Step 2:
Click the midpoint of the vertical line

FIGURE 4-1.6 Move tool used to stretch a rectangle

1' - 6"

FIGURE 4-1.7 Stretched rectangle (using Move tool)

The rectangle is now resized, or stretched, to be half its original width.

You will notice that the horizontal lines automatically adjusted.

Revit assumes a special relationship between a line being edited and any line whose endpoint is directly touching it.

TIP: You can select "Disjoin" on the Options Bar while in the Move command if you don't want other lines to move or stretch with it. You will not do that here though.

17. **Save** your project.

view name: **Dresser-1**

18. Draw the dresser using the following tip:

    TIP: Simply draw two rectangles. Move the smaller rectangle into place using the Move tool and Snaps.

view name: **Dresser-2**

19. Draw this smaller dresser.

view name: **Desk-2**

20. Draw this desk in the same way you drew *Dresser-1*.

view name: **File Cabinet**

21. Draw this file cabinet.

view name: **Chair-1**

22. Draw this chair per the following tips:

Draw the 2′x2′ square first, and then draw three separate rectangles as shown to the right. Move them into place with *Move* and *Snaps*. Next, delete the extra lines so your drawing looks like the one shown on the left. Pay close attention to the dimensions!

view name: **Sofa**

23. *Duplicate* and *Rename* the *Chair-1* view to start this drawing.

TIP: See the next page for more information on creating this drawing.

You can create the *Sofa* in a similar way that you created the *Night Table*; that is, you will use the *Move* tool. Rather than selecting one vertical line, however, you will select all the lines on one side of the chair.

You can select all the lines on one side in a single step, rather than clicking each one individually while holding the Ctrl key. You will select using a *window* selection, not a *crossing window* selection.

24. **Select** all the lines on the right side (Figure 4-1.8).

> *TIP: Pick from left to right for a* window *selection.*

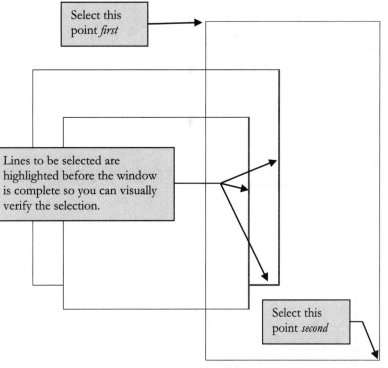

Select this point *first*

Lines to be selected are highlighted before the window is complete so you can visually verify the selection.

Select this point *second*

FIGURE 4-1.8 Stretch chair using Move tool

25. Use the ***Move*** tool to extend the chair into a sofa.

> *TIP: The difference between the chair width and the sofa width is the distance the lines are to be moved.*

You have just successfully transformed the chair into a sofa! Do not forget to *Save* often to avoid losing work. Also, use the *Measure* tool to verify your drawing's accuracy.

view name: **Bed-Double.dwg**

26. Draw this bed using lines and rectangles; the exact sizes of items not dimensioned are not important.

FIGURE 4-1.9 Floor Plan example using similar furniture to that drawn in this exercise.

Image courtesy of Stanius Johnson Architects
www.staniusjohnson.com

Exercise 4-2:
Sketching Objects With Curves

Similar to the previous exercise, you will draw several shapes; this time the shapes will have curves in them.

You will look at the various commands that allow you to create curves, like *Arc*, *Circle* and *Fillet*.

Again, you will not draw the dimensions as they are for reference only; each drawing should be drawn in its own *Drafting View*. Name the view with the label provided.

Finally, you can ignore the black dot on each of the drawings below. This dot simply represents the location from which the symbol would typically be inserted or placed.

view name: Laundry-Sink

This is a simple rectangle that represents the size of a laundry sink, with a circle that represents the drain.

1. **Open** a new Revit project and name it **Ex4-2.rvt**.

2. Draw the rectangle shown; refer to Exercise 4-1 for more information.

3. Use the *Measure* tool to verify the size of your rectangle.

Next you will draw a circle for the drain. The drain needs to be centered left and right and 5" from the back edge. The following steps will show you one way in which to do this.

4. Select the *Detail Line* tool from the *Annotate* tab.

5. Select the *Circle* icon from the *Ribbon* (Figure 4-2.1).

FIGURE 4-2.1 Sketch Options for detail lines

6. Pick the midpoint of the top line (Figure 4-2.2).

   FYI: This is the center of the circle.

7. Type **0 1** for the radius and press **Enter** (0 1 = 0′ – 1″).

   FYI: This creates a 2″ diameter circle.

FIGURE 4-2.2 Creating a circle and moving it into place.

At this point you may get an error indicating the "Element is too small on screen" (Figure 4-2.3). This is supposed to prevent a user, like yourself, from accidentally drawing a very small line when you click the mouse twice right next to each other or trying to change the dimension to a previously drawn line to something less than 1/32″. If you get this error, you simply zoom in on your drawing more so the circle is more prominently visible on the screen.

FIGURE 4-2.3 Revit error message when creating the circle IF you are zoomed out too far

8. If you did get the error message just described, click *Cancel, Zoom In* and then draw the circle again.

9. Select the circle and then the **Move** tool.

10. **Move** the circle straight down 5″ (Figure 4-2.2).

That's it! Do not forget to save your *Ex4-2* project often.

view name: Dryer

Here you will draw a dryer with rounded front corners. This, like all the other symbols in this lesson, is a plan view symbol, as in "viewed from the top."

11. Draw a 30″x26″ Rectangle.

12. Use the **Measure** tool to verify your dimensions.

Next, you will draw the line that is 2½″ from the back of the dryer. You will draw the line in approximately the correct position and then use the temporary dimensions to correct the location.

13. Select the **Detail Line** tool and then pick a point approximately 3″down from the upper-left corner; a temporary dimension will be displayed before you click your mouse button (Figure 4-2.4).

14. Complete the horizontal line by picking a point perpendicular to the vertical line on the right (Figure 4-2.4).

15. With the temporary dimensions still displayed, click the text for the 0′-3″ dimension, type **0 2.5** and then press **Enter** (Figure 4-2.5).

16. Click *Modify* to clear the selection and make the *Temporary Dimensions* go away.

FIGURE 4-2.4 Drawing a line

0 2.5

1' - 11 3/4

Pick these lines
– Step 19

FIGURE 4-2.5 Adjusting new lines position via temporary dimensions

Next you will round the corners. You still use the *Detail Line* tool, but use a *Draw* option called *Fillet Arc*, pronounced "Fill it." You will try this next.

17. With the ***Detail Lines*** tool active, select the **Fillet Arc** *Draw* option on the *Ribbon* (Figure 4-2.6).

18. Check **Radius** and enter **0' 2"** in the text box on the *Options Bar* (Figure 4-2.6).

FIGURE 4-2.6 Ribbon and Options Bar; options for Detail Lines in Fillet mode

19. Pick the two lines identified in Figure 4-2.5.

The intersection of the two lines is where the arc is placed; notice the two lines you picked have been trimmed back to the new *Fillet Arc*.

20. Repeat the previous step to **Fillet** the other corner.

view name: **Washer**

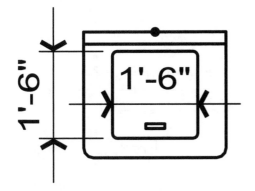

This drawing is identical to the *Dryer* except for the door added to the top. You can duplicate the *Dryer Drafting View* to get a jump start on this drawing.

To draw the door you will use the **Offset** option, which is part of the *Detail Line* tool.

The *Offset* tool is easy to use; to use it you:
o   Select the *Detail Line* tool
o   Select the *Pick Lines* icon on the *Ribbon*
o   Enter the *Offset* distance on the *Options Bar*
o   Select near a line, and on the side to offset

21. Select the *Detail Line* tool.

22. Select the **Pick Lines** icon on the *Ribbon* (Figure 4-2.7).

FIGURE 4-2.7 Ribbon and Options Bar: options for Detail Lines in Pick Lines mode

Note that the *Pick Lines* icon toggles you from *Draw* mode to *Pick Lines* mode. The *Pick Lines* mode allows you to use existing linework to quickly create new linework. You should notice the available options on the *Options Bar* have changed after selecting *Pick Lines*; you can switch back by selecting the *Draw* icons on the *Ribbon* (Figure 4-2.7).

23. Enter **0′ 6″** for the *Offset* distance (Figure 4-2.7).

Next you will need to select a line to offset. Which side of the line you click on will indicate the direction the line is offset. Revit provides a visual reference line indicating which side the line will be offset to and its location based on the offset distance entered.

Without clicking the mouse button, move your cursor around the drawing and notice the visual reference line. Move your mouse from side-to-side over a line to see the reference line move to correspond to the cursor location.

24. **Offset** the left vertical line towards the right.

> *TIP: Make sure you entered the correct offset distance in the previous step (Figure 4-2.8).*

You will need to look at the washer drawing and the dryer drawing dimensions to figure out the door size.

25. **Offset** the other three sides; your sketch should look like Figure 4-2.9.

26. Use the *Fillet Arc* sketch mode, in the *Detail Line* tool, to create a 1″ radius on the four corners.

27. Click *Modify* to finish the current command.

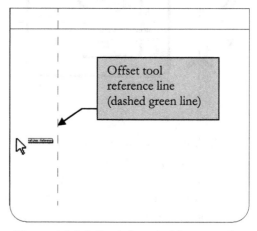

Figure 4-2.8 Offset left vertical line towards the right 6″

Offset tool reference line (dashed green line)

All four corners should now be rounded off.

28. Draw a small 4″x1″ rectangle to represent the door handle. Draw it anywhere. Then using *Snaps*, move it to the midpoint of the bottom door edge, and then move the handle 2″ up.

29. **Save** your project. Make sure the view name is *Washer*.

FIGURE 4-2.9 All four lines offset inward to create outline for washer door

TIP: Revit also provides an Offset *tool on the* Modify *tab of the* Ribbon. *The steps required are very similar to those just described.*

view name: **Range**

Now you will draw a kitchen *Range* with four circles that represent the burners.

In this exercise you will have to draw temporary lines, called *construction lines*, to create reference points needed to accurately locate the circles. Once the circles have been drawn, the construction lines can be erased.

30. Draw the range with a 2″ deep control panel at the back; refer to the steps described to draw the dryer if necessary.

31. Draw the four construction lines shown in Figure 4-2.10. Use the **Ref Plane** tool on the *Architecture* tab.

32. Draw two 9½″ Dia. circles and two 7½″ Dia. circles using the intersection of the construction lines to locate the centers of the circles (Figure 4-2.10).

FIGURE 4-2.10 Range with four temporary construction lines (shown dashed for clarity)

TIP: Refer back to the Laundry-Sink for sketching circles.

33. **Erase** the four **Ref Plane** lines (construction lines).

34. **Save** your project.

TIP: When using the Measure *tool, you can select* Chain *on the* Options Bar *to have Revit calculate the total length of several picks. For example, you can quickly get the perimeter of a rectangle by picking each corner. Notice, as you pick points, the* Total Length *is listed on the* Options Bar.

view name: **Chair-2**

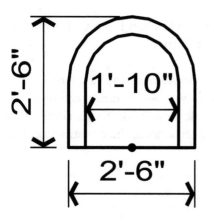

Now you will sketch another chair. You will use *Detail Line* with *Offset* and the *Arc* settings.

First you will draw the arc at the perimeter.

35. Select *Detail Line* and then **Center – Ends Arc** from the *Ribbon* (Figure 4-2.1).

Notice on the *Status Bar* you are prompted to "**Click to enter arc center**."

36. *First Pick*: Pick a point somewhere in the middle of a new *Drafting View* named *Chair-2* (Figure 4-2.11).

You are now prompted, on the *Status Bar*, "**Drag arc radius to desired location**."

37. *Second Pick*: Move the cursor towards the left, while snapped to the horizontal, until the temporary dimension reads **1'-3"** (Figure 4-2.11).

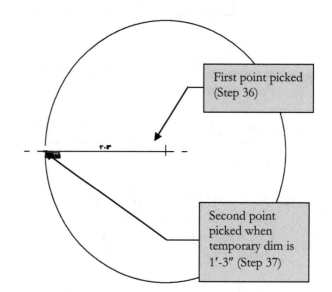

FIGURE 4-2.11 Sketching an arc; picking second point

NOTE: As you can see, Revit temporarily displays a full circle until you pick the second point. This is because Revit does not know which direction the arc will go or what the arc length will be. The full circle allows you to visualize where your arc will be (Figure 4-2.11).

38. *Third Pick*: Move the cursor to the right until the arc is 180 degrees and snapped to the horizontal again (Figure 4-2.12).

TIP: Notice that your cursor location determines on which direction or side the arc is created; move the cursor around before picking the third endpoint to see how the preview arc changes on screen.

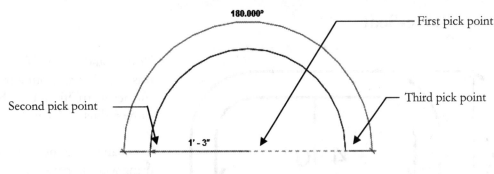

FIGURE 4-2.12 Pick points for arc command

Next you will draw the three *Detail Lines* to complete the perimeter of the chair.

39. Draw two vertical lines **1'-3"** long; attached to the arc endpoints.

   TIP: Do not forget to use Medium Lines *when sketching detail lines; if you forgot you can select the lines, while in* Modify *mode, and select* Medium Lines *from the* Element Type Selector *on the* Ribbon.

40. Draw the **2'-6"** line across the bottom.

Notice the radius is 1'-3". You did not have to enter that number because the three points you picked were enough information for Revit to determine it automatically.

If you had drawn the three lines in Steps 39 and 40 before the arc, you would not have had the required center point to pick while creating the arc. However, you could have drawn a temporary horizontal line across the top to set up a center pick that would allow you to draw the circle in its final location; or even better, use the **Start-End-Radius** *Detail Line* option.

You have now completed the perimeter of the chair.

41. Use the ***Offset*** tool to offset the arc and two vertical lines the required distance to complete the sketch.

42. **Save** your project.

view name: **Love-Seat**

You should be able to draw this *Love-Seat* without any further instruction. Use the same radius as *Chair-2*.

You can create the drawing using a combination of the following tools:
- o *Detail Line*
- o *Fillet Arc*
- o *Offset*
- o *Move*

view name: **Tub.dwg**

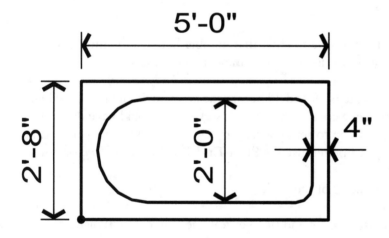

Now you will draw a bathtub. You will use several commands previously covered.

You will use the following tools:
- o *Detail Line*
- o *Fillet Arc*
- o *Offset*
- o *Move*

You may also wish to draw one or more construction lines to help locate things like the large radius, although it can be drawn without them.

view name: **Lav-1**

Draw this lavatory per the following specifications:

- o Larger arcs shown shall have a 2½″ radius
- o Smaller arcs shown shall have a 1″ radius, outside corners
- o Sides and Front of sink to have 1½″ space, offset
- o Back to have 4″ space, offset
- o Small rectangle to be 4½″x1″ and 1½″ away from the back
- o 2″ Dia. drain, 8″ from back

view name: **Lav-2**

Next you will draw another lavatory. This time you will use the *Ellipse* tool.

43. Create a new *Drafting View.*

44. Select *Detail Lines* and then **Ellipse** from the *Options Bar* (Figure 4-2.1).

Notice the *Status Bar* prompt: **"Click to enter ellipse center."**

45. Pick near the middle of the screen.

46. With the cursor snapped to the vertical, point the cursor straight down and then type **0 9.5**; press **Enter.**

   NOTE: 9½″ is half the HEIGHT, which is 1′-7″.

Now you need to specify the horizontal axis of the ellipse.

47. Again, snapping to the horizontal plane, position the cursor towards the right then type **0 11** and then press the **Enter** key.

   NOTE: 11″ is half the width: 1′-10″.

That's all it takes to draw an ellipse!

48. ***Copy*** the ellipse vertically downward **3½"** (Figure 4-2.13).

FIGURE 4-2.13 Ellipse copied downward 3½"

Next you will use the *Scale* tool to reduce the size of the second ellipse. To summarize the steps involved:

- Select the ellipse to be resized
- Select the *Scale* icon
- Pick the origin
- Pick the opposite side of the ellipse
- Enter a new value for the ellipse.

49. Select the lower ellipse.

50. Select the **Scale** icon on the *Ribbon,* on the *Modify* tab.

Notice the *Status Bar* prompt: **"Pick to enter origin."** The origin, or base point, is a point on, or relative to, the object that does not move.

51. *First Pick:* Pick the top edge, midpoint, of the selected ellipse (Figure 4-2.14).

52. *Second Pick:* Pick the bottom edge, midpoint, of the same ellipse (Figure 4-2.14).

53. Type **1 2** (i.e., 1'-2") and press **Enter;** this will be the new distance between the two points picked.

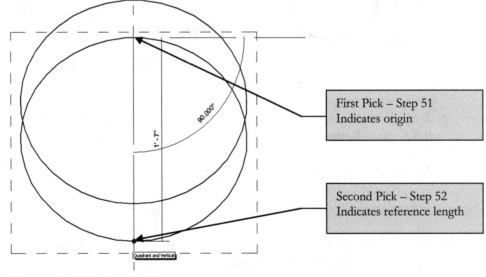

First Pick – Step 51
Indicates origin

Second Pick – Step 52
Indicates reference length

FIGURE 4-2.14 Scaling the ellipse

Next you need to draw the faucet and drain. As it turns out, the faucet and drain for *Lav-1* are in the same position relative to the middle and back (black dot). So to save time, you will *Copy/Paste* these items from the *Lav-1* drafting view into the *Lav-2* view.

54. Open **Lav-1** *Drafting View*.

55. Select the entire *Lav-1* sketch.

56. Pick **Modify | Lines → Clipboard → Copy** while the *Lav-1* linework is selected.

57. Switch back to the *Lav-2* view and press **Ctrl + V** on the keyboard. Press both keys at the same time.

58. Pick a point to the side of the *Lav-2* sketch (Figure 4-2.15).

59. Select the faucet, the small rectangle, and the drain (i.e., the circle).

   TIP: Use a window *selection, picking from left to right.*

60. Select the *Move* tool; pick the middle/back of the *Lav-1* sketch and then pick the middle/back of the *Lav-2* sketch.

   NOTE: These two points represent the angle and distance to move the selected items.

61. **Erase** the extra *Lav-1* linework from the *Lav-2* view.

You should now have the faucet and drain correctly positioned in your *Lav-2* view.

FIGURE 4-2.15 Lav-2 view: moving items from copied sketch

view name: **Sink-1**

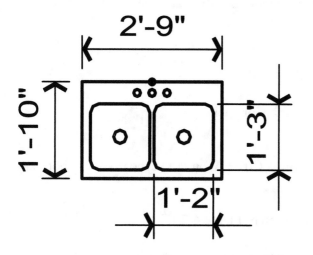

Draw this lavatory per the following specifications:

- o 2″ space, offset at sides and front
- o 3″ Dia. Circles centered in sinks
- o 2″ rad. for Fillets
- o 1½″ Dia. at faucet spaces; 3½″ apart

view name: **Water-Closet**

You should be able to draw this symbol without any help.

TIP: Draw a construction line from the Origin (i.e., black dot) straight down 11″ (2′-4″ – 1′-5″ = 11″). This will give you a point to pick when drawing the ellipse.

view name: **Tree**

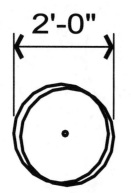

62. Draw one large circle and then copy it similar to this drawing.

63. Draw one small 1″ diameter circle at the approximate center.

64. **Save** your project.

view name: **Door-36**

This symbol is used to show a door in a floor plan. The arc represents the path of the door as it opens and shuts.

A symbol like this, 90 degrees open, helps to avoid the door conflicting with something in the house like cabinets or a toilet. Existing doors are typically shown open 45 degrees so it is easier to visually discern new from existing.

Revit has an advanced door tool, so you would not actually draw this symbol very often. However, you may decide to draw one in plan that represents a gate in a reception counter or one in elevation to show a floor hatch. Refer back to Figure 4-1.9 for a floor plan example with door symbols.

65. Draw a **2″x3′-0″ rectangle**.

66. Draw an arc using **Center – Ends Arc**; select the three points in the order shown in Figure 4-2.16.

> *TIP: Be sure your third pick shows the cursor snapped to the horizontal plane.*

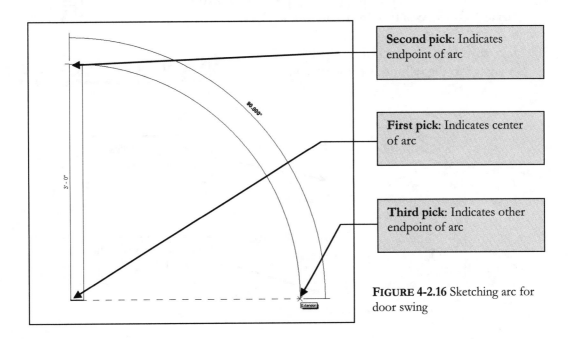

Second pick: Indicates endpoint of arc

First pick: Indicates center of arc

Third pick: Indicates other endpoint of arc

FIGURE 4-2.16 Sketching arc for door swing

view name: **Door2-36**

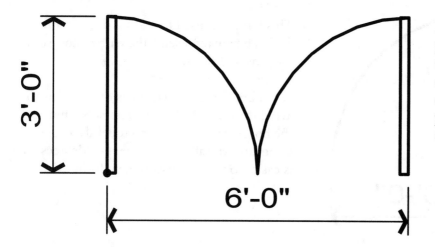

Here you will use a previous drawing and the *Mirror* tool to quickly create this drawing showing a pair of doors in a single opening.

67. Right-click on **Door-36** view label in the *Project Browser*, select "**Duplicate with detailing**" from the pop-up menu.

68. **Rename** the new *Detail View* **Door2-36**.

Next you will mirror both the rectangle and the arc. By default, Revit wants you to select a previously drawn line to be used as the "axis of reflection," but you do not have a line that would allow you to mirror the door properly to the left, so you have to pick the "*Draw Mirror Axis*" option on the *Ribbon*.

69. Select the rectangle and the arc, use a *crossing window* by picking from right to left, and then pick the **Modify | Lines → Modify → Mirror - Draw Axis** tool from the *Ribbon*.

70. Make sure *Copy* is checked on the *Options Bar*. See image to the right; this is the default.

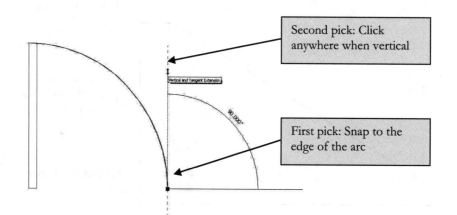

Second pick: Click anywhere when vertical

First pick: Snap to the edge of the arc

FIGURE 4-2.17 Creating axis of reflection

Notice the *Status Bar* is prompting you to "**Pick Start Point for Axis of Reflection.**"

71. Pick the two points shown in **Figure 4-2.17**.

At this point the door symbol, the rectangle and arc, is mirrored and the *Mirror* tool is done.

72. Select *Modify* to end the command and unselect everything.

73. **Save** your project as "Ex4-2.rvt".

view name: **Clg-Fan-1**

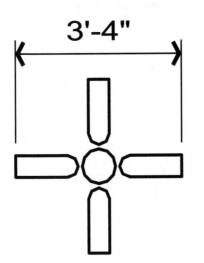

You will use the *Array* command while drawing this ceiling fan.

The *Array* command can be used to array entities in a rectangular pattern (e.g., columns on a grid) or in a polar pattern (i.e., in a circular pattern).

You will use the polar array to rotate and copy the fan blade all in one step!

74. Start a new drawing and create the portion of drawing shown in the figure to the right.

75. Select the fan blade and then select **Array** from the *Ribbon*.

Similar to the *Rotate* tool, you will relocate the *Center of Rotation Symbol* to the center of the 8″ circle. This will cause the fan blade to array around the circle rather than the center of the first fan blade.

76. Click *Radial* on the *Options Bar* and then click and *drag* the **Rotation grip** to the center of the 8″ circle (or click the *Place* button on the *Options Bar*); make sure Revit snaps to the center point before clicking (see Figure 4-2.19).

77. Make the following changes to the *Options Bar* (Figure 4-2.18).

FIGURE 4-2.18 Array options on the Options Bar

78. After typing the angle in the *Options Bar*, press **Enter**.

You should now see the three additional fan blades and a temporary array number. This gives you the option to change the array number if desired.

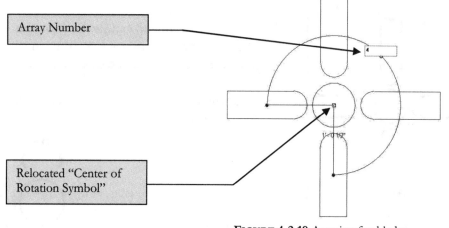

FIGURE 4-2.19 Arraying fan blades

79. Click **Modify** to complete the *Array* and finish the ceiling fan.

Because you left *Group and Associate* checked on the *Options Bar* when you created the array, you can select any part of a fan blade and the array number will appear, like a temporary dimension, and allow you to change the number. You can select *Ungroup* from the *Ribbon* to make each item individually editable as if you had drawn everything from scratch.

80. **Save** your project.

FYI: You can export each Drafting View to a file and import it back into any project file. It can then be placed as a symbol into floor plans. This would make for smaller files on large projects, such as a large hospital complex. The major downside is that you would not see anything in your 3D views for furniture. Thus, you will not likely use these for your Revit plans, but you will be able to utilize every skill learned in this section!

Self-Exam:

The following questions can be used as a way to check your knowledge of this lesson. The answers can be found at the bottom of the page.

1.   Revit does not allow you to copy *Detail Views*. (T/F)

2.   Entering 4 3.25 in Revit means 4'-3¼". (T/F)

3.   Reference Planes (aka, construction lines) are useful drawing aids. (T/F)

4.   Use the _____ tool to sketch an oval shape.

5.   When you want to make a previously drawn rectangle wider you would use

     the _____ tool.

Review Questions:

The following questions may be assigned by your instructor as a way to assess your knowledge of this section. Your instructor has the answers to the review questions.

1.   Use the *Offset* option to quickly create a parallel line(s). (T/F)

2.   If Revit displays an error message indicating a line is too small to be drawn, you simply zoom in more and try again. (T/F)

3.   Use the _____ command to create a reverse image.

4.   With the *Move* tool, lines completely within the selection window are actually only moved, not stretched. (T/F)

5.   You can relocate the "center of rotation" when using *Radial Array*. (T/F)

6.   Occasionally you need to draw an object and then move it into place to accurately locate it. (T/F)

7.   The _____ is an option within the *Detail Line* tool which allows you to create a rounded corner where two lines intersect.

8.   When using the *Mirror* tool, you occasionally need to draw a temporary line that represents the *Axis of Reflection*. (T/F)

9.   Which line style was required to be selected in the *Type Selector*, in the *Properties Palette*, for all the linework in this Lesson? _____

10. In the *Detail Line* tool, how many options allow you to draw arcs? _____

Notes:

Lesson 5
Residence: FLOOR PLAN (First Floor):

In this lesson you will draw the first floor plan of a single family residence. The project will be further developed in subsequent chapters. It is recommended that you spend adequate time on this lesson as later lessons build upon this one.

Be sure to check out the videos on the disc for more information on modeling walls, doors and windows using Autodesk® Revit®.

Exercise 5-1:
Project Setup

The Project:

You will model a two-story residence located in a suburban setting. Just to the North of the building site is a medium sized lake. For the sake of simplicity, the property is virtually flat.

The main entry is from the South side of the building. You enter the building into a large foyer. The second floor has a railing that looks down onto the foyer.

This building is not meant to meet any particular building code. It is strictly a tool to learn how to use Autodesk Revit 2016. Having said that, however, there are several general comments as to how codes may impact a particular part of the design; each must be verified with your local rules and regulations.

Creating the Project File:

A Building Information Model (BIM), as previously mentioned, consists of a single file. This file can be quite large. For example, the prestigious architectural design firm SOM used Autodesk Revit to design the Freedom Tower in New York. As you can imagine, a skyscraper would be a large BIM file, whereas a single family residence would be much smaller.

Large databases are just starting to enter the architectural design realm. However, banks, hospitals, etc. have been using them for years, even with multiple users!

When Autodesk Revit is launched, the *Recent Files* view is loaded. Template files have several items setup and ready to use (e.g., some wall, door and window types). Starting with the correct template can save you a significant amount of time.

Autodesk Revit provides a handful of templates with particular project types in mind. They are *Commercial*, *Construction* and *Residential*.

In this exercise you will use the *Residential* template. It has several aspects of the project file pre-setup and ready for use. A few of these items will be discussed momentarily.

As your knowledge in Revit increases, you will be able to start refining a custom template, which probably originated from a standard template. The custom template will have things like a firm's title block and a cover sheet with abbreviations, symbols etc. all set up and ready to go.

Next you will create a new project file.

1. Select *Application Menu → New → Project*.

   You are now in the *New Project* dialog box. Rather than clicking *OK*, which would use a stripped-down default architectural template, you will select *Browse* so you can select a specialized template (Figure 5-1.1).

FIGURE 5-1.1 New Project dialog

2. Click the **Browse...** button.

3. Select the template named **Residential-Default.rte** from the list of available templates (Figure 5-1.2).

4. Click **Open** to select the highlighted template file.

5. Click **OK** to complete the *New Project* dialog.

FIGURE 5-1.2 Choose Template dialog

You have just set up a project file that you will use for the **remainder of this book**, so be sure you selected the correct template file!

Next, you will take a look at the predefined wall types that have been loaded with the template file.

FIGURE 5-1.3 Preloaded wall types

6. Select **Architecture → Build → Wall**.

7. Click the *Type Selector* down-arrow on the *Properties Palette* (Figure 5-1.3). When done looking at the wall types, press the **Esc** key three times to close the *Type Selector* and cancel the command.

Wall Types:

Notice the wall types that have been preloaded as part of the *Residential* template. These wall types are many of the types of walls one would expect to find on a typical residential construction project.

The walls are mostly wood stud walls, both interior and exterior. If you look at the *Default* or *Commercial* templates, you will see mostly metal stud and concrete block (CMU) wall types.

Additionally, the thicknesses of materials can vary between commercial and residential; this is also accounted for in the templates. For example, gypsum board is typically ⅝″ thick on commercial projects whereas it is usually only ½″ on residential work.

To reiterate the concept, consider the following comparisons between a typical commercial interior wall and a typical residential interior wall.

- Typical Commercial Wall
  - ⅝″ Gypsum Board
  - 3⅝″ Metal Stud
  - ⅝″ Gypsum Board
    - Total thickness: **4⅞″**

- Typical Residential Wall
  - ½″ Gypsum Board
  - 2x4 Wood Stud (3½″ actual)
  - ½″ Gypsum Board
    - Total Thickness: **4½″**

Project Browser:

Take a few minutes to look at the *Project Browser* and notice the views and sheets that have been set up via the template file you selected (Figure 5-1.4).

Many of the views that you need to get started with the design of a residence are set up and ready to go.

Practically all the sheets typically found on a residential project have been created; see Figure 5-1.4 under the *Sheets (all)* heading of the *Project Browser*. Also, notice the sheets with a plus symbol next to them. These are sheets that already have views placed on them. You will study this more later, but a view, such as your *East Elevation* view, is placed on a sheet at a scale you select. This means your title block sheets will have printable information as soon as you start sketching walls in one of your plan views.

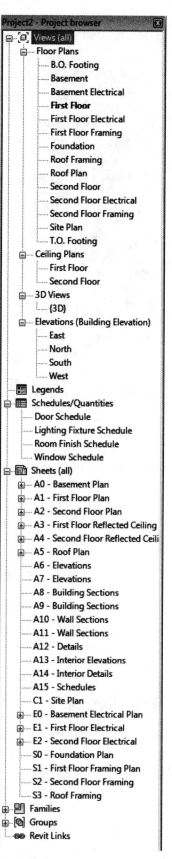

FIGURE 5-1.4 Project Browser: various items preloaded

Project Information:

Revit provides a dialog to enter the basic project information, such as client name, project address, etc. Next you will enter this information.

8. Select **Manage → Settings → Project Information**.

Project
Information

9. Enter the *Project Information* shown in Figure 5-1.5.

FYI: For now you will enter three question marks for the date.

Project Issue Date:	**???**
Project Status:	**Preliminary**
Client Name:	**John Brown**
Project Name:	**New Residence**
Project Number:	**2015-048**

FIGURE 5-1.5 Project Information dialog

10. Click in the field next to the *Project Address* parameter and then click the small icon that appears to the right (Figure 5-1.5).

11. Enter the project address shown in Figure 5-1.6.

FYI: This is the address where the house is going to be built, not the client's current address.

Enter:
2138 East Superior Street
Duluth, MN 55812

NOTE: You can enter any address you want to at this point; the address suggested is made up.

FIGURE 5-1.6 Adding Project Address (partial view)

Edit Text

2138 East Superior Street
Duluth, MN 55812

12. Click **OK**.

13. Click the **Edit** button next to the *Energy Settings* parameter (Figure 5-1.7).
    a. Enter/select the information shown.
    b. Notice that the address must be entered a second time here.

14. Click **OK**.

15. Click **OK** to close the *Project Information* dialog box.

The project information is now saved in your Revit project database. Revit has already used some of this information to infill in a portion of your title block on each of your sheets. You will verify this next.

Note that the *Energy Data* information is mainly used by external applications or *Revit MEP* to perform energy analyses like

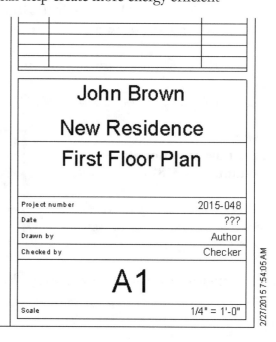

FIGURE 5-1.7 Adding Energy Data (partial view)

heating and cooling loads. Using Revit in conjunction with programs like *Autodesk Green Building Studio*, *Sefaira* or *IES Virtual Environment* can help create more energy efficient buildings because you can study the design impacts on energy consumption earlier in the project when changes are still possible.

16. Under the **Sheets** heading, in the *Project Browser*, double-click on the sheet **A1 – First Floor Plan**.

17. **Zoom** in to the lower right area of the title block (Figure 5-1.8).

Notice that much of the information is automatically filled in, and this is true for every sheet!

Your project database is now set up.

18. **Save** your project as **Ex5-1.rvt**.

John Brown

New Residence

First Floor Plan

Project number	2015-048
Date	???
Drawn by	Author
Checked by	Checker

A1

| Scale | 1/4" = 1'-0" |

2/27/2015 7:54:05 AM

FIGURE 5-1.8 Sheet A1 – First Floor Plan: Title block with Project Information added automatically

Exercise 5-2:
Exterior Walls

You will begin the first floor plan by drawing the exterior walls. Like many projects, early on you might not be certain what the exterior walls are going to be. So, you will start out using the generic wall styles. Then you will change them to a custom wall style, which you will create once you have decided what the wall construction is.

Often a residence is designed with a specific site in mind. However, to keep in line with most drafting and design classes, where floor plans are studied before site plans, you will develop the plans now.

Completed Plans – For Reference:

The following two images show the floor plans as they will look when you are done with this book. You should not need to use any information from these images; they are simply meant to introduce you to the project.

First Floor:
Living Room, Kitchen, Formal Dining, Coat Closet, ½ Bath, Mud Room, Garage

Second Floor:
Master Bath & Bedroom, Two Bedrooms,
Bathroom, Linen Closet, Office

Adjust Wall Settings:

1. Switch to *First Floor* view; select **Wall** from the *Architecture* tab.

2. Make the following changes to the wall options within the *Ribbon*, *Options Bar* and *Properties Palette* (Figure 5-2.1):

   - *Wall style:*   Basic Wall: **Generic – 8"**
   - *Height:*   **Unconnected**
   - *Height:*   **19′ 0″**
   - *Location Line:*   **Finish Face; Exterior**
   - *Chain:*   **checked**

FIGURE 5-2.1 Ribbon and Option bar – Wall command active

Draw the Exterior Walls:

3. **Draw** the walls shown in Figure 5-2.2. Make sure your dimensions are correct. Use the *Measure* tool, on the *QAT*, to double check your dimensions. Center the building between the elevation tags (see Figure 1-2.1). Move the elevation tags as needed by selecting the square part of the tag and using the *Move* tool (do not delete them).

    NOTE: If you draw in a clockwise fashion, your walls will have the exterior side of the wall correctly positioned. You can also use the spacebar to toggle which side the exterior face is on.

    TIP: In the Options Bar, while you are in the Wall tool, you can click Chain to continuously draw walls. When Chain is not selected you have to pick the same point twice: once where the wall ends and again where the next wall begins.

FIGURE 5-2.2 Exterior walls

Modifying Wall Dimensions:

Now that you have the exterior walls drawn, you might decide to adjust the building size for masonry coursing if you have a concrete block foundation, or subtract square footage to reduce cost.

Editing walls in Revit is very easy. You can select a wall and edit the temporary dimensions that appear, or you can use the *Move* tool to change the position of a wall. Any walls whose endpoints touch the modified wall are also adjusted (i.e., they grow or shrink) automatically.

Next, you will adjust the dimensions of the walls just drawn. You will assume the house will have a concrete block (CMU) foundation.

4. Click the **Modify** button (not the tab) and then select the far left wall (Figure 5-2.3).

Clicking *Modify* cancels the current command and de-selects everything. Sometimes you have to press it twice to completely clear everything.

5. Select the temporary dimensions text (35'-0″) and then type **34 8** (Figure 5-2.3).

> *FYI: Remember you do not need to type the foot or inch symbol; the space distinguishes between them.*

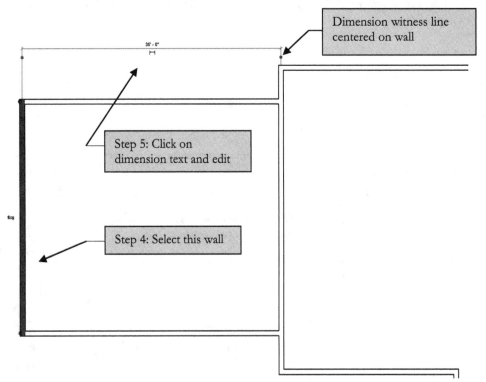

FIGURE 5-2.3 Editing wall dimensions

> *TIP: Whenever you want to adjust the model via temporary/permanent dimensions, you need to select the object you want to move first and then select the text, or number, of the temporary or permanent dimension.*

6. In the lower right corner of the floor plan, select the wall shown in Figure 5-2.4.

7. Edit the 4'-4″ dimension to **4'-0″**.

> *TIP: Just type 4 and press Enter; Revit will assume feet when a single number is entered.*

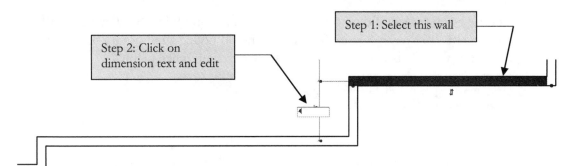

FIGURE 5-2.4 Editing exterior walls

FYI: You can edit the location of the witness lines if desired by going to Manage → Additional Settings → Temporary Dimensions. Here you can set the default to "Faces" rather than "Centerlines." Do not change any settings at this time.

TIP:

Concrete blocks (or CMU) come in various widths, and most are 16″ long and 8″ high. When drawing plans, there is a simple rule to keep in mind to make sure you are designing walls to coursing. This applies to wall lengths and openings within CMU walls.

Dimension rules for CMU coursing in floor plans:
- e'-0″ or e'-8″   where e is any even number (e.g., 6′-0″ or 24′-8″)
- o'-4″   where o is any odd number (e.g., 5′-4″)

Using the Align Tool with Walls:

Revit has a tool called *Align* that allows you to quickly make one element align with another. You will make the South wall of the garage align with the wall you just modified. After they are aligned, you will *Lock* the relationship so the two walls will always move together, which is great when you know you want two walls to remain aligned but might accidentally move one, maybe while zoomed in and you cannot see the other wall.

8. Select the **Modify** (tab) → **Modify** (panel) → **Align** icon.

> *TIP:* Or just type **AL** to start the Align tool

Notice the *Status Bar* is asking you to select a reference line or point. This is the wall, or linework, that is in the correct location; the other wall(s) will be adjusted to match the reference plane.

9. Select the exterior face of the horizontal wall you just modified: Set *Prefer* to **Wall Faces** on the *Options Bar* (Figure 5-2.5).You should notice a temporary dashed line appear on screen. This will help you to visualize the reference plane.

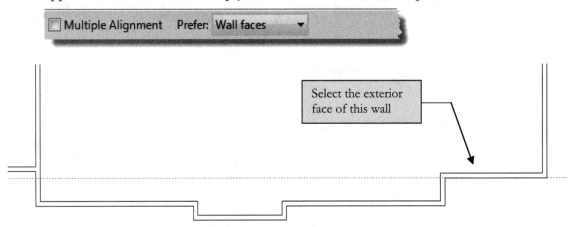

FIGURE 5-2.5 Align tool: wall selected

Notice the *Status Bar* is prompting you to select an entity to align with the temporary reference plane.

10. Now, select the exterior face of the South garage wall (Figure 5-2.6).

FIGURE 5-2.6 Align tool: select wall(s) to be aligned

Note that if you would have selected the interior face of the wall that side of the wall would have aligned with the reference plane rather than the exterior as it did. If you made a mistake, click *Undo* and try it again.

Also, notice that you have a padlock symbol showing. Clicking the padlock symbol will cause the alignment relationship to be maintained, a parametric relationship. Next you will lock the alignment relationship and experiment with a few edits to see how modifying one wall affects the other.

11. Click on the **padlock** symbol (Figure 5-2.6).

The padlock symbol is now in the locked position.

12. Click the **Modify** button to unselect the walls (or just press the **Esc** key).

13. Select the garage wall identified in Figure 5-2.6.

Next you will make a dramatic change so you can clearly see the results of that change on both locked walls.

14. Change the 4'-0" dimension to **20'-0"** (Figure 5-2.7).

Notice that both walls moved together (Figure 5-2.7). Also notice that when either wall is selected, the padlock is displayed, which helps in identifying "locked" relationships while you are editing the project. Whenever the padlock symbol is visible, you can click on it to unlock it, or remove the aligned relationship.

FIGURE 5-2.7 Wall edit: Both walls move together

Next you will make a few more wall modifications, on your own, to get the perimeter of the building to masonry coursing.

15. Modify wall locations by selecting a wall and modifying the temporary dimensions; the selected wall will move to match Figure 5-2.8; do not draw the dimensions at this time.

TIP: Make sure you use the Measure *tool to verify all dimensions before moving on!*

TIP: Clicking the grip on the witness line of a Temporary Dimension causes the witness line to toggle locations on the wall (i.e., exterior face, interior face and center). You can also drag the grip to a different wall. See page 5-27 for more information on this.

FIGURE 5-2.8 Exterior walls with final dimensions

Changing a Wall Type:

In the next several steps, you will learn how to change the generic walls into a more refined wall type. Basically, you select the wall(s) you want to change and then you pick a different wall type from the *Type Selector* on the *Properties Palette*. Remember, the *Ribbon*, *Options Bar* and *Properties Palette* are context sensitive, which means the wall types are only listed in the *Type Selector* when you are using the *Wall* tool or you have a wall selected.

16. Select all the walls in your *First Floor* plan view.

    TIP: You can select all the walls at once: click and drag the cursor to select a window. Later in the book you will learn about "Filter Selection" which also aids in the selection process.

FIGURE 5-2.9 Type Selector

17. From the *Type Selector* on the *Properties Palette*, select **Exterior – Wood Shingle over Wood Siding on Wood Stud** (Figure 5-2.9).

18. Click **Modify** to unselect the walls.

If you zoom in on the walls, you can see their graphic representation has changed a little. It would have changed a lot, of course, if you had selected a brick and CMU cavity wall. But you typically try to start with a wall closest to the one you think you will end up with, though you may never even have to change the wall type.

Even though the wall did not change much graphically in this plan view, it did change quite a bit. In a 3D view, which you will look at in a moment, the wall now has siding and trim! The image to the right is a snapshot of the 19'-0" tall wall you now have in your model.

Next, you will create a custom wall type for the walls around the garage. You will need a wall type similar to the one you just selected, but with 2x4 studs rather than 2x6s. You will start by making a copy of the existing wall type and then modify the copy.

Create a Custom Wall Type:

As previously mentioned, Revit provides several predefined wall styles, from wood studs with gypsum board to concrete block and brick cavity walls. However, you will occasionally need a wall style that has not yet been predefined by Revit. You will study this process next.

First, you will take a close look at the predefined wall type you are using for the exterior walls.

19. Select the *Wall* tool, pick the wall type **Exterior – Wood Shingle over Wood Siding on Wood Stud** from the *Type Selector* drop-down list (Figure 5-2.9).

20. Click the **Edit Type** button on the *Properties Palette*.

FIGURE 5-2.10 Edit Type button

21. You should be in the *Type Properties* dialog box (Figure 5-2.11).

22. Click the **Edit** button next to the *Structure* parameter (Figure 5-2.11).

FIGURE 5-2.11 Type Properties

FYI:
Here is the difference between the two Element Properties dialogs:

Properties Palette (Instance Properties): This is information that can vary by instance (i.e., individual walls, doors, windows, etc.). For example, the height to the bottom of a window or the fire rating of a wall or door; these values can vary from instance to instance.

Type Properties: This is information that is the same for every instance of a specific type. For example, the width and height of window type "W1" should be the same for all, and the width of wall type "S6" should be the same for all. Any changes to these values changes all previously drawn, and to be drawn, objects in the model.

23. Finally, you are in the *Edit Assembly* dialog box. This is where you can modify existing wall types. Click **<<Preview** to display a preview of the selected wall type (Figure 5-2.12).

Here, the *Edit Assembly* dialog box allows you to change the composition of an existing wall or to create a new wall.

Things to notice (Figure 5-2.12):

- The exterior side is labeled at the top and interior side at the bottom.

- You will see horizontal lines (i.e., *Layers*) identifying the core material. The core material can be used to place walls and dimension walls. For example, the *Wall* tool will let you draw a wall with the interior or exterior core face as the reference line. On an interior wall you might dimension to the face of stud rather than to the finished face of gypsum board; this would give the contractor the information needed for the part of the wall he will build first.

- Each row is called a *Layer*. By clicking on a *Layer* and picking the **Up** or **Down** buttons, you can reposition materials within the wall assembly.

FIGURE 5-2.12 Edit Assembly

24. Click **Cancel** to close the open dialog box.

Next, you will instruct Revit to create a new wall type which will be based on a copy of the currently selected wall type.

25. Click the **Duplicate** button (Figure 5-2.11).

26. Enter **Exterior – Wood Shingle over Wood Siding on 2x4 Wood Stud** for the new wall type name, and then click **OK** (Figure 5-2.13).

> *FYI: Notice that you have simply added "2x4" as a descriptor, making the name distinguishable from the others. Be sure to remove the "2" at the end, which was automatically added by Revit in case you did not change the name.*

FIGURE 5-2.13 New wall type name

27. Click the **Edit** button next to the *Structure* parameter.

Next you will simply change the size of the wood stud layer and then save your changes.

28. Change the *Thickness* of the **Softwood, Lumber** *Layer* (Row 6) to **0' 3 ½"**.

29. Your dialog should look like **Figure 5-2.14**. Notice the total wall thickness is listed near the top. Also note the *Total Thickness* and *R-Value* updated.

30. Click **OK** to close all dialog boxes.

You now have access to your newly defined wall. You can sketch new walls using the *Wall* tool or you can change existing walls to your new wall type using the *Modify* tool.

FIGURE 5-2.14 Edit Assembly; change stud size to 2x4

The next step is to change the wall type for the three walls around the garage.

31. Select the **Modify** button from the *Ribbon*; this cancels any active commands and allows you to select elements in your model.

32. **Zoom out** so you can see the entire plan. Dragging your mouse from upper-right to lower-left, make a *crossing window* to select the three garage walls, **or** hold down **Ctrl** and click each wall.

33. With the walls selected, pick **Basic Wall: Exterior – Wood Shingle over Wood Siding on 2x4 Wood Stud** from the *Type Selector* drop-down; see tip below.

You should notice the wall thickness change; the reference line (face, center, etc.) does not move. You had *Finish Face: Exterior* selected when you drew the walls, so the exterior side of the wall does not move, which is good.

TIP: If, after selecting all the walls, the Type Selector *is grayed out and the contextual tab says* Multi-Select, *you have some other type of element selected, such as text or dimensions (although you have not been instructed to draw anything but walls yet) or one of the four elevation tags. Try to find those objects and delete them, but DO NOT delete the elevation tags. You can also click on the* Filter *button, located on the Ribbon when objects are selected, and uncheck the types of elements to exclude from the current selection.*

For many of the walls, Revit can display more refined linework and hatching within the wall. This is controlled by the *Detail Level* option for each view. At the moment, making this change will only reveal the exterior sheathing, but this is helpful information. You will change the *Detail Level* for the *First Floor Plan* view now.

34. Click on the **Detail Level** icon in the lower-left corner of the drawing window (Figure 5-2.15).

35. Select **Medium**.

FYI: This view adjustment is only for the current view, as are all changes made via the View Control Bar.

FIGURE 5-2.15 Detail Level; set to medium

You may need to zoom in, but you should now see a line added for the exterior sheathing. If you did not pay close enough attention when drawing the walls originally, some of your walls may show the sheathing to the inside of the building.

TIP: On the View tab you can select Thin Lines *to temporarily turn off the line weights; this has no effect on plotting.*

36. Select **Modify** (or press **Esc**); select a wall. You will see a symbol appear that allows you to flip the wall orientation by clicking on that symbol (Figure 5-2.16).

Click this symbol to
flip wall orientation

FIGURE 5-2.16 Selected Wall

37. Whether you need to adjust walls or not, click on the flip symbol to experiment with its operation.

   TIP: The flip symbol is always on the exterior side, or what Revit thinks is the exterior side, of the wall.

38. If some walls do need to be adjusted so the sheathing and flip symbol are to the exterior, do it now. You may have to select the wall(s) and use the *Move* tool to reposition the walls to match the required dimensions.

   TIP: Walls are flipped about the Location Line, which can be changed via the Properties Palette. So changing the Location Line to Wall Centerline before flipping the wall will keep the wall in the same position. Be sure to change the Location Line back to Exterior Face.

TIP: You can use the MOVE tool on the Ribbon to accurately move walls. The steps are the same as in the previous chapters!

Follow these steps to move an element:
- *Select the wall*
- *Click the Move icon*
- *Pick any point on the wall*
- *Start the mouse in the correct direction; do not click!*
- *Start typing the distance you want to move the wall and press Enter.*

39. You can see your progress nicely with a 3D view. Click the **Default 3D View** icon on the *QAT*. In the enlargement image, walls are shaded to make the image more clear (Figure 5-2.17).

FIGURE 5-2.17 Default 3D View; zoomed in to detail (image on the right)

If you zoom in on the walls, you can see how much detail Revit can store in a wall type. By picking a few points, you defined the wall's width, height and exterior finish materials.

The last thing you will do in this exercise is to adjust the height of the walls at the garage and a portion of the living room; refer to image on the book's cover. Revit allows you to modify the building model in any view. You will make the wall height adjustments in the current 3D View, per the following steps.

40. In the *3D View*, click to select the three exterior garage walls.

   TIP: Holding down the Ctrl key allows you to select multiple elements, while holding down the Shift key allows for subtraction from the current selection set. The total number of selected items is listed in the lower right, on the Status Bar; make sure it is says "3."

You will notice, similar to other views, when an element is selected in a 3D view the entire object temporarily turns blue and becomes transparent. This helps to see which objects are in the current selection set when several items are selected.

You should also see the *Ribbon* has been populated with options for the selected walls, just like the plan views. You will adjust the height setting in the *Properties Palette* next.

41. In the *Properties Palette*, change the *Unconnected Height* parameter to **12'-0"** and then press **Enter**.

42. Make the same height adjustment to the three exterior walls at the Eastern most portion of the living room (Figure 5-2.18).

43. Close the *3D View* and switch back to the *First Floor Plan* view.

44. Using the **Save As** command, save your project as **ex5-2.rvt**.

Figure 5-2.18 Completed exercise

TIP: *Holding down the Shift key while pressing the wheel button on the mouse allows you to orbit around the building. You will have to experiment with how the mouse movements relate to the building orbit. Selecting an item first causes that item to remain centered on the screen during orbit.*

Exercise 5-3:
Interior Walls

In this lesson you will draw the interior walls for the first floor. Using the line sketching and editing techniques you have studied in previous lessons, you should be able to draw the interior walls with minimal information.

Overview on How Plans are Typically Dimensioned:

The following is an overview of how walls are typically dimensioned in a floor plan. This information is intended to help you understand the dimensions you will see in the exercises, as well as prepare you for the point when you dimension your plans, in a later lesson.

Wood or metal stud walls are typically dimensioned to the centers of the walls. This is one of the reasons the walls do not need to be the exact thickness. Here are a few reasons why you should dimension to the center of the stud rather than to the face of the gypsum board:

o   The contractor is laying out the walls in a large "empty" area. The most useful dimension is to the center of the stud; that is where they will make a mark on the floor. If the dimension was to the face of the gypsum board, the contractor would have to stop and calculate the center of the stud, which is not always the center of the wall thickness; for example, a stud wall with one layer of gypsum board on one side and two layers of gypsum board over resilient channels on the other side of the stud.

Dimension Example
– Two Stud Walls

o   When creating a continuous string of dimensions, the extra dimensions indicating the thickness of the walls would take up an excessive amount of room on the floor plans, space that would be better used by notes.

Occasionally, you should dimension to the face of a wall rather than the center; here's one example:

o   When indicating design intent or building code requirements, you should reference the exact points/surfaces. For example, if you have uncommonly large trim around a door opening, you may want a dimension from the edge of the door to the face of the adjacent wall. Another example would be the width of a hallway; if you want a particular width you would dimension between the two faces of the wall and add the text "clear" below the dimension to make it known without question that the dimension is not to the center of the wall.

Dimensions for masonry and foundation walls:

- o Foundation and masonry walls are dimensioned to the nominal face and not the center. These types of walls are modular (e.g., 8″x8″x16″) so it is helpful, for both designer and builder, to have dimensions that relate to the masonry wall's "coursing."

Dimension Example
– Two masonry Walls

Dimensions from a stud wall to a masonry wall:

- o The rules above apply for each side of the dimension line. For example, a dimension for the exterior foundation wall to an interior stud wall would be from the exterior face of the foundation wall to the center of the stud on the interior wall.

Dimension Example
– Stud to masonry

Again, you will not be dimensioning your drawings right away, but Revit makes it easy to comply with the conventions above.

Adjust Wall Settings:

1. Select **Wall** form the *Architecture* tab on the *Ribbon*.

2. Make the following changes to the wall options in the *Properties Palette* and *Options Bar* (similar to Figure 5-2.1):
   - Wall style: **Interior – 4 ½″ partition**
   - Height: **Second Floor** (rather than unconnected)
   - Location Line: **Wall Centerline**

Contos Residence

Image courtesy of Anderson Architects
Alan H. Anderson, Architect, Duluth, MN

Drawing the Interior Walls:

Now that you have the perimeter drawn, you will draw a few interior walls. When drawing floor plans it is good practice to sketch out the various wall systems you think you will be using; this will help you determine what thickness to draw the walls. Drawing the walls at the correct thickness helps later when you are fine-tuning things.

Although Revit provides most of the wall types required, it is a good idea for the student to understand exactly what is being drawn.

Take a moment to think about the basic interior wall in a residential project. It typically consists of the following:
- o 2x4 wood studs
  (actual size is 1½″ x 3½″)
- o ½″ gypsum board

4 ½″

2x4 WOOD STUDS at 16″ O.C.

ONE LAYER OF ½″ GYPSUM BOARD EACH SIDE

FIGURE 5-3.1
Sketch – Plan view of interior wall system

The wall system described above is shown in Figure 5-3.1.

Note: All your interior walls should be drawn **4½″** <u>for each floor</u>.

3. Draw a wall approximately as shown in Figure 5-3.2. You will adjust its exact position in the next step. *TIP: Click near the center of each exterior wall and make sure the wall is snapped to the vertical reference plane (vertical relative to the computer screen).*

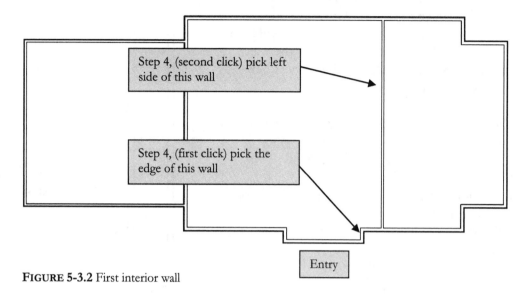

Step 4, (second click) pick left side of this wall

Step 4, (first click) pick the edge of this wall

Entry

FIGURE 5-3.2 First interior wall

4. Use the ***Align*** tool to align the interior wall you just drew with the edge of the exterior wall (Figure 5-3.2). Set *Prefer* to *Wall Faces* on the *Options Bar*. When you are done, the wall should look like Figure 5-3.3.

FYI: You do not need to lock this alignment.

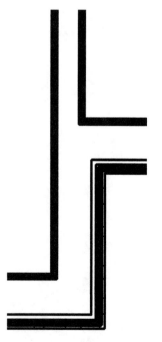

5. Create the same wall for the West side of the entry, repeating the steps above.

Next, you will draw a handful of walls per the given dimensions. You will use the same partition type (4½″ partition).

6. Draw the interior walls shown in Figure 5-3.4; see the tips below which should help you sketch the walls more accurately.

    a. All dimensions are from exterior face of exterior walls and centerline of interior walls.

FIGURE 5-3.3 Aligned wall

FIGURE 5-3.4 Layout dimensions for first floor interior walls

TIP - DIMENSION WITNESS LINE CONTROL:

When sketching walls, you can adjust the exact position of the wall after its initial placement. However, the temporary dimensions do not always reference the desired wall location (left face, right face, or center). You will see how easy it is to adjust a dimension's witness line location so you can place the wall exactly where you want it.

First, you will be introduced to some dimension terminology. The two "boxed" notes below are only for permanent dimensions, the others are for both permanent and temporary.

Next you will adjust the witness lines so you can modify the inside clear dimension, between the walls, in the above illustration.

When you select a wall you will see temporary dimensions, similar to the image on the next page.

TIP - DIMENSION WITNESS LINE CONTROL: (CONTINUED FROM PREVIOUS PAGE)

NOTE: Some elements do not display temporary dimensions; in that case you can usually click the "Activate Dimensions" button on the Options Bar to see them.

Clicking, not dragging, on the witness line grip causes the witness line to toggle between the location options (left face, right face, center). In the example below, the grip for each witness line has been clicked until both witness lines refer to the "inside" of the room.

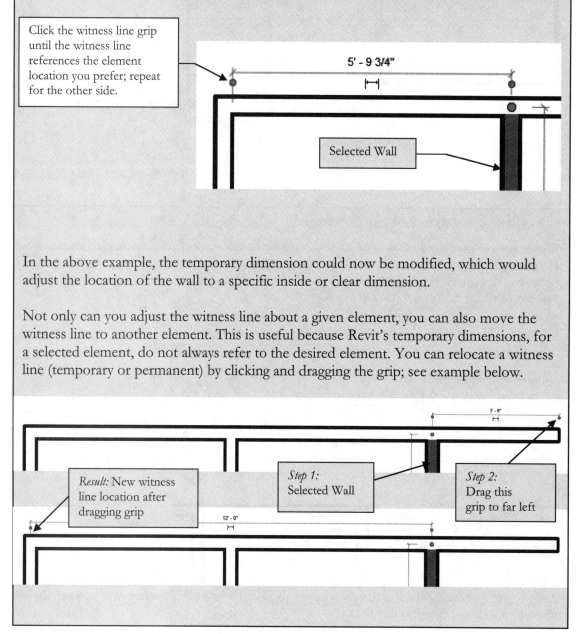

Click the witness line grip until the witness line references the element location you prefer; repeat for the other side.

5' - 9 3/4"

Selected Wall

In the above example, the temporary dimension could now be modified, which would adjust the location of the wall to a specific inside or clear dimension.

Not only can you adjust the witness line about a given element, you can also move the witness line to another element. This is useful because Revit's temporary dimensions, for a selected element, do not always refer to the desired element. You can relocate a witness line (temporary or permanent) by clicking and dragging the grip; see example below.

Result: New witness line location after dragging grip

Step 1: Selected Wall

Step 2: Drag this grip to far left

3' - 9"

12' - 0"

Next you will use the *Trim* tool to remove a portion of wall that is not needed.

7. Select **Trim** from the *Modify* tab.

8. Select the two walls identified in Figure 5-3.5.

   FYI: The walls can be selected in either order.

Portion of wall
to be removed

Pick this wall

Pick this wall

Figure 5-3.5 Trimmed wall

Modify an Existing Wall:

Next you want to change the portion of wall between the house and the garage. Currently, the wall is your typical exterior wall which includes siding on the garage side. The entire vertical wall is one element, so to only change the interior portion you will need to split the current wall, trim the corners and then draw a new interior wall.

9. **Zoom** in on the interior garage wall and select the **Modify → Modify → Split Element** tool.

   FYI: This will break a wall into two; when used in plan it splits the wall vertically and when used in a section a horizontal split results.

10. Pick somewhere in the middle of the wall (Figure 5-3.6a).

11. Use the **Trim** tool to trim the corners so the exterior wall only occurs at exterior conditions. Select **Unjoin Elements** (see "Warning Prompt" section on the next page).

    TIP: Select the portion of wall you wish to retain (Figure 5-3.6b).

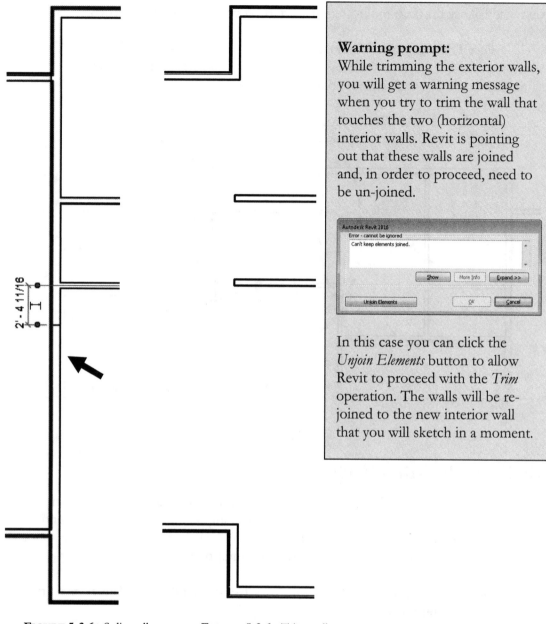

Warning prompt:
While trimming the exterior walls, you will get a warning message when you try to trim the wall that touches the two (horizontal) interior walls. Revit is pointing out that these walls are joined and, in order to proceed, need to be un-joined.

In this case you can click the *Unjoin Elements* button to allow Revit to proceed with the *Trim* operation. The walls will be re-joined to the new interior wall that you will sketch in a moment.

FIGURE 5-3.6A Split wall   **FIGURE 5-3.6B** Trim wall

Additional Custom Wall Types:

Next, you will create a new interior partition type using a copy of the original exterior wall type as a starting point. It is easier to start with a wall that is similar to the one you wish to create.

Structurally, this wall could probably only require 2x4 studs. However, directly above this wall will be an exterior wall (the portion above the garage roof) that wants to have 2x6 studs to allow for adequate insulation. Additionally, you will want to insulate the interior garage wall; this helps with noise and heat loss when the large garage door is opened in -20 degree weather!

Truthfully, in this case it may be easier to start with a new wall, given the complexity of the exterior wall you are about to modify. However, this will give you a little more insight on how the exterior wall is constructed and the interworking of Revit's wall assembly.

12. Using wall type: **Exterior – Wood Shingle over Wood Siding on Wood Stud** as a starting point, create a new wall type named **Exterior – Garage Wall (Interior)**. *(Remember to click Edit Type and then Duplicate; see page 5-15.)*

13. Click the **Edit** button next to the *Structure* parameter.

Typically you will want to give walls more generic names so they can be used elsewhere in the project. Because you know this wall will only be used once, it is easier to give it a more descriptive name so it is not confused with other wall types later.

FIGURE 5-3.7 Edit Assembly dialog

The *Edit Assembly* dialog shown in Figure 5-3.7 will be modified in the following way. This is just an overview; the detailed instructions will follow:

- First, you will delete the horizontal sweeps.
  - A sweep is a closed 2D shape that is extruded along the length of a wall at a given height; a unique material can be specified.
  - This wall type currently has two sweeps (refer back to Figure 5-2.17): one at the base of the wall and another near the second floor line.

- Second, you will merge the two "vertically stacked" exterior finish layers so you can delete the exterior finish layers.
  - A layer can be split vertically into multiple regions; the exterior layer of this wall style is split into two regions. One has the material "Wood-Shakes" assigned to it and the other has "Finishes – Exterior – Siding / Clapboard" assigned to it.
  - Looking at Figure 5-3.7, you can visually see which layers are spilt vertically by looking at the Thickness column; the shaded "Thickness" cells are "vertically stacked" layers.
  - Vertically stacked layers must be *Merged* back into one region before they can be deleted from the layers list.

- Finally, you will change the plywood sheathing to gypsum board and move the air barrier between the gypsum board and the studs.

14. In the *Edit Assembly* dialog make sure the *Preview* pane is visible (*click on the <<Preview button*) and then select **Section: modify type attributes** from the *View* list (Figure 5-3.7).

15. Click the **Sweeps** button to load the *Wall Sweeps* dialog.

16. Delete both *Wall Sweeps*: click on the row number, to select the row, and then click the **Delete** button (Figure 5-3.8). Click **OK** to close the dialog box when done.

FIGURE 5-3.8 Wall Sweeps to be deleted

The two rectangular shaped sweeps, which represented the horizontal trim, are now removed from the preview section.

Also, notice in Figure 5-3.8, this is where the material is assigned to the sweep.

Next you will merge the two "vertically stacked" layers into one region. The tricky part here is that Revit will let you merge any two regions. So you need to keep an eye on the cursor and the pop-up tooltip.

17. Select the **Merge Regions** button.

18. Using the *scroll wheel* on the mouse, zoom in on the region split line at the top edge of the vertical dimension; you need to click in the *Preview* window to activate that area first (Figure 5-3.7).

19. Move your cursor over the short horizontal line and then tap the **Tab** key until the cursor changes to a horizontal line with an arrow pointing downward and the tooltip states that **Layer 1 and Layer 2 will be merged** (see Figure 5-3.7), and then click.

    FYI: You can also Pan *in the Preview pane using your scroll wheel button.*

20. Individually select the *Layer* numbers 1 and 2, to select the row, and **Delete** them. This will delete the two exterior finish layers: shakes and siding.

    FYI: Watch the Preview pane while you do this.

21. Click the *Air Infiltration Barrier* **Membrane Layer** (row 1) and then click the **Down** button to move the location of the air barrier within the wall.

22. Do not change the wood stud layer; leave it at 5½″.

23. Change the ¾″ sheathing layer by clicking in each cell in that row and then clicking the down-arrow that appears to the right; change the *Function* to **Finish 1** [4], *Material* to **Gypsum Wall Board**, *Thickness* to ½″ (Figure 5-3.9).

FIGURE 5-3.9 Modified edit assembly dialog

Now that you have created a new wall type, you can sketch the wall in the first floor plan view.

24. With your new wall type selected in the *Type Selector*, use the **Wall** tool to sketch a wall between the garage and the house.

    a.   Set the wall *Height* to **Second Floor**.

    b.   Set the *Location Line* to **Finish Face: Interior** and then select the interior corner of the exterior wall.

FIGURE 5-3.10 New interior garage wall added

It is important to remember that the "flip control" symbol is displayed on the exterior side of the wall when the wall is selected; this corresponds to the *Exterior Side* and *Interior Side* designations with the wall type editor. If your symbol is on the wrong side, click it to flip the wall and the symbol to the other side. You will then have to *Move* or *Align* the wall so it is flush with the adjacent exterior wall.

25. Save your project as **Ex5-3.rvt**.

Exercise 5-4:
Doors, Openings and Windows

This lesson will take a closer look at inserting doors and windows.

Now that you have sketched the walls, you will add some doors. A door symbol indicates which side the hinges are on and the direction the door opens.

New doors are typically shown open 90 degrees in floor plans, which helps to avoid conflicts such as the door hitting an adjacent base cabinet. Additionally, to make it clear graphically, existing doors are shown open only 45 degrees.

Door symbol Example – New Door drawn with 90 degree swing

Door symbol Example – Existing Door shown with 45 degree swing

One of the most powerful features of any CAD program is its ability to reuse previously drawn content. With Revit you can insert entire door systems (door, frame, trim, etc). You drew a 2D door symbol in Lesson 4; however, you will now use Revit's powerful *Door* tool which is fully 3D.

For those new to drafting, you may find this comparison between CAD and hand drafting interesting: when hand drafting, one uses straight edges or a plastic template that has doors and additional often used symbols to trace.

Hand Drafting Template – Plastic template with holes representing common residential shapes, at ¼″ = 1′-0″

Image used by permission, Timely Templates
www.timelytemplates.com

Doors in stud walls are dimensioned to the center of the door opening. On the other hand and similar to dimensioning masonry walls, doors in masonry walls are dimensioned to the face (see example below).

Door Dimension Example – Dimension to the center of the door opening

Door Dimension Example – Dimension the opening size and location

Loading Additional Door Families:

Revit has done an excellent job providing several different door families. This makes sense seeing as doors are an important part of an architectural project. Some of the provided families include bi-fold, double, pocket, sectional (garage), and vertical rolling to name a few. In addition to the content found on your local hard drive, many more are available via Autodesk SEEK—which requires an internet connection.

The default template you started with *(Residential-Default.rte)* only provides four door *families*; each family contains multiple door sizes. If you want to insert other styles, you will need to load additional *families* from the library. The reason for this step is that, when you load a family, Revit actually copies the data into your project file. If every possible family was loaded into your project at the beginning, not only would it be hard to find what you want in a large list of doors, but also the project file would be several megabytes in size before you even drew the first wall.

You will begin this section by loading a few additional families into your project.

1. Open project ex5-3.rvt and **Save-As ex5-4.rvt**.

2. With the *Door* tool selected, select **Load Family** on the *Ribbon* (Figure 5-4.1).

Load Family

3. Browse through the **Doors\Residential** folder for a moment. The *Doors* folder is a sub-folder of the *US Imperial* library; Revit should have taken you there by default; if not, you can browse to: C:\ProgramData\Autodesk\RVT 2016\Libraries\US Imperial\Doors

FIGURE 5-4.1 Load content from Library

Each file represents a *family*, each having one or more *Types* of varying sizes.

FIGURE 5-4.2 Door families on hard drive

4. Click **Cancel** to close the *Load Family* dialog.

All New Door Content

This version of Revit replaced the entire door library with new content. However, the content in the template is still based on the original content style. The new library does not currently have a bi-fold door. Given these issues in this release, the original door library will be accessed from Autodesk SEEK and used through the book. The reader is encouraged to explore the new door content.

Downloading Additional Door Families from the Internet:

Now you will explore Autodesk's online content website: **seek.autodesk.com**. You will learn how to download door families that are not available locally on your hard drive.

This content distribution site is geared toward all of Autodesk's design software. If you browse directly to the site using your web browser you can search for several types of design files, including AutoCAD and 3DS Max. However, you can also initiate a search from within Revit and automatically narrow your search down to Revit content.

5. Switch to the **Insert** tab on the *Ribbon*.

Notice the *Autodesk Seek* panel on the *Insert* tab (Figure 5-4.3).

Normally you might type something such as closet door and sort through the options that appear. You are encouraged to try this on your own. In this case you will enter specific family names to gain quick access to content required for this lesson.

> Search Autodesk Seek
>
> **Find and download building product models, drawings, and specs**
>
> **Autodesk Seek**

FIGURE 5-4.3 Insert tab, Seek panel

6. Click in the text box and enter "**Bifold-2 Panel**" (Figure 5-4.4).

FIGURE 5-4.4 Insert tab, Seek panel

7. Press **Enter**.

Your default web browser is automatically opened and any matching items are listed (Figure 5-4.5). In this case there should only be one element that matches the name you entered (there are multiple but of the same family). Of course, this website could change, so the results may vary. If this door family is not available, search for another closet door.

FIGURE 5-4.5 Autodesk Seek opened in web browser

8. Click "**Bifold-2 Panel**" to for more details and a download link.

You now have the option to download several Revit versions of the family; you can download any version as long as it is not newer than the version of Revit software you are using. You will be downloading the files to your computer's hard drive.

FIGURE 5-4.6 Autodesk Seek opened in web browser

9. Check the **Revit 2012 Imperial File** check-box.

FYI: Revit can always open an older Revit file format but never a newer one. So it is possible to load the 2009 or 2010 content, but it will take a little longer as Revit will have to upgrade it first.

10. Ensure **Download selected to Local** is selected in the upper right, rather than *Download to A360 Drive*.

11. Enter your Autodesk user name and password – or create one (see image to right).

12. Click the down-arrow and select **Save As** (Figure 5-4.7).

13. *Save* the file to your computer's *Desktop* using the default name provided.

FYI: You will be prompted to specify a location to save the downloaded files. Make sure you pay attention to where the files are being saved so you can load them into your project later.

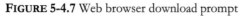

FIGURE 5-4.7 Web browser download prompt

You will repeat the previous steps to load the remaining content, or enter your search text in the current *Seek* page.

14. Repeat the previous steps to download six more door families from SEEK:
    a. **Single-Panel 4**
    b. **Sliding-2 panel**
    c. **Double-Raised Panel with Sidelights**
    d. **Single-Entry 3**
    e. **Single-Pocket**
    f. **Opening-Elliptical Arch**

15. In the *Project Browser*, expand the *Families* category and then *Doors* to see the loaded door families (Figure 5-4.8).

If you expand the *Doors* families in the *Project Browser* you see the predefined door sizes (i.e., Family Types) associated with that family. Right-clicking on a door size allows you to rename, delete or duplicate it. To add a door size, you

FIGURE 5-4.8 Loaded door families

duplicate and then modify properties for the new item, similar to how you created a new wall.

You may want to create a folder where you save all the families you download. This would make future access more convenient, especially if you did not have internet access at that time. This folder should probably not be in Revit's standard folder location as it may be difficult to migrate the data after an upgrade (i.e., sorting the custom files from the default files).

One more thing on families via the web: you have access to content via sources other than Autodesk. You can try an internet search with text that reads something like "*autodesk revit families.*" As Revit's popularity grows, more and more product manufacturers are starting to making families available that represent their products, thus making it easier for designers to incorporate those products into a project. For example, one can also download an extensive wall and ceiling library from United States Gypsum (USG) at www.usgdesignstudio.com. Additionally, you can visit www.augi.com (Autodesk Users Group International), or www.revitcity.com for Revit related resources and content.

Rather than loading content with the *Door* tool active, first you will just use the *Load Family* tool directly from the *Insert* tab.

16. Select **Insert → Load From Library → Load Family** from the *Ribbon*.

17. Browse to the location where you saved the family files and select **Double-Raised Panel with Sidelights.rfa**, and then click **Open**.

18. Repeat the previous two steps to load the other four families, from Step 16, into your project.

    TIP: *You can press the Ctrl key and select more than one family to load.*

19. In the *Project Browser*, expand the *Doors* category, under *Families*, again to verify all the doors have been loaded into your project (Figure 5-4.9)

Note that the *Opening-Elliptical Arch* does not display here; it actually shows up under *Generic Model*.

Doors
- Bifold-2 Panel
- Double-Glass 1
- Double-Raised Panel with Sidelights
- Single-Entry 3
- Single-Flush
- Single-Panel 4
- Single-Pocket
- Single-Raised Panel with Sidelights
- Sliding-2 panel
- Sliding-Closet

FIGURE 5-4.9 All door families loaded for this exercise

Next you will start inserting the doors into the first floor plan.

20. With the *Door* tool selected, pick **Single-Entry 3: 36″ x 80″** from the *Type Selector* on the *Properties Palette*.

21. Select **Tag on Placement** on the *Ribbon*, and then place one door in the North wall of the garage as shown in Figure 5-4.10.

Immediately after the door is inserted, or when the door is selected, you can click on the horizontal or vertical flip-controls to position the door as desired.

Since "Tag on placement" was selected on the *Ribbon*, Revit automatically adds a *Door Tag* near the newly inserted door. The door itself stores information about the door that can then be compiled in a door schedule. The doors are automatically numbered in the order they are placed. The number can be changed at any time to suit the designer's needs; you will do this later in the door schedule section. Most architects and designers use 1x or 1xx (i.e., 12 or 120) numbers for the first floor and 2x or 2xx numbers for the second floor door numbers.

The *Door Tag* can be moved simply by clicking on it to select it, and then clicking and dragging it to its new location. You may need to press the *Tab* key to pre-highlight the tag before you can select it.

Also, with the *Door Tag* selected you can set the vertical/horizontal orientation and whether a leader should be displayed when the tag is moved; it is done via the settings on the *Options Bar*. The tag must be selected.

FIGURE 5-4.10 First door placed at rear of garage

22. Click *Modify* and then select the newly placed door; take a moment to review the information displayed in the *Properties Palette*.

    TIP: *If the Properties Palette is not visible, simply type "pp" on the keyboard; do not press Enter.*

Notice, in Figure 5-4.11, you see the *Instance Parameters* which are options that vary with each door, e.g., *Sill Height* and *Door Number (Mark)*. These parameters control selected or to-be-created items.

The *Type Parameters* are not visible in this dialog. To be sure you want to make changes that affect all doors of that type, Revit forces you to click the *Edit Type* button and make changes in the *Type Properties* dialog. Also, in the *Type Properties* dialog, you can add additional pre-defined door sizes to the *"Single-Entry 3"* door family by clicking the *Duplicate* button, providing a new name and changing the "size" dimensions for that new *Type*.

FIGURE 5-4.11
Properties for door

23. Finish inserting doors for the first floor (Figure 5-4.12). Use the following guidelines:

   a. Use the door styles shown in Figure 5-4.12.

   b. Doors across from each other in the *Mud Room* should align with each other.

   c. Place doors approximately as shown; exact location is not important.

   d. See the next page for information on sliding pocket doors.

   e. While inserting doors, you can control the door swing by moving the cursor to one side of the wall or the other and by using the spacebar on the keyboard.

   f. The order in which the doors are placed does not matter; this means your doors may have different numbers than the ones shown below.

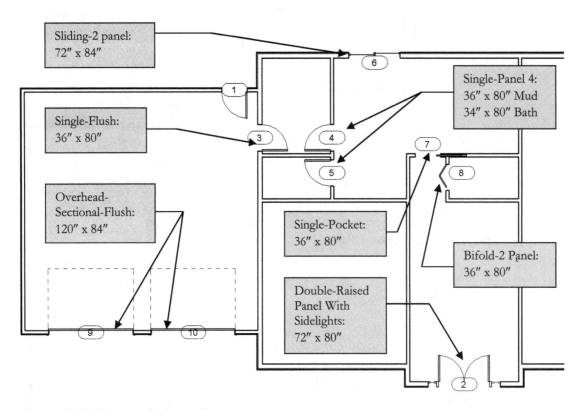

FIGURE 5-4.12 Doors to be inserted

Sliding Pocket Doors:

Sliding pocket doors are doors that slide into the wall rather than swinging open into a room. This type of door is convenient when the door will be open most of the time and you do not want, or have room for, an open door. On the other hand, if the door will be used often, like the door from the hallway into the bath room, you should use a swinging door for ease of use and long-term durability.

One important thing to keep in mind when designing a room with a sliding door: the entire width of the door is in the wall when the door is fully open. That means you need space in the wall next to the door that equals the width of the door plus a few inches depending on the manufacturer. This includes plumbing and electrical that might be in the wall.

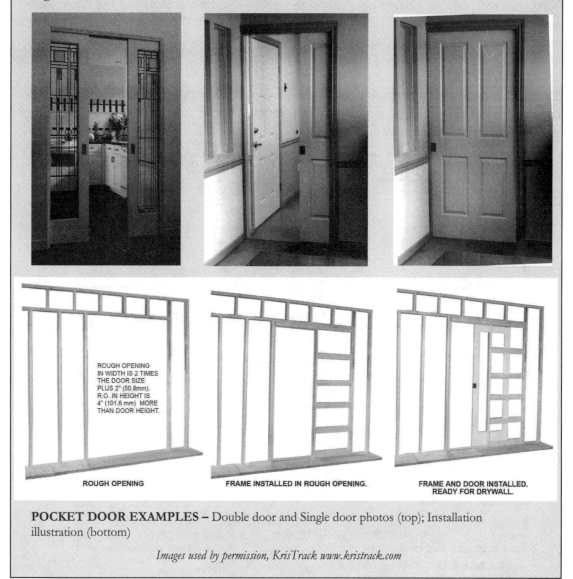

ROUGH OPENING IN WIDTH IS 2 TIMES THE DOOR SIZE PLUS 2" (50.8mm). R.O. IN HEIGHT IS 4" (101.6 mm) MORE THAN DOOR HEIGHT.

ROUGH OPENING   FRAME INSTALLED IN ROUGH OPENING.   FRAME AND DOOR INSTALLED. READY FOR DRYWALL.

POCKET DOOR EXAMPLES – Double door and Single door photos (top); Installation illustration (bottom)

Images used by permission, KrisTrack www.kristrack.com

Insert Openings:

With the first floor doors in place, you will add three openings. An opening is similar to a door in that, when placed, it removes a portion of wall automatically creating a circulation route. Also, like doors, openings come in different predefined shapes and sizes.

One common mistake is to break a wall so the floor plan appears to have an opening. However, when a section is cut through the opening there is no wall above the opening. This is also problematic for the room tagging feature and the *Ceiling Placement* tool.

One of the keys to working successfully in Revit is to model the building project just like you would build it because that is the way Revit is designed to work.

Next, you will place two larger openings in the walls between the *Foyer* and the *Living Room* and the *Dining Room*. A smaller opening will be placed in the wall between the *Dining Room* and the *Kitchen*. All three openings are from a family you previously loaded: *Opening-Elliptical Arch*.

The *Type Properties* dialog is shown below (Figure 5-4.13). Notice the various fields that can be filled in. For example, you could enter how much it would cost to construct an opening with an arched top in the *Cost* field.

FIGURE 5-4.13 Type Properties for *Passage-Elliptical Arch* family.
Note: If downloaded from the web, this family is named *Opening-Elliptical Arch*

24. Select **Architecture → Build → Component**; just click the upper part of the icon which defaults to the *Place a Component* option, seen via down-arrow selection.

25. Place the three **openings** as shown in Figure 5-4.14.

> *TIP: Select the appropriate opening (family/type) from the Type Selector on the Properties Palette.*

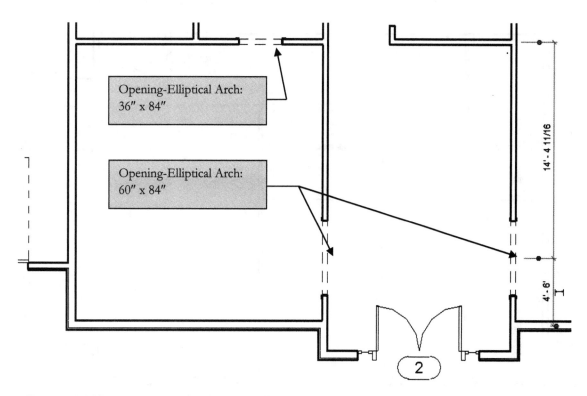

FIGURE 5-4.14 Openings placed in first floor plan

Insert Windows:

Adding windows to your project is very similar to adding doors. The template file you started from has three families preloaded into your project: <u>Casement with Trim</u>, <u>Double Hung with Trim</u> and <u>Fixed with Trim</u>. Looking at the *Type Selector* drop-down you will see the various sizes available for insertion. Additional families can be loaded, similar to how you loaded the doors, although your project will only use two families total and they are already loaded: *Double Hung* and *Fixed*.

26. Click the **Window** button on the *Architecture* tab, select **Double Hung with Trim: 36" x 72"** in the *Type Selector* and then select **Tag on Placement** on the *Ribbon*.

27. Insert 9 windows as shown in **Figure 5-4.15**; be sure to adjust the window locations to match the dimensions shown, but do not add the dimensions. Be sure to click towards the exterior side of the wall, so the window has the proper orientation.

TIP: To edit location: Modify → select window → adjust temporary dimension witness lines → edit temporary dimension text.

FIGURE 5-4.15 (9) windows added: Double Hung with Trim: 36″ x 72″

With a window *Type*, within a family, not only is the window size pre-defined, but the vertical distance off the ground is as well. Next you will see where this setting is stored.

28. Select one of the windows that you just placed in the walls and then notice the information presented in the *Properties Palette*.

Figure 5-4.16a Element Properties

As previously discussed, this palette shows the various settings for the selected item: a window in this case (Figure 5-4.16).

As you might guess, the same size window could have more than one sill height (i.e., distance from the floor to the bottom of the window). So Revit lets you adjust this setting on a window-by-window basis; this is called an *Instance Parameter*.

Another setting you might have noticed by now is *Phase Created*. This is part of what makes Revit a 4D program; the fourth dimension is time. Again, you might have several windows that are existing and several new ones in an addition, all the same size window. Revit lets you do that!

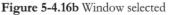

Figure 5-4.16b Window selected

Notice a Flip Control icon is shown when the window is selected, similar to doors. This icon should be on the exterior side of the wall. If not, simply click on the icon to flip the window's orientation within the wall.

29. Make sure the *Sill Height* is **1'-0"** and the **Flip Control** icon is on the exterior side of the wall; if not, change all nine windows.

Next, you will insert several double hung windows that are not as tall in the less prominent rooms, also in the *Kitchen* so cabinets will fit below the window. However, if you did place the tall windows in the *Kitchen*, you would realize it as soon as you tried to place the base cabinets and generate interior elevations or sections in the *Kitchen*. This is because the entire Revit project is one 3D database.

Compare the above mentioned conflict with traditional CAD, where the 2D elevations have nothing to do with the floor plans, sections, or interior elevations. With traditional CAD, you could draw the exterior elevations with the tall windows and place cabinets under it in plan view and then draw an interior elevation showing the cabinets and a shorter window. The windows are usually ordered and rough openings framed based on the exterior elevations. Revit helps to avoid these types of costly mistakes.

30. Insert window **Double Hung with Trim: 36″ x 48″** as shown in **Figure 5-4.17**; use *Instance Properties* to make sure the *Sill Height* is set to **3′-0″**; place 9 windows total.

FIGURE 5-4.17 (9) windows added: Double Hung with Trim: 36″ x 48″

Creating a New Window Type:

You will add four more windows to the East wall. These will be high windows, two on either side of a fireplace. Rather than using one of the predefined window sizes, you will create a new size within an existing family.

These windows will be fixed, non-operable, so you will be adding a new type to the *Fixed with Trim* family.

31. Select the **Window** tool and then select the **Edit Type** button on the *Properties Palette*.

32. Set the *Family* drop-down to **Fixed with Trim** and then set the *Type* drop-down to **36″ x 24″** (Figure 5-4.18). **Do not select the Double Hung window!**

> *FYI: You could have selected this in the* Type Selector *before clicking the* Edit Type *button.*

FIGURE 5-4.18 Type Properties – *Family*: Fixed with Trim; *Type*: 36″ x 24″

33. Click the **Duplicate** button.

34. Enter **36″ x 20″** for the name and then click **OK**.

You are now viewing the *Type Properties* for the new 36″ x 20″ type you just created. However, the name has nothing to do with actually changing the window size. You will do this next.

35. Change the *Height* parameter to **1′-8″**.

36. Change the *Default Sill Height* to **5′-4″**. *(This makes the top of all your windows align at 7′-0″.)*

37. Click **OK** to close the *Type Properties* dialog.

38. Add the windows as dimensioned in Figure 5-4.20.

    a. Before placing the first window, make sure the *Sill Height* is set to **5′-4″** in the *Properties Palette*.

FIGURE 5-4.19 Type Properties: New predefined window size

You are probably wondering where the windows are? They are tagged and you can select them. However, they are not visible.

With your project being a 3D model, Revit has to cut through the model at a certain elevation when generating the plan view. The default *Cut Plane* is 4'-0" above the floor line.

As you should recall, the sill of the new window type you just created is 5'-4" (Figure 5-4.19). If it is not, you should select the 36"x20" windows and adjust the sill height in the *Properties Palette*, so the window occurs above the cut line.

The windows will show up just fine in elevation and section views. Next you will see where the *Cut Plane* is set for each plan view.

POWER TIP: If you want the windows to be visible, or a high stair landing to show, you can create a Plan Region, which allows you to override the cut plane within the selected area. See Help for more on this.

FIGURE 5-4.20
First floor plan: last four windows added

39. Click the **Modify** tool on the *Ribbon* to unselect elements and cancel any active commands. This will cause the *Properties Palette* to show information about the current view.

40. Scroll down, in the *Properties Palette*, and select **Edit** next to *View Range*.

Notice the *Cut Plane* is set to 4'-0" (Figure 5-4.21). Try changing it and closing the dialog to see the various effects it has on your *Floor Plan* view; also look at the high windows.

Be sure to set the *Cut Plane* back to 4'-0" before proceeding.

41. Click **OK** to close the *View Range* dialog box.

View Range

Primary Range

Top: Associated Level (First Floo ▼   Offset: 7' 6"

Cut plane: Associated Level (First Floo ▼   Offset: 4' 0"

Bottom: Associated Level (First Floo ▼   Offset: 0' 0"

View Depth

Level: Associated Level (First Floo ▼   Offset: 0' 0"

[OK] [Cancel] [Apply] [Help]

FIGURE 5-4.21 View Range properties

Cleaning House:

As previously mentioned, you can view the various *Families* and *Types* loaded into your project via the *Project Browser*. The more families and types you have loaded the larger your file is, whether or not you are using them in your project. Therefore, it is a good idea to get rid of any door, window, etc., that you know you will not need in the current project. You do not have to delete any at this time, but this is how you do it:

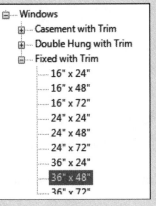

- In the *Project Browser*, navigate to Families → Windows → Fixed with Trim. Right-click on **36" x 48"** and select **Delete**.

Figure: Project Browser

Another reason to delete types is to avoid mistakes. As you have seen, loading a door family brings in 6'-8" and 7'-0" tall doors. On a residential project you would rarely use 7'-0" tall doors, so it would be a good idea to delete them from the project so you don't accidentally pick them.

That concludes the exercise on adding doors, openings and windows to the first floor plan.

Exercise 5-5:
Adding a Fireplace

The last thing you will do in this lesson is to add a fireplace to the *Living Room*. Creating a fireplace is beyond the scope of this introductory book, so you will download one from the *Web Library* (http://seek.autodesk.com).

1. Using techniques previously described to download doors from *Seek* (page 5-39), download the following items (Figure 5-5.1):
    a. **Mantel 1**
    b. **Masonry Chimney-Wall**

FIGURE 5-5.1 Seek content – download: Mantel and Chimney

2. **Load** the downloaded families into your project (see page 5-41).

You are now ready to place the fireplace in the first floor plan.

3. With the *First Floor Plan* view current, select **Architecture → Build → Component** from the *Ribbon*.

4. From the *Type Selector*, pick **Masonry Chimney-Wall : Chimney**.

The chimney will be looking for a wall to be inserted into; this is a *wall hosted family*. When your cursor is near a wall, you will see a "ghost" chimney to help you visually place the element; when the cursor is not near a wall, Revit does not display the "ghost" image because it is not a valid location to place the selected element.

Try moving the cursor around the plan for a minute. Notice, again, that when the cursor is near a wall you see the "ghost" image and the image orients itself with the wall (e.g., vert., horiz., angled). When the element encounters another element placed within a wall, you will see a small circle with a diagonal line through it indicating the two elements cannot overlap. Furthermore, the element flips to the side of the wall the cursor is on. Try moving the cursor from one side of the wall to the other and observe the image flip back and forth.

5. Move your cursor to the middle portion of the easternmost wall, between the high windows; with your cursor on the exterior side of the wall, click to place the fireplace.

6. Adjust the temporary dimensions so the chimney is centered on the wall (Figure 5-5.2).

Next you will place the mantel in the plan view. This is less automatic as it does not attach to the wall. So you will insert the mantel in the middle of the living room, rotate it and then move it into place.

FIGURE 5-5.2 Chimney added

7. Use the **Component** tool to insert **Mantel 1:80″ x 58¾″** into the middle of the *Living Room*.

8. Select the *Mantel* and use the *Rotate* tool to rotate the mantel 90 degrees in the clockwise direction.

    TIP: You could have also pressed the spacebar during placement in step 7 and then skipped step 8.

FIGURE 5-5.3 3D view of mantel

9. With the *Mantel* still selected, use the **arrow keys** on your keyboard to "nudge" the element into place, or try using the *Align* tool (Figure 5-5.4).

10. Take a minute to look at the *3D View* of all that you have completed so far (Figure 5-5.5).

Fireplace

Mantel

11. **Save** your project as **Ex5-5.rvt**.

FIGURE 5-5.4 Mantel added in plan view

FIGURE 5-5.5 3D View of completed chapter

Self-Exam:

The following questions can be used as a way to check your knowledge of this lesson. The answers can be found at the bottom of the page.

1. The *Options Bar* allows you to select the height at which your wall will be drawn. (T/F)

2. It is not possible to draw a wall with the interior or exterior face of the core as the reference point. (T/F)

3. Objects cannot be moved accurately with the *Move* tool. (T/F)

4. The _____ tool, on the *Ribbon*, has to be selected in order to select an object in your project.

5. A wall has to be _____ to see its flip icon.

Review Questions:

The following questions may be assigned by your instructor as a way to assess your knowledge of this section. Your instructor has the answers to the review questions.

1. Revit comes with many predefined doors and windows. (T/F)

2. The *Project Information* dialog allows you to enter data about the project, some of which is automatically added to sheet borders. (T/F)

3. You can delete *families* and *types* in the *Project Browser*. (T/F)

4. It is not possible to add a new window *type* to a window *family*. (T/F)

5. It is not possible to select which side of the wall a window should be on while you are inserting the window. (T/F)

6. What tool will break a wall into two smaller pieces? _____

7. The _____ tool allows you to match the surface of two adjacent walls.

8. Use the _____ key, on the keyboard, to flip the door swing while placing doors using the *Door* tool.

9. You adjust the location of a dimension's witness line by clicking on, or dragging, its _____.

10. The _____ file has a few doors, windows and walls preloaded in it.

Notes:

Lesson 6
Residence: SECOND FLOOR and BASEMENT PLANS:

In this lesson you will develop the second floor plan as well as the basement. This will involve copying objects from the first floor with some modifications along the way. You will also add stairs and dimensions to your plans. Be sure to check out the video on *Stairs* on the disc.

Exercise 6-1:
View Setup and Enclosing the Shell

Discussion: Second Floor View Current Conditions

1. Switch to the **Second Floor** view under *Floor Plans* in the *Project Browser*; double-click on the view name.

You should see a plan view similar to Figure 6-1.1. The geometry you are seeing is a result of two things:

- First, the height of walls drawn on the first floor:
    i. Some of the exterior walls that you sketched in the first floor plan are 19'-0" tall.
    ii. From the elevation views, you can see that the second floor is 9'-0" above the first.
    iii. As you may recall from the last chapter, the default *View Range* – Cut Line is 4'-0" above the floor.
    iv. So, relative to the first floor, the second floor Cut Plane is 13'-0" above it (9'-0" + 4'-0").
    v. Therefore, the 19'-0" tall walls extend past the second floor Cut Plane; that is why they are bold (elements in section automatically have a heavier line weight).
    vi. The exterior walls of the garage and east living room walls are only 12'-0", which is below the Cut Plane. It is still within the *View Range* so it shows up in "elevation" or projection. Elements in *projection* (i.e., beyond the Cut Plane) have lighter lines than those in section (i.e., at the Cut Plane).
- Second, the *Underlay* feature:
    i. In the *Properties Palette* (View Properties) for the *Second Floor Plan* view you will see a parameter labeled *Underlay* (Figure 6-1.2).
    ii. This feature is currently set to *First Floor*.

iii. The *Underlay* feature causes the selected view's walls to be displayed as light gray lines for reference.

iv. The walls shown as part of an underlay cannot be selected using a *window* selection but can be selected, and even deleted, by picking directly on a wall or anything else.

FIGURE 6-1.1 Second Floor: initial view

You do not need to see the first floor walls at the moment, so you will turn them off.

2. In the *Properties Palette* dialog set **Underlay** to **none**. *(Click Modify first if the View Properties are not currently shown.)*

Now you should only see the exterior walls (Figure 6-1.3).

Next, you will sketch two more exterior walls to enclose the second floor. These walls only occur above the second floor line so they will only have wood shakes for siding.

FIGURE 6-1.2 View Properties: Second Floor view

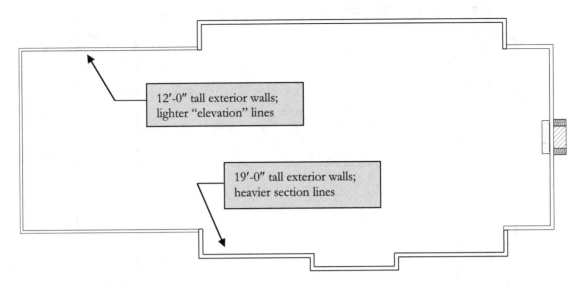

12'-0" tall exterior walls; lighter "elevation" lines

19'-0" tall exterior walls; heavier section lines

FIGURE 6-1.3 Second Floor: underlay turned off

3. Using the *Wall* tool, select **Exterior – Wood Shingle on Wood Stud** from the *Type Selector*.

If you look at the properties for this wall you will see that it is very similar to your primary exterior wall assembly. The main difference is that the vertical elements are stripped away: horizontal siding and two sweeps. You will see another wall type with just horizontal siding as well. These two walls are loaded in the template for the reason you are about to use one: as infill between the main, more complex, wall type. The image to the right shows, from left to right, horizontal siding only, shakes only and then the main wall you have previously used.

If you tried to use the wall type "Basic Wall: Exterior – Wood Shingle over Wood Siding on Wood Stud," the horizontal wood siding would start at the second floor line for any wall placed on the second floor. This is why you need a wall that just has wood shingles and no sweeps (i.e., horizontal trim boards).

4. Draw the two walls as shown in Figure 6-1.4, using the following information:
   - Set the *Height* to **Roof** (*Options Bar*).
   - Set the *Location Line* to **Finished Face: Interior** (*Options Bar*).
   - Pick the interior side of the existing wall; press the *spacebar* if you need to flip the wall before picking the wall end point.

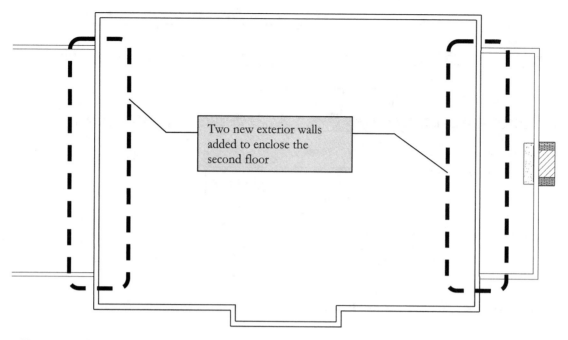

Two new exterior walls added to enclose the second floor

FIGURE 6-1.4 Second Floor: two exterior walls added

The height of the walls will change later when the roof is drawn. In fact, the height will vary as it extends up to the underside of the gable end roof; see image on the book cover.

The two walls just drawn will be supported by the second floor, which has not been drawn yet. The bottom of the walls is aligned with *Level 2* because of the view you are in.

You may have noticed that the exterior face of the wall does not appear to align perfectly with the adjacent walls. You will explore this problem and correct it in the next steps.

5. Select one of the walls just placed.

6. Click the **Edit Type** button on the *Properties Palette*.

7. In the *Type Properties* dialog, click **Edit** next to the ***Structure*** parameter.

8. Take note of the overall wall thickness and the thickness of the various layers (Figure 6-1.5A).

9. Close the dialog boxes, *Edit Assembly* and *Type Properties*, by clicking **OK**.

10. Follow the previous steps to look at the structure properties for the **Exterior – Wood Shingle over Wood Siding on Wood Stud**.

    NOTE: The sheathing thickness is not the same (Figures 6-1.5a and b). You will change one so they both match.

FIGURE 6-1.5A & B Comparing two walls' properties; sheathing thickness varies

11. Modify the *Sheathing* from ½″ to ¾″ for *Exterior – Wood Shingle on Wood Stud.*

12. **Save** your project as **Ex6-1.rvt**.

FYI:

Just as a reminder: the four elevation tags should not be deleted. You will study these more thoroughly later. This is what they represent:

The default template has four elevation tags shown in plan view. These symbols represent what the four preset views listed in the *Project Browser* will see. Therefore, you should always start drawing your plan in the approximate center of the four symbols. The symbols can be moved by dragging them with your mouse.

Again, do not delete these elevation tags as that will delete the actual views from the *Project Browser*.

Any view (e.g., plan, elevation or section) can be recreated but all the notes and dimensions, which are view specific, would have to be manually recreated.

Exercise 6-2:
Adding the Interior Walls

This short exercise will help reinforce the commands you have already learned. You will add walls, doors and windows to your project.

Copying Walls From the First Floor:

Often, you will have walls occur in the same location on each floor. The easiest thing to do is copy/paste between floors. You will try this now.

1. Switch to the *First Floor Plan* view.

2. Hold down the **Ctrl** key; select the four walls identified in Figure 6-2.1.

FIGURE 6-2.1 First Floor: Selected walls, (4) total, to be copied/pasted to the Second Floor

3. With the four walls selected, select **Modify | Walls → Clipboard → Copy**; this command is different than *Copy* in the *Modify* panel which only works in the current view.

4. Click **Modify** to unselect the first floor walls and then switch back to the ***Second Floor Plan*** view.

   TIP: Press Ctrl + Tab to switch between open views.

5. Select **Modify → Clipboard → Paste → Aligned to Current View** (Figure 6-2.2).

You should now see the four walls in your *Second Floor Plan* view (Figure 6-2.3).

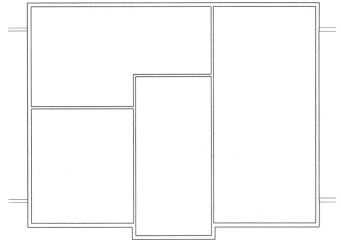

Why did we not just draw these four first floor walls 19′-0″ high like the exterior walls?

FIGURE 6-2.2
Modify tab: Paste Aligned fly-out

Simulating real-world construction is ideal for several reasons. Mostly, you can be sure exterior walls align from floor to floor. Although the four walls align, they do not necessarily have to because they are separated by floor construction; this allows one floor to later be modified easily. However, if an exterior wall is moved in any plan view, you want to make sure it moves everywhere, so these walls are drawn full height.

6. Select **Modify** to deselect the walls via the *Ribbon*.

Any time a wall is copied, or copy/pasted, any hosted elements attached to the wall(s) are copied with the wall. Next, you will delete the openings that were copied with the walls from the first floor.

7. Individually select each of the four openings and delete them.

FIGURE 6-2.3 Second Floor: walls copied, doors deleted

Your first floor walls have their *top constraint* set to the second floor, so when you copied the walls from the first floor to the second floor Autodesk® Revit® Architecture automatically sets the *top constraint* to the next level above the first floor: the *Roof* level. This is fine for now.

Next you will add a few more interior walls.

8. Using the ***Wall*** tool, draw the walls shown in Figure 6-2.4 using the following information:
   a. Wall type: **Interior – 4½″ Partition**
   b. Location Line: *use whatever is appropriate*
   c. Height: **Roof**
   d. Do not draw the dimensions at this time.
   e. Notice that one of the interior walls from Figure 6-2.3 gets extended and another gets trimmed; the walls previously created have a heavy dashed line over them (Figure 6-2.4).

FIGURE 6-2.4 Second Floor: additional walls added

Joining Geometry:

Occasionally the intersection of two walls will not clean up, so you can use the *Join Geometry* icon on the *Tools* toolbar. The steps are as follows:

- Click *Modify* → *Geometry* → *Join*.

- Select the two walls.

- That's it; the walls are joined.

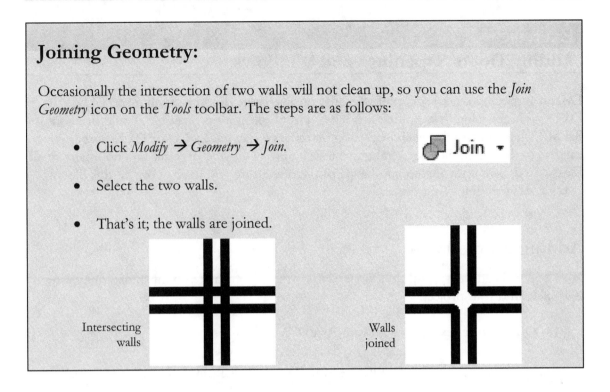

Intersecting
walls

Walls
joined

Controlling the View Scale

The size of the dimensions and door and window tags is controlled by the *View Scale*. Each *View* has its own scale setting. To facilitate the creation of this book, the *View Scale* has been set to 3/32″ = 1′-0″ typical. At that scale, Revit makes the text and symbols larger so it is legible at the smaller scale. However, the images in this book are not to scale.

The default *View Scale* is ¼″ = 1′-0″ for the plan views, floor, ceiling and framing plans. This is good and should not be changed for this tutorial. In addition to controlling the text and symbols, it also controls the size, or scale, of that drawing on the plot sheet (i.e., one of the sheets in a set of drawings). This only makes sense seeing as *View Scale* has everything to do with what scale that view is intended to be printed at.

The *View Scale* can be controlled via the *View Properties* dialog or more conveniently on the *View Control Bar* at the bottom of the drawing window (Figure 6-2.5).

9. Save your project as **ex6-2.rvt**.

FIGURE 6-2.5
View Scale

Exercise 6-3:
Adding Doors, Openings and Windows

Do not forget to keep a backup of your files on a separate disk (i.e., flash drive, CD or DVD) or in the Cloud via Autodesk A360 or Dropbox. Your project file should be about 8.5 MB when starting this exercise. Most computers today have a CD or DVD burner you can use to save large files. Remember, your Revit project is one large file and not many small files. You do not want anything to happen to it. Make sure you have a copy of this file in two places at all times – do this daily!

Adding More Doors

Now you will add the second floor doors and openings, but first you must load one more *door family* into your project.

1. Open project ex6-2.rvt and **Save-As ex6-3.rvt**.

2. Load the door Family **Bifold–4 Panel.rfa** into your project.

    Reminder: *Insert → Load Family, and then browse to folder containing the doors you downloaded.*

3. Add the doors as shown in Figure 6-3.1:
    a. Center the closet doors in the closet.

    TIP: *With the inserted door selected, you can "nudge" the door using the arrow keys.*

    FYI: *The more zoomed in you are, the more accurate the "nudge" increments are.*

Residential Door Sizes!
Doors come in many shapes and sizes.

Thickness: $1\frac{3}{8}''$, $1\frac{3}{4}''$ and $2\frac{1}{4}''$
The $1\frac{3}{8}''$ door is most often used in residential construction and the $2\frac{1}{4}''$ door is typically only used on exterior doors for high-end projects, i.e., big budget.

Size: ranges from $1'-0''$ x $6'-8''$ to $4'-0''$ x $9'-0''$
The height of a residential door is usually $6'-8''$. This writer recently worked on a project where $7'-0''$ high doors were specified. The contractor was so used to the standard $6'-8''$ dimension; he framed all the exterior openings at $6'-8''$. To top it off, the exterior walls were concrete (ICF system), so the openings could not be modified. Thus, $6'-8''$ doors were used.

You can find more information on the internet; two examples are
    algomahardwoods.com and madawaska-doors.com
     (wood veneer door mfr.)   *(custom solid wood door mfr.)*

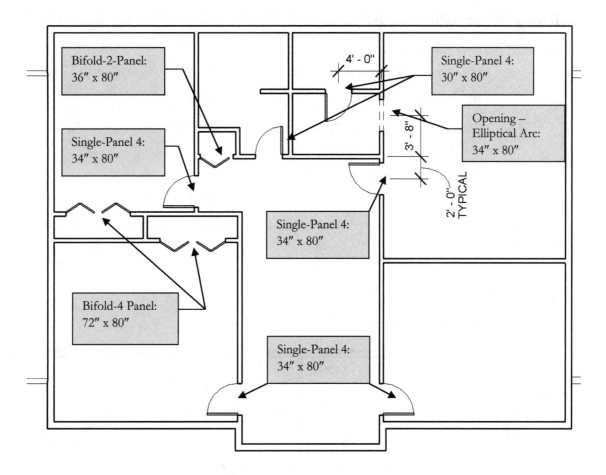

FIGURE 6-3.1 Second Floor; doors added

The door numbers were temporarily hidden from view for clarity. On your plans you notice that the new doors have different numbers while the windows have the same number. Why is this? It relates to industry standards for architectural drafting. Each window that is the same size and configuration has the same type number throughout the project. Each door has a unique number because doors have so many variables (i.e., locks, hinges, closer, panics, material, and fire rating). To make doors easier to find, many architectural firms will make the door number the same as the room number the door opens into. You can change the door number by selecting the tag and then clicking on the text. The door schedule will be updated automatically.

Adding More Windows:

4. Add the windows as shown in Figure 6-3.2.

   a. Verify via the *Properties Palette* that each window's *Head Height* is set to 7'-0".

      TIP: *Type* PP *if you accidentally closed the* Properties Palette.

   b. All windows are **Double Hung with Trim: 36″ x 48″** unless otherwise noted in Figure 6-3.2.

   c. Similar to the previous image, the door and window tags have been temporarily hidden from view; you will learn how to do this next.

   d. All dimensions are from the center of the window to the exterior face of wall.

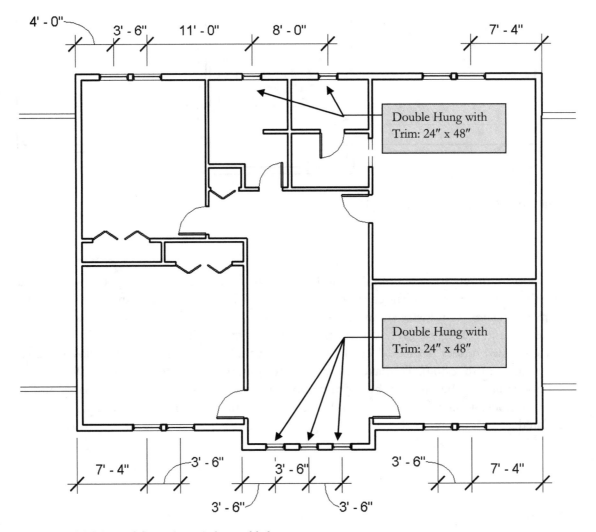

FIGURE 6-3.2 Second floor plan: windows added

Using Hide/Isolate to Control Visibility:

Now you will shift gears for a moment and look at the *Hide/Isolate* feature. This allows you to temporarily hide or isolate the selected elements or all the elements in the same category as those selected.

This feature is accessed via the *View Control Bar*, similar to the *View Scale* feature previously discussed.

5. Holding the **Ctrl** key, select one door tag and one window tag.

6. On the *View Control* bar click the **Temporary Hide/Isolate** icon (looks like sunglasses).

7. From the pop-up menu, select **Hide Category** (Figure 6-3.3).

FIGURE 6-3.3 View Control bar: Hide/Isolate selected

You should notice two things. First, all the door and window tags are gone. Second, the *Hide/Isolate* icon has a cyan background and the drawing window has a heavy cyan border around it, with text in the upper left stating "Temporary Hide/Isolate," which reminds you that some thing(s) is temporarily removed from the current view.

As implied by the feature name, the tags are temporarily hidden from view; they have not been deleted.

If you would have selected *Hide Element*, only the selected elements would have been hidden from view rather than the entire category.

To restore this temporary setting, do the following:

8. Click the **Temporary Hide/Isolate** icon again (nothing has to be selected).

9. Select **Reset Temporary Hide/Isolate** from the pop-up menu.

> *FYI: Hiding items does affect printing. If you close the project and reopen it the temporary override will be gone.*

All is now back to normal. Try a few other variations on this feature and observe the results. Select *Reset Temporary Hide/Isolate* before proceeding.

Apply Hide/Isolate to View:

If you temporarily hide a few elements or categories and you want those items to be permanently hidden, you can select **Apply Hide/Isolate to View** from the *Hide/Isolate* icon menu shown in Figure 6-3.3.

This feature allows you to hide (or isolate) individual items; for example, you could select a single window tag and hide it. The only way to see it again in that view is to select the **Reveal Hidden Elements** icon on the *View Control Bar* (Figure 6-3.4a).

You should notice two things. First, all the hidden window tags are magenta and everything else is light gray. Second, the *Reveal Hidden Elements* icon has a magenta background and the drawing window has a heavy magenta border around it with a label in the upper left which reminds you that the current view settings are currently being modified.

FIGURE 6-3.4A
View Control Bar: Reveal Hidden Elements

Restoring Hidden Elements:

To restore a hidden item you first click the *Reveal Hidden Elements* (Figure 6-3.4a) icon and then select the element(s) to be restored to view. Once the item(s) is selected, you click **Unhide Element** or **Unhide Category** from the *Ribbon (Figure 6-3.4b).* Finally, you select the *Reveal Hidden Elements* icon again to return to the normal "current view" settings.

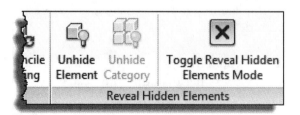

FIGURE 6-3.4B
Ribbon: Reveal Hidden Elements panel

Exercise 6-4:
Basement Floor Plan

Basement Floor Plan:

Now you will sketch the basement floor plan. Not all residences have basements; they mostly occur in cold climates where the foundation walls are deep to avoid frost heave. Once you have dug out for the deep foundation walls along the entire perimeter of the building, it does not take much more effort or resources to create a basement. Drawing a basement is the same as the other floors; you draw the exterior walls, concrete foundation walls in this case, the interior walls, etc. Once again, with the residential template that you started with being set up for the typical residential project, it should not surprise you that a typical foundation wall type is already set up and ready to be sketched; both 10″ and 12″ walls have been predefined.

1. Open your project file ex6-3.rvt and **Save As ex6-4.rvt**.

2. Switch to the *Foundation* floor plan view; <u>not</u> the *Basement* plan.

You should see a grayed out representation of the first floor.

3. In *View Properties* do the following two steps:

   a. Note the **Underlay** parameter is set to **First Floor**; if not set properly, you should change it now so *First Floor* is the current *Underlay*.

   b. Set the **Discipline** to **Architectural**.

This underlay setting gives you an outline of your building that can be used to sketch the foundation walls.

4. Using the *Wall* tool, draw the foundation walls using the following information (see *Type Selector* and *Options Bar* image below):
   a. *Wall type*:   **Foundation – 12″ Concrete**
   b. *Location Line*:   **Finish Face: Exterior**
   c. *Depth*:   **T.O. Footing** (i.e., Top of Footing).

   FYI: Notice this setting on the Options Bar changes from "Height" to "Depth" when a "foundation" wall is selected!

   d. Check **Chain** on the *Options Bar*.
   e. Start anywhere by snapping to one of the exterior corners of the *Underlay*; work in a clockwise direction.

When finished, your plan should look like Figure 6-4.1. The garage area will be slab-on-grade (i.e., no basement under it), so make sure you sketch a foundation wall between the garage and basement as shown.

FIGURE 6-4.1 Foundation Floor Plan; with First Floor Underlay turned on

5. Set the *Underlay* parameter for "Foundation" floor plan to **None** in the *Properties Palette*.

So What Exactly Did You Just Draw?

You just drew a foundation where the **top** is based on the current level, a level named Foundation in this example, and the "Depth" parameter on the *Options Bar* controls the **bottom** of the wall (T.O. Footing in this example).

The image to the right should make this concept perfectly clear (Figure 6-4.2).

FYI: Each level datum has a corresponding floor plan view when the target is blue (as seen in the image to the right). You may not need all of these views in a set of construction documents, but they are useful for creating the Building Information Model (BIM).

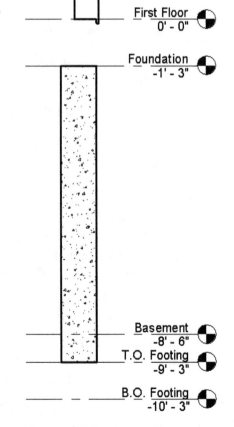

FIGURE 6-4.2
Foundation wall in section

Creating a New Foundation Wall Type:

Because the garage area is slab-on-grade, both sides of the foundation wall will have earth against them. The main basement walls act like a retaining wall because they only have earth on one side of the wall. Therefore, you will change the three exterior foundation walls, at the garage area, to 8″ concrete. You will have to create a new wall type to accommodate this need.

NOTE: When the "Wall Function" is set to Retaining in the "Type Parameters" for a wall, the wall cannot be room bounding, so Room/Room Tags cannot be added.

Disclaimer:
All dimensions and sizes shown in this book are solely for the purpose of learning to use the software. Under no circumstances should any information be assumed to be appropriate for a real-world project. A structural engineer should be consulted if you do not have adequate expertise in that area.

---

6. Select the *Wall* tool and then select **Foundation – 12″ Concrete** from the *Type Selector*.

7. Create a new wall type based on the current selection; name it **Foundation – 8″ Concrete**.

   REMEMBER: Properties Palette → Edit Type → Duplicate

8. Adjust the *Type Parameters* of the new wall so the Width is **8″**.

   FYI: This is through Properties Palette → Edit Type → Edit Structure.

9. Select the three exterior garage foundation walls while holding down the Ctrl key, and then select your new wall in the *Type Selector*.

   REMEMBER: Click Modify first to cancel the Wall tool.

   TIP: Hover your cursor over one wall, press Tab to highlight all three walls (a chain of walls), and then click to select all three walls at once!

Your basement plan should look like Figure 6-4.3.

Because the *Location Line* was set to Finish Face: Exterior, the exterior side of the foundation wall is stationary when walls of a different width are selected; this is the desired result in this situation.

FYI: You will add footings below the foundation walls in Exercise 10-2.

FIGURE 6-4.3 Basement Floor Plan; with 8″ foundation walls at the garage

Adding Interior Walls in the Basement:

To make things simple, for this tutorial and structurally, you will copy all the walls from the first floor to the basement. In the process of accomplishing this task you will also study the selection **Filter** function.

First you will switch to the first floor and select a large area using a *crossing window* (i.e., picking from right to left), and then use the *Filter* function to strip the selection down to just the walls.

10. Switch to the ***First Floor*** view and select all the interior walls using a *crossing window* (Figure 6-4.4).

Everything within or passing through the *crossing window* is now selected. Next you will filter out everything except for the walls.

FIGURE 6-4.4 First Floor Plan; selecting all walls with a crossing window

11. With everything from the previous step still selected, click the **Filter** icon on the *Status Bar* (Figure 6-4.5).

FIGURE 6-4.5 Filter Selection icon

You are now in the *Filter* dialog (Figure 6-4.6). This lists all the element types or categories that are in the current selection set. When you click OK, only the items checked will be part of the current selection set.

Filter

Category:	Count:
☐ Door Tags	4
☐ Doors	4
☐ Generic Models	3
☑ Walls	8

[Check All]
[Check None]

Total Selected Items: 8

[OK]   [Cancel]   [Apply]

TIP:
If you only wanted the walls selected, but had 20+ items in the list, you could click the "Check None" button and then check only "Walls" in the list. This would be faster than individually clicking each item in the list to unselect it.

FIGURE 6-4.6 Filter dialog

12. Uncheck everything except the **Walls** item in the *Filter* dialog (Figure 6-4.6).

13. Click **OK** to update the current select set.

TIP: Notice the number of selected items is listed in the lower right corner of the program window (image to the right). If you know you want to delete 3 doors and the count shows 4 items, you would not want to click Delete before you unselect the fourth item!

Now only the walls are selected. Next you will copy them to the *Clipboard* and then *Paste* them into the basement floor plan.

This selection technique can be used in many ways. For example, you could select all the walls and change their *Top Constraint* via the *Properties* dialog.

14. From the *Ribbon* select **Modify | Walls → Clipboard → Copy**.

15. Switch to the **Basement** view, not the Foundation view.

16. Select **Modify** on the *Ribbon*, and then **Modify → Clipboard → Paste → Aligned to Current View**.

You should get the following warning (Figure 6-4.7):

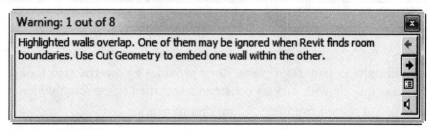

FIGURE 6-4.7 Wall placement warning

This error is indicating that the wall(s) you just placed overlaps another wall (vertically or horizontally). In this case it may be that the *Top Offset* is not set to 0″, but to 6″, which causes the wall to extend 6″ above the *Top Constraint* (which is the first floor line). So, if the first floor walls start at the first floor line, the basement walls extend up into the first floor walls by 6″, and the two walls would be overlapping vertically.

17. If you get this warning, click the "X" in the upper right corner of the warning window; this will close it. Then select all the interior walls in the basement and make sure the *Top Offset* is set to 0″ via the *Properties Palette*.

When finished, your plan should look like Figure 6-4.8.

FIGURE 6-4.8 Walls added to the basement floor, copied from the first floor

Even though the doors were not selected, they were still copied with the walls just as before. This is fine; to save time you will leave the doors as they are.

18. **Save** your project as **ex6-4.rvt**.

Exercise 6-5:
Stairs

Next you will add stairs to your floor plans. Revit provides a powerful stair tool that allows you to design stairs quickly with various constraints specified in the *family* which was loaded with the template you started from (e.g., 7″ maximum riser).

Stair Type Parameters:

Before you draw the stair, it will be helpful to review the options available in the stair family.

1. Open ex6-4.rvt and *Save As* **ex6-5.rvt**. Open the **First Floor** plan.

2. From the *Project Browser*, expand the *Families* → *Stairs* → *Stair* (i.e., click the plus sign next to these labels).

3. Right-click on the stair type **Residential – Closed 2 Sides**, and select the **Type Properties…** option from the pop-up menu.

You should now see the options shown in Figure 6-5.1.

Take a couple minutes to see what options are available. We will quickly review a few below.

- Tread Depth: Treads are typically 12″ deep (usually code min.) and 1″ of that depth overlaps the next tread; so only 11″ is visible in plan view. This overlap is called the *nosing*.
- Riser: This provides Revit with the maximum dimension allowed (by code, or if you want it, less). The actual dimension will depend on the floor-to-floor height.
- Stringer dimensions: These dimensions usually vary per stair depending on the stair width, run and materials, to name a few.
- Cost: Estimating placeholder.

FYI: Closed 2 Sides (part of the name of the stair family) means there will be a wall on each side of the stair; thus a stringer will be visible above the stair.

FIGURE 6-5.1 Stair type properties

Calculate Tread and Riser Size:

Although Revit automatically calculates the rise and tread dimensions for you, it is still a good idea to understand what is happening.

The *riser* is typically calculated to be as large as building codes will allow. Occasionally a grand stair will have a smaller riser to create a more elegant stair.

Similarly, the *tread* is usually designed to be as small as allowable by building codes.

The largest riser and shortest tread create the steepest stair allowed. This takes up less floor space (Figure 6-5.2). A stairway that is too steep is uncomfortable and unsafe.

Building codes vary by location; for this exercise you will use 7" (max.) for the risers and 9" (min.) for the treads.

Codes usually require that each tread be the same size, likewise with risers.

Calculate the number and size of the risers:

    Given:
    Risers: **7"** max.   Floor to floor height: **9'-0"**.

    Calculate the number of risers:
        9'-0" divided by 7" (or 109" divided by 7") = 15.429

Seeing as each riser has to be the same size we will have to round off to a whole number. You cannot round down because that will make the riser larger than the allowed maximum (9'-0" / 15 = 7.2"). Therefore you have to round up to 16. Thus: 9'-0" divided by 16 = 6.75.

So you need **16** risers that are **6¾"** each.

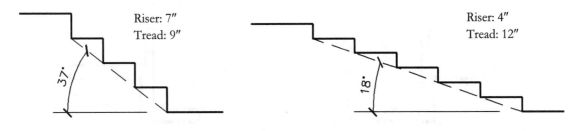

FIGURE 6-5.2 Stair rise/run comparison

Drawing the Stairs in Plan:

You will be drawing a U-shaped stair from the first floor to the second and an L-shaped stair from the basement to the first floor. At first, when using Revit to draw stairs, it may be helpful to manually figure out the number of risers and landings. That information will be helpful when drawing the stair. As you become more familiar with the *Stair* tool, you will not need to do those calculations to draw a stair.

To get an idea about what you are going to draw next, take a moment to look at Figure 6-5.3. The image below is at the first floor, and the "UP" label indicates where you would access the stair on the first floor. (Everything else rises from there, of course, to the second floor.)

FIGURE 6-5.3 Stair information overview

The first thing you will do, to prepare to draw the stair from the first floor to the second floor, is to draw a temporary reference line. This line will be used to accurately pick a starting point while using the *Stair* command (you will be picking a starting point near the middle of the room – next to the "UP" label in Figure 6-5.3). After the stair is drawn, you will erase the line.

You have had plenty of practice drawing lines in previous chapters, so you will be given minimal instruction on how to draw the line.

4. Make sure you are in the ***First Floor Plan*** view.

5. **Zoom in** to the front *Entry Foyer*.

6. Using the ***Detail Line*** tool from the *Annotate* tab, draw the temporary line in the ***First Floor Plan*** view, as shown in Figure 6-5.4.

FIGURE 6-5.4 Draw a temporary detail line

7. Click on the ***Architecture*** tab on the *Ribbon*.

8. Select **Architecture → Circulation → Stair → Stair by Component**.

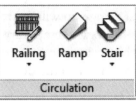

9. Click on the ***Edit Type*** icon in the *Properties Palette*.
   Notice the *Minimum Run Width* is 3'-0". Click **OK**. Also notice the **Actual Run Width** is set to **3'-0"** on the *Option Bar*.

FIGURE 6-5.5 Stair tool active; Select Edit Type from the Properties Palette

10. Notice the *Top Level* is set to **Second Floor** (Figure 6-5.6).

11. Click the endpoint of your temporary detail line as shown in **Figure 6-5.7**; you are selecting the start point for the first step. Make sure you are snapping to the line for accuracy; a tooltip will appear stating "endpoint" before you click.

12. Pick the remaining points as shown in Figures 6-5.7, 6-5.8 and 6-5.9.

*FYI: For the second run, set the Location Line to **Left** on the Options Bar.*

TIP:

Notice the palette to the left is the Instance Properties *which controls selected or to-be-created instances. In this case, of course, we are talking about a to-be-created instance.*

Clicking the Edit Type *button here would make changes to this stair and any others previously created. Your project does not have any previously created stairs at this time.*

FIGURE 6-5.6 Stair instance properties

Notice as you draw the stairs, Revit will display the number of risers drawn and the number of risers remaining to be drawn to reach the next level, or whatever level is selected as *Top Level* in *Properties*.

If you click *Finish Stairs*, the green check mark on the *Ribbon*, before drawing all the required risers, Revit will display a warning message. You can leave the problem to be resolved later.

Pick #2: After picking the first point below, begin moving the cursor straight up; click when the label below the stairs reads "8 Risers Created, 8 Remaining."

Pick #1: Pick the endpoint of your temporary line as the starting point for the stair.

8 RISERS CREATED, 8 REMAINING

FIGURE 6-5.7 Beginning to sketch the stair

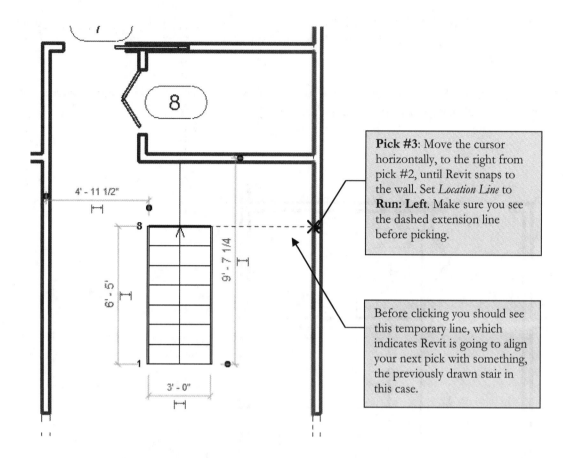

Pick #3: Move the cursor horizontally, to the right from pick #2, until Revit snaps to the wall. Set *Location Line* to **Run: Left**. Make sure you see the dashed extension line before picking.

Before clicking you should see this temporary line, which indicates Revit is going to align your next pick with something, the previously drawn stair in this case.

FIGURE 6-5.8 Continuing to sketch the stair

Pick #4: Move the cursor straight down until Revit indicates "8 Risers Created, 0 Remaining."

TIP: You can move the mouse past that point; you do not need to click directly on it.

FIGURE 6-5.9 Last step in sketching the stair

13. Click the **green check mark** to *Finish* the stair on the *Ribbon* (Figure 6-5.5).

14. **Erase** the temporary detail line; you may need to tap the Tab key (i.e., tap, not hold down) to select it rather than the stair.

Your stair should now look like Figure 6-5.10! Notice that Revit adds a break-line at the *Cut Plane* and everything above that is dashed in.

As soon as you click *Finish Stair*, Revit will automatically add the landing, creating it between the two stair runs sketched. The width of the landing will match the stair width, which is 3'-0". This is true for any stair configuration using the above method. You will see this momentarily when you sketch an L-shaped stair in the basement.

The second floor plan also shows this stair but with a down arrow and no break lines because it does not pass through that view's *Cut Plane*!

FIGURE 6-5.10 Finished stair

Modeling the Basement Stairs:

Now you will draw the L-shaped stairs from the basement to the first floor.

To get an idea about what you are going to draw next, take a moment to look at Figure 6-5.11. The image below is at the basement level, and the "UP" label indicates where you would access the stair on the basement level. Everything else rises from there, of course, to the first floor.

15. Save your project as **ex6-5.rvt**; remember to save often.

16. Switch to the **Basement** floor plan view.

17. Select the **Stair** tool.

FIGURE 6-5.11 Stair information overview

18. In the *Properties Palette* make the following changes:

    a. Change the *Type Selector* to **Residential – Open 2 Sides**.

    b. Make sure the *Top Level* is set to **First Floor**; the *Stair* tool defaults to the next *Level* up – which is "foundation" level and not "first floor" in your case.

19. Select the **Railing** button on the *Ribbon*.

20. Select **None** and **OK** (see image to right).

21. Using the same techniques you employed to sketch the first floor stair, draw the basement stair per the information given in Figure 6-5.11.

TIP: While sketching the stairs, you can select a window (picking from left to right) around a run of stairs and move it. Also, do not forget to draw a temporary line(s) if you think it will help.

Your stair should look like Figure 6-5.12. If not, select one of the riser/tread lines and press the *Delete* key on the keyboard to erase the stair and try again. It can get a little frustrating when you are not familiar with the ins-and-outs of what Revit is doing or what information it needs to proceed. Take your time; take a break if necessary.

Next you will draw three walls next to the stair. This will close off the two open sides and the bottom of the stair.

TIP: If a stair needs to be modified at any time in the future, you do not actually have to delete the stair and start over; it is recommended above for practice. If you select a stair, you can click the Edit Sketch icon on the Ribbon to re-enter Sketch mode for that stair.

FIGURE 6-5.12 Finished basement stair

22. Using the *Wall* tool, draw the three interior walls as shown in **Figure 6-5.13**.

- Use the standard interior wall you used for the other floors.

  TIP #1: You can select one and see what type it is in the Type Selector.

  TIP #2: You can also select a wall and right-click, and then select "Create Similar" from the pop-up menu to add another wall of the type selected.

- Click the *Chain* option if not already checked.

- Set *Location Line* to one of the finished wall faces.

- *Top Constraint* set to **First Floor**.

- Click the inside points of the stair. Press the *spacebar* if needed to flip the wall so it is created outside of the stair footprint.

- Draw the third wall under the stair, at the fifth riser line.

FIGURE 6-5.13 Three walls added at stairs

A cutaway 3D view of your model looks something like this; you will learn to do cutaway views later in the book.

You should notice two things about this 3D view:

First: The basement wall you just added extends through the basement stair. You will fix that in the building sections lesson.

Second: No floors have been drawn yet. You will draw floor systems in the next chapter.

23. **Save** your project.

FIGURE 6-5.14 3D view of stair

FYI: Normally you would not rename your project file. You do it here in the book for grading and restore options, should things get really corrupted.

Make sure to examine the stair sample file available on Autodesk's online content library (seek.autodesk.com – search for "Revit samples" and select the stair option). You can download this file and see examples of several different stair types side-by-side (see image below). You can select one and view its properties to see how it was done. You can also Copy/Paste one into your project; select your stair, and then select the newly imported type(s) from the *Type Selector*. The partial view of the sample file, shown below, has open riser, single stringer, no stringer, spiral…

FIGURE 6-5.15 Partial view of sample stair file from Revit's website

Modify the Building's Floor-to-Floor Height:

You will not need to do this for this tutorial, but you can modify the building's floor-to-floor height (or Level). The reasons for doing this vary. Some examples might be to make the building shorter or taller, to accommodate ductwork in the ceilings or the depth of the floor structure; the longer the span, the deeper the structure. The default floor-to-floor height in the template file you started from is 9'-0", which is fine for this project. However, should you want to change this for another project, here is how to do it:

- Open any exterior elevation from the *Project Browser*.

- Change the floor-to-floor height to be 12'-0" for each level; in this example, to the right.

- Select the floor elevation symbol, and then select the text displaying the elevation. You should now be able to type in a new number. Press Enter to see the changes. Notice the windows move because the sill height has not been changed (Figure A).

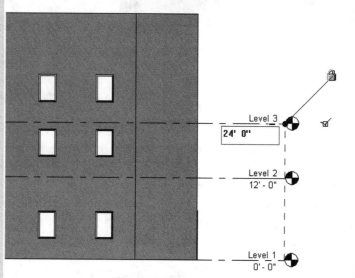

FIGURE A Exterior elevation: modifying Level 3 elevation

- The floor-to-floor height is a good thing to figure out, when possible, before drawing the stairs, as it affects the number of risers and treads required, not to mention floor area.

Exercise 6-6:
Dimensions

Next you will add dimensions to your floor plans. Revit provides a powerful dimension tool that allows you to quickly dimension drawings. This process is much easier than other CAD programs. Revit has a dimension style all set up and ready to use, which works for most designers. Furthermore, the size of the text and ticks are tied to the *View Scale* feature to make sure the dimensions always print at the correct size. For example, a dimension's text and ticks would get twice as big just by changing the *View Scale* from ¼″ = 1′-0″ to ⅛″ = 1′-0″. You will try this in a moment.

Industry standard dimensioning conventions were covered in the previous lesson. You may want to take a minute and review that information (see page 5-23).

Drawing dimensions in Revit involves the following steps:

- Select the *Aligned* dimension tool from the *Annotate* tab.

- *Ribbon*, *Options Bar* and *Type Selector*:
  o Select one of the predefined styles from the *Type Selector*.
  o Select the kind of dimension you want: Linear, Angular, Radial, Arch Length.
  o Tell Revit what part of the wall you want to dimension to: Wall centerlines, Wall Face, Center of Core, Face of Core; this can change for each side of a dimension's line.

- Select two, or more, walls to dimension between.

- Select a location for the dimension line.

Adding Dimensions to the First Floor Plan:

1. Open ex6-5.rvt and **Save-As ex6-6.rvt**.

2. Switch to the *First Floor Plan* view.

3. **Zoom in** on the North wall of the garage.

4. Select the **Annotate → Dimension → Aligned** tool.

Notice the *Ribbon, Options Bar* and *Type Selector* changes to give you control over the various options mentioned above (Figure 6-6.1).

FIGURE 6-6.1 Ribbon, Option Bar and Type Selector: Dimension tool active

5. Set the *Type Selector* to **Linear – 3/32″ Arial**.

6. Click the **Edit Type** button on the *Properties Palette*.

Notice the various properties you can adjust for the selected dimension type (Figure 6-6.2).

Creating a new, custom, dimension type is the same as for walls, doors, etc.; just click the *Duplicate* button, provide a name and then adjust the properties.

All the dimensions you see here are multiplied by the *View Scale*. For example, the 3/32″ text is multiplied by 48 when the *View Scale* is set to ¼″ = 1′-0″; thus, the text is 4½″ tall in ¼″ drawings. When the ¼″ view is placed on a *Sheet*, Revit automatically scales the view down 1/48. At this point the text is 3/32″ again. This makes the view actually a ¼″ = 1′-0″ on the *Sheet*, which is actual sheet size

FIGURE 6-6.2 Properties for selected dimension type

– say 22″ x 34″. Finally, all this is changed automatically whenever the *View Scale* is changed: dimension and text size as well as the *View* size on sheets! You will learn about *Sheets* later in the book.

7. Click **OK** to close the dialog box.

The Aligned dimension tool allows you to place dimensions by picking walls. You will try this now.

Aligned

8. Next, select **Wall Faces** on the *Options Bar* (Figure 6-6.1).

9. Draw your first dimension by clicking the three points as identified in **Figure 6-6.3**.

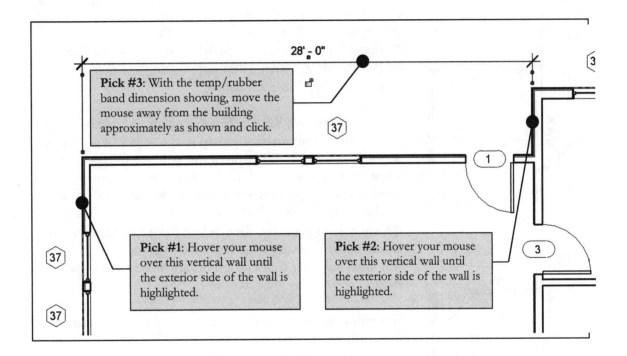

FIGURE 6-6.3 First Floor plan: first dimension added

FYI: In the figure above (6-6.3), you can select points 1 and 2 in the opposite order as well.

10. Dimension the rest of the North exterior wall as shown in Figure 6-6.4. You may not be able to read the dimensions in the image provided, but you can still determine the number of dimensions required and Revit provides the dimension text anyway. See the next page for dimension comments.

Once you have drawn one dimension, as in Step 10, the remaining dimensions in that "string" should align with the first. Revit helps you make the third pick (as in Figure 6-6.3) by automatically snapping to the previous dimension when you move your cursor to it.

You can add a "string" of dimensions by simply clicking on parallel walls. When done, click somewhere away from any Revit elements to position and finish the dimension string. To edit a string of dimensions after it has been placed, simply select it and pick the **Edit Witness Lines** tool on the *Ribbon*. You can also *Tab/Select* a single dimension within a dimension string and delete it without deleting the entire string.

Yet another feature Revit offers that other programs do not is the ability to automatically snap to the center of a door or window opening. In other programs you might have to draw a line from one door jamb to the other, use the dimension command to snap to the midpoint of the line and then delete it. Then you are left with dimensions that just look like they dimension to the center. Remember, Revit's dimensions are able to modify the drawing, kind of a two-way road if you will, whereas other CAD programs are mostly a one-way road.

In addition to snapping to the center of doors and windows, Revit will also snap to the jambs; depending on where your mouse is relative to the element being dimensioned.

You will notice that Revit does not care if a dimension's witness line overlaps a door or window tag. The tags need to be selected and moved manually, individually or in groups.

Next you will dimension the west side of the building.

FIGURE 6-6.4
First Floor: rotated 90 degrees
to increase image size in book

11. Dimension the West exterior walls and openings as shown in **Figure 6-6.5**.

> **TIP:**
> If you click on this dimension, you can drag its grip to the left to shorten the witness line. Revit will still reference the correct wall.

FIGURE 6-6.5 First Floor: dimensions added to the West wall

The last two images in the exercise give you an idea of what each dimension type which was loaded with the residential template looks like. Similar to other elements in Revit, you can select a dimension and verify what type it is by looking at the *Type Selector* on the *Properties Palette*. Also, you can change the type by selecting the desired type from the *Type Selector*.

FIGURE 6-6.6 Dimension type comparison

FIGURE 6-6.7 Dimension type comparison

This should be enough for you to understand how to dimension your plans. If you want more practice, you can dimension the rest of the *First Floor Plan* and then the other two floors; your instructor may require this. See Revit's *Help System* if you want to dig a little deeper in to Revit's dimensioning options.

12. **Save** your Project as **ex6-6.rvt**.

Self-Exam:

The following questions can be used as a way to check your knowledge of this lesson. The answers can be found at the bottom of the page.

1. The default settings for the floor plan view shows the walls for the floor below. (T/F)

2. The size of dimension text and arrows are set by the *View Scale* feature. (T/F)

3. You should start drawing your floor plan generally centered on the default elevation marks in a new project. (T/F)

4. You can use the *Align* tool to align one wall with another. (T/F)

5. Where do you change the maximum riser height? _____

Review Questions:

The following questions may be assigned by your instructor as a way to assess your knowledge of this section. Your instructor has the answers to the review questions.

1. It is not possible to copy/paste elements from one floor to another and have them line up (with the original objects). (T/F)

2. Revit's dimension tool can snap to the middle of a door opening without the need to draw a temporary line to snap to. (T/F)

3. Each Revit view is saved as a separate file on your hard drive. (T/F)

4. You select the part of the wall to be deleted when using the *Trim* tool. (T/F)

5. You cannot "finish stair" if you have not drawn all the treads or risers that are required between the two specified levels. (T/F)

6. What parameter should be set to none, in the *View Properties* dialog, if you

    do not want to see the walls from the floor below? _____

7. The _____ controls the size of dimensions and text, plus the scale that view is placed on a sheet.

8. You can use the _____ tool to quickly select a certain type of element from a large group of selected objects.

9. The number of _____ remaining is displayed while sketching a stair.

Notes:

Lesson 7
Residence: ROOF:

This lesson will look at some of the various options and tools for designing a roof for your building. You will also add skylights. Be sure to check out the video on Roofs located on the disc.

Exercise 7-1:
Roof Design Options (Style, Pitch and Overhang)

In this lesson you will look at the various ways to use the *Roof* tool to draw the more common roof forms used in architecture today.

Start a New Revit Project:

You will start a new project for this lesson so you can quickly compare the results of using the *Roof* tool.

1. Start a new project using the **default.rte** template: *New → Project → Browse*.

2. Switch to the **North** elevation view and rename the level named *Level 2* to **T.O. Masonry**. This will be the reference point for your roof. Click **Yes** to rename corresponding views automatically.

    TIP: Just select the Level *datum and click on the level datum's text to rename.*

3. Switch to the **Level 1** *Floor Plan* view.

T.O. Masonry
10' - 0"

Drawing the Buildings:

4. Set the Level 1 *"Detail Level"* to **medium**, so the material hatching is visible within the walls.

    TIP: Use the View Control Bar at the bottom.

5. Using the **Wall** tool with the wall *Type* set to **"Exterior - Brick on Mtl. Stud,"** draw a **40'-0" x 20'-0"** building (Figure 7-1.1).

    FYI: The default Wall height is OK; it should be 20'-0".

Be sure to draw the building
within the elevation tags.

*TIP: You can draw the building
in one step if you use the
Rectangle option on the Ribbon
while using the Wall tool.*

Elevations tags – (4) are shown which
correspond to the (4) elevation views
listed in the *Project Browser.*

FIGURE 7-1.1 Bldg. and Elev. tags

You will copy the building so that you have a total of four buildings. You will draw a
different type of roof on each one.

6. Drag a window around the walls to select them. Then use the **Array** command to set
    up four buildings **35'-0" O.C.** (Figure 7-1.2). See the *Array Tip* below.

*TIP: Zoom in and make
sure the brick is on the
exterior side of the wall. If
not, you can select each wall
and click its* flip *icon.*

*ARRAY TIP: Select the
first building, select Array,
and then, just like the
Copy command, define a
copy 35' to the right; then
enter the number of copies.*

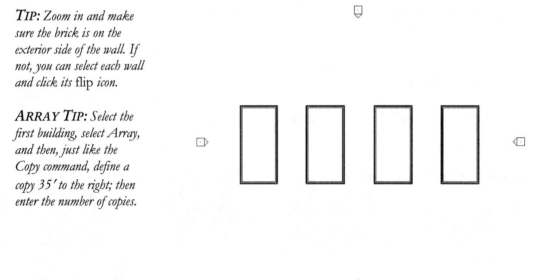

FIGURE 7-1.2 Four buildings

7. Select all of the buildings and click **Ungroup**
    from the *Ribbon.*

Ungroup

Hip Roof:

The various roof forms are largely defined by the *"Defines slope"* setting. This is displayed in the *Options Bar* while the *Roof* tool is active. When a wall is selected and the *"Defines slope"* option is selected, the roof above that portion of wall slopes. You will see this more clearly in the examples below.

8. Switch to the **T.O. Masonry** *Floor Plan* view.

9. Select the **Architecture** → **Build** → **Roof** *(down-arrow)* → **Roof by Footprint** tool.

10. Set the overhang to **2'-0"** and make sure **Defines slope** is selected (checked) on the *Options Bar*.

11. Select the four walls of the West building, clicking each wall one at a time.

    TIP: Make sure you select towards the exterior side of the wall; notice the review line before clicking.

12. Click **Finish Edit Mode** (i.e., the green check mark) on the *Ribbon* to finish the *Roof* tool.

13. Click **Yes** to attach the roof to the walls.

14. Switch to the **South** elevation (Figure 7-1.3).

FIGURE 7-1.3 South elevation – Hip roof

You will notice that the default wall height is much higher than what we ultimately want. However, when the roof is drawn at the correct elevation and you attach the walls to the roof, the walls automatically adjust to stop under the roof object. Additionally, if the roof is raised or lowered later, the walls will follow; you can try this in the South elevation view by simply using the *Move* tool. **REMEMBER:** *You can make revisions in any view.*

15. Switch to the **3D** view using the icon on the *QAT* (Figure 7-1.4).

You can change the "model graphics style" to **Shading** if you would like. Select the *Visual Style* icon on the *View Control Bar* at the bottom.

FIGURE 7-1.4 3D view – hip roof

Gable Roof:

16. Switch back to the **T.O. Masonry** view (not the ceiling plan for this level).

17. Select the **Roof** tool, and then **Roof by Footprint**.

18. Set the overhang to **2'-0"** and make sure **Defines slope** is selected (checked) on the *Options Bar*.

19. Only select the two long (40'-0") walls.

20. **Uncheck** the **Defines slope** option.

21. Select the remaining two walls (Figure 7-1.5).

22. Pick the **green check mark** on the *Ribbon* to finish the roof.

23. Select **Yes** to attach the walls to the roof.

24. Switch to the **South** elevation view (Figure 7-1.6).

FIGURE 7-1.5 Gable – plan view

FIGURE 7-1.6 South elevation – gable roof

25. Switch to the **3D** view (Figure 7-1.7).

Notice the wall extends up to conform to the underside of the roof on the gable ends.

FYI: You may be wondering why the roofs look odd in the floor plan view. If you remember, each view has its own cut plane. The cut plane happens to be lower than the highest part of the roof – thus, the roof is shown cut at the cut plane. If you go to Properties Palette → View Range (while nothing is selected) and then adjust the cut plane to be higher than the highest point of the roof, then you will see the ridge line.

FIGURE 7-1.7 3D view – gable roof

Shed Roof:

26. Switch back to the **T.O. Masonry** view.

27. Select the **Roof** tool, and then **Roof by Footprint**.

28. Check **Defines slope** on the *Options Bar*.

29. Set the overhang to **2'-0"** on the *Options Bar*.

30. Select the East wall (40'-0" wall, right-hand side).

31. Uncheck **Defines slope** in the *Options Bar*.

32. Select the remaining three walls (Figure 7-1.8).

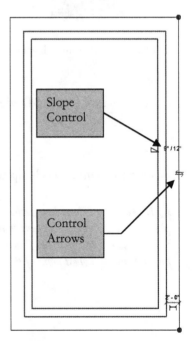

FIGURE 7-1.8 Selected walls

33. Set the **Slope**, or roof pitch, to 3/12 (Figure 7-1.9) on the *Properties Palette*.

34. Click **Apply** on the *Properties Palette*.

35. Pick the **green check mark** on the *Ribbon* to finish the roof.

36. Select **Yes** to attach the walls to the roof.

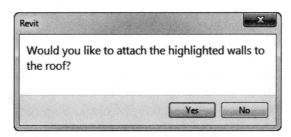

FIGURE 7-1.9
Properties for Roof tool

FYI: You can also change the slope of the roof by changing the Slope Control text (see Figure 7-1.8); just select the text and type a new number.

TIP: You can use the Control Arrows, while the roof line is still selected, to flip the orientation of the roof overhang if you accidentally selected the wrong side of the wall and the overhang is on the inside of the building.

37. Switch to the **South** elevation view (Figure 7-1.10).

FIGURE 7-1.10 South elevation – shed roof

38. Switch to the **Default 3D** view (Figure 7-1.11).

FIGURE 7-1.11 Default 3D view – shed roof

Once the roof is drawn, you can easily change the roof's overhang. You will try this on the shed roof. You will also make the roof slope in the opposite direction.

39. In **T.O. Masonry** view, Select **Modify** from the *Ribbon*, and then select the shed roof.

40. Click **Edit Footprint** from the *Ribbon*.

Edit
Footprint

41. Click on the East roof sketch-line to select it.

42. Uncheck **Defines slope** from the *Options Bar*.

43. Now select the West roofline and check **Defines slope**.

If you were to select the green check mark now, the shed roof would be sloping in the opposite direction. But, before you do that, you will adjust the roof overhang at the high side.

44. Click on the East roofline again to select it.

45. Change the overhang to **6'-0"** in the *Options Bar*.

Changing the overhang only affects the selected roofline.

46. Select the **green check mark**.

47. Switch to the South view to see the change (Figure 7-1.12).

FIGURE 7-1.12 South elevation – shed roof (revised)

Thus you can see it is easier to edit an object than to delete it and start over. Just remember you have to be in sketch mode (i.e., *Edit Sketch*) to make changes to the roof. Also, when a sketch line is selected, its properties are displayed in the *Properties Palette*. That concludes the shed roof example.

Flat Roof:

48. Switch back to the **T.O. Masonry** *Floor Plan* view.

49. Select **Architecture → Roof → Roof by Footprint**.

50. Set the overhang to **2'-0"** and make sure **Defines slope** is not selected (i.e., un-checked) in the *Options Bar*.

51. Select all four walls.

52. Pick the **green check mark**.

53. Select **Yes** to attach the walls to the roof.

FIGURE 7-1.13 South elevation – flat roof

54. Switch to the South elevation view (Figure 7-1.13).

55. Also, take a look the **Default 3D view** (Figure 7-1.14).

FIGURE 7-1.14 Default 3D view – flat roof

56. Save your project as **ex7-1.rvt**.

Want More?

Revit has additional tools and techniques available for creating more complex roof forms. However, that is beyond the scope of this book. If you want to learn more about roofs, or anything else, take a look at one of the following resources:

- Revit **Web Site**: http://help.autodesk.com/view/RVT/2015/ENU/
- Revit **Newsgroup**: potential answers to specific questions
  www.augi.com; www.revitcity.com; www.autodesk.com; www.revitforum.org
- Revit **Blogs**: information from individuals (some work for Autodesk and some don't)
  www.revitoped.com, revitclinic.typepad.com, do-u-revit.blogspot.com

Exercise 7-2:
Gable Roof

The template file you started with already has a *Roof Plan* view created. You can think of this as the top plate height for your wall. This *Roof Plan* view creates a working plane for the *Roof* tool. After creating a high roof over the two story areas, you will create a *Low Roof* view and design roofs over the one story areas: garage and portion of the family room.

Create Gable Roof:

1. Open ex6-6.rvt and **Save As ex7-2.rvt**.

2. Switch to the ***Roof Plan*** view.

Your image should look something like Figure 7-2.1. The walls you can see in the *Roof Plan* view were created in Lesson 5. The specified height extends into the *Roof Plan's View Range*, whereas the two walls you cannot see were created on the second floor, in Lesson 6, and the specified height does not extend up into the *Roof Plan's View Range*. This does not really matter because, as you will see in a moment, you have enough information visible to create the footprint of the roof; also, you will *Attach* the walls to the roof, just like the previous exercises, which causes them to conform to the underside of the roof.

Because the walls do not connect, neither will the overhang lines you will be sketching. Before you can "finish" a roof sketch, you must have the entire perimeter of the roof drawn with line endpoints connected. Revit allows you to sketch additional lines and use tools like *Trim* to complete the perimeter of the roof sketch.

3. Select the ***Roof*** tool drop-down from the *Architecture* tab.

4. Select ***Roof by Footprint*** from the drop-down menu.

5. Make sure ***Pick Walls*** is selected on the *Ribbon*.

FIGURE 7-2.1 Roof Plan; initial view

First you will specify the roof overhang for the entire roof.

6. Set the *Overhang* to **1′-6″** on the *Options Bar*.

You only need to select four walls to define the extents of the gable roof you are about to create. However, the perimeter will not be closed after selecting the four walls.

7. With *Defines slope* **checked** on the *Options Bar*, select the two walls as shown in Figure 7-2.2; make sure the overhang lines are on the exterior side of the building.

    TIP: Use the flip control icon while the line is still selected if your overhang is on the wrong side (i.e., interior).

8. With *Defines slope* **NOT checked** on the *Options Bar*, select the two walls as shown in Figure 7-2.2; make sure the overhang lines are on the exterior side of the building.

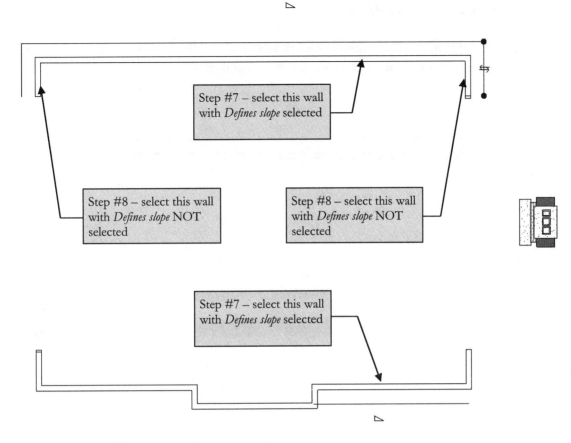

FIGURE 7-2.2 Roof Plan; four walls selected for sketching roof footprint

9. Change the roof pitch, or *Slope*, to **8″** on the *Properties Palette* (Figure 7-2.3).

10. Click **Apply**.

Note that the four walls, just selected, can be selected in any order. Of course it would be easier to select all the sloping edges first and then all the non-sloping edges second. That way you do not have to keep toggling the *Defines slope* option on and off.

Next you will use the *Trim* tool to close the perimeter of the roof footprint. Many of your 2D drafting skills learned early in this book can be applied to this type of *Sketch* mode.

Finally, notice the roof type is set to **Generic – 12″** as seen in the image to the right. This can be modified similar to walls via the *Edit Type* button.

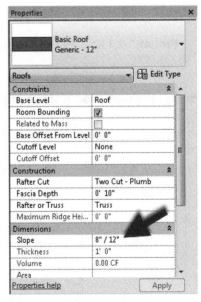

FIGURE 7-2.3 Roof Properties

11. Select *Modify* from the *Ribbon*.

12. Select the *Trim* icon from the contextual tab on the *Ribbon*, and then select the roof lines that are not yet connected to make them connected (Figure 7-2.4).

FIGURE 7-2.4 Roof Plan; entire roof perimeter defined

Now that the roof footprint is complete you can finish the roof.

13. Select the **green checkmark** from the *Ribbon*.

14. Click **Yes** to attach the walls (Figure 7-2.5).

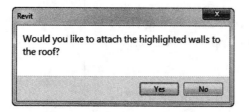

FIGURE 7-2.5 Roof Plan; attachment warning

15. Switch to your *Default 3D* view.

Your project should look like Figure 7-2.6. Notice that the walls that were visible in the *Roof Plan* view are now attached to the roof. The East and West walls that have not been attached can be attached manually.

Select this wall in step 16

FIGURE 7-2.6 3D View; gable roof added

16. While in the 3D view, select the East wall that has not been attached to the roof yet. Notice how the wall is transparent when selected.

17. Select the *Attach Top/Base* button from the *Ribbon*; then **select the roof** (Figure 7-2.7).

18. Repeat the previous two steps with the West wall.

   TIP: Click in the upper left corner of the Front face of the ViewCube to quickly view that side of the building (see image to right).

FIGURE 7-2.7 3D View; wall attached to roof

Main Entry Gable:

Next you will draw the gable roof element over the main entry.

You can modify the existing roof to add this design feature.

19. Switch back to the **Roof Plan** view.

20. Select the existing **roof**, and then **Edit Footprint** from the *Ribbon*.

21. Select **Pick Walls** and then make sure the overhang is still **1'-6"** and the pitch is **8"/12"**.

22. Edit the roof sketch to look like Figure 7-2.8.

TIP: Use the Split *and* Trim *tools to modify the existing sketch.*

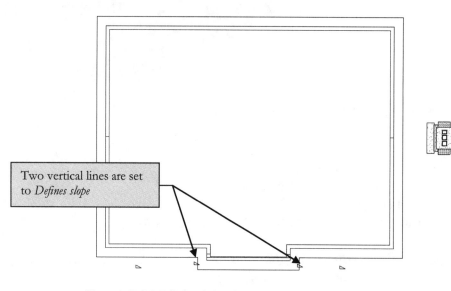

Two vertical lines are set to *Defines slope*

FIGURE 7-2.8 Edit roof sketch

23. Select the **green checkmark** to finish the roof.

NOTE: If you get any errors, make sure all the "defines slope" sketch lines have the same slope.

This is where the power of Revit really begins to shine. As you can see in the *Roof Plan* view (Figure 7-2.9 below), Revit was able to interpret the sketch using the *Pitch* and *Defines slope* information to create the proper roof complete with ridgelines and valleys.

Next you will change the *View Range* of the *Roof* view so you can see the low roof, which will be added in the next exercise.

24. Select **Edit** next to *View Range* in the *Properties Palette* (make sure nothing is selected in the model first – this will make sure the *View Properties* are shown).

25. Change both *Bottom* and *View Depth* to **Unlimited**.

26. Click **OK**.

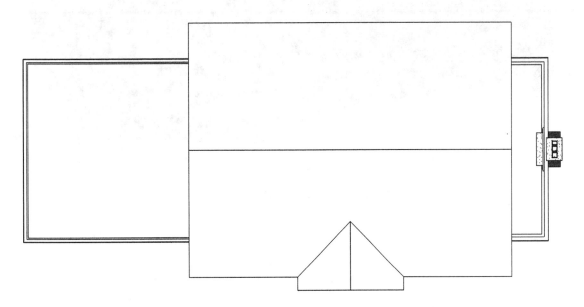

FIGURE 7-2.9 Site plan view; revised roof created

27. Switch to the ***Default 3D*** view.

When finished, your 3D view should look like Figure 7-2.10.

> **TIP:**
> Custom fascias, gutters and soffits are beyond the scope of this tutorial. However, you can take a look at the *Help* system for more information on this.
>
> After reviewing the *Help* system, try adding these techniques to your Revit project.

This entry roof element could have been drawn as a separate element. This would be useful if the fascia/eaves did not align, for example.

FIGURE 7-2.10 3D view; Entry roof element added

28. Save your project as **Ex7-2.rvt**.

> **TIP:** *You have probably figured this out by now: the last view open when you close will be the current view the next time the project is opened.*

Exercise 7-3:
Low Roof Elements

In this exercise you will add the lower roof elements, which will involve adding a new level datum for reference.

Create a New Level:

1. Open ex7-2.rvt and **Save As ex7-3.rvt**.

2. Open the *South* elevation view.

3. Click **Architecture → Datum → Level** from the *Ribbon*.

4. Draw a *Level* symbol at the top of the low exterior walls, at elevation 12'-0". Draw the symbol so both ends align with the other symbols below and above it (Figure 7-3.1).

   TIP: Hover your cursor over the top of the garage wall (do not click). Next, move your cursor towards the left and pick two points across from each other horizontally, picking from left to right.

FIGURE 7-3.1 South elevation; new level added

Notice that Revit automatically names the level and creates a floor plan and reflected ceiling plan views with the same name (Figure 7-3.2). Next, you will rename the *Level* datum.

5. Press **Esc** or select *Modify* from the *Ribbon*.

6. Now select the *Level* symbol you just created in the drawing window.

FIGURE 7-3.2 South elevation; new level added (named Level 8 in this example)

7. With the *Level* symbol selected, **drag the small circle grip** near the target symbol (see image below) to the right. This will relocate all the level targets away from the building.

8. With the *Level* symbol still selected, click on the text to rename the level label. Press *Undo* if you accidentally click an icon and change the level position; you may need to zoom in to click the text.

9. Change the label to **Low Roof** (Figure 7-3.3).

FIGURE 7-3.3 South elevation; renaming a level datum

10. Click **Yes** when prompted to rename corresponding views (Figure 7-3.4).

Notice the *Low Roof* label is now listed in the *Floor Plans* and *Ceiling Plans* sections of the *Project Browser*.

> Revit
>
> Would you like to rename corresponding views?
>
> Yes   No

FIGURE 7-3.4 Rename prompt

Add another gable roof:

11. Open the newly created **Low Roof Floor Plan** view.

> TIP: *You may want to close the Ceiling Plan views so you don't accidentally click on them.*

12. Select the **Roof** tool (down-arrow) from the *Ribbon*.

13. Select **Roof by footprint** from the drop-down list.

14. Set the overhang to **1'-6"** on the *Options Bar*.

15. You are now prompted to select exterior walls to define the footprint. Select ONLY the three wall segments that define the *Living Room* area per **Figure 7-3.5**. Only the horizontal sketch lines are to be *Defines slope* as shown.

> REMEMBER: *Pick the exterior side of the walls.*

You will notice in Figure 7-3.5 that there is one section that still needs to be sketched to close the footprint or outline.

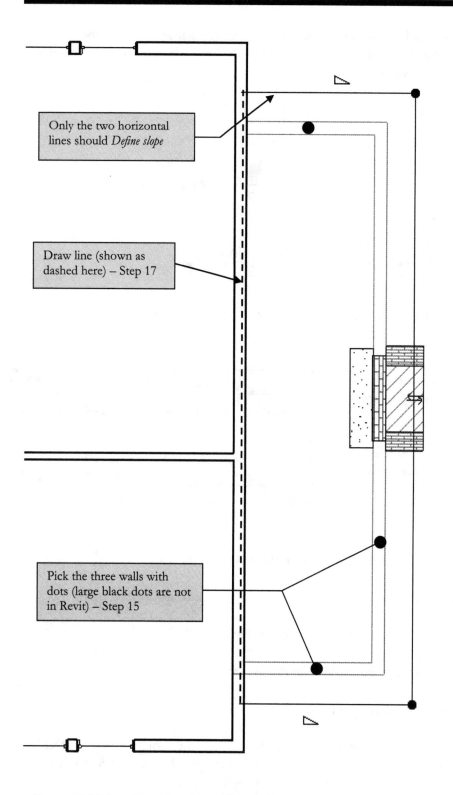

Only the two horizontal lines should *Define slope*

Draw line (shown as dashed here) – Step 17

Pick the three walls with dots (large black dots are not in Revit) – Step 15

FIGURE 7-3.5 Low Roof plan view; adding roof

16. Select the **Line** tool from the *Ribbon* (Figure 7-3.6).

17. Draw the line to create a complete rectangle (i.e., footprint), making sure you use *Snaps* to accurately snap to the endpoints of the lines already present (Figure 7-3.5). Use *Trim* if needed. *Defines Slope* should be off here.

18. Change the *Slope* to **8″ / 12″** in the *Properties Palette*.

19. Click **Apply** in the *Properties Palette*.

FIGURE 7-3.6 Roof sketch options

Again, this will make the roof pitch 8/12, which means for every 12″ of horizontal run, the roof will *rise* 8″ vertically.

20. Now click the **green checkmark** from the *Ribbon* to finish the roof.

21. Click **Yes** when prompted to attach the highlighted walls to the roof (Figure 7-3.7).

FIGURE 7-3.7 Prompt

You will now see a portion of the roof in your plan view. The cutting plane is 4′-0″ above the floor level, so you are seeing the roof thickness in section at 4′-0″ above the *Low Roof* level (Figure 7-3.8 on next page).

- Switch to an elevation view to see the roof, the South elevation, shown in Figure 7-3.9.

- You can also switch to the **Default 3D** view to see the roof in isometric view.

FIGURE 7-3.9 South elevation

After looking at the roof you have created, switch back to the plan view: **Low Roof.** You will now add a roof over the garage.

FIGURE 7-3.8 Low Roof plan view

22. **Zoom in** on the garage area.

23. Select the *Roof* tool and click *Roof by Footprint*.

24. With *Defines slope* checked in the *Options Bar*, pick the two horizontal walls: North and South (Figure 7-3.10).

25. Uncheck *Defines slope*, select the West wall, and then use the *Line* tool to sketch a line to close the footprint, as shown in Figure 7-3.11. Be sure to use *Snaps* to accurately draw the enclosed area.

26. Make sure the *Slope* is set to **8"/12"** and then select the **green checkmark** from the *Ribbon* (Figure 7-3.6).

27. Click **Yes** when prompted to attach the highlighted walls to the roof (Figure 7-3.7).

FIGURE 7-3.10 Low Roof plan view at garage

28. Switch to the *South* elevation view (Figure 7-3.11).

FIGURE 7-3.11 South elevation view; garage roof added

The 3D model is shown shaded and has *Ambient Shadows* turned on (Figure 7-3.12).

Revit content is set up to make glass in windows and curtain walls transparent.

FIGURE 7-3.12 Shaded model

Changing to a Hip Roof:

Now that you have drawn the roof, you will see what is involved to modify the gable roof to a hip roof. In the first exercise in this Lesson, you learned how to create a hip roof from scratch. Here you will modify a previously drawn gable roof into a hip roof.

29. Switch to the **Roof Plan** view.

30. Click on the main roof element to select it.
    TIP: Select one of the lines at the perimeter of the roof.

Edit Footprint

31. Select **Edit Footprint** from the *Ribbon*.

32. Select the vertical line on the left.

33. With the left vertical line selected, check **Defines slope** on the *Options Bar*.

34. Repeat these steps for the right vertical line.

Your screen should look like Figure 7-3.13.

FIGURE 7-3.13 Roof Plan; vertical lines set to *Defines slope*

35. Select the **green check mark** from the *Ribbon.*
36. Switch to the *South* exterior elevation view.

You now have a hip roof. However, there is a little problem with the lower roofs; they do not properly intersect. This could be a problem when it rains!

FIGURE 7-3.14 South Elevation; main roof changed to a hip roof

37. Switch to the *Default 3D* view.

38. Select **Modify → Geometry → Join/Unjoin Roof** tool from the *Ribbon.*

39. *Join* the lower roof over the garage to the upper roof.

> ***TIP:*** *Select the edge of the low roof and then select the face of the upper roof, which will be the face you wish to extend the roof to. Hover your cursor over the icon on the ribbon to see the extended tooltip for more information.*

40. Now *Join* the low roof over the *Living Room* with the upper roof.

Your model should look similar to Figure 7-3.15.

FIGURE 7-3.15 3D view; low roofs joined to upper roof

Here you can see that the bottoms of the roofs, to be joined, do not have to align with each other.

After looking at the two roof options, the client decides they like the gable option so you will change it back. Do not simply click *Undo*; the next steps will show you how to *Unjoin* the roof.

    41. Switch to the *Roof Plan* view.

    42. Select **Modify** → **Geometry** → **Join/Unjoin Roof**.

This tool, as its name implies, allows you to both *Join* and *Unjoin* roof elements. To *Unjoin*, you simply click on a line that has been created by a *Join* and the entire *Join* will go away.

    43. Select the valley line as shown in **Figure 7-3.16**.

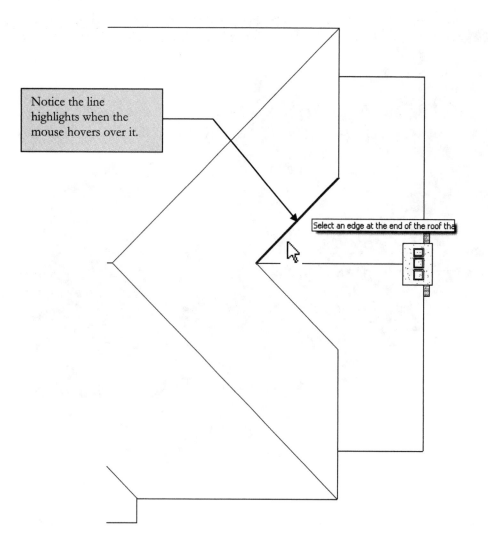

Notice the line highlights when the mouse hovers over it.

Select an edge at the end of the roof tha

FIGURE 7-3.16 Roof plan; Unjoining the lower roof from the upper roof

As soon as you click the valley line, the roof is unjoined.

44. Repeat this process to *Unjoing* the West lower roof.

45. Change the hip roof back to a gable using the techniques previously covered.

When finished, your 3D view should look like 7-3.12 again.

46. **Save** your project.

Exercise 7-4:
Skylights

This short exercise covers inserting skylights in your roof. The process is much like inserting windows. In fact, Revit lists the skylight types with the window types, so you use the *Window* tool to insert skylights into your project.

Inserting Skylights:

You will place the skylights in an elevation view.

**Load
Family**

1. Load project file **ex7-3.rvt**.

2. Switch to the ***North*** elevation view.

3. Select the ***Window*** tool and use the *Load Family* icon to import the *skylight* family (skylight.rfa) into the current project; it can be found in the *Windows* folder.

4. Select **Skylight: 24" x 27"** from the *Type Selector*.

You are now ready to place skylights in the roof. Revit will only look for roof objects when placing skylights; this is what is called a *roof hosted family*, so you do not have to worry about a skylight ending up in a wall.

5. Roughly place two skylights as shown in Figure 7-4.1.

    FYI: *This can be done directly in the elevation view.*

FIGURE 7-4.1 North elevation, skylights added

6. Press **Esc** or click the *Modify* tool to cancel the *Window* tool.

Next, you will want to align the skylights with each other.

7. Switch to the *East* elevation view.

8. Select one of the visible skylights.

You should now have the skylight selected and see the reference dimensions that allow you to adjust the exact location of the object. Occasionally, the dimension does not go to the point on the drawing that you are interested in referencing from. Revit allows you to adjust where those temporary dimensions reference.

9. Click and drag the grip shown in Figure 7-4.2 to (wait until it snaps) the ridge of the main roof (Figure 7-4.3).

Skylight selected

FIGURE 7-4.2 East elevation; temporary dimension shown after selecting the skylight.

10. Click on the dimension text and change the text to **18'-0"**.

   NOTE: *This will adjust the position of the skylight relative to the ridge.*

11. Select the other skylight and adjust it to match the one you just revised.

FIGURE 7-4.3 East elevation; temp dimension witness line adjusted.

Your skylights now align vertically on the roof. The same step would allow you to align the skylight horizontally.

12. Use the temporary dimensions to center the skylight over the second floor windows that are below it, on the North elevation.

13. **Zoom in** on one of the skylights.

The number may vary; it is not a problem if it does vary.

14. Select the skylight's tag. You should see a symbol appear near the bottom of the tag; this is the *Move* icon (Figure 7-4.4).

15. Drag on the *Move* icon to position the skylight tag so the tag does not overlap the skylight (Figure 7-4.5).

This can be done with any tag (i.e., Door tag, Room tag, etc.).

FIGURE 7-4.4 Enlarged view of skylight

16. Adjust the other skylight tag which is a *Window Tag*. As you reposition these tags, you may see a reference line appear indicating the symbol will automatically align with an adjacent symbol.

> **REMEMBER:** *The size of the tag is based on the View Scale setting.*

Take a minute to look at your shaded 3D view and try changing the view so you can see through the skylight glass into the space below (Figure 7-4.6).

17. **Save** as **ex7-4.rvt**.

FIGURE 7-4.5 Enlarged skylight view – revised

FIGURE 7-4.6 Shaded skylight view

FIGURE 7-4.7 Roof plan

Reference material: Roof position relative to wall

The remaining pages in this chapter are for reference only and do not need to be done to your model. You are encouraged to study this information so you become more familiar with how the *Roof* tool works.

The following examples use a brick and concrete wall example. The image below shows the *Structure* properties for said wall type. Notice the only item within the *Core Boundary* section is the *Masonry – Concrete Block* (i.e., CMU) which is 7⅝" thick (nominally 8"). Keep this in mind as you read through the remaining material.

The following examples will show you how to control the position of the roof system relative to the wall below, both vertically and horizontally. The roof properties that dictate its position basically involve relationships between three things: the **Level Datum**, the exterior **Wall System** and the bottom edge of the **Roof System**. There are several other properties (e.g., pitch, construction, fascia, etc.) related to the roof that will not be mentioned at the moment so the reader may focus on a few basic principles.

The examples on this page show a sloped roof sketched with *Extend into wall (to core)* enabled and the *Overhang* set to 2'-0″. Because *Extend into wall (to core)* was selected, the bottom edge of the roof is positioned relative to the *Core Boundary* of the exterior wall rather than the finished face of the wall. See the discussion about the wall's *Core Boundary* on the previous page.

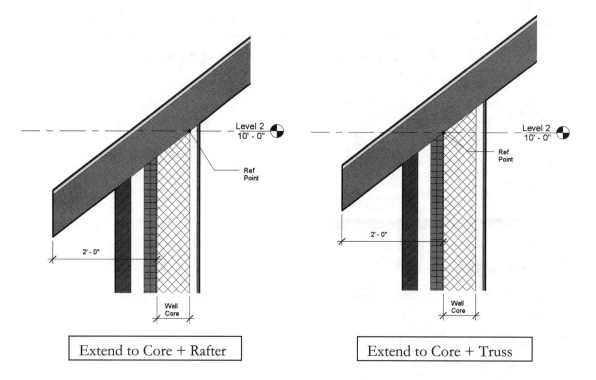

| Extend to Core + Rafter | Extend to Core + Truss |

Revit Roof Properties under Consideration:

Extend Into Wall:
(To Core)   This option was *checked* on the *Options Bar* while sketching the roof.

Rafter Or Truss: This option is an *Instance Parameter* of the roof object; the example on the above left is set to *Rafter* and the other is set to *Truss*.

NOTE: The Extend into Wall (to core) *option affects the relative relationship between the wall and the roof, as you will see by comparing this example with the one on the next page.*

Base Level: Set to *Level 2*: By associating various objects to a level, it is possible to adjust the floor elevation (i.e., *Level Datum*) and have doors, windows, floors, furniture, roofs, etc., all move vertically with that level.

Base Offset:
From Level   Set to *0'-0″*: This can be a positive or negative number which will be maintained even if the level moves.

The examples on this page show a sloped roof sketched with *Extend into wall (to core)* NOT enabled and the *Overhang* set to 2'-0". Notice that the roof overhang is derived from the exterior face of the wall (compared to the *Core Boundary* face on the previous example when *Extend into wall* was enabled).

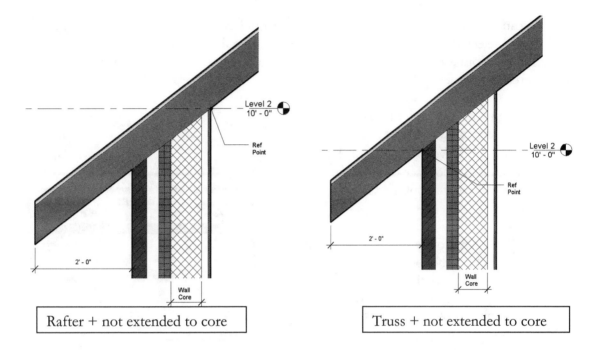

| Rafter + not extended to core | Truss + not extended to core |

Revit Roof Properties under Consideration:

Extend Into Wall: This option was *NOT checked* on the *Options Bar* while sketching the
(To Core) roof.

Rafter Or Truss: This option is an *Instance Parameter* of the roof object; the example above on the left is set to *Rafter* and the other is set to *Truss*. This parameter only appears if the *Pick Wall* option is used to sketch the roof perimeter.

NOTE: The Extend into wall (to core) *option affects the relative relationship between the wall and the roof, as you will see by comparing this example with the one on the previous page.*

Base Level: Set to *Level 2*. By associating various objects to a level, it is possible to adjust the floor elevation (i.e., *Level Datum*) and have doors, windows, floors, furniture, roofs, etc., all move vertically with that level.

Base Offset: Set to *0'-0"*. This can be a positive or negative number which will be
From Level maintained even if the level moves.

As you can see from the previous examples, you would most often want to have *Extend to wall (to core)* selected while sketching a roof because it would not typically make sense to position the roof based on the outside face of brick or the inside face of gypsum board for commercial construction.

Even though you may prefer to have *Extend to wall (to core)* selected, you might like to have a 2'-0" overhang relative to the face of the brick rather than the exterior face of concrete block. This can be accomplished in one of two ways:

(A) You can modify the overhang, while sketching the roof, to include the wall thickness that occurs between the face of wall and face of core: 2'-0" + 9⅝" = 2'-9⅝". See the image to the right.

(B) The second option is to manually edit the sketch lines. You can add dimensions while in *Sketch* mode, select the sketch line to move, and then edit the dimension. The dimension can also be *Locked* to maintain the roof edge position relative to the wall. When you finish the sketch the dimensions are hidden.

Energy Truss:

In addition to controlling the roof overhang, you might also want to control the roof properties to accommodate an energy truss with what is called an *energy heel*, which allows for more insulation to occur directly above the exterior wall.

To do this you would use the *Extend into wall (to core)* + *Truss* option described above and then set the *Base Offset from Level* to 1'-0" (for a 1'-0" energy heel). See the image and the *Properties Palette* shown on the next page.

Level 2
10' - 0"

Ref
Point

Wall
Core

1' - 0"

2' - 0"

2' - 9 5/8"

Properties

Basic Roof
Generic - 12"

Roofs   Edit Type

Constraints	
Base Level	Level 2
Room Bounding	✓
Related to Mass	☐
Base Offset From Level	1' 0"
Cutoff Level	None
Cutoff Offset	0' 0"
Construction	
Rafter Cut	Plumb Cut
Fascia Depth	0' 0"
Rafter or Truss	Truss

Many other properties and techniques exist which one can use to develop the roof for a project, things like the *Rafter Cut* and *Fascia Depth* which control the fascia design. Also, you can apply a sweep to a roof edge to add a 1x fascia board around the building. These are intermediate to advanced concepts and will not be covered here.

This concludes the study of the *Roof* tool!

Self-Exam:

The following questions can be used as a way to check your knowledge of this lesson. The answers can be found at the bottom of the page.

1. You do not have to click the *green check mark* to finish a roof. (T/F)

2. The wall below the roof automatically conforms to the underside of the roof when you join the wall to the roof. (T/F)

3. The roof overhang setting is available from the *Options Bar*. (T/F)

4. To create a gable roof on a building with four walls, two of the walls should not

    have the _____ option checked.

5. Is it possible to change the reference point for a temporary dimension that is displayed while an element is selected? (Y/N)

Review Questions:

The following questions may be assigned by your instructor as a way to assess your knowledge of this section. Your instructor has the answers to the review questions.

1. When creating a roof using the "*create roof by footprint*" option, you need to create a closed perimeter. (T/F)

2. The *Defines slope* setting can be changed after the roof is finished. (T/F)

3. Skylights need to be rotated to align with the plane, or pitch, of the roof. (T/F)

4. Skylights have the glass transparent in shaded views. (T/F)

5. While using the **Roof** tool, you can use the _____ tool from the *Ribbon* to fill in the missing segments to close the perimeter.

6. You use the _____ parameter to adjust the vertical position of the roof relative to the current working plane (view).

7. While using the *Roof* tool, you need to select the _____ tool from the *Ribbon* before you can select a roofline for modification.

8. You need to use the _____ to flip the roofline when you pick the wrong side of the wall and the overhang is shown on the inside.

9. The _____ from the *Modify* tab (on the *Ribbon*) allows you to extend one roof element over, and into, another.

10. Changing the name of a level tag (in elevation) causes Revit to rename all the corresponding views (plan, ceiling, etc.) if you answer yes to the prompt.

SELF-EXAM ANSWERS:
1 - F, **2** – T, **3** – T, **4** – defines slope, **5** – Y

Lesson 8
Residence: FLOOR SYSTEMS AND REFLECTED CEILING PLANS:

In this lesson you will learn to create floor structures and reflected ceiling plans.

Even though you currently have floor levels defined, you do not have an object that represents the mass of the floor systems. You will add floor systems with a hole for the stair.

Ceiling systems allow you to specify the ceiling material by room and the height above the floor. Once the ceiling has been added, it will show up in section views. Sections are created later in this book.

Be sure to view the videos on modeling floors and ceilings located on the disc. Many of the videos cover additional material not found in the book.

Exercise 8-1:
Floor Systems

Similar to other Autodesk® Revit® elements, you can select from a few predefined floor types. You can also create new floor types. In your residence you will use a predefined floor system for the first and second floors and then create a new type for the basement and garage.

Basement Floor, Slab on Grade:

Sketching floors is a lot like sketching roofs; you can select walls to define the perimeter and draw lines to fill in the blanks, and add holes, or cut-outs, in the floor object.

1. Open ex7-4.rvt and **Save As ex8-1.rvt**.

2. Switch to the **Basement** *Floor Plan* view.

3. Select **Architecture → Build → Floor** *(just the icon, not the down-arrow)*.

Floor

4. Click the **Edit Type** button on the *Properties Palette*.

5. Select **Concrete Slab – 4"** from the *Type* drop-down list near the top.

6. Click **Duplicate**.

7. Type **4″ Slab on Grade over Vapor Barrier**, then **OK**.

8. Click the **Edit** button next to the *Structure* parameter.

Here you could change the thickness of the slab, but you will leave it at 4″ for the basement.

Next you will add a vapor barrier and sand bed below the slab.

9. Insert a new layer:
   a. *Function:* **Membrane Layer**
   b. *Material:* **Vapor Retarder**
   c. *Thickness:* **0″**

NOTE: *Vapor barriers do have a thickness, of course (4mil, 6mil, etc). However, the thickness is typically ignored on drawings. A Membrane is the only layer which can have no thickness; that is, a zero value.*

10. Add another layer:
    a. *Function:* **Substrate [2]**
    b. *Material:* **Sand** *(see TIP below)*
    c. *Thickness:* **4″** (Figure 8-1.0).

NOTE: *The sand is sometimes placed over the vapor barrier. The sand helps to protect the vapor barrier until the rebar and concrete slab are in place. Additionally, the sand allows the concrete to cure more evenly with less chance of cupping. On the other hand, a vapor barrier directly below the slab helps prevent some floor finishes from delaminating due to moisture in the sand.*

TIP: *You can change the position of layers within a system. Simply select the row and then click the Up or Down button until positioned.*

TIP: *To load the Sand material, search for sand in the box at the top of the Material Browser (via Manage tab → Materials tool), and then double-click the Sand option in the Autodesk Library near the bottom. See Figure 8-1.1.*

11. Click **OK** to close the open dialog boxes.

12. Select the walls in the ***Basement Plan*** as shown in Figure 8-1.2.

FIGURE 8-1.0 New floor system

FIGURE 8-1.1 Materials Dialog

TIP: Select the interior side of the wall. You can use the control arrows if needed, opposite of what you did for the roof.

13. Click the **green check mark** on the *Ribbon*.

TIP: If you get any errors, see the information in the box below.

Common Errors Finishing a Floor Sketch:

If you get an error message when trying to finish a floor sketch, it is probably due to a problem with the sketched perimeter lines. Here are two common problems:

Perimeter not closed:

You cannot finish a floor if there is a gap, large or small, in the perimeter sketch. *FIX:* Sketch a line to close the loop.

Sketch lines – perimeter not closed because line is missing

Error message after clicking finish sketch

Perimeter lines intersect:

You cannot finish a floor if any of the sketch lines intersect. *FIX:* Use *Trim* to make it so all line endpoints touch.

Sketch lines – lines extend past each other; not good

Error message after clicking finish sketch

FIGURE 8-1.2 Basement floor plan; floor slab sketched

14. Click **No** when prompted to join the floor to the walls (Figure 8-1.3).

FIGURE 8-1.3 Floor prompt

You now have a floor at the basement level. You should see a stipple pattern representing the floor area. You would most likely want to turn that pattern off for a floor plan. You will do that next.

15. In the **Basement Floor Plan** view, type **VV**; this is the keyboard shortcut for *Visibility/Graphic Overrides*.

   TIP: You may have to click within the drawing window before typing the keyboard shortcut for Revit to recognize it.

16. In the *Visibility/Graphic Overrides* dialog, on the *Model Categories* tab and in the **Floors** row, click the empty cell in the **Projection/ Surface → Patterns** column (Figure 8-1.4).

17. With the word *Override* now showing, click the exact same location again.

FIGURE 8-1.4 Visibility/Graphics Overrides: Editing the floor surface pattern visibility

18. Uncheck **Visible**, which will make the floor surface pattern not visible in the current view (Figure 8-1.5).

19. Click **OK** to close the dialogs.

FIGURE 8-1.5 Fill Pattern Graphics

The stipple pattern is no longer visible. The *Visibility/Graphic Overrides* dialog now indicates that the surface pattern is hidden (Figure 8-1.6). Keep in mind, this override is only for the current view. If you create another floor using the same 4″ concrete type you just created in the Level 1 floor plan view, it would have the stipple pattern. It would even show up if in another basement level floor plan, as it is possible to create more than one view which references the same *Level Datum*.

FIGURE 8-1.6 Visibility/Graphics Overrides

Garage Floor, Slab on Grade:

Now you will sketch the floor slab for the garage area. Because this floor will have vehicles parking on it, you will create a new slab type that is 6″ thick.

20. Switch to the *First Floor Plan* view.

21. Select the *Floor* tool.

22. Using the floor type you just created as a starting point, create a new floor type named **6″ Slab on Grade over Vapor Barrier**.

> *TIP: Properties Palette → Edit Type → Duplicate*

FIGURE 8.1-7 Changing the conc. slab thickness

23. Click the **Edit** button next to the *Structure* parameter.

24. Change the *Concrete* thickness from 4″ to **6″** (Figure 8-1.7).

25. Click **OK** to close the open dialog boxes.

26. With *Pick Walls* selected on the *Ribbon*, select the interior side of the four walls surrounding the garage (Figure 8.1-8).

27. Click the **green check mark** to finish the floor. Click **No** when prompted to join the wall and the floor.

You now have a floor slab in the garage area. You will notice that the floor element has a stipple pattern, even though you turned that stipple pattern off in the *Basement* view. Remember: the visibility settings are controlled by view, not project-wide, although they can be. You will turn this off later.

Notice the **Span Direction** symbol identified in the image to the right. This can be ignored for this type of floor. It is meant to define the flute direction for a metal floor/roof deck, which your residential floors will not have.

FYI: The Span Direction button on the Ribbon, visible while in the Floor tool, will allow you to change the span direction by picking a different sketch line.

FIGURE 8.1-8 First floor: floor slab sketched

When floors are created, the top of the floor aligns with the level (see image below). Each floor plan view is associated with a level (which cannot be changed), so the view in which you create the floor determines the default level the floor references. The referenced floor level can be changed at any time. The top of the floor will stay aligned with the level even if the floor thickness is changed. However, it is possible to select the floor and change its "Height Offset From Level" parameter to change the default behavior.

Top of floor aligns with level

First Floor (Wood Joists):

28. Use the floor type *Wood Joist 10" - Wood Finish* as a starting point to create a new floor type named **Wood Joist 14" - Wood Finish**.

29. Change the *Structure* settings per the following image (Figure 8-1.9).

    FYI: *This has all been covered previously.*

FIGURE 8.1-9 Floor properties

Creating the first and second floors will be a little more involved than were the basement and garage floors. This is because the upper floors require openings. For example, you need to define the openings for the stair. Revit makes the process very simple.

You should still be in the *Floor* tool.

30. On the *Options Bar*, check **Extend into wall (to core)**.

    FYI: *The* Extend into wall (to core) *option will extend the slab under your wall core (wood stud and sheathing are in the core in our example) and go under the gypsum wall board. This is similar to the information presented at the end of the previous chapter.*

31. Select the exterior walls indicated in Figure 8-1.10. Select the exterior side of the wall; use the flip control arrows if needed.

FIGURE 8-1.10 First Floor – floor system sketched

Next you will define the hole in the floor for the stair that leads down to the basement. You will need to use the *Lines* option from the *Draw* panel to define this area.

32. While the *Floor* tool is still active, **Zoom In** to the stair area.

33. Select the **Rectangle** icon on the *Ribbon*; see image below.

34. Draw a rectangle defining the stair opening; use Revit's snaps to accurately pick the points as shown in **Figure 8-1.11**.

FIGURE 8-1.11 First Floor – sketching floor opening

FYI: This floor opening has a big problem. You will see this problem when you get to the building sections exercise later in this book.

35. Click the **green check mark** to finish the floor.

Next, you will get two prompts: one asks if you want the walls below, whose tops are set to terminate at the first floor, to attach to the new floor. The other prompt asks if you want the floor to attach to the exterior walls. You will answer **Yes** to both.

36. Click **Yes** to the prompt *"Would you like the walls that go up to this floor's level to attach to its bottom?"* (Figure 8-1.12). Also, click **OK** if prompted with a "highlighted walls are attached, but miss…" warning.

    FYI: *This will allow the walls to dynamically change if the floor elevation or thickness is changed.*

37. Click **Yes** for the prompt to join the walls that overlap the floor system (Figure 8-1.13).

FIGURE 8-1.12 Join walls below to new floor prompt

FIGURE 8-1.13 Join walls that overlap the new floor prompt

Now that the floor is placed, you should see a dense horizontal line pattern that represents the finished wood floor. This would be nice for presentation drawings, but like the basement, you will turn the floor hatch off so the floor plan is not too cluttered.

38. Change the first floor's *Visibility* to turn off the floor hatch.

Copy/Paste the First Floor to the Second:

That completes the first floor system. Next you will copy the floor you just created to the second floor. It would probably be easier to just create a floor from scratch, but you will get more practice editing existing elements.

39. Select the floor you just created, in the first floor plan view, and select **Modify | Floors → Clipboard → Copy to Clipboard** on the *Ribbon*. See *TIP* on next page.

TIP: *Selecting elements that overlap, like the exterior walls and the edge of floor system, may require the use of the Tab key. The only way to select a floor element is by picking its edge. Revit temporarily highlights elements when you move your cursor over them. But, because the floor edge may not have an "exposed" edge to select, you will have to toggle through your selection options for your current cursor location. With the cursor positioned over the edge of the floor, probably with an exterior wall highlighted, press the Tab key to toggle through the available options. A tooltip will display the elements. When you see* floors: floor:floor-name, *click the mouse; also watch the Status Bar.*

40. Pick **Modify → Clipboard → Paste → Aligned to Selected Levels**.

41. Select **Second Floor** and then **OK**.

TIP: *You can press Ctrl and select more than one level.*

42. Switch to the **Second Floor**.

You now have a copy of the first floor's "floor system" in the *Second Floor Plan* view (Figure 8-1.14); keep in mind that all the views are looking at a single 3D model. You will edit the sketch lines of the second floor slab to make the stair hole larger and remove a portion of the floor that extends past the East exterior wall.

FIGURE 8-1.14 New floor added to level 2 using the paste aligned option

43. Select the floor element in the **Second Floor Plan** view.

> *TIP: The edge of the floor is "exposed" at the stair opening; this would be the easiest place to select the floor.*

Edit Boundary

44. Click **Edit Boundary** from the *Ribbon*. See icon to right.

You are now in *Sketch* mode, where you can change the perimeter and holes for the selected floor element. You can select lines and delete them, sketch new lines, and use *Trim* to modify lines.

45. Modify the lines at the far right, using *Delete* and *Trim*, so your sketch looks like Figure 8-1.15.

46. *Stair opening: Move* the West vertical line **4'-10"** farther West; the horizontal sketch lines should automatically extend, as shown in Figure 8-1.15. The overall width of the stair opening should be 8'-0"; if not, you should go back and double check your stair dimensions with Chapter 6, page 6-25.

47. Click the **green check mark** to recreate the floor element.

FIGURE 8-1.15 Second floor: sketch lines modified

Now that Revit is recreating the floor, it notices the walls below and at the exterior so you get the "join" prompts.

48. Click **Yes** to the two "join" prompts, if you get them.

Your *Second Floor Plan* view should look like Figure 8-1.16.

FIGURE 8-1.16 Second Floor: sketch lines modified

FIGURE 8-1.17 3D view: cutaway view showing floor elements added

49. Change the second floor's *Visibility* to turn off the floor hatch.

Turning off Surface Pattern at the Source:

If you do not want a portion of your plan to show a surface pattern, you might want to remove the surface pattern associated with the floor system. That way you could leave the surface pattern setting turned on. Set the *Surface Pattern* to **None** in the *Material Editor*.

Basically you remove the surface pattern for the *Finish* layer in a floor system.

FIGURE 8-1.18
Surface pattern setting for floor assembly

50. Save your project as **ex8-1.rvt**.

Exercise 8-2:
Ceiling Systems (Susp. ACT and Gypsum Board)

This lesson will explore Revit's tools for drawing reflected ceiling plans. This will include drawing different types of ceiling systems.

Traditionally, residential projects do not typically include reflected ceiling plans. The ceilings are generally straightforward, with all required information coming from a *Room Finish Schedule* and *Sections*. However, in Revit you will sketch the ceiling profile in the ceiling plan views, similar to how you drew the floor systems. You want to add the ceilings so they show up in sections. So, seeing as you have ceiling plans, why not include them in the construction documents set? Your design intent will be clearer, and you can make sure the lighting design is coordinated and laid out the way you want it.

The use of suspended acoustical ceiling tile in residential projects is somewhat limited. However, it is occasionally used so it will be covered here. In this lesson you will add it to the second floor office and a family room in the basement.

Suspended Acoustical Ceiling Tile System:

1. Open ex8-1.rvt and **Save As ex8-2.rvt**.

2. Switch to the **Second Floor Ceiling Plan** view, from the *Project Browser*, ceiling plans are just below the floor plans.

Notice the doors and windows are automatically "turned off" in the ceiling plan views. Actually, the ceiling plan views have a cutting plane similar to floor plans, except they look up rather than down. You can see this setting by right-clicking on a view name in the *Project Browser* and selecting *Properties*, and then selecting **View Range**. The default value is 7'-6". You might increase this if, for example, you had 10'-0" ceilings and 8'-0" high doors. Otherwise, the doors would show because the 7'-6" cutting plane is below the door height (Figure 8-2.1).

View Range				
Primary Range				
Top:	Level Above (Roof)	▼	Offset:	0' 0"
Cut plane:	Associated Level (Second F	▼	Offset:	7' 6"
Bottom:	Associated Level (Second F	▼	Offset:	7' 6"
View Depth				
Level:	Level Above (Roof)	▼	Offset:	0' 0"
	OK	Cancel	Apply	Help

FIGURE 8-2.1 Properties: View Range settings

3. Close the *View Range* dialog box, if open, and then select **Architecture → Build → Ceiling**.

Ceiling

You have four ceiling types, by default, to select from (Figure 8-2.2).

FIGURE 8-2.2 Type Selector: Ceiling: types

4. Select *Compound Ceiling:* **2'x4' ACT System**.

Next you will change the ceiling height. The default setting is 8'-0" above the current level. You will change the ceiling height to 8'-4"; this will give about 6½" of space above the ceiling to the bottom of the rafters for recessed light fixtures and any required wiring. This setting can be changed on a room by room basis; that is why it is an *Instance Parameter*.

5. In the *Properties Palette*, set the *Height Offset From Level* setting to **8'-4"** (Figure 8-2.3).

FIGURE 8-2.3 Ceiling: Properties

You are now ready to place ceiling grids. This process cannot get much easier, especially compared to 2D CAD programs.

6. Move your cursor anywhere within the office in the lower-right corner of the building. You should see the perimeter of the room highlighted.

7. Pick within the room; Revit places a ceiling grid in the room (Figure 8-2.4).

FIGURE 8-2.4: Second Floor Ceiling Plan view: 2'x4' suspended acoustical ceiling tile added to office

You now have a 2x4 ceiling grid at 8'-4" above the floor, the second floor in this case. Later in the book, when you get to the exercise on cutting sections, you will see the ceiling with the proper height and thickness.

Next, you will add the same ceiling system to the family room in the basement. But, you will notice the ceiling plan section in the *Project Browser* does not have a *Basement* view.

Many residential basements do not have any finished ceilings, so that view was not included in the template from which you started. Next you will create a view for this.

8. Select **View → Create → Plan Views → Reflected Ceiling Plan**.

9. Select the **Basement** view from this list and then click **OK** (see image to the right).

10. You are taken to the **Basement Ceiling Plan** view automatically.

Your view should look a little funny, no walls. You will have to adjust the *View Range* settings.

11. Click **Modify** and then set the *View Range* to **6'-6"**.

You should now see the walls and doors. The doors show because the cut plane is lower than the top of the door. You will ignore that for now.

12. Use the **Ceiling** tool to place 2'x 4' acoustic ceiling tile in the *Family Room*, the large room to the far East. See the following notes (Figure 8-2.5):
   a. You will probably get a symbol at the cross-hairs that indicates you cannot place a ceiling anywhere; the symbol is a circle with a slash through it. This has to do with the ceiling height.
   b. Via the *Properties Palette*, change the ceiling height to **7'-0"**.
   c. You should be able to place the ceiling system now.
   d. Revit automatically rotates and centers the ceiling grid within each room.

FIGURE 8-2.5: Basement Ceiling Plan view: 2'x4' suspended acoustical ceiling tile added to Family Rm.

When you place a ceiling grid, Revit centers the grid in the room. The general rule-of-thumb is you should try to avoid reducing the tile size by more than half of a tile. You can see in Figure 8-2.5 that the East and West sides look OK. However, the North and South sides are small slivers. You will adjust this next.

Looking at Figure 8-2.6, you can see why it was not possible to place a ceiling until the ceiling height was lowered and why the walls did not show up; the foundation wall is only 7'-3" above the basement floor. Thus, a floor cut plane of 7'-6" would not show walls and an 8'-4" ceiling could not find walls to form a perimeter to contain it.

FIGURE 8-2.6
Section at basement / foundation wall

13. Select *Modify* from the *Ribbon*.

14. **Select** the ceiling grid. Only one line will be highlighted.

15. Use the **Move** tool to move the grid 24″ to the North (Figure 8-2.7).

FIGURE 8-2.7
Basement: Ceiling Grid moved

You should notice that only the grid moved, not the ceiling perimeter.

Modifying the Suspended Acoustical Ceiling Tile System:

Making modifications to the grid is relatively easy. Next, you will adjust the ceiling height and rotate the grid.

16. In the *Basement* view, select the ceiling grid in the *Family Room*.

17. Within the *Properties Palette*, change the height to **7′-2″**. *(Every inch counts!)*

18. Click **Apply** to accept the new height change (or just move your cursor back into the drawing area).

19. Again, with the grid still selected, use the **Rotate** tool from the *Ribbon* to rotate the grid **30 degrees**.

   FYI: Notice, while in the Rotate command, the <u>Center of Rotation</u> icon appears, and like in the earlier lessons, this can be dragged to a different location if needed.

TIP: *When using the Rotate tool you need to pick two points. The first point is your reference line. The second point is the number of degrees off that reference line. In this example, try picking your first point to the right as a horizontal line. Then move the cursor counter-clockwise until 30 degrees is displayed. You can also type the angle rather than clicking the second point.*

Your drawing should look similar to **Figure 8-2.8**. Notice how the perimeter of the room acts like a cropping window when you use *Move* or *Rotate* on a ceiling grid.

Deleting a Ceiling Grid:
When selecting a ceiling grid, Revit only selects one line. This does not allow you to delete the ceiling.

To delete: hover cursor over a ceiling grid line and press the TAB key until you see the ceiling perimeter highlight, then click the mouse. The entire ceiling will be selected. Press Delete.

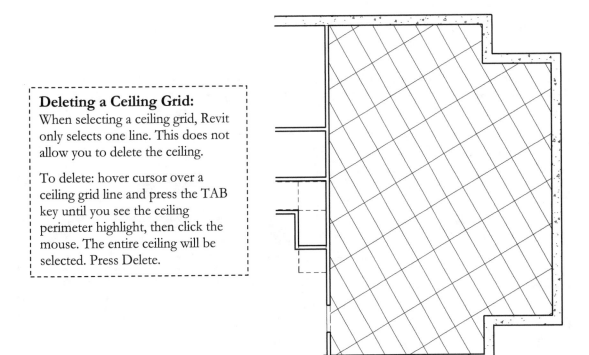

FIGURE 8-2.8 Basement: Modified Ceiling

Next, you will look at drawing gypsum board ceiling systems. The process is identical to placing the grid system. Additionally, you will create a ceiling type.

Gypsum Board Ceiling System:

You will create a new ceiling type for a gypsum board (gyp. bd.) ceiling. To better identify the areas that have a gyp. bd. ceiling, you will set the ceiling type to have a stipple pattern. This will provide a nice graphical representation for the gyp. bd. ceiling areas. The ceiling you are about to create would lean more towards a commercial application. However, it will give you a better understanding of how to create custom ceilings. You will add this ceiling to a room in the basement; assume it is being installed below HVAC ductwork, to finish the room.

20. Select **Manage → Settings → Materials**. *This is the list of materials you select from when assigning a material to each layer in a wall system, etc.*

Materials

21. Select *Gypsum Wall Board* in the name list, right-click and then select **Duplicate.** Enter the name **Gypsum Ceiling Board**.

22. In the *Surface Pattern* area, pick the preview and select **Gypsum-Plaster** from the list, and then click **OK** twice (Figure 8-2.9).

FIGURE 8-2.9 Materials dialog

The *Surface Pattern* setting is what will add the stipple pattern to the gyp. bd. ceiling areas. With this set to *none*, the ceiling has no pattern, like the basic ceiling type.

Thus, if you wanted "Carpet 1" finish to never have the stipple hatch pattern, you could change the surface pattern to none via the *Materials* dialog and not have to change each view's visibility override.

23. Select the ***Ceiling*** tool from the *Ribbon*.

24. Set the *Type Selector* to **GWB on Metal Stud**.

> *FYI: You are selecting this because it is similar to the ceiling you will be creating.*

25. Click the **Edit Type** button in the *Properties Palette*.

26. Click *Duplicate* and type the name **Susp GB on Metal Stud**.

27. Select **Edit** next to the *Structure* parameter.

28. Create a *Layer* and set the *Values* as follows (Figure 8-2.10):
    a. **1½″ Mtl. Stud**
    b. **¾″ Mtl. Stud**
    c. **Gypsum Ceiling Board** *(This is the material you created in Step 21.)*

29. Click **OK** two times.

FYI: The ceiling assembly you just created represents a typical suspended gyp. bd. ceiling system. The metal studs are perpendicular to each other and suspended by wires, similar to an ACT (acoustical ceiling tile) system.

You are now ready to draw a gypsum board ceiling.

30. Make sure **Susp GB on Metal Stud** is selected in the *Type Selector* on the *Properties Palette*.

31. Set the ceiling height to **7′-0″**.

Edit Assembly

Family:	Compound Ceiling
Type:	Susp GB on Metal Stud
Total thickness:	0′ 2 3/4″
Resistance (R):	13.0915 (h·ft²·°F)/BTU
Thermal Mass:	0.5774 BTU/°F

Layers

	Function	Material	Thickness	Wrap
1	Core Boundary	Layers Above Wrap	0′ 0″	
2	Structure [1]	Metal Stud Layer	0′ 1 1/2″	
3	Structure [1]	Metal Stud Layer	0′ 0 3/4″	
4	Core Boundary	Layers Below Wrap	0′ 0″	
5	Finish 2 [5]	Gypsum Ceiling Board	0′ 0 1/2″	

Insert	Delete	Up	Down

<< Preview	OK	Cancel	Help

FIGURE 8-2.10 New ceiling – Edit assembly

32. Pick the lower left room as shown in **Figure 8-2.11**. If you don't see the ceiling, you may have forgot to change the material to *Gypsum Ceiling Board* back in step 28.

FIGURE 8-2.11 Gyp. Bd. Ceiling

You now have a gypsum board ceiling at 7'-0" above the basement floor slab.

Adding a Bulkhead:

Next, you will draw a ceiling in the area at the bottom of the steps. However, you cannot simply pick the room to place the ceiling because Revit would fill in the stair area. First, you will need to draw a bulkhead at the bottom of the steps. A bulkhead is a portion of wall that hangs from the floor above and creates a closed perimeter for a ceiling system to tie into. The bulkhead will create a perimeter that the *Ceiling* tool will detect for the proper ceiling placement.

33. While still in the *Basement Reflected Ceiling Plan* view, select the **Wall** tool.

Properties ×

Basic Wall
Interior - 4 1/2" Partition

New Walls ▾ ⊞ Edit Type

Constraints ⊗ ▲

Location Line	Finish Face: Interi...
Base Constraint	Basement
Base Offset	7' 0"
Base is Attached	☐
Base Extension Distance	0' 0"
Top Constraint	Up to level: First ...
Unconnected Height	1' 6"
Top Offset	0' 0"
Top is Attached	☐
Top Extension Distance	0' 0"
Room Bounding	☑
Related to Mass	☐

Structural ⊗

Structural	☐
Enable Analytical Model	☐
Structural Usage	Non-bearing

Dimensions ⊗

| Area | |
| Volume | |

Identity Data ⊗

Image	
Comments	
Mark	

Properties help | Apply

FIGURE 8-2.12 Bulkhead (wall) properties

34. Set the *Type Selector* to **Interior – 4 1/2"**
    Partition.

35. In the *Properties Palette* set the *Base Offset* to
    7'-0" (Figure 8-2.12).

This will put the bottom of the wall at 7'-0"
above the current floor level, the basement in
this case.

36. Set the *Top Constraint* to **Up to level:**
    First Floor (Figure 8-2.12).

    *IMPORTANT TIP: The next time you draw a wall
    you will have to change the Base Offset back to 0'-0"
    or your wall will be 7'-0" off the floor; this can be
    hard to remember!*

37. **Draw the bulkhead**; make sure you snap
    to the adjacent walls (Figure 8-2.13).

Bulkhead added here; a wall
with the bottom starting at
7'-0" above the basement floor

FIGURE 8-2.13 Bulkhead drawn

38. Select the **Ceiling** tool.

You could just pick within this room and Revit would automatically create a ceiling; however, you will look at another way to place a ceiling. Next you will sketch the perimeter of the ceiling, just like you did for the floor slabs in the previous lesson.

39. Select **Sketch Ceiling** from the *Ribbon*.

Sketch Ceiling

40. Sketch a line around the perimeter of the room using *Snaps* (Figure 8-2.14). Settings should be *Susp GWC* ceiling at 7'-0".

   TIP: Remember to use the Chain option.

41. Click the **green check mark** to finish the sketch.

FIGURE 8-2.14 Sketching Ceiling

Your ceiling should look like Figure 8-2.15. You will see what is happening here a little better in the sections exercise.

FIGURE 8-2.15 Ceiling added at bottom of steps

Modifying a Floor System to Include the Ceiling:

Next you will modify the floor systems, already in place, to have gypsum board attached to the bottom of the joists. This is what is typically done in a residence, unless room is needed above the ceiling for ductwork.

42. Switch to the **Second Floor Plan** view (not the ceiling plan).

43. Select the floor.

   TIP: Clicking near the stair opening may be the easiest way to select the floor.

44. Via *Edit Type*, create a *Duplicate* floor from the one selected; name it **Wood Joist 14″ – Wood Finish – Gyp Bd Ceiling**.

45. Edit the floor structure via *Type Properties* (Figure 8-2.16).
   a. Insert a new *Layer* at the bottom of the floor assembly
   b. Set the *Function* to **Finish 1 [4]**
   c. Set the *Material* to **Gypsum Ceiling Board**
   d. Set the *Thickness* to ½″

Why Did You Create a New Floor Type?

You needed to create a new floor type for the second floor because the first floor does not need gypsum board on the underside. When you modify a *family type*, all instances of that type are changed throughout the project. This is very powerful when you actually want to change several instances of a type. However, if you modify a type and only want the selected one to change, you are in for a big surprise when you look at the other instances of that type elsewhere in your project, because they will all change. That is why you had to create a new floor type, because that same floor type is also placed on the first floor.

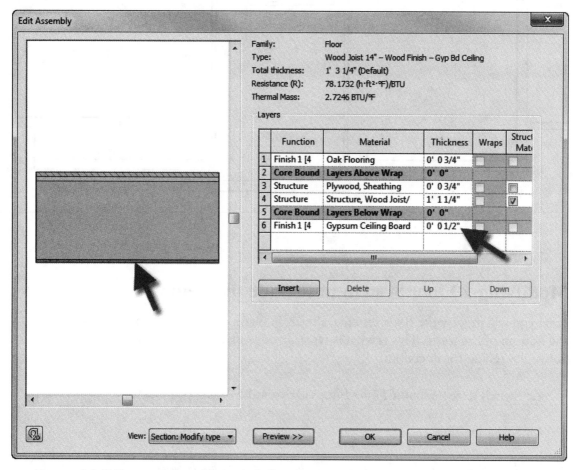

FIGURE 8-2.16 Floor system modified to include ceiling

46. Close the open dialog boxes.

Now switch to the *First Floor Ceiling Plan* (Figure 8-2.17) and notice that the gypsum ceiling board surface pattern is showing everywhere the floor occurs. If not, make sure the second floor system has been changed to the new type. That takes care of the ceiling for the first floor.

47. Switch to the *Second Floor Ceiling Plan* and add your **Susp GB on Metal Stud** at 8'-0" high to the remaining rooms (Figure 8-2.18).

    FYI: Once a ceiling is placed you can select it and click Edit Boundary on the Ribbon. Then you can change the perimeter or add an enclosed area within the main perimeter to create a hole. This is how you would accommodate the skylights in the roof: by adding holes to the ceiling to let the light in.

48. **Save** your project as **ex8-2.rvt**.

FIGURE 8-2.17 First floor ceiling plan: gypsum board added to bottom of floor structure

Real-Time Design Validation

Notice how the ceiling, which is a 3D object, covers the roof ridge line and skylights? This is very powerful in that you see all aspects of the design. If you could see ductwork in the view below, that would mean it was added to the model too low and needs to be raised or moved. Being able to see everything in context helps the designers validate their design solution. Also, not seeing the skylights is a problem. This means the light is being blocked by the ceiling and needs to be addressed. However, we will not be doing that in this tutorial.

FIGURE 8-2.18 Second Floor Ceiling Plan: gypsum board ceiling system suspended at 8'-0" AFF

Exercise 8-3:
Placing Light Fixtures

In this exercise, you will learn to load and place light fixtures in your reflected ceiling plans.

Loading Families:

Before placing fixtures, you need to load them into your project.

1. While in the **Second Floor** *Ceiling Plan*, select **Component** from the *Architecture* tab on the *Ribbon*.

2. Select **Load Family** on the contextual *Ribbon* (Figure 8-3.1).

FIGURE **8-3.1** Component tool active; contextual Ribbon options

3. Double-click the *Lighting\Architectural\Internal* folder, and then double-click **Troffer Light - 2x4 Parabolic.rfa** (Figure 8-3.2).

FIGURE **8-3.2** Load component

Placing Instances of Components:

You are now ready to place the fixtures in your ceiling plans.

4. With **Component** still selected, pick **Troffer Light – 2′ x 4′ Parabolic: 2′x4′ (2 Lamp) – 120 V** from the *Type Selector* drop-down on the *Properties Palette*.

5. On the **Second Floor Ceiling Plan** view, place fixtures as shown in **Figure 8-3.3**.

   FYI: Adjust the ceiling grid position if needed.

FIGURE 8-3.3 Light fixtures added to ceiling

You will have to use the *Move* command, or even better the *Align* tool, to move the fixture so it fits perfectly in the ACT grid.

6. Switch to the *Basement Ceiling Plan* view.

7. Now place another **2x4 light fixture** as shown in **Figure 8-3.4**.

FIGURE 8-3.4 Basement ceiling plan; light fixture added

Notice the fixture does not automatically orient itself with the ceiling grid. There may be an occasion when you want this.

Also, notice the light fixture hides a portion of the ceiling grid. This is nice because the grid does not extend through a light fixture.

8. Use *Rotate* and *Move* to rotate the fixture to align with the grid (Figure 8-3.5). The *Align* tool will also work.

> *TIP: You can use the normal* Rotate *and* Move *tools in conjunction with the Snaps.*

FIGURE 8-3.5 Basement Ceiling Plan; light fixture moved/rotated into place

9. Once you have one fixture rotated, it is easier to use the *Copy* tool and the *Snaps* to add rotated light fixtures. **Copy** the light fixture to match the layout in **Figure 8-3.6**.

TIP: Check Multiple *on the Options Bar when the Copy command is active.*

FIGURE 8-3.6 Basement Ceiling Plan; light fixture copied

10. **Save** your project as **ex8-3.rvt**.

These 2x4 light fixtures have *Rendering* settings already set up. That means the room will automatically have lights when you get to creating a photo-realistic rendering using this built-in feature!

The example image below shows a reflected ceiling plan with supply and return diffusers added. These are not used too often in residential work. They are loaded similarly to the light fixture via component tool.

FIGURE 8-3.7 Example image; supply and return diffusers added

Reflected Ceiling Plan Symbols:

Revit provides many of the industry standard content necessary in drawing reflected ceiling plans (RCP). As shown in Figure 8-3.7, supply air diffusers are represented with an X and return air has a diagonal line. It is typical to have an RCP symbol legend showing each symbol and material pattern and listing what each one represents. The *Legend* feature makes this a snap!

Component Properties

If you want to adjust the properties of a component, such as a light fixture, you can browse to it in the *Project Browser* and right click on one of the *Types* listed. *Notice the right click menu also has the option to select all instances of the item in the drawing.* Select *Properties.* You will see the dialog below for the 2x4 (2 lamps)-120V.

You can also click *Duplicate* and add more sizes (e.g., a 4'x4' light fixture).

Type Properties		
Family:	Troffer Light - 2x4 Parabolic	Load...
Type:	2'x4'(2 Lamp) - 120V	Duplicate...
		Rename...

Type Parameters

Parameter	Value
URL	
Description	
Cost	
Assembly Description	Lighting - Fluorescent
Type Mark	
OmniClass Number	23.80.70.11.14.11
OmniClass Title	Downlights
Code Name	
Photometrics	
Light Loss Factor	0.88
Initial Intensity	80.00 W @ 78.75 lm/W
Initial Color	4230 K
Emit from Rectangle Width	1' 10"
Emit from Rectangle Length	3' 10"
Emit Shape Visible in Rendering	
Dimming Lamp Color Temperatu	<None>
Color Filter	White
Light Source Definition (family)	Rectangle+HemiSpherical

<< Preview	OK	Cancel	Apply

You can also select an inserted component and look at the *Properties Palette* for additional properties for that particular instance.

Exercise 8-4:
Annotations

This short section will look at adding notes to your RCP.

Adding Annotations:

1. In the *Basement Reflected Ceiling Plan* view, select the **Annotate → Text → Text** tool from the *Ribbon*.

A

Text

2. Pick **Text: 3/32″ Arial** from the *Type Selector* (Figure 8-4.1).

3. Select the **Leader** (Curved) button highlighted in **Figure 8-4.1**.

FIGURE 8-4.1 Text; Ribbon options

Next, you will add a note indicating that a room in the basement does not have a ceiling. First you will draw a leader, and then Revit will allow you to type the text.

4. Add the note "**NO CEILING - TYPICAL**" shown in **Figure 8-4.2**.

NO CEILING - TYPICAL

FIGURE 8-4.2 Text with Curved leader

Notice that immediately after adding the text or while it is selected, you see the *Move* icon, the *Rotate* icon and *Grips* to edit the arrow/leader.

When the text is selected you can click the "add leader" tools on the *Ribbon* (shown on the left above) to add additional leaders.

Adding Text Styles to Your Project:

You can add additional text styles to your project. Some firms prefer a font that has a hand lettering look and others prefer something like the Arial font. These preferences can be saved in the template file so they are consistent and always available. Next, you will add a new style to your Revit project.

5. Click on the *Text* tool.

6. Next, click **Edit Type** in the *Properties Palette*.

7. Select **Duplicate** and enter **1/4″ OUTLINE TEXT** (Figure 8-4.3).

8. Next, make the following adjustments to the *Type Properties* (Figure 8-4.4).
    a. Text Font: **Swis721 BdOul BT**
    b. Text Size: ¼″

    NOTE: You can use any Windows True-Type font. If you do not have this font, select another that best matches (Figure 8-4.5).

FIGURE 8-4.3 New text name

The text size you entered in Step 9 is the size of the text when printed. Revit automatically scales the text, in each view, based on the *View Scale* setting. For example, if you are adding 3/32″ text to a ⅛″ floor plan view, the text placed will be 9″ tall. If you add text to a ¼″ plan view, the text will be 4½″ tall. When both the ¼″ and ⅛″ plan views are placed on a sheet, the text for each is 3/32″ tall. Here is what happens: adding text to the ¼″ plan causes the 3/32″ text to be scaled up 48 times, and when the plan view is placed on a *Sheet*, the entire view, including the text, is scaled down 1/48 times; thus, the text makes a full loop back to being 3/32″ tall.

If you change the *View Scale* of the drawing, the text size will automatically change, so the text is always the correct size when printing. It is best to set the drawing to the correct scale first, as changing the *View Scale* can create a lot of work repositioning resized text that may be overlapping something or too big for a room.

9. Select **OK** to close the open dialog.

You should now have the new text style available in the *Element Type Selector* on the *Ribbon*.

10. Use the new text style to create the text shown below (Figure 8-4.5).

> *TIP: Select the text only option on the Ribbon – i.e., No Leader.*

When typing text, you simply click somewhere in the view to complete the text string; pressing *Enter* just adds more lines.

11. Save as **ex8-4.rvt**.

Type Properties			
Family:	System Family: Text		Load...
Type:	1/4" OUTLINE TEXT		Duplicate...
			Rename...

Type Parameters

Parameter	Value
Graphics	
Color	■ Black
Line Weight	1
Background	Opaque
Show Border	☐
Leader/Border Offset	5/64"
Leader Arrowhead	Arrow 30 Degree
Text	
Text Font	Swis721 BdOul BT
Text Size	1/4"
Tab Size	1/2"
Bold	☐
Italic	☐
Underline	☐
Width Factor	1.000000

<< Preview   OK   Cancel   Apply

FIGURE 8-4.4 New text properties

FIGURE 8-4.5 New text style added

Self-Exam:

The following questions can be used as a way to check your knowledge of this lesson. The answers can be found at the bottom of the page.

1. You must pick walls to define floor areas. (T/F)

2. Use the Ctrl key to cycle through the selection options. (T/F)

3. When you add a floor element in plan view, the floor does not show up right away in the other views, i.e., 3D, Sections, etc. (T/F)

4. You use the _____ feature if you need to add a new product, like exterior plaster, so you can add it to wall types and other systems.

5. You have _____ different types of leader options with the *Text* tool (not including the 6 leader location icons).

Review Questions:

The following questions may be assigned by your instructor as a way to assess your knowledge of this section. Your instructor has the answers to the review questions.

1. It is not possible to create new text styles. (T/F)

2. You can add additional light fixture sizes to the family as required. (T/F)

3. The light fixtures automatically turn to align with the ceiling grid. (T/F)

4. You can adjust the ceiling height room by room. (T/F)

5. Revit allows you to model bulkheads by adjusting the bottom position of the wall. (T/F)

6. You can use any Windows True Type font in Revit. (T/F)

7. Use the _____ tool if the ceiling grid needs to be at an angle.

8. Use the _____ tool to adjust the ceiling grid location if a ceiling tile is less than half its normal size.

9. Use the _____ tool to adjust whether an element's surface pattern is displayed (i.e., the stipple for the gypsum board ceiling).

10. What is the current size of your project (after completing exercise 8-4)?

    _____ MB.

Notes:

Lesson 9
Residence: ELEVATIONS:

This lesson will cover interior and exterior elevations. The default template you started with already has the four main exterior elevations set up for you. You will investigate how Autodesk® Revit® generates elevations and the role the elevation tag plays in that process. Be sure to review the video on elevations which came with this book.

Exercise 9-1:
Creating and Viewing Exterior Elevations

Here you will look at setting up an exterior elevation and how to control some of the various options.

Setting up an Exterior Elevation:

Even though you already have the main exterior elevations set, you will go through the steps necessary to set one up. Many projects have more than four exterior elevations, so all exterior surfaces are elevated.

1. Open your project, ex8-4.rvt, and **Save As ex9-1.rvt**.

2. Switch to your *First Floor* plan view.

3. Select **View → Create → Elevation** *(not the down-arrow)*.

4. Make sure the *Type Selector* is set to *Elevation:* **Building Elevation** and then place the elevation tag in plan view as shown in Figure 9-1.1.

   NOTE: As you move the cursor around the screen, the Elevation Tag automatically turns to point at the building.

You now have an elevation added to the *Project Browser* in the *Elevations* section. **The first thing you should do after placing an elevation is rename it**; the default name is not very descriptive. These generic names would get very confusing on larger projects with dozens of views.

Add this ——→ elevation tag

FIGURE 9-1.1 Added elevation tag

5. **Right-click** on the new view name, in the *Project Browser*, and select **Rename** (Figure 9-1.2).

6. Type: **South – Main Entry**.

The name should be fairly descriptive so you can tell where the elevation is just by the name in the *Project Browser*.

7. Double-click on **South –Main Entry** in the *Project Browser*.

The elevation may not look correct right away (Figure 9-1.3). You will adjust this in the next step. Notice, though, that an elevation was created simply by placing an *Elevation Tag* in plan view.

8. Switch back to the ***First Floor Plan*** view.

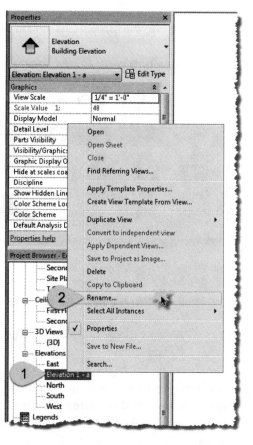

FIGURE 9-1.2 Renaming new view name

FIGURE 9-1.3 Initial elevation view

Next, you will study the options associated with the elevation tag. This, in part, controls what is seen in the elevation.

9. The elevation tag has two parts: the pointing triangle and the square center. Each part will highlight as you move the cursor over it. **Select the square center part**.

You should now see the symbol shown on the right.

View direction boxes:
The checked box indicates which way the elevation tag is looking. You can check, or uncheck, the other boxes. Do NOT do that at this time. Each checked box adds another view name to the *Project Browser*.

Rotation Control icon visible when Elevation Tag is selected

.**Rotation Control:**
Clicking and dragging on this allows you to look perpendicular to an angled wall in plan, for example.

Interior Elevations:
When adding an interior elevation tag to the floor plan, you should select *Interior Elevation* from the *Type Selector*. This will use a different symbol to help distinguish the interior tags from the exterior tags in the plan views. Also, the interior and exterior views are separated in the *Project Browser*, making it easier to manage views as the project continues to develop.

10. Press the **ESC** key to unselect the elevation tag.

11. Select the "pointing" portion of the elevation tag.

Your elevation tag should look similar to Figure 9-1.4.

Far clip plane

Cutting plane/ extent of view

Adjustment grips

FIGURE 9-1.4 Selected elevation tag

The elevation tag, as selected in Figure 9-1.4, has several features for controlling how the elevation looks. Here is a quick explanation:

- **Cutting plane/extent of view line:** This controls how much of the 3D model is elevated from left to right (i.e., the width of the elevation).

- **Far clip plane:** This controls how far into the 3D model the elevation view can see.

- **Adjustment grips:** You can drag this with the mouse to control the features mentioned above.

12. Next you will take a look at the new elevation's *View Properties*. You can do this in one of the following ways:

    a. Select the "pointing" portion of the elevation tag (which should currently be selected based on the previous step).

    b. Select the view label (South – Main Entry in this example) in the *Project Browser*.

    c. Open the view, with nothing in the model selected.

You have several options in the *Properties Palette* (Figure 9-1.5). Notice the three options with check boxes next to them; these control the following:

- **Crop View**: This crops the width and height of the view in elevation.
  Adjusting the width of the cropping window in elevation also adjusts the "extent of view" control in plan view.

- **Crop Region Visible**: This displays a rectangle in the elevation view indicating the extent of the cropping window, described above.
  When selected in elevation view, the rectangle can be adjusted with the adjustment grips.

- **Far Clipping**: If this is turned off, Revit will draw everything visible in the 3D model, *within the "extent of view."*

FIGURE 9-1.5 South – Mail Entry Elev view properties

You will manipulate some of these controls next.

13. With the elevation tag still selected (as in Figure 9-1.4), drag the "cutting plane/ extent of view" line up **into** the main entry as shown in Figure 9-1.6.

FIGURE 9-1.6 Relocated cutting plane

14. Now switch to the elevation view **South – Main Entry**. Adjust the **Crop Region** so the entire roof is visible; click the *Crop Region* to select it and drag the top grip upward. **FYI:** The roof's ridge line will not be visible yet.

Your elevation should look similar to Figure 9-1.7.

The main entry wall and roof are now displayed in section because of the location of the *cutting plane* line in plan.

FIGURE 9-1.7 Elevation with cutting plane thru front entry

Notice that the roof is not fully visible. This is not related to the cropping window shown in Figure 9-1.7. Rather, it is related to the *Far Clip Plane* set in the plan view.

15. Adjust the *Far Clip Plane* in the **First Floor Plan** view so that the entire roof shows in the **South – Main Entry** view.

 TIP: Click on the grip and drag the Far Clip Plane *North until it is past the ridge line, which is at the middle of the building. You may need to adjust the crop region again.*

Now when you switch back to the **South – Main Entry** elevation view, you should see the entire roof.

Next, you will adjust the elevation tag to set up a detail elevation for the main entry area.

16. In the **First Floor Plan** view, adjust the elevation tag to show only the main entry wall (Figure 9-1.8).
    - The cutting plane/extent of view line is moved South so it is outside of the building footprint.
    - Use the left and right grips to shorten the same line.

17. Switch to the **South – Main Entry** view to see the "detail" elevation you are setting up (Figure 9-1.9).

18. Set the **View Scale** to ½" = 1'-0" on the *View Control Bar* at the bottom of the screen.

Notice how the *Level Datum* tags have changed to a smaller size. *Undo* and try it again if you missed it. You did notice the levels were automatically added, right?

19. Click the **Hide Crop Region** icon on the *View Control Bar* to make the *Crop Region* disappear.

FIGURE 9-1.8
Main Entry wall detail elevation

Once you modify the view constraints in plan view (Figure 9-1.8) and you switch to the new elevation view, you can click on the *crop region* and use the grips to make the view wider. You might want to do this to make sure the roof overhang shows.

When you drag the *crop region* to the right, the *Level Datum* tags move so they do not overlap the elevation. This is another example of Revit taking the busy work out of designing a residence!

Crop region; visibility should be turned off in Step 19.

DETAIL ELEVATION:
A detail elevation like this might be used to dimension various items like the mail box, sign, special siding/ trim, etc. The scale would typically be larger than the full South elevation so you can fit more notes and dimensions.

This view might be placed on a sheet with the other elevations or any sheet where you can find room.

FIGURE 9-1.9 Main Entry wall detail elevation; View Scale is set to ¼" = 1'-0" so the level labels would be legible in this book

Many designers like to change the line weight around portions of the building which protrude out from the main elevation. This helps the builder and client to more easily read the drawings. However, Revit does not do this automatically. It can be done manually using the **Linework** tool on the *Modify* tab. When the tool is active you can select a line style from the *Ribbon* and then begin clicking lines in the model to override their default settings. These lines will adjust as the model is changed. Selecting **<by category>** for a line style and then clicking an overridden line will set it back to its original state. Give it a try!

20. **Save** your project as **ex9-1.rvt**.

Exercise 9-2:
Modifying the Project Model: Exterior Elevations

The purpose of this exercise is to demonstrate that changes can be made anywhere and all other drawings are automatically updated.

Modify an Exterior Elevation:

1. Open ex9-1.rvt and **Save As ex9-2**.

2. Open the *West* exterior elevation view. Adjust the start and end locations of the *Level Datum* lines to be closer to the edge of the building (Figure 9-2.1).

3. Using the **Ctrl** key, select the two double-hung windows on the right, two of the four windows in the garage wall.

You will delete the two selected windows and move the remaining two windows to the center of the wall.

4. Press the **Delete** key to erase the selected windows.

5. Select the remaining two windows and use the *Move* tool to <u>approximately</u> center them on the wall/roof ridge, keeping the vertical alignment unchanged (Figure 9-2.1). The next page will discuss how to center them more precisely.

FIGURE 9-2.1 Modifying windows on the West elevation

9-9

Now you will switch to the *First Floor Plan* view to see your changes.

6. Switch to the ***First Floor*** plan view and zoom in on the garage area (Figure 9-2.2). Adjust the window position per the information mentioned below.

Notice how the windows in plan have changed to match the modifications you just made to the exterior elevations? This only makes sense seeing as both the floor plan and the exterior elevation are projected 2D views of the same 3D model. Both views are directly manipulating the 3D model.

Also, notice that even the dimensions adjusted! Revit is all about reducing drafting time and maximizing design time. Step 5 had you approximately locate the windows; now you can select the windows in plan and type the exact dimension you want; 12'-3" centers them on the building.

FIGURE 9-2.2 Changes automatically made to the floor plan

Next, you will insert a window in elevation. This will demonstrate, first, that you can actually add a window in elevation not just plan view, and second, that the other views are automatically updated.

7.   Switch to the *North* exterior elevation view.

8.   Select the *Window* tool from the *Architecture* tab.

Notice, with the window selected for placement, you have the usual dimensions helping you accurately place the window. As you move the window around, you should see a dashed horizontal cyan colored line indicating the default sill height, although you can deviate from this in elevation views.

9.   From the *Type Selector*, choose *Double Hung with Trim:* **36"x48"**.

10. Place a window as shown in **Figure 9-2.3**; make sure the bottom of the window *Snaps* to the dashed, cyan colored sill line.

   TIP: The window should be about centered between the existing windows.

FIGURE 9-2.3 Placing a window on the North elevation

If you laid out the interior walls as described in Lesson 5, you should get a warning message when inserting the window. This is because the interior wall between the kitchen and the living room conflicts with the exterior window. Revit is programmed to see that conflict and bring it to your attention. You can ignore this error because it is possible to build a wall up to the center of a window; some errors you cannot ignore because they will have a negative impact on Revit's functionality.

11. Click the "X" in the upper-right corner to ignore the wall/window conflict warning (Figure 9-2.4).

> **Warning** [X]
>
> Insert conflicts with joined Wall.

FIGURE 9-2.4 Conflict warning

12. Switch to the *First Floor* plan view to see the problem (Figure 9-2.5).

FIGURE 9-2.5 First Floor – kitchen area

13. While in plan view, select the new window and **Delete** it.

Why did the window location dimensions update in Figure 9-9.2 and not in Figure 9-2.5? The first had dimensions associated with the windows and the latter did not. When you dimension something in Revit, the witness lines "remember" what they are dimensioning to and move with that element. Also, notice how the window was tagged in elevation view, but not in plan view like the previously placed windows? The tag is only added in the view the element was placed in, but can be manually tagged in any view (even multiple times).

TIP: When working in the exterior elevation view, you can quickly see where the interior walls are simply by selecting the exterior wall (Figure 9-2.6).

Whenever something is selected, it turns blue and becomes transparent. Thus, the things behind the element are temporarily visible.

FIGURE 9-2.6 Transparent selections

Adding Shutters to the South Elevation:

Next you will add shutters to the South elevation. You will need to load a family from the online Revit Content website.

14. Switch back to the **North** elevation view and notice that the new window is gone, per your plan change.

15. Switch to the **Insert** tab on the *Ribbon*.

16. Using *Autodesk Seek*, search for **shutter (high-res)**; save it to your hard drive and then *Load* it.

    TIP: Refer to previous lessons for more instruction.

17. With the **Component** tool active and **Shutter (high-res): 18″ x 48″** selected in the *Type Selector*, place a shutter in elevation as shown in Figure 9-2.7 (upper-left window on North Elevation).

    TIP: If the shutter does not land in the correct spot, select it and use the arrow keys (on the keyboard) to nudge it into place, or use the Align tool per the tip below.

18. Use the same technique to place the remaining shutters shown in **Figure 9-2.8**.

19. Add shutters to the South elevation per **Figure 9-2.9**.

TIP: USING THE ALIGN TOOL

Don't forget about the Align tool. Simply drop your shutter somewhere near the window and use the Align tool to move it into place. After placing the shutter, click Align, select the edge of the window and then select the edge of the shutter to move the shutter into place. If the window moves, you picked in the wrong order – click Undo and try again. Also, immediately after you use Align you can click the Padlock to maintain a parametric relationship; meaning if the window moves, even via a plan view, the shutters will move with it!

FIGURE 9-2.7 Placing a shutter on the North elevation

The shutter element has been set up so that it can only be placed on a wall (this is called a *wall hosted family*). If you move the cursor over a door or window, you get the (⊘) symbol meaning it cannot be placed there.

FIGURE 9-2.8 (8) Shutters added to the North elevation

FIGURE 9-2.9 (4) Shutters added to the South elevation

20. **Save** your Project as ex9-2.rvt.

REMINDER: ENTERING DIMENSIONS IN REVIT

As your experience with Revit grows, you will want to learn some of the shortcuts to using the program. One of those shortcuts is how you enter dimensions when drawing. You probably already know, maybe by accident, that if you enter only one number (e.g., 48) and press Enter, Revit interprets that number to be feet (e.g., 48'-0"). So, if you want to enter 48", you may be typing 0'-48" or 48". Both work, but having to press the Shift key to get the inch symbol takes a little longer.

Here are some options for entering dimensions:

0 48	*Revit reads this as 48" (zero space forty-eight)*
48	*Revit reads this as 48'-0"*
5.5	*Revit reads this as 5'-6"*
0 5.5	*Revit reads this as 5 ½"*
2 0 1/4	*Revit reads this as 2'-0¼" (two space zero space fraction)*

Exercise 9-3:
Creating and Viewing Interior Elevations

Creating interior elevations is very much like exterior elevations. In fact, you use the same tool. The main difference is that you are placing the elevation tag inside the building, rather than on the exterior.

Adding an Interior Elevation Tag:

1. Open project ex9-2.rvt and **Save As ex9-3.rvt**.

2. Switch to the *First Floor* plan view, if necessary.

3. Select the *Elevation* tool from the *View* tab.

In the next step you will place an elevation tag. Before clicking to place the tag, try moving it around to see how Revit automatically turns the tag to point at the closest wall.

4. Select *Elevation:* **Interior Elevation** and then place an elevation tag, looking East, or to the right, in the living room area (Figures 9-3.1a and b).

FIGURE 9-3.1A Element Type Selector

REMEMBER: *The first thing you should do after adding an* Elevation Tag *is to give it an appropriate name in the* Project Browser *list.*

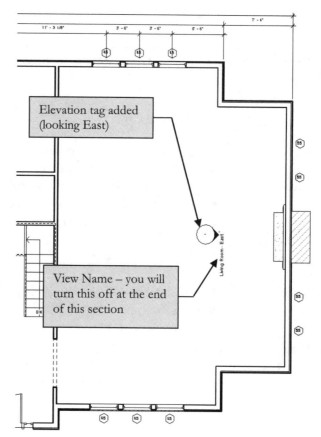

FIGURE 9-3.1B First floor: Elev tag added in Living Rm

5. Change the name of the new elevation to **Living Room – East** in the *Project Browser*.

6. Switch to the ***Living Room – East*** view.

> *TIP: Try double-clicking on the elevation tag, the pointing portion.*

Initially, your elevation should look something like Figure 9-3.2; if not, you will be adjusting it momentarily so do not worry. You will adjust this view next. *Notice how Revit automatically controls the lineweights of things in section versus things in elevations.*

FIGURE 9-3.2 Living Room - East, initial view

7. Switch back to the ***First Floor Plan*** view.

8. Pick the "pointing" portion of the elevation tag, so you see the view options (Figure 9-3.3).

You should compare the two drawings on this page (Figures 9-3.2 and 9-3.3) to see how the control lines in the plan view dictate what is generated and visible in the elevation view for both width and depth.

Revit automatically found the left and right walls, the floor and ceiling in the elevation view.

Notice the *Far Clip Plane* is also acceptable. If you cannot see the fireplace in the elevation view, that means the *Far Clip Plane* needs to be moved farther to the right.

FIGURE 9-3.3 Elevation tag selected

FYI: *The elevation tags are used to reference the sheet and drawing number so the client or contractor can find the desired elevation quickly while looking at the floor plans. This will be covered in a later lesson. It is interesting to know, however, that Revit automatically does this, fills in the elevation tag when the elevation is placed on a sheet and will update it if the elevation is moved.*

9. Switch back to the *Living Room - East* view.

Just to try adjusting the *crop region* to see various results, you will extend the top upward to see the second floor.

10. Select the *cropping region* and drag the top middle grip upward, to increase the view size vertically (Figure 9-3.4).

FIGURE 9-3.4 Living Room - East elevation: crop region selected and modified

Here you are getting a sneak peak ahead to the "sections" portion of this book. Notice that additional level datums were added automatically as the view grew to include more vertical information (i.e., second floor, roof).

11. Now select **Undo** to return to the previous view state (Figure 9-3.2).

As you probably noticed, the interior elevation shows the *Foundation* level datum below the *First Floor* level datum. The *Foundation* level datum is not necessary in this view, so you will remove it from this view.

> **IMPORTANT:** You cannot simply delete the level datum because it will actually delete all related views from the entire project (i.e., floor and ceiling plan views). This will delete any model elements that are hosted by that level (walls, doors, windows) and any tags, notes and dimensions in that view.

To remove a level datum, you select it and tell Revit to hide it in the current view. You will do this next.

12. Click on the horizontal line portion of the *First Floor* level datum.

13. Right-click and select **Hide in View → Elements** from the pop-up menu.

> *TIP: Selecting* Category *would make all level datum elements disappear from the current view.*

14. Adjust the bottom of the *crop region* to align with the *First Floor* level (horizontal line).

15. On the *View Control Bar*, make sure the *View Scale* is set to ¼"=1'-0".

Your elevation should look like Figure 9-3.5.

FIGURE 9-3.5 Living Room - East Elevation

You can leave the *crop region* on to help define the perimeter of the elevation. You can also turn it off; however, some lines that are directly under the *crop region* might disappear. You could use the *Detail Line* tool to manually define the perimeter using a heavy line.

TIP: If perimeter lines disappear when you print interior elevations, try unchecking Hide Crop Regions in the Print dialog, and turn off the ones you don't want to see.

Turning off the View Name on the Elevation Tag:

The interior elevation tag currently has the view name showing (in plan view). You will turn this off as it is not required on the construction drawings.

16. Select **Manage → Settings → Additional Settings** (down-arrow)**→ Elevation Tags**

17. Set the *Type* to ½″ **Circle** (Figure 9-3.6).

18. Select **Elevation Mark Body_Circle: Filled Arrow** from the *Elevation Mark* drop-down list (Figure 9-3.6).

19. Click **OK** to close the dialog box.

The view name is now gone from the *elevation tags* in the floor plan view.

FIGURE 9-3.6 Adjusting the interior elevation tag

FYI: If you right-click on an elevation view name in the Project Browser, you will notice you can Duplicate the view (via Duplicate View → Duplicate). This is similar to how a floor plan is duplicated with one major variation: when an elevation view is duplicated, Revit actually just copies another elevation tag on top of the one being duplicated in the plan view. This is because each elevation view requires its own elevation tag. If two views could exist based on one elevation tag, then Revit would not know how to fill in the drawing number and sheet number if both views are placed on a sheet.

Adding Annotation:

Now you will add a note and dimensions to the interior elevation view.

> 20. Add the (2) dimensions and (1) text (3/32″ text style) with leader shown in Figure 9-3.7.

FIGURE 9-3.7 Living Room - East elevation: annotation added

It is possible to add *Detail Lines* to this view to represent baseboard or other details such as wall bracing. This is often done for finer details which are not modeled. This approach helps with model performance, but will not show up in sections or renderings.

> 21. On the *View Control Bar*, set the **View Scale** to ½″=1′-0″.

Notice the text and dimensions automatically resize to match the new scale. When space permits, most residential interior elevations are ½″ = 1′-0″.

> 22. Save your project as **ex9-3.rvt**.

Exercise 9-4:
Modifying the Project Model: Interior Elevations

This short exercise, similar to Exercise 9-2, will look at an example of Revit's parametric change engine. All drawings are generated from one 3D model.

Modify the Interior Elevations:

1. Open ex9-3.rvt and **Save As ex9-4.rvt**.

2. Open the *Living Room - East* elevation view.

You will move the windows and add an exterior door.

3. Select both of the windows on the right; use the **Ctrl** key to select multiple objects at one time.

4. Use the *Move* tool to move the windows 6″ to the right, or South.

5. Repeat the previous steps to *Move* the other two windows 6″ towards the left, or North.

6. In the *Living Room - East* elevation view, use the *Door* tool to place a **Single Entry 3: 32″ x 84″** door in the wall to the far left (North). See Figure 9-4.1.

FIGURE 9-4.1 Living Room - East - modified

You moved the windows out from the mantel so they provide a little more space between them. Revit allows you to design in all views!

You should notice, in Figure 9-4.1, that the door bottom is below the floor level; this is a problem only if your cursor was near the bottom of the wall when you clicked. You will fix it next.

7. Select the new door in the *Living Room – East* view.

8. In *Properties*, change the **level** from *Foundation* to ***First Floor*** if needed.

The interior elevation should now look correct (Figure 9-4.2).

FIGURE 9-4.2 Living Room - East elevation: door height adjusted

Notice, back in the *Properties Palette* for the new door, a setting called *Sill Height*. This setting allows you to move the door vertically, relative to the specified level. For example, you might have a second floor door that opens onto a low roof, but the door needs to be 1'-0" above the second floor for this door to work correctly (roof insulation, flashing, etc.). You simply select the door and adjust its *Sill Height* to 1'-0", with the level set to *Second Floor* via the *Properties Palette*.

Now it is time to see the effects to the plan views.

9. Switch to the ***First Floor Plan*** view (Figure 9-4.3).

When placing a door in elevation, you may have to switch to plan view to verify the door swing is the way you want it. You can control the door swing in elevation: right-click and select "flip hand" or "flip facing."

In elevation, you can adjust many things this way. Some examples are ceiling height, interior and exterior windows, wall locations, perpendicular to the current view, etc.

Notice that the door does not have a door tag like the other doors in the plan view. This is because the door was not placed in this view. You will learn how to add this tag later.

Added door

FIGURE 9-4.3 First Floor plan with changes

10. Save your project as **ex9-4**.

Exercise 9-5:
Design Options

This exercise will look at a feature called *Design Options*. This feature allows you to present two or more options for a portion of your design without having to save a copy of your project and end up having to maintain more than one project until the preferred design option is selected.

Design Options Overview:

A Revit project can have several design option studies at any given time; you might have an (A) entry porch options study, (B) a kitchen options study and a (C) master bedroom furniture layout options study in a project. Each of these studies can have several design options associated with them. For example, the entry porch study might have three options: 1. flat roof, 2. shed roof and 3. shed roof with a dormer type embellishment.

A particular study of an area within your project is called a *Design Option Set*, and the different designs associated with a *Design Options Set* are each called an *Option*. Both the *Design Options Set* and the *Options* can be named (see the examples below).

One of the *Options* in a *Design Option Set* is specified as the *Primary* option (the others are called *Secondary Options*); this is the option that is shown by default in all new and existing views. However, you can adjust the *Visibility* of a *View* to show a different option. Typically you would duplicate a *View*, adjust the *Visibility*, and *Rename* it to have each option at your finger-tips.

When the preferred design is selected by you and/or the owner, you set that *Option* to *Primary*. Finally, you select a tool called *Accept Primary* which deletes the *Secondary Options* and the *Design Option Set*, leaving the *Primary Option* as part of the main building model.

Design Option Set

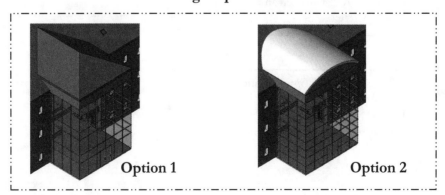

Option 1   Option 2

The following images (Figures 9-5.1a and b) provide an overview of the *Design Options* dialog box and *Status Bar* tools. See Step 2 to access this dialog.

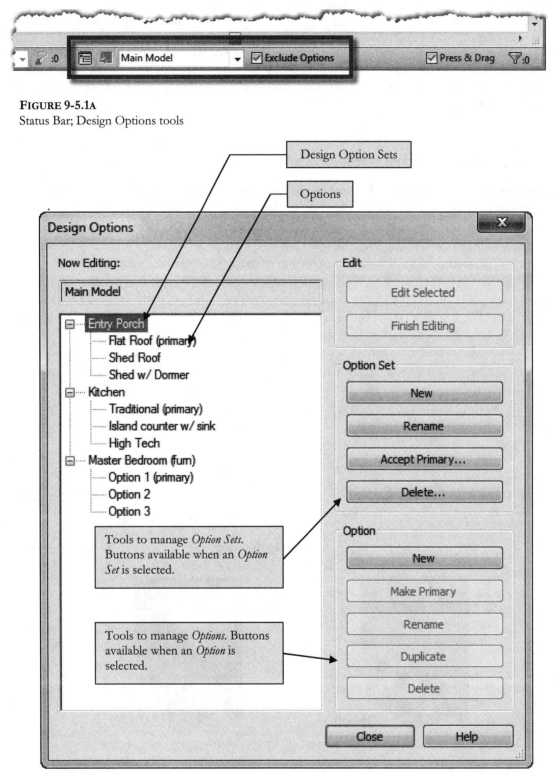

FIGURE 9-5.1A
Status Bar; Design Options tools

FIGURE 9-5.1B Design Options Dialog

Notes about the *Design Options* dialog box:

Edit buttons:
You can edit a *Design Option* by selecting an *Option* (in the window area on the left) and then clicking the **Edit Selected** button. Next you add, move and delete elements in that *Design Option*.

When finished editing a *Design Option*, you reopen the *Design Options* dialog and click the **Finish Editing** button.

If you are currently in an *Option Editing* mode, the *Now Editing* area in the *Design Options* dialog displays the *Option* name being modified; otherwise it displays *Main Model*.

Option Set buttons:
The **New** button is always available. You can quickly set up several *Option Sets*. Each time you create a new *Option Set*, Revit automatically creates a *Primary Option* named *Option 1*.

The other buttons are only available when an *Option Set* label is highlighted (i.e., selected) in the window list on the left.

The **Accept Primary** button causes the *Primary Option* of the selected set to become a normal part of the building model and deletes the set and secondary options. This is a way of "cleaning house" by getting rid of unnecessary information which helps to better manage the project and keeps the file size down.

Option buttons:
These buttons are only available when an *Option* (primary or secondary) is selected within an *Option Set*. You can quickly set up several *Options* without having to immediately add any content (i.e., walls, components, etc.) to them.

The **Make Primary** button allows you to change the status of a *Secondary Option* to *Primary*. As previously mentioned, the *Primary Option* is the *Option* that is shown by default in existing and new views. You can only have one *Primary* option in an *Option Set*.

The **Duplicate** button will copy all the elements in the selected *Option* into a new *Option*; this makes the file larger because you are technically adding additional content to the project. You can then use the copied elements (e.g., walls, furniture, etc.) as a starting point for the next design option. This is handy if the various options are similar.

Now you will put this introductory knowledge to use!

Setting up a Design Option Set:

In this exercise you will create two *Design Option Sets*: one for the Main Entry Roof and another for the windows above the Entry Door. You will create an alternate roof and window design for your project.

You could just create one *Design Option Set* and have two design options total. However, by placing the roof options in one *Option Set* and the windows in another, you actually get four design options total; you can mix and match the window and roof options.

Setting up Design Options in Your Project:

First you will set up the *Option Sets* and *Options*.

1. Open ex9-4.rvt and **Save As ex9-5.rvt**.

2. Click the **Design Options** icon on the *Status Bar* (Figure 9-5.1a).

You are now in the *Design Options* dialog box (Figure 9-5.2). Your dialog will look like this one, basically empty:

3. In the *Option Set* area click **New**.

FIGURE 9-5.2 Design Options Dialog; initial view

Notice an *Option Set* named *Option Set 1* has been created. Revit also automatically created the *Primary Option* named *Option 1* (Figure 9-5.3). Next you will rename the *Option Set* to something that is easier to recognize.

FIGURE 9-5.3 Design Options dialog; new option set created

4. Select the *Option Set* currently named *Option Set 1* and then click the **Rename** button in the *Option Set* area.

    WARNING! *Be sure you are not renaming the* Option *but rather the* Option Set.

5. In the *Rename* dialog type: **Entry Windows** (Figure 9-5.4).

6. Click **OK** to rename.

Giving the *Option Set* a name that is easy to recognize helps in managing the various options later, especially if you have several.

Next you will create a *Secondary Option* for the *Entry Windows* option set.

FIGURE 9-5.4 Rename Option Set dialog

7. With the *Entry Windows* option set selected, click **New** in the *Option* area (Figure 9-5.5).

Notice a secondary *Option* was created and automatically named *Option 2*. If you have descriptive names for the options in a set, you should apply them. In this example you can leave them as they are.

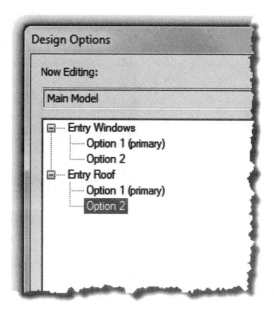

FIGURE 9-5.5
Design Options dialog; secondary option created

FIGURE 9-5.6
Design Options dialog

8. Create an *Option Set* for the roof (Figure 9-5.6):
   a. Name the set ***Entry Roof***
   b. Create a secondary option

The basic thinking with the *Design Options* feature is that you set up the *Option Set* and *Option*s and then start drawing the elements related to the current *Option*. So, you select the *Option* from the drop-down list on the *Status Bar*, make the additions and modifications relative to that *Design Option*, and finally switch the drop-down back to *Main Model* to finish editing the option and then be able to make changes in the main model.

However, in your case, you want to move content already drawn to *Option 1*. Revit has a feature that allows you to move content to a *Design Option Set*, which means the content gets copied to the *Options* in the *Set* you select.

Entry Windows Design Option:

You are now ready to set up the different design options.

9. Close the *Design Options* dialog and switch to the **3D** view; adjust the view so you are looking at the main entry (South elevation).

Unfortunately, you cannot just select the windows and add them to a *Design Option Set* because they are hosted elements that require a wall to be inserted in. Therefore, you will also add the entry walls and door to the *Design Option Set*.

10. **Select** the three walls at the main entry, three windows and main entry door; orbit as required.

11. Click the **Add to Set** icon on the *Status Bar*.

12. Select *Entry Windows* from the dialog drop-down and then click **OK** (Figure 9-5.7).

The selected items are now in both *Option 1* and *Option 2* under the option set *Entry Windows* because both options were selected in the previous dialog, Figure 9-5.7.

Add to Design Option Set

Add selection to:

Entry Windows

☑ Option 1 (primary)
☑ Option 2

OK   Cancel   Help

FIGURE 9-5.7 Add to Design Option Set Dialog

From this point forward you can only modify the entry windows, door and walls when in *Option 1* or *Option 2 Edit* mode. In which case, the tables are turned and you cannot edit the main building model; this is because *Active Only* is checked on the *Status Bar*.

13. In the **Design Options** drop-down list, on the *Status Bar*, select **Entry Windows: Option 2** as shown in the image below.

Main Model — ☑ Exclude Options

Main Model
Entry Windows
Option 1 (primary)
Option 2
Entry Roof
Option 1 (primary)
Option 2

Now you should notice that the main building model is slightly grey and not editable; it is not editable because *Active Only* is selected on the *Status Bar*. All hosted elements for the wall were also moved into the *Design Option*; three windows and a door in this case. You will change the windows per Figure 9-5.8.

14. Zoom in on the main entry, particularly the second floor window area in your **3D** view.

15. Select the three windows above the main entry door and change their type to **Double Hung with Trim: 16″ x 72″** from the *Type Selector*.

16. Make sure the window head (i.e., top) is at **7′-0″** via the *Properties Palette* for the selected windows.

17. Change the *Design Options* drop-down list, on the *Status Bar*, back to **Main Model**.

FIGURE 9-5.8 3D View: second floor windows modified

It now appears like all your changes disappeared, right? Well, if you recall from the introduction to this exercise, the *Primary Option* is displayed by default for all new and existing views. So when you finished editing *Entry Windows: Option 2* the *3D* view switched back to the *Primary Option*, which is currently set to *Option 1* (Figure 9-5.6).

Next, you will create a new view and adjust its *Visibility* to display *Option 2* of the *Entry Windows* options set.

First you will create a duplicate copy of the *3D* view.

18. In the *Project Browser*, under *3D Views*, right-click on the **{3D}** label.

19. Select **Duplicate View → Duplicate** from the pop-up menu.

You now have a copy of the *3D* view named *Copy of {3D}*.

20. **Rename** the new 3D view to *Entry Windows Option 2.*

21. Switch to your new view, if needed.

22. Select **View → Graphics → Visibility/Graphics** (or type **VV**).

23. Click on the **Design Options** tab at the top of the dialog.

24. Change the *Design Option* parameter for *Entry Windows* to **Option 2** (Figure 9-5.9).

FIGURE 9-5.9 Visibility/Graphic Overrides dialog: modified Entry Windows design option visibility

25. Click **OK** to close the dialog.

Now, with the *Default 3D* view and the *Entry Windows: Option 2* view, you can quickly switch between design options. Both views could be placed on the same sheet and printed out for a design critique.

Entry Roof Design Option:

Now you will add an option for a roof over the entry door.

26. Select *Entry Roof: Option 2* from the *Design Options* drop-down list on the *Status Bar*.

You will add a roof shortly.

27. Switch to the **South** elevation view.

28. Zoom in to the area below the entry windows, just above the front door.

Next you will create an *in-place family* to represent a curved roof option over the entry area. Basically, you will create a solid by specifying a depth and then drawing a profile of the curved roof with lines.

29. Click **Architecture → Build → Component (down-arrow) → Model In-Place**.

Immediately, you are prompted to select a *Family Category*. This allows Revit to understand how other elements should interact with the object(s) you are about to create and control visibility.

30. Select **Roofs** from the *Family Category* list (Figure 9-5.10).

31. Click **OK**.

Now you are prompted to provide a name for the new *in-place family*.

FIGURE 9-5.10 Family Category and Parameters dialog

32. For the family *Name*, type **Entry Roof** (Figure 9-5.11).

FIGURE 9-5.11 Family name prompt

You are now in a mode where you draw the *Entry Roof*. Notice that the *Ribbon* has changed to have special buttons on the *Architecture* tab which has all the tools needed to create a family. You are continuously in the *Model In-Place* mode until you select *Finish Model* (green check mark) or *Quit Model* (red x) from the *Ribbon*.

FIGURE 9-5.12 Form Ribbon; select Extrude

You will now select the type of solid you wish to create.

33. Select **Architecture → Forms → Extrusion**.

Finally, you are prompted to select a plane in which to start drawing the profile of the solid to be extruded. Even though the view is a 2D representation of a 3D model, Revit needs to know where you want the 3D solid created so it knows how to show it in other views (both 2D representations and 3D). You will select the entry wall as a reference surface to establish a working plane.

34. Select **Pick a Plane** and click **OK** (Figure 9-5.13).

FIGURE 9-5.13 Work Plane dialog; select Pick a Plane

35. Move the cursor near the edge of the entry wall and then click to select it.

> *TIP: If needed, click the Tab key until a heavy line appears around the perimeter of the wall. Then click the mouse to select (Figure 9-5.14). Do not hold the Tab key down.*

Hover cursor here and press the Tab key until the wall is highlighted as shown.

(Entry Windows : Option 1) : Walls : Basic Wall : Exterior - Wood Shingle over Wood Siding on Wood Stud : Reference

FIGURE 9-5.14 South Elevation; select wall to establish work plane

Next, you will draw an arc to specify the bottom edge of the curved roof design option. Notice the *Ribbon* changed again to show tools related to drawing an extruded solid.

36. On the *Options Bar*, enter **2'-0"** for the **Depth** (Figure 9-5.15).

> *FYI: A negative number for the depth would cause the solid to project in towards the building from the work plane.*

Depth 2' 0"   ☑ Chain Offset: 0' 0"   ☐ Radius: 1' 0"

37. Click the **Start – End – Radius Arc** icon from the *Draw* panel on the contextual tab: *Modify | Create Extrusion*.

38. Pick the three points shown in Figure 9-5.15 to draw the arc. The angle 71.343° is not critical; get as close as possible. The ends of the arc are approximately straight up from the edge of the entry door below.

TIP: Try typing SO *before clicking the third point to temporarily turn off the Snaps for one pick (SO = Snap Off).*

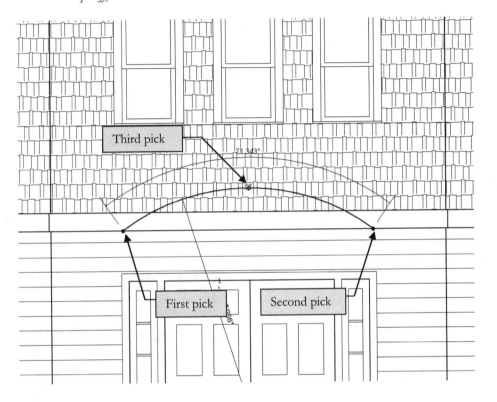

FIGURE 9-5.15 South Elevation; drawing arc to define roof

Now you will draw another arc 7¼″ above the previous one.

39. Press **Esc** on the *Options Bar*, and with the *Start-End-Radius Arc* still selected, enter **0 7.25** for the *Offset*.

40. Draw another **Arc** picking the same three points; be sure to snap to the end points and midpoint of the previous arc (Figure 9-5.15).

Notice that an arc is drawn offset 7¼″ from the points you picked. If you pick the first two points in the other direction, the arc would be offset in the other direction, downward in this case.

Next, you will draw two short lines to connect the endpoints of the two arcs. This will create a closed area, which is required before finishing the sketch. Think of it this way: you need to completely define at least two dimensions before Revit can create the third.

41. Click the "straight line" icon on the *Draw* panel (see image on previous page); this will switch you from drawing arcs back to drawing straight line segments. Set the *Offset* back to **0″**.

42. Zoom in and sketch a short line on each end of the arc as shown in Figure 9-5.16; be sure to use your *Endpoint* snaps (type SE).

FIGURE 9-5.16 South elevation; two arcs and two short lines define roof profile

43. Click the **green checkmark** from the *Ribbon*.

> **TIP:** *If you get any warnings, it may be because one or more of the profile's corners do not create a perfect intersection; zoom in to see and use the Trim tool to close the corners. Delete any stray lines.*

You are still in the *Model In-Place Family* mode. Before you finish you will apply a material to the roof element.

44. Click the roof to select it.

45. In the *Properties Palette*, click in the *Material* value field and then click the "**...**" icon that appears.

The *Materials* dialog opens.

46. Select **Roofing, Metal** from the list of predefined *Materials* (i.e., the AEC Materials library). See Fig 9-5.17.

> **FYI:** *Notice the Appearance asset material is set to anodized aluminum with a dark bronze color for Metal – Roofing.*

47. Click **OK** to close the *Materials* dialog.

You are now ready to finish the family.

Finish Model

48. From the *Ribbon* click **Finish Model**.

FIGURE 9-5.17 Materials dialog
Step one, in the image, toggles the visibility of the external Autodesk material library. You need to see this library in order to load materials from it into your model.

Next you will move the roof down a little. At this point, the only "mode" you are in is for editing the *Entry Roof: Option 2*.

49. Click on the roof to select it.

50. Use the arrow keys on the keyboard to nudge the roof element down until it looks similar to Figure 9-5.18.

FIGURE 9-5.18 South elevation; roof element moved to a lower position

Notice the arrow-grips on each end of the roof element when it is selected? Clicking one of these grips allows you to extend that solid perpendicular to the arrow. Try it; just *Undo* (Ctrl+Z) when you are done experimenting. It works better on rectilinear objects.

You are now ready to finish editing the current design option for the time being.

51. Set the *Design Options* drop-down back to **Main Model**.

As before, the option you were just working on was not the *Primary Option* in the *Entry Roof* design set, so the current view reverted back to *Entry Roof: Option 1*, which is the primary view.

You will create a 3D view that has *Option 2* set to be visible for both the *Entry Window* option set and the *Entry Roof* option set.

52. Right-click on the **Default 3D** view and click **Duplicate View → Duplicate**.

53. Rename the duplicated view to **Entry – Option 2**.

54. Switch to the new view (*Entry – Option 2*); you should already be in that view.

55. Click **Visibility/Graphics** from the *View* tab (or type **VV**).

56. On the *Design Options* tab, set both *Option Sets* to ***Option 2*** in the *Design Option* column.

57. Click **OK** to close the dialog.

FIGURE 9-5.19 Entry – Option 2 view with shadows on

You can now see a 3D view of your new entry roof option. The previous image has shadows turned on. This can provide a very dramatic result with almost no extra effort. The shadows can be useful while designing; however, you will probably have them turned off most of the time just to maintain system performance.

To turn on shadows, you simply click the *Shadows* toggle icon on the *View Control Bar* at the bottom of the screen.

Because the new entry roof element is a roof to Revit, you can attach walls to it, meaning a wall top would conform to the underside of the curved roof.

Another entry roof option might be a more traditional shed type porch roof like the one shown above. You might try adding this roof to the *Option 1* place holder. Simply sketch a roof by footprint, with only the South edge set to *Defines slope*.

58. **Save** your project as **ex9-5.rvt**.

TIP: The Design Options feature can also be used to manage alternates, where both the base bid and the alternate(s) need to be drawn.

Self-Exam:

The following questions can be used as a way to check your knowledge of this lesson. The answers can be found at the bottom of the page.

1. The plan is updated automatically when an elevation is modified, but not the other way around. (T/F)

2. You can use the *Elevation* tool to place both interior and exterior elevations. (T/F)

3. You can rename elevation views to better manage them. (T/F)

4. You have to resize the level datums and annotations after changing a view's scale. (T/F)

5. How do you enter 5½" without entering the foot or inch symbol? _____

Review Questions:

The following questions may be assigned by your instructor as a way to assess your knowledge of this section. Your instructor has the answers to the review questions.

1. The visibility of the *crop region* can be controlled. (T/F)

2. You **have to** manually adjust the lineweights in the elevations. (T/F)

3. As you move the cursor around the building, during placement, the elevation tag turns to point at the building. (T/F)

4. There is only one part of the elevation tag that can be selected. (T/F)

5. You cannot adjust the "extent of view" using the *crop region*. (T/F)

6. What is the first thing you should do after placing an elevation tag?

   _____

7. Although they make the drawing look very interesting, using

   the _____ feature can cause Revit to run extremely slow.

8. With the elevation tag selected, you can use the _____ icon to adjust the tag orientation to look at an angled wall.

9. You need to adjust the _____ to see objects, in elevation, that are a distance back from the main elevation.

10. What feature allows you to develop different ideas? _____

Lesson 10
Residence: SECTIONS:

Sections are one of the main communication tools in a set of architectural drawings. They help the builder understand vertical relationships. Architectural sections can occasionally contradict other drawings, such as mechanical or structural drawings. One example is a beam shown on the section is smaller than what the structural drawings call for; this creates a problem in the field when the duct does not fit in the ceiling space. The ceiling gets lowered and/or the duct gets smaller, ultimately compromising the design to a certain degree.

Autodesk® Revit® takes great steps toward eliminating these types of conflicts. Sections, like plans and elevations, are generated from the 3D model. So it is virtually impossible to have a conflict between the architectural drawings. Many structural, mechanical and electrical engineers are starting to use Autodesk Revit for even greater coordination; this is helping to eliminate conflicts and redundancy in drawing.

The disc has a video on sections you should take the time to review.

Exercise 10-1:
Specify Section Cutting Plane in Plan View

Similar to elevation tags, placing the section "graphics" in a plan view actually generates the section view. You will learn how to do this next.

Placing Section Marks:

1. Open ex9-5.rvt and **Save As ex10-1.rvt**.

2. Switch to the *First Floor* plan view.

3. Select **View → Create → Section**.

   Section

   TIP: You may also select the Section icon from the Quick Access Toolbar, which would be more convenient.

4. Draw a **Section** mark as shown in Figure 10-1.1. Start on the left side in this case. Use the *Move* tool if needed to accurately adjust the section after insertion. The section line should go through the stair landings (Figure 10-1.1).

FIGURE 10-1.1 Section mark (selected)

You can see that the *Far Clip Plane* location in the plan view is out past the building perimeter; this means you will see everything (Figure 10-1.1). Anything passing through the section line is in section; everything else you see is in elevation (Revit calls it "projection"). Also, you can see the roof is shown in section exactly where the section line is shown in plan. Figure 10-1.2 also shows the *crop region*.

The *Section* tool is almost exactly like the *Elevation* tool.

FIGURE 10-1.2 Longitudinal section view

Notice in the *Project Browser* that a new category has been created: *Sections (building Section)*. If you expand this category, you will see the new section view listed; it is called *Section 1*. You should always rename any new view right after creating it. This will help with navigation and when it comes time to place views on sheets for printing.

5.   Rename section view *Section 1* to **Longitudinal Section**.

6.   Switch to the new section view, **Longitudinal Section**.

> *TIP: Double-click on the section bubble head to open that view. The section needs to be unselected first; double-click on the blue part.*

7.   Change the *View Properties* so the *Detail Level* is set to **Medium**.

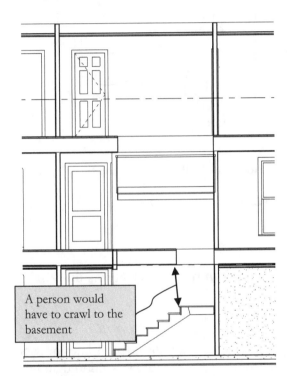

A person would have to crawl to the basement

Notice how the walls change to show more detail. You can set this on the *View Control Bar* at the bottom of the screen.

8.   Zoom in on the portion of the section through the stairs.

You should notice an added level of detail in the section view.

You may also notice a big problem, as first mentioned on page 8-10: in Figure 10-1.3, the stair to the basement is obstructed by the first floor system. You will fix this soon.

The image below lists the additional terms related to the section mark graphics in the plan view, as compared to elevation tags.

FIGURE 10-1.3 Section view – zoomed in

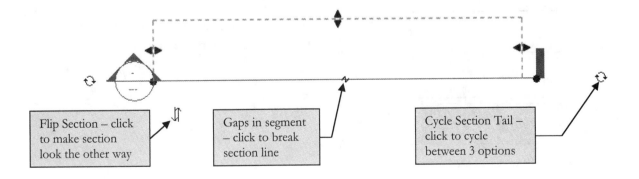

Flip Section – click to make section look the other way

Gaps in segment – click to break section line

Cycle Section Tail – click to cycle between 3 options

9. Create another **section** in the *First Floor* plan view as shown in **Figure 10-1.4**.

   TIP: You can use the control arrows to make the section look the other direction.

FIGURE 10-1.4 Plan view; Section tag (selected)

10. Rename the new section view to **Cross Section 1** in the *Project Browser*.

11. Switch to the **Cross Section 1** view.

12. Set the *Detail Level* to **Medium** and turn off the **crop region** visibility via the *View Control Bar* (Figure 10-1.5).

FIGURE 10-1.5 Cross Section 1 view

Revit automatically displays lines heavier for elements that are in section than for elements beyond the cutting plane and shown in elevation.

Also, with the *Detail Level* set to *Medium*, the walls and floors are hatched to represent the material in section.

Notice that the *Longitudinal Section* mark is automatically displayed in the *Cross Section 1* view. If you switch to the *Longitudinal Section* view, you will see the *Cross Section 1* mark. Keeping with Revit's philosophy of changing everything anywhere, you can select the section mark in the other section view and adjust its various properties, like its *Far Clip Plane*.

FYI: In any view that has a section mark in it, you can double-click on the round reference bubble to quickly switch to that section view. However, the section cannot be selected.

Modifying the First Floor Stair Opening:

Next, you will fix the problem with the stair opening in the first floor system. Basically, you will switch to the *First Floor Plan* view and select the floor. Then you will click *Edit Boundary* from the *Ribbon* and modify the sketch so the stair opening is larger.

13. Switch to the **First Floor** plan view.

14. Select the floor; use *Tab* if required to highlight the floor element for selection.

    TIP: You can also toggle on Select Element by Face on the Status Bar and select the floor anywhere within its boundary.

15. Click **Edit Boundary** on the *Ribbon* (see image below).

16. Use the *Line* and *Edit* tools, such as *Split* and *Trim*, to modify the sketch of the floor opening as shown in Figure 10-1.6.

17. Click the **green check mark** and choose **No** to the *attach walls* prompt.

18. Switch back to the **Longitudinal Section** view.

Notice the stair no longer has a problem (Figure 10-1.7).

19. **Save** your project as **ex10-1.rvt**.

FIGURE 10-1.6 Plan view – Floor, sketch edit

FIGURE 10-1.7 Longitudinal view – First floor element modified

Exercise 10-2:
Modifying the Project Model in Section View

Again, similar to elevation views, you can modify the project model in section view. This includes adjusting door locations and ceiling heights.

Modifying Doors in Section View:

In this section you will move a door and delete a door in section view.

1. Open ex10-1.rvt and **Save As ex10-2.rvt**.

2. Open *Cross Section 1* view.

Looking back to Figure 10-1.5, you should notice the wall below the basement stair still extends up through the stair. You will move the wall over in the section view and then note that the adjacent wall and ceilings all automatically adjust in other views.

3. Use the *Align* tool to make the wall align with the edge of the floor opening (Figure 10-2.1).

    TIP: Pick the edge of the floor first and then the face of the wall to align with the selected edge.

FIGURE 10-2.1 Cross Section 1 view; wall below stair moved

4. Switch to the ***Basement*** <u>ceiling plan</u> view.

Notice the wall below the stair moved South and the ceiling automatically adjusted as well (Figure 10-2.2).

As long as a wall that defines the perimeter of a ceiling does not get deleted or shortened so that the ceiling perimeter is no longer defined, Revit will automatically update the ceiling. If the perimeter does become undefined, you may have to edit it manually. **Avoid deleting objects** just to redraw them because "hosted" elements, such as lights and dimensions, will be deleted.

Next, looking at Figure 10-2.1, you see that the arched opening in the basement is too tall; you will make it shorter. This will require a new *Type* within the *Opening-Elliptical Arch* family.

FIGURE 10-2.2 Basement Floor Plan view; notice changes

5. Switch back to **Cross Section 1**.

6. **Select** the **arched opening** in the basement.

7. Click **Edit Type** on the *Properties Palette* and then **Duplicate**.

8. Enter **60″ x 80″** for the name.

9. Change the **Height** *Parameter* to **6′-8″** (Figure 10-2.3).

10. Click **OK** to close the open dialog box.

Your arched opening should now look like Figure 10-2.4 in *Cross Section 1* view. This change would not be apparent in a plan view because the only change was to the opening's height.

FIGURE 10-2.3 Changing the arched opening height

FIGURE 10-2.4 Cross Section 1 view; arched opening modified

Next you will adjust a ceiling height via your *Longitudinal Section* view.

11. Switch to **Longitudinal Section** view.

12. At the basement level, select the suspended acoustical ceiling tile system in the *Family Room* (lower right room).

Notice that while a ceiling is selected in a section view, a temporary dimension appears. This dimension allows you to directly change the ceiling height.

FYI: The dimension may be overlapping a wall.

13. Change the ceiling height to **6'-8"** using the temporary dimension. If required, adjust the witness lines to go from the top of the basement floor slab to the bottom of the ceiling.

Now, as you can see in the section view (Figure 10-2.5), the ceiling has lowered and there is more room for the recessed light fixtures shown; notice the lights lowered automatically.

FIGURE 10-2.5 Cross Section 1 view; ceiling height modified

Adding the Strip Footing Below the Foundation Wall:

A strip footing, in Revit, can be just a wall type set up as concrete. The width of the "wall" is set to be the width of your footing, as is the height. Revit provides a predefined wall and plan view in the residential template; this makes it very easy.

14. Switch to the plan view called ***T.O. Footing***.

    FYI: *T.O. means "Top Of," i.e., "Top Of Footing."*

15. Select the ***Wall*** tool and then select *Basic Wall:* ***24″ Footing*** from the *Type Selector*.

16. Set the *Location Line* to **Wall Centerline** and make sure the *Depth* is set to **B.O. Footing** (i.e., Bottom of Footing) on the *Options Bar*.

17. Select **Chain** on the *Options Bar*.

18. Start picking the intersection of wall centerlines, working around the perimeter of the building; also add a footing below the wall between the garage and the house. You want the 24″ footing to be centered on the foundation wall (Figure 10-2.6).

    TIP: *Setting the Location Line to Wall Centerline is for the wall you are about to draw. Revit will automatically "snap" to the centers of walls previously drawn. Hover your cursor over the center of the wall until you see a dashed magenta/purple reference line, letting you know you are snapped to the center of the wall, and then move your cursor towards the end of that wall/purple reference line and click.*

After drawing the footings, you will notice the interior side of the footing will disappear because it is below the basement floor slab; it is visible in the garage area because it is unexcavated.

Figure 10-2.6 T.O. Footing view; 24″ footing added

19. Switch back to the section view *Cross Section 1*.

As you can see (Figure 10-2.7), the footings have been added.

FIGURE 10-2.7 Cross Section 1 view (modified)

If you look at the properties for the 24″ footing wall type, you can see how the wall was created relative to the *T.O. Footing* view in which you drew it.

Notice the *Base* and *Top Constraints* are selected. The *Base Constraint* is set to *B.O. Footing* and the *Top Constraint* is set to *Up to level: T.O. Footing.* Also notice the *Unconnected Height* is grayed-out, meaning you cannot change this setting, which makes sense seeing as you have defined both the top and bottom of the wall.

The distance between the two levels is 1′-0″, so the footing is 1′-0″ high.

In *Cross Section 1* view, try clicking on the *B.O. Footing* text (i.e., the -10′-3″ text) and change it to -11′-3″ and notice the footing size will automatically change.

Figure 10-2.8 Properties for 24″ Footing wall

If you try this, make sure you *UNDO* so that when you finish this exercise your footing is only 1′-0″ thick (see image to the right).

Adding the Strip Footing Using the Foundation Tool on the Structure tab:

Revit offers another tool to add continuous strip footings below your foundation wall. On the *Foundation* panel (on the *Structure* tab) you can select the **Wall Foundation** tool. Then you simply select foundation walls and Revit automatically places a footing, centered, and directly under the wall. If you want to try this option, you can delete a portion of footing and use the *Structure* tool to replace it. If you try this, make sure you *Undo* before proceeding.

Modifying the Footing Linework in Plan View:

Revit has predefined settings for line styles and lineweights. Most of the time, the developers have selected settings that will be satisfactory to most designers, which is great because this saves much time. However, you will occasionally want to tweak these prescribed settings. As mentioned in the previous chapter, Revit makes this easy with the *Linework* tool on the *Modify* tab. Basically, you select the *Linework* icon, select the desired setting from the *Type Selector* (e.g., lineweight or line style) and then select the lines to change. This change only applies to the current view.

You will try this next, switching the footing lines to dashed.

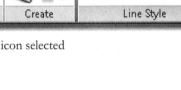

20. Switch back to the ***T.O. Footing*** view.

21. Select **Modify → View → Linework**.

22. Select **Hidden** from the *Line Style Panel* on the *Ribbon* (Figure 10-2.9).

23. Click all the visible footing lines. Click Ctrl+Z if you pick another line by accident; that will *Undo* the previous pick.

Figure 10-2.9 Linework icon selected

The footing lines are now the hidden line style (i.e., dashed) in the current view (Figure 10-2.10).

24. Save your project as **ex10-2.rvt**.

FIGURE 10-2.10 Footing lines dashed

*FYI: The Linework tool will work on most lines generated by the model that are visible in a view. In the above example, the **Filter** feature of Revit might be more appropriate because you can set up a view to make all the walls with the word "footing" in the name be dashed; this is just one example of how Filter can be used. This will affect current walls and future walls that are visible in the current view. This filter can then be applied to other views if desired.*

Stepped Footings:

Foundation walls and footings often need to step on sloped sites and around utilities. This is a little more work to set up in Revit but is still very doable. You will not actually do this at this time, but the concept will be covered here to get you started in the right direction when the time comes that you need to implement this type of design.

Basically, you *Split* the footings where the steps occur and edit the vertical position of each section of footing.

You do not need to Split the foundation wall; you will see why in a moment.

- In elevation or plan view, use the **Split** tool to break the footings up where each step needs to occur.

FIGURE 10-2.11
Footing Split and heights adjusted

- Modify the *Base* and *Top Constraints* as required for each wall so they are in the correct position vertically (Figure 10-2.11).

- In an elevation or section view, select the foundation wall and pick the **Edit Profile** button on the *Ribbon*.

- Use the **Lines** tool, on the *Ribbon*, and any of the edit tools (*Split, Trim, Mirror,* etc.) to redefine the perimeter of the wall in elevation. Modify the bottom magenta sketch line to follow the tops of the footings. Click **Finish Edit Mode** (i.e., green checkmark) when done (Figure 10-2.12).

FIGURE 10-2.12
Foundation wall modified (via Edit Profile)

- Using the same technique as for the footing "wall" (i.e., *Edit Profile*), you can edit the profile of the footings so they appear correctly in elevation making sure the adjacent edges touch.

- When you **Finish Edit Mode** on the footings, you should see the footings join together and appear monolithic. If not, you can use the **Join Geometry** tool unless the edges do not touch perfectly, in which case you need to use *Edit Profile* again and fix the problem.

FIGURE 10-2.13
Footing "wall" modified (via Edit Profile)

Exercise 10-3:
Wall Sections

So far in this lesson you have drawn building sections. Building sections are typically ⅛″ or ¼″ scale and light on the detail and notes. Wall sections are drawn at a larger scale and have much more detail. You will look at setting up wall sections next.

Setting up the Wall Section View:

1. Open ex10-2 and **Save As ex10-3.rvt**.

2. Switch to the *Cross Section 1* view.

Callout

3. From the *View* tab on the *Ribbon*, click the rectangular **Callout** tool and then select *Section:* **Wall Section** from the *Type Selector*.

4. Place a **Callout** as shown in Figure 10-3.1.

   TIP: Pick in the upper left and then in the lower right to place the Callout tag; do not drag.

   TIP: You can use the control grips *for the Callout tag to move the reference bubble if desired; for example, move it way from notes/dimensions.*

FIGURE 10-3.1 Cross Section 1 view with Callout added

Notice that a view was added in the *Sections (Wall Section)* category of the *Project Browser*. Because *Callouts* are detail references off of a section view, it is a good idea to keep the new callout view name similar to the name of the section.

Additionally, *Callouts* differ from section views in that the callout is not referenced in every related view. This example is typical, in that the building sections are referenced from the plans, and wall sections are referenced from the building sections. The floor plans can get pretty messy if you try to add too much information to them.

5. Double-click on the reference bubble portion of the *Callout* tag to open the **Callout of Cross Section 1** view (Figure 10-3.2).

Notice, down on the *View Control Bar*, that the scale is set to ½″ = 1'-0″. This affects the elevation tags, text, datums and any annotation you add.

6. On the *View Control Bar* set:
   a) *View Scale* to **¾″ = 1'-0″**
   b) *Detail Level* to **Fine**.

Notice the level datum's size changed.

If you zoom in on a portion of the *Callout* view, you can see the detail added to the view. The wall's interior lines are added and the materials in section are hatched (see Figure 10-3.4, at the second floor line).

You can use the *Detail Lines* tool to add more detailed information to the drawing. For example, you could show the truss, wall base, and flashing. Walls can be configured to have wall bases, which are set up as sweeps.

FIGURE 10-3.2 Callout of Cross Section 1

As before, you can turn off and adjust the *crop region*. If you set the *Detail Level* to **Coarse**, you get just an outline of your structure. The *Coarse* setting is more appropriate for building sections than wall sections. Figure 10-3.3 is an example of the *Coarse* setting.

FIGURE 10-3.3 Callout view (zoomed in); detail level: Coarse

FIGURE 10-3.4 Callout view (zoomed in); detail level: Fine

Refining the Walls:

Now that the residence is more developed, you will modify various wall properties to make them more accurate to what they would be in the real world. Both the main building walls and the garage need a little attention.

In the larger scale wall section you can see a few problems that need to be addressed.

A – The siding and sheathing need to extend down and over the edge of the flooring.

B – The top of the foundation wall needs to be modified to accommodate a 2x plate for the floor joists to bear on and attach to.

FIGURE 10-3.5 First floor condition in Wall Section view

7. In the wall section view, *Callout of Cross Section 1*, click to select the **Foundation** datum and then click to select the elevation text **-1'-3"** and change it to **-1'-4 ½"**.

You have now provided space for a continuous 2x board (which is 1 ½" high). This board will be added later.

Note that **all** of the foundation walls in the model have been changed by this one modification!

FIGURE 10-3.6 Top of foundation wall modified

Next you will adjust the sheathing and siding. Revit provides a way in which specific "layers" (i.e., the sheathing and siding in this example) can extend down farther than the rest of the wall (i.e., the wood studs and gypsum board). You will modify your exterior walls, except at the garage, so that the sheathing and siding extend down to the top of the foundation wall. To do this you need to make one change within the wall type.

8. In the wall section view, select the exterior wall *Basic Wall:* **Exterior - Wood Shingle over Wood Siding on Wood Stud**.

9. Select **Edit Type** on the *Properties Palette* and then click **Edit** next to the *Structure* parameter.

10. Make sure the preview pane is displayed by clicking the **Preview** button in the lower left.

11. Below the preview pane, set the **View** to **Section: Modify type attributes** so the wall is shown in section (Figure 10-3.7).

FIGURE 10-3.7 Wall structure – edit assembly

Next, you will zoom in on the bottom of the wall in the preview pane and unlock the bottom edge of the siding and sheathing layers. This will allow the unlocked material to extend up or down apart from the bottom location of the wall.

12. Click in the preview pane to make sure it is active and then scroll the wheel on your mouse to zoom in on the bottom of the wall; you can also press the wheel button while moving the mouse to pan.

13. Click the **Modify** button (Figure 10-3.8).

14. Click the bottom edge of the siding "layer" (Figure 10-3.8).

Be sure you have the bottom edge of the siding layer selected. You should see a padlock symbol above it. Next you will click that symbol to unlock it. As soon as you make this change you will have a new parameter associated with that wall type named *Base Extension Distance*, which is an *Instance Parameter*, allowing you to change this value on a wall-by-wall basis. Entering a positive number moves the sheathing and siding up that distance from the bottom of the wall and a negative number moves it down.

15. Click the padlock symbol so it is shown in the **unlocked** position.

FIGURE 10-3.8 Enabling base extension for selected wall type

You will repeat the previous two steps for the sheathing layer as well.

16. Click on the bottom edge of the sheathing layer.

17. Click the padlock symbol to unlock it.

   FYI: Only one contiguous section of layers can be set up to move up and down like this. Contiguous means the layers have to touch each other.

18. **Close** the open dialog boxes.

19. Switch to the *First Floor Plan* view.

In the next step you will select all the exterior walls except the three at the garage. In order to select the three walls at the front entry, you will need to uncheck an option on the *Status Bar*; you will do this next.

20. Uncheck **Exclude Options** on the *Status Bar* (lower right).

21. Hover your cursor over one of the exterior walls to highlight it, but do not click, and then press the **Tab** key, which will highlight all the exterior walls. Click to select the highlighted walls.

   FYI: Alternately you can simply hold down the Ctrl key and individually pick each wall.

22. Press the **Shift** key and select the <u>four</u> garage walls, one at a time while holding the Shift key down, to un-select them (if they are selected).

23. With all the exterior walls selected, except the <u>four</u> garage walls, draw your attention to the *Properties Palette*.

24. Set the *Base Extension Distance* to **-1'-4"**. Do not forget to add the negative sign at the beginning. See Figure 10-3.9.

This will make the sheathing and siding extend down 1'-4" below the bottom of the wall.

Properties	
	Basic Wall Exterior - Wood Shingle over Wood Siding on Wood ▼ Stud
Walls (10)	▼ ⊞ Edit Type
Constraints	⋀
Location Line	Wall Centerline
Base Constraint	Second Floor
Base Offset	0' 0"
Base is Attached	☐
Base Extension Distance	-1' 4"
Top Constraint	Unconnected
Unconnected Height	20' 0"
Top Offset	0' 0"
Top is Attached	☐
Top Extension Distance	0' 0"

FIGURE 10-3.9 Base Extension Distance

25. Switch back to *Callout of Cross Section 1* to see the modified wall (Figure 10-3.10).

FIGURE 10-3.10 Results of 'Base Extension Distance' modification

26. Switch back to plan view and enter edit mode *Entry Windows – Option 2*, via the *Status Bar*, so you can make the same change to the three entry walls located in the second design option for the entry windows. Refer to previous sections for more information on editing *Design Options*.

Wall Section at Garage:

Next you will set up a wall section view at the garage wall.

27. Switch to the *Longitudinal Section*.

28. Add a "wall section" type **Callout** at the garage wall (Figure 10-3.11).

29. Rename the new view to *Garage Wall Section*.

30. **Open** the *Garage Wall Section* view.

As you can see, the top of the foundation wall is not correct for the garage area. The foundation wall typically comes up to the top of the floor slab or 8-16″ above that. You will make this change next.

FIGURE 10-3.11 Callout added to longitudinal section

31. Switch to the *Basement Floor Plan* and select the three foundation walls at the garage.

32. In *Properties Palette*, set the *Top Constraint* to **Up to level: First Floor**.

33. Switch back to the *Garage Wall Section* view.

As you can see in the figure below, the foundation wall and floor slab overlap each other. You will fix this next.

FIGURE 10-3.12
Garage Wall Section – edge of slab condition

34. Click **Modify → Geometry → Join**.

35. Select the foundation wall and then the floor slab.

Your wall section should now look like Figure 10-3.13. You can use the *Linework* tool if desired to edit any line styles or weights.

36. **Save** your project as **ex10-3.rvt**.

FIGURE 10-3.13
Garage Wall Section

TIP: *The wall section in Figure 10-3.13 shows two level datums that are not required in this view (Low Roof and Foundation). You cannot delete them, but you can select them; right-click and then pick* Hide in View → Elements *from the pop-up menu. Click* Reveal Elements *on the View Control Bar to see them again.*

Exercise 10-4:
Annotation and Detail Components

This exercise will explore adding notes, dimensions and detail components to your wall section.

Add Notes and Dimensions to Callout of Cross Section 1:

1. Open ex10-3.rvt and *Save As* **ex10-4.rvt**.

2. Switch to *Callout of Cross Section 1* view.

3. Click the *Hide Crop Region* icon on the *View Control Bar*.

4. Add the three dimensions as show in **Figure 10-4.1**.

    TIP: Revit lets you dimension to the window opening even though you are not cutting directly through a window in the current view.

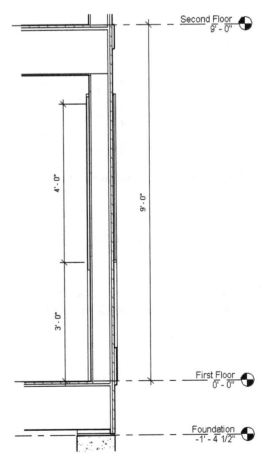

These dimensions are primarily for the carpenters framing the stud wall. Typically, when a window opening is dimensioned in wood stud framing, the dimension has the suffix R.O. This stands for Rough Opening, clearly representing that the dimension identifies an opening in the wall. You will add the suffix next.

5. Select the dimension at the window opening.

6. Click directly on the blue dimension text (i.e., 4'-0″).

7. Type **R.O.** in the *Suffix* field and then click **OK**.

FIGURE 10-4.1 Added dimensions

Dimension Text

Note: this tool replaces or appends dimensions values with text and has no effect on model geometry.

Dimension Value

◉ Use Actual Value   4' - 0"

◯ Replace With Text

Text Fields

Above:

Prefix: Value: Suffix:

                4' - 0"   R.O.

Below:

Segment Dimension Leader Visibility: By Element ▼

     OK   Cancel   Apply

FIGURE 10-4.2 Selected dimension properties

FIGURE 10-4.3 Dimension with suffix

Figure 10-4.3 shows the dimension with the added suffix.

8. Use the same process to add the text "WINDOW BEYOND" in the *Below* field (Figure 10-4.4).

FIGURE 10-4.4 Text added below dimension

9. Turn the *crop region* back on for a moment.

10. Select the ***crop region***.

Notice the dashed line that shows around the *crop region*? It has its own set of positioning grips. This dashed lined area allows you to control the visibility of various elements in the current view, such as text. You will adjust the right-hand side so it will accommodate more text and notes.

11. Drag the control grips for the vertical dashed line on the right as per **Figure 10-4.5**.

12. Turn the *crop region* off again.

FIGURE 10-4.5 Crop Region Edits

13. Add the notes with leaders shown in Figure 10-4.6 (See Step 14); the text *Type* should be 3/32" Arial.

TIP: Select the Text tool and then one of the leader icons on the Ribbon (see image to right).

FIGURE 10-4.6 Notes added to wall section

14. The text style should be set to **3/32" Arial**; it may still be set to the last text style you used in this book: ¼" Outline Text.

15. Select the text and use the grips and the justification buttons to make the text look like **Figure 10-4.6**.

Adding Detail Components:

Revit provides a way in which you can quickly add common 2D detail elements like dimensional lumber in section, anchor bolts, and wall base profiles to "embellish" your sections. These are just a few loaded with your template file (Figure 10-4.7); many others can be created or downloaded from the internet.

Next, you will add just a few *Detail Components* so you have a basic understanding of how this feature is used.

You will add a 2x6 sill plate and double top plate. You will also add the batt insulation symbol in the stud cavity.

16. Select **Annotate → Detail → Component → Detail Component**.

17. From the *Type Selector*, pick *Dimension Lumber-Section* **2 x 6**.

18. Add the sill plates as shown in Figure 10-4.8.

FIGURE 10-4.7
Detail Components; Type Selector open

TIP: When placing the 2x6 you will need to press the spacebar to Rotate, and then Move to properly position the element. The sill plate should be directly on the ¾" wood sheathing. Note that the horizontal line that extends through the sill plate is the level datum.

3' - 0"

1/2" GYPSUM WALL BOARD

VAPOR BARRIER

First Floor
0' - 0"

Foundation
-1' - 4 1/2"

FIGURE 10-4.8 Callout of Cross Section 1 view; 2 x 6 sill plates added

Detail Components can be copied once you have placed one in the view. This saves the step of rotating the stud in this example.

19. Use **Copy** and **Snaps** to add the double top plate (Figure10-4.9).

Second Floor
9' - 0"

2"x14" WOOD JOISTS a

2" x 6" WOOD STUDS a

FULL-FIT BATT INSULA

FIGURE 10-4.9 Callout of Cross Section 1 view; 2 x 6 dbl. top plate added

Next you will add the batt insulation.

20. Select **Annotation → Detail → Insulation.**   **Insulation**

21. Pick the midpoint of the sill plate and the top plate to draw a line that represents the center of the batt insulation symbol; you can pick in either direction (Figure 10-4.10).

Second Floor
9' - 0"

2"x14" WOOD JOISTS at 16" O.C.

2" x 6" WOOD STUDS at 16" O.C.

FULL-FIT BATT INSULATION

3/4" PLYWOOD SHEATHING

AIR INFILTRATION BARRIER

1/2" GYPSUM WALL BOARD

VAPOR BARRIER

WINDOW BEYOND

4' - 0" R.O.

9' - 0"

3' - 0"

First Floor
0' - 0"

FIGURE 10-4.10 Callout of Cross Section 1 view; Insulation added

Next you will change the width of the insulation so it fits the space of the stud cavity (i.e., 5½" wide).

22. Click **Modify** and then click to select the insulation just drawn.

23. Adjust the **Width** on the *Options Bar* to **5½"**.

Note that this change can also be made via the *Properties Palette* (Figure 10-4.11).

FIGURE 10-4.11 Insulation properties

FIGURE 10-4.12
Insulation width changed

These tools we just used are on the *Annotate* tab of the *Ribbon* because they are 2D graphics and only show up in the current view.

Drawing some elements like this, rather than modeling them three-dimensionally, can save time and system resources. A file could get very large if you tried to model everything. Of course, every time you skip drawing in 3D, you increase the chance of error. It takes a little experience to know when to model and when not to model.

FYI: Architectural text is typically all uppercase.

Loading Additional Detail Components:

In addition to the *Detail Components* that are preloaded with the template file you started with, you can load more from the Revit content folder on your hard drive.

24. Select **Component → Detail Component** from the *Annotate* tab.

25. Click the **Load Family** button from the *Ribbon*.

26. Double-click on the *Detail Items* folder and then the following sub-folders: *Div 06-Wood* and *Plastic\064000-Architectural Woodwork\064600-Wood Trim*.

27. Double-click the file named *Crown Molding-Section.rfa*.

You now have access to the newly imported crown molding. Take a minute to observe some of the other *Detail Components* that may be loaded into the project; for example, in the *Div 05-Metals\05200-Structural Steel Framing* folder you can load a steel beam family which has all the standard shapes contained within it as types (Figure 10-4.13).

28. Add the *Crown Molding* to the intersection between the wall and the ceiling using the **Component** tool on the *Annotate* tab (not the *Architecture* tab).

FIGURE 10-4.13 Load Detail Component dialog, wide flange beams selected

Using Repeating Details:

Many details and sections have components that occur multiple times, one right after another. Some examples are brick, siding and floor joists in section. Revit provides a tool, called *Repeating Details*, which can basically copy any *Detail Component* the required number of times to fill the space between two pick points you select with the mouse. The spacing of the *Detail Component* being copied has to be predefined when setting up the *Repeating Detail* style.

29. Click **Annotate → Detail → Component → Repeating Detail.**

30. From the *Type Selector*, select *Repeating Detail:* **Lap Siding 6″.**

Repeating Detail Component

For now, you will draw the siding off to one side just to test this feature. Make sure you are within the *crop window* area or you will not see the results.

31. Pick two points similar to those shown in Figure 10-4.14.

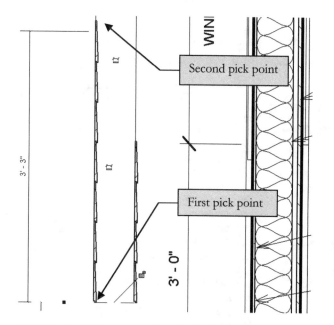

The example to the left shows two *Repeating Details* added. You can adjust them via the grips or the temporary dimensions.

FIGURE 10-4.14 Repeating Detail added: lap siding

32. Try adjusting the length of the siding by selecting it and clicking on the dimension text.

One way to quickly study several *Repeating Details* is to download the sample file for repeating details from SEEK (Figure 10-4.15).

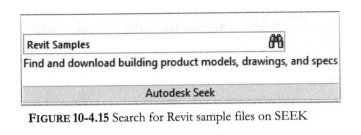

FIGURE 10-4.15 Search for Revit sample files on SEEK

FIGURE 10-4.16 Sample file downloaded from Revit content website

Once you download the file you can open it and examine how the repeating details work.

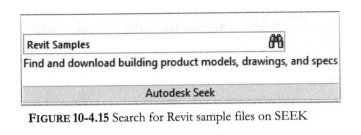

FIGURE 10-4.17 Type Properties dialog box

The sample file shows Brick, CMU, Lap Siding, Stone Wall (plan), Metal Deck, 2x Floor Framing, Concrete Pavers, Cut Stone, Brick Paver (Figure 10-4.16).

Selecting a *Repeating Detail* and opening its *Type Properties* dialog reveals the handful of settings associated with it (Figure 10-4.17).

33. **Delete** the *Lap Siding* repeating detail.

34. **Save** your project as **10-4.rvt**.

Self-Exam:

The following questions can be used as a way to check your knowledge of this lesson. The answers can be found at the bottom of the page.

1. The controls for the section mark, when selected, are similar to the controls for the elevation tag. (T/F)

2. *Detail Components* added in this lesson were 3D. (T/F)

3. The footings drawn in this lesson were a Revit wall type. (T/F)

4. The *crop region* is represented by a rectangle in the section view. (T/F)

5. Use the _____ tool to reference a larger section off a building section.

Review Questions:

The following questions may be assigned by your instructor as a way to assess your knowledge of this section. Your instructor has the answers to the review questions.

1. The visibility of the *crop region* can be controlled. (T/F)

2. It is not possible to draw a leader without placing text. (T/F)

3. When a section mark is added to a view, all the other related views automatically get a section mark added to them. (T/F)

4. It is possible to modify elements such as doors, windows and ceilings in section views. (T/F)

5. You cannot adjust the "depth of view" using the *crop window*. (T/F)

6. What is the first thing you should do after placing a section mark?

   _____

7. If the text appears to be excessively large in a section view, the view's

   _____ is probably set incorrectly.

8. The abbreviation R.O. stands for _____.

9. Describe what happens when you double-click on the section bubble:

   _____.

10. Revit provides _____ different leader options within the *Text* command, not including the leader location options.

Lesson 11
Residence: INTERIOR DESIGN:

This lesson explores some interior design elements of a floor plan, such as toilet room layouts and kitchen cabinets. Additionally, you will look at placing furniture and guardrails into your project.

Exercise 11-1:
Bathroom Layouts

Bathroom layouts involve placing toilets, tubs and sinks. You will start with the half bath on the first floor.

   1.   Open ex10-4.rvt and **Save As ex11-1.rvt.**

The template you started with has everything you need to lay out this room. You will create the layout shown in Figure 11-1.1.

FIGURE 11-1.1 First Floor plan view: half bath layout

   2.   Switch to *First Floor* plan view and zoom in on the half bath next to the garage, North of the dining room.

The first step will be to place the toilet.

3. With the *Component* tool selected on the *Architecture* tab, pick **Toilet-Domestic-3D** from the *Type Selector*. Click **No** when prompted to load a *Plumbing Fixture* tag.

4. **Place** the toilet in the middle of the room and then *Move* and *Rotate* into place utilizing *Snaps* (Figure 11-1.2).

   TIP: Press the spacebar to rotate the toilet before placing it.

The toilet is 1″ out from the wall, which is typical for floor mounted – tank type toilets.

The overlapping letters, C and L, is the symbol for "centerline." This means that the middle of the toilet is 1′-4″ from the wall. Actually, if you were to add this dimension, Autodesk® Revit® Architecture would automatically add this symbol if the *Centerline Symbol* parameter is turned on in the properties of the dimension!

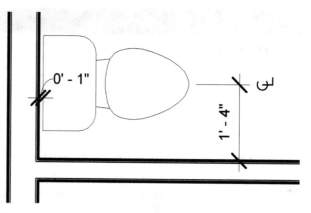

FIGURE 11-1.2 Toilet location

If you want to make sure the 1′-4″ dimension never changes, you can add the dimension shown and then click the padlock symbol to *Lock* that dimension. Then, anytime the wall moves, the toilet will move with it. If you want the constraint but do not want the dimension, you can delete the dimension and Autodesk® Revit® Architecture will ask you if you want to maintain the constraint after the dimension is deleted.

Next, you will add the sink. This consists of three separate components: a base cabinet, a countertop and a sink, which is similar to what you would have in the "real-world." First you will add the base cabinet.

5. Place a *Vanity Cabinet-Double Door Sink Unit: 24″* using the *Component* tool (Figure 11-1.3).

   TIP: Use the spacebar to rotate.

   TIP: It is hard to tell which side is the front of the cabinet in plan view; the side the cursor is attached to is the back of the cabinet. If you add it incorrectly you will see the problem when you set up the interior elevation.

FIGURE 11-1.3 Vanity base cabinet added

Next, you will add the countertop. Autodesk Revit has one that even has a hole in it for the sink. You will have to adjust the length to fit your cabinet.

6. Using the *Component* tool, place the <u>*Vanity Counter Top w Round Sink Hole*</u>: **24"** depth in the middle of the room.

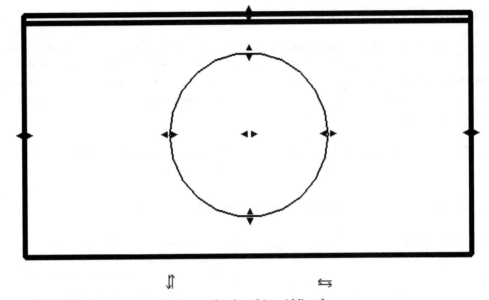

FIGURE 11-1.4 Vanity counter top temporarily placed in middle of room

FIGURE 11-1.5 Vanity counter top properties

You will notice that the counter top is 48" long; you will change this to 24" in a moment. When selected, you see several arrow-grips which allow you to graphically adjust the size of the selected element.

7. With the counter top selected, note the **Properties Palette** options.

8. Change the *Length* to **2'-0"** and the *Sink Location* to **1'-0"** (Figure 11-1.5).

9. Click **Apply**, or just move your cursor back into the drawing window.

The counter top is now the correct size for your base cabinet.

10. Use **Move** and **Rotate** to position the counter top over the vanity base cabinet; use **Snaps** for accuracy.

11. Again, using the *Component* tool, add <u>*Sink Vanity-Round:*</u> **19" x 19"**. Press the spacebar to rotate the sink 90 degrees and then visually place the sink in the center of the hole in the countertop.

Your plan should now look like Figure 11-1.1, less the elevation tag which you will add next.

Interior Elevation View:

Next, you will set up an interior elevation view for the half bath. You will also add a mirror above the sink in elevation view. As you can see, the tasks in this book are building on previously learned material; refer back to previous chapters if you need a refresher. Using these features multiple times will help you to become more efficient and to better understand the tools.

12. Place an **Elevation** tag, with the *Type Selector* set to **Interior Elevation**, looking towards the "wet" wall, the wall with fixtures on it (Figure 11-1.6).

   FYI: A "wet" wall is any wall that has plumbing fixtures on it and piping behind it.

   TIP: When placing the Elevation Tag, Revit turns the pointer to look at the closest wall, so you will have to place the tag close to the West wall (overlapping the plumbing fixtures) and then move the tag back as a separate step.

13. Rename the new view to **1/2 Bath** in the *Project Browser*.

FIGURE 11-1.6 Elevation tag added

14. Switch to the new view; click the *crop region* and drag the bottom up so the floor system does not show. Your view should look like Figure 11-1.7.

FIGURE 11-1.7 ½ Bath elevation

15. Change the *View Scale* to **½" = 1'-0"**.

16. Load the component **Mirror** from the Autodesk Seek library; it will be from the *Revit Architecture* **library** rather than a manufacturer such as Bradley Corp.

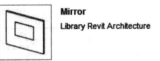

TIP: Check the "Generic:" option on the left, under Content Source heading.

17. Create a *Duplicate* of the mirror family just loaded and name the new *Type*: **24" x 36"**; Change the *Width* to **24"** and the *Height* to **36"**.

18. While in the *1/2 Bath* elevation view, place the mirror as shown in Figure 11-1.8.

19. Add the notes and dimensions shown in Figure 11-1.8.

TIP: As you are drawing the leaders, Revit will help you align your pick points vertically so the leaders and notes align; just watch for the dashed vertical reference line before picking your points.

20. Using the same techniques just covered, lay out the two second floor bathrooms per **Figure 11-1.9**; use the tub loaded with the template.

    a. Make the larger vanity cabinet and counter top 4'-0" wide.

FIGURE 11-1.8 Interior elevation with mirror and notes added

FYI: Keep in mind that many of the symbols that come with Revit, or any program for that matter, are not necessarily drawn or reviewed by an architect. The point is that the default values, such as mounting heights, may not meet ADA, national, state or local codes. Items such as accessible mirrors have a maximum height off the floor to the reflective surface that Revit's standard components may not comply with. However, as you apply local codes to these families, you can reuse them in the future.

FIGURE 11-1.9 Second Floor Bath Rooms

21. **Save** your project as **ex11-1.rvt**.

Exercise 11-2:
Kitchen Layout

In this exercise you will look at adding kitchen cabinets and appliances to your project. As usual, Revit provides several predefined families to be placed into the project.

Placing Cabinets:

You will add base cabinets and appliances first.

1. Open ex11-1.rvt and **Save As ex11-2.rvt**.

2. Switch to the *First Floor* plan view and zoom into the kitchen.

    FYI: As with other families (i.e., doors and windows), Revit loads several Types to represent the most valuable and useful sizes available. Cabinets typically come in 3" increments with different types (i.e., single or double door unit) having maximum and minimum sizes.

3. With the ***Component*** tool selected, place the families, cabinets **and appliances**, as shown in Figure 11-2.1; use *Snaps* for accuracy. Remember that the cursor is at the back of the cabinet when placing the component.

    FYI: Most of the specified families are already loaded into your project from your template you started with; the others can be loaded manually from the local or online libraries.

4. Select one of the base cabinets and click **Edit Type** from the *Properties Palette*.

Notice the height is 2'-10½" which, when combined with a 1½" standard counter top, gives you a 3'-0" surface.

Next, you will add the counter tops to the base cabinets. You will place three separate counter top elements (Figure 11-2.2). You will adjust the lengths of the counter tops to fit the cabinets below.

FIGURE 11-2.1 First Floor Plan View: base cabinets added to kitchen

5. Per the steps listed below, add the counter tops shown in Figure 11-2.2, using *Snaps* to accurately place them.

    a. Load the elements not currently loaded in your project from the *Casework* folder.

    b. Place the bottom-right corner unit (use *Move, Mirror* and *Snaps*) and then, with the unit selected, drag one of the end grips back to align with the edge of the cabinet below.

    c. Load and place the other corner unit with the sink hole.
        i.   Adjust the edge locations (use *Properties* for accuracy)
        ii. Adjust sink hole via *Properties Palette*: *Sink Location*: **5'-4"**

    d. Add the two straight counter tops as shown.

    e. Verify the *Height* is **3'-0"** via the *Properties Palette*.

FIGURE 11-2.2 First Floor Plan View: counter tops added

6. Select the counter top with the sink hole and go to the **_Properties Palette_**.

7. Change the following (Figure 11-2.3):
   a. Sink Location to Wall: **5"**
   b. Sink Opening Depth: **1'-5"**
   c. Sink Opening Width: **3'-4"**

**TIP:** Some settings are per instance (i.e., the settings in the palette to the left) and others are per type (i.e., clicking the Edit Type _button – Type Parameters); the Instant Parameters only affect the selected item. So, if you place another instance of this family in the basement, the sink can be in a different location._

FIGURE 11-2.3 Properties for Counter Top with Sink Hole: 24" Depth

8. Using the *Component* tool, add **Sink Kitchen-Double: 42″ x 21″** to your project – centered on the sink hole (Figure 11-2.4).

FIGURE 11-2.4 Sink placed in countertop, centered on hole

Placing Wall Cabinets:

Next you will add a couple wall cabinets to see how they work. They are similar to adding base cabinets, with the exception that they are dependent on walls (i.e., they are *wall hosted*). You can only place an upper cabinet on a wall, not in the middle of a room like you did with the base cabinets. The base cabinets are set up to sit on the floor and the upper cabinets are assigned a height above the floor, on the wall, via *Properties*.

9. Using the ***Component*** tool, add the upper cabinets as shown in **Figure 11-2.5**:

    a. Move the cursor close to a wall until you see the cabinet, which means Revit found a wall.

    b. Center the upper cabinet above the range, leaving an equal space on each side of the cabinet; these spaces will get a filler that matches the cabinets.

    c. The numbers (which represent the cabinet width) and Xs in the cabinets are for clarity of this step only; you do not need to add these items.

    d. Use both single and double upper cabinets as necessary.

    e. If you have trouble adding the uppers at the pocket door location, add them to the right and move them into place.

Use the *Measure* tool to figure out how wide each upper cabinet needs to be. First, add the corner units and then list the distance from the edge of the corner cabinet to the edge of the base cabinet below that the upper cabinet will align with, or to the window jamb.

FIGURE 11-2.5 First Floor plan view: upper cabinets added (Xs added for clarity in this image)

The heights of the cabinets will be adjusted when you get to the interior elevation view.

FYI: Wall cabinets are typically dashed in plan because they are above the floor plan cut plane.

Adding the Interior Elevation Tag:

10. Add an interior **Elevation Tag** as shown in Figure 11-2.6.

    TIP: Make sure you select Interior Elevation *from the Type Selector.*

11. Rename the new elevation view to *Kitchen (east)*.

12. Select the **circle** portion of the symbol; the symbol should look like Figure 11-2.7 when selected correctly.

13. Click the *North* and *South* check-boxes as shown in Figure 11-2.7.

14. **Rename** the two new views to *Kitchen (north)* and *Kitchen (south)*.

The single elevation tag in plan view is associated with the three kitchen elevation views.

15. Double-click the pointer portion of the elevation tag pointing towards the East to open that view.

FIGURE 11-2.6 Elevation tag added to kitchen

16. Adjust the ***crop region*** so the floor system is not visible.

17. Set the *View Scale* to ½″ = 1′-0″; your interior elevation view should look like **Figure 11-2.8**.

Depending on where, exactly, you placed the *Elevation Tag*, you may see the side of the refrigerator or a section through it, as in Figure 11-2.8. In this case you will want to adjust the view so you see the cabinets beyond, which is more important to show. You will switch back to the plan view and adjust the views settings.

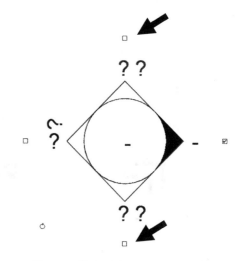

FIGURE 11-2.7 Elevation tag selected

18. Switch back to the ***First Floor*** plan view.

19. Click to select the *East view's* pointer portion of the elevation tag so you see the *Extent of View/Far Clip Plane* lines.

FIGURE 11-2.8 Kitchen (east); initial view

20. Click and drag to adjust the location of the *Extent of View* line as shown in Figure 11-2.9; also adjust the *Far Clip Plane* if necessary.

Notice the *Extent of View* line has been moved to the east of the refrigerator and the *Far Clip Plane* is in the middle of the wall.

21. Switch back to the ***Kitchen (east)*** view and note the changes (Figure 11-2.10).

You will modify one more thing in this view before moving on. The height of the wall cabinets needs a little work (Figure 11-2.10); the corner wall cabinets are too short and the cabinet over the range is too tall. You can adjust these in either the plan or elevation view. You will adjust them in the elevation view so you can immediately see the changes.

FIGURE 11-2.9 First Floor; elev. tag selected

FIGURE 11-2.10 Kitchen (east) view; view settings adjusted

22. Select both **corner** upper cabinets and change their height to **2'-6"** and the Elevation to **4'-6"** (2'-6" + 4'-6" = 7'-0" to top). Make these changes via the *Properties Palette* and *Type Properties*.

23. Select the upper cabinet above the range and change its height to **15"** and the elevation so the top stays at 7'-0".

24. Search **Autodesk SEEK** for a range hood; load and then place it.

Range Hood
Library Revit Architecture

Your elevation should now look like Figure 11-2.11. Notice that the cabinets on the right and left, which are actually in section, have heavier lines than the cabinets which are in elevation. Again, Revit saves time by assuming the industry standard. However, you can use the *Linework* tool to change this if you so desire!

FIGURE 11-2.11 Kitchen (east) view; view settings adjusted

You will add notes and dimensions to the elevation.

25. Add the notes and dimensions per **Figure 11-2.12**.

26. Select the *Linework* tool from the *Modify* tab, and set the *Line Style* (on the *Ribbon*) to **Wide lines**. Select the perimeter lines so they stand out more.

RANGE HOOD

WOOD WALL CABINETS
- 12" DEEP

SOLID POLYMER COUNTER
TOP WITH BACKSPLASH

30" WIDE RANGE (N.I.C.)

WOOD BASE CABINETS
- 24" DEEP

RUBBER BASE

First Floor
0' - 0"

FIGURE 11-2.12 Interior elevation with annotations

That is it for the East elevation! Next, you will take a quick look at the other two elevations you set up in the kitchen.

27. Switch to the *Kitchen (north)* view.

28. Adjust the *crop region* and the perimeter lines per the previous elevation (Figure 11-2.13).

29. Change the *View Scale* to ½" = 1'-0".

You will notice right away that the windows are in conflict with the cabinets and the countertop does not extend over the dishwasher. Both of these required changes can be made in either the plan or the elevation; again, you will make changes in the elevation view so you can see the results.

First you will fix the windows. An error like this could easily be overlooked using a traditional CAD program because the exterior elevation and the interior elevations are separate/independent drawings files; so you could fix the height of the windows in the interior elevation, but forget to change the exterior elevation, where the windows are specified and ordered from. In Revit, it is not even possible to have one window be two different sizes in the same project file.

FIGURE 11-2.13 Kitchen (north); initial view

30. Select the *Section* line, right-click and pick **Hide in View → Elements**. You do not need to see that section mark here.

31. Select the two windows in the ***Kitchen (north)*** view.

32. Via *Properties*, create a new window *Type*, via *Edit Type → Duplicate*, named
    <u>*Double Hung with Trim:*</u> **36″ x 42″**:
    a.   Set the *Height* to **3′-6″** (from 4′-0″) – *Type Parameter*
    b.   See the *Sill Height* to **3′-6″** (From 3′-0″) – *Instance Parameter*
    c.   Click **OK** and then adjust the sill height for the selected windows to **3′-6″**.

Now the windows do not conflict with the countertop's backsplash. Next, you will adjust the counter top.

33. In the ***Kitchen (north)*** view, zoom in on the dishwasher area.

34. Select the **Counter Top** over the **15″** wide base cabinet, to the left of the dishwasher, and press the **Delete** key to erase it.

35. Using the ***Align*** tool, select the left-edge of the 15″ wide base cabinet and then select the left edge of the countertop. The countertop should now align with the edge of the cabinets.

    FYI: You must pick these items in the order specified.

36. Edit the perimeter using the ***Linework*** tool and adjust the *Crop Region* to hide the floor.

Your modified *Kitchen (north)* should look like Figure 11-2.14.

FIGURE 11-2.14 Kitchen (north); modified view

37. Open ***Kitchen (south)***.

38. Modify the ***crop region*** and the perimeter linework.

If you cannot see the refrigerator doors, you would now realize that the refrigerator was inserted backwards (Figure 11-2.15). You will fix this next.

FIGURE 11-2.15 Kitchen (south); initial view

39. Set the scale to **½" = 1'-0"** and ***Hide*** the building section mark.

40. If needed, ***Rotate*** the refrigerator (in plan view) 180 degrees (if required – the door handles should be visible if facing the correct way).

41. Modify the upper cabinet above the refrigerator to be **12"** tall, with the top at **7'-0"**.

> ***TIP:*** *If this cabinet were used anywhere else in the project, you would have had to make a duplicate before changing the height; otherwise, all the cabinets would have changed as well, because it is a Type Parameter you are changing, not an Instance Parameter.*

Often, you have a portion of a wall that does not have very much on it, so it is not worth elevating. In the *Kitchen (south)* view you will crop a portion of the wall on the right.

42. Click the ***crop region*** and drag the right side of the *crop region* rectangle towards the left so only the portion of elevation shown in Figure 11-2.16 is visible.

Your *Kitchen (south)* view should now look like Figure 11-2.16.

FIGURE 11-2.16 Kitchen (south); modified view

The last things you will adjust are the lines in the cabinet elevations that indicate the swing of the cabinet door; these lines are typically dashed lines.

There are two ways to accomplish this. One way will only affect the current view (View → *Visibility/Graphics*) and the other will affect the entire project (Manage →*Settings* → *Object Styles*). You want this change to be applied everywhere, so you want to implement per the latter method.

43. Select **Manage → Settings → Object Styles**.

Object Styles

44. On the *Model Objects* tab, click the plus symbol next to **Casework** in the *Category* column (Figure 11-2.17).

45. Change the **Line Pattern** for *Elevation Swing* to **Hidden 1/8″** (Figure 11-2.17).

46. Click **OK** to see the results in the three kitchen elevations.

FIGURE 11-2.17 Object Styles dialog box; controls project wide graphics settings

That is it for the kitchen! With a little practice, you could design a kitchen in very short order.

47. **Save** your project as **ex11-2.rvt**.

TIP: The Woodwork Institute (http://www.aws-cds.com/) has Revit families for most of the industry standard cabinets. You can download the cabinets from their website. You can even print out a small flyer that shows an image of each cabinet that can be downloaded.

Exercise 11-3:
Furniture

This lesson will cover the steps required to lay out furniture. The processes are identical to those previously covered for toilets and cabinets. First you will start with the office on the second floor.

Loading the Necessary Families:

1. Open ex11-2.rvt and **Save As ex11-3.rvt**.

2. Select the **Load Family** tool, on the *Insert* tab, and load the following items into the current project:

    Local Files *(i.e., on your hard drive)*
    a. **Work Station Desktops** (Furniture System)
    b. **Chair-Executive** (Furniture\Seating)
    c. **Sofa-Pensi** (Furniture\Seating)
    d. **Table-Round** (Furniture\Tables)

    Online Files *(i.e., Autodesk Seek on the internet via the Insert tab)*
    e. Search SEEK for **Copier-Floor**

    TIP: You can type "copier" in SEEK and find a few options.

TIP: You can set the View *mode for the Open dialog box, which is displayed when you click Load from Library. One option is* Thumbnail *mode; this displays a small thumbnail image for each file in the current folder. Press Ctrl + spin your mouse wheel to adjust preview size. This makes it easier to see the many symbols and drawings that are available for insertion.*

Above: View set to List mode

Right: View set to Thumbnail mode

Designing the Office Furniture Layout:

3. Switch to the *Second Floor* plan view.

4. Using the **Component** tool, place the furniture as shown in Figure 11-3.1.

   TIP: Use Snaps to assure accuracy; use Rotate and Mirror as required.

FIGURE 11-3.1 Second Floor – Office furniture layout

Look at the type properties, via *Edit Type*, for the Work Station Desktop to see the *Desktop Height* setting which controls how high the surface is above the current floor.

You may want to browse through the component library and the web library for miscellaneous residential furniture. You can add dining room tables and chairs, bookshelves, washer and dryer, etc. Your instructor may require you to complete this suggested step. An example of a few items placed can be seen in Figure 11-3.2.

FIGURE 11-3.2 First Floor; one possible furniture layout

3D View of Office Layout:

Next, you will look at a 3D view of your office area. This involves adjusting the visibility of the roof and skylights.

5. Switch to the ***Default 3D*** view via the *QAT*.

6. Click anywhere in the drawing window to activate the view.

7. Type **VV** to access the *Visibility/Graphics Overrides* dialog box. Remember, these settings are only for the current view.

8. Uncheck the *Ceiling* and the *Roof* category then click **OK**.

The ceilings and roof should not be visible now. However, you should still see the light fixtures floating in space. You will make those disappear next.

9. Select one of the 2′ x 4′ light fixtures floating above the office.

10. Click the ***Temporary Hide/Isolate*** tool from the *View Control Bar*.

You should see the menu shown in **Figure 11-3.3** show up next to the *Hide/Isolate* icon. This allows you to isolate an element, so it is the only thing on the screen. Or you can hide it, so the element is temporarily not visible.

FIGURE 11-3.3 Hide/Isolate pop-up menu

11. Click **Hide Category** in the menu (Figure 11-3.3).

> *FYI: This makes all the lights temporarily hidden.*

12. Adjust your **3D** view to look similar to **Figure 11-3.4**; try looking at the room from other angles as well.

> *TIP: While pressing the Shift key, also press the wheel button on the mouse and drag the mouse around to "orbit" the model without selecting any icons. Also, selecting an object in the view makes the model pivot about the selected object.*

You will now restore the original visibility settings for the **3D** view. Notice the *Hide/Isolate* icon now has a colored background, which means something in the project is temporarily hidden from view.

13. Click the *Hide/Isolate* icon and then select ***Reset Temporary Hide/Isolate*** from the pop-up menu.

14. Reset the **3D** view's visibility settings so the ceilings and roof are visible (type VV).

15. Click the *Home* icon via the ***ViewCube*** to reset the view (Figure 11-3.5).

16. **Save** your project as **ex11-3.rvt**.

> *FYI: Not all families found online are drawn in full 3D. Some may have been brought over from a CAD program where all the symbols are drawn in 2D only.*

FIGURE 11-3.4 3D view with ceiling/roof/lights hidden

Online Content:

A few locations on the internet provide additional content for use in Revit; some is free and some is not. Some product manufacturers are starting to provide content based on the products they make. This is making it easier for designers to include that manufacturer's product in their project, both in the virtual and real projects.

You have already spent a little time looking at Revit's online content library (seek.autodesk.com). You should spend some more time there so you know what is generally available. This will help you to reduce duplicated effort.

As previously mentioned in this text, the Autodesk SEEK initiative is meant to facilitate the dissemination of high quality manufacturer Revit content, as well as content for other Autodesk products: AutoCAD, Inventor, etc. The screen shot below shows the seek.autodesk.com homepage. This site can be directly accessed from within Revit via the *Insert* tab and then the *Autodesk Seek* panel.

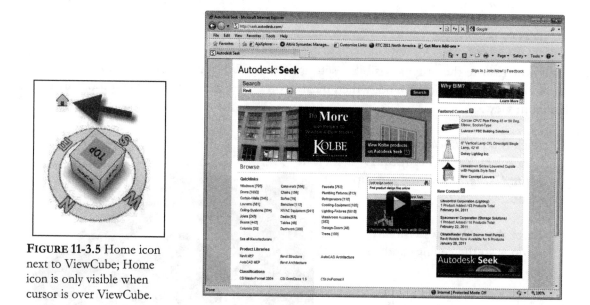

FIGURE 11-3.5 Home icon next to ViewCube; Home icon is only visible when cursor is over ViewCube.

The following sites also contain content that can be downloaded:
- www.revitcity.com *(free content provided by other users)*
- www.turbosquid.com *(buy, sell and trade other user's content)*
- www.arcat.com, www.revit-content.com, *and* www.smartbim.com

You should occasionally search the internet to see if additional content becomes available. You can do an internet search for "revit content"; make sure to include the quotation marks. Rendering content, such as that offered by www.archvision.com, will be covered in Chapter 13.

Exercise 11-4:
Adding Guardrails

This lesson will cover the steps required to lay out guardrails. The steps are simple; you select your style and draw its path.

Adding a Guardrail to the Second Floor Stair Area:

1. Open ex11-3.rvt and **Save As ex11-4.rvt**.

2. Switch to the **Second Floor** plan view.

3. Select **Architecture → Circulation → Railing → Sketch Path**.

4. **Zoom** into the stair area.

At this point you will draw a line representing the path of the guardrail. The railing is offset to one side of the line, similar to walls. However, you do not have the *Location Line* option as you do with the *Wall* tool, so you have to draw the railing in a certain direction to get the railing to be on the floor and not hovering in space just beyond the floor edge.

5. Draw a line along the edge of the floor as shown in **Figure 11-4.1**.

   TIP: Select Chain *from the Options Bar to draw the railing with fewer picks.*

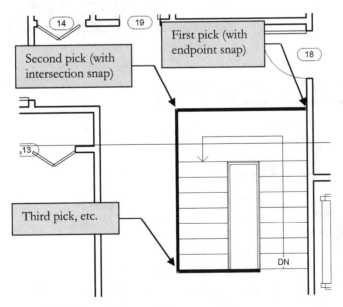

FIGURE 11-4.1 Second Floor: adding a guardrail

6. Click the **green checkmark** from the *Ribbon* to finish the railing.

The railing has now been drawn. In the next step you will switch to a 3D view and see how to quickly change the railing style. This will also involve changing the height of the railing. Most building codes require the railing height be 42″ when the drop to the adjacent surface is more than 30″; this is called a guardrail.

7. Switch to the **3D** view.

8. Turn off the ceilings and roof as previously reviewed (*TIP: Temp. Hide/Isolate*), and then zoom into the railing just added to the second floor. Notice the railing style shown in Figure 11-4.2.

9. Select the railing. You may have to use the *Tab* key to cycle through the various selection options.

10. With the railing selected, select the other railing types available in the *Type Selector* on the *Properties Palette*. When finished make sure *Railing:* **Handrail – Rectangular** is selected.

FIGURE 11-4.2 Added railing – 3D view

Modify Railing via the *Properties Palette*

When the alternate style was selected, your railing should have looked like Figure 11-4.3. Even the railing for the stair could be changed by a similar step. This style is too contemporary for this design so you will not use it at this time.

FYI: You can change the height via Type Properties.

Notice stair handrail buried within the wall; see discussion below.

FIGURE 11-4.3 Railing with alternate style

Editing the Sketch Lines for the Stair Railing:

You will notice, in the image above (Figure 11-4.3), that a portion of the railing added with the stair is buried in the wall. You will edit the railing sketch lines to remove this conflict.

11. Switch to the ***First Floor Plan*** view.

12. Select the outer <u>railing</u> for the upper stair; use the *Tab* key to cycle through your selection options.

13. Click the **Edit Path** button on the *Modify | Railings* tab.

14. Delete the sketch lines on the north and east walls, shown dashed in Figure 11-4.4.

FYI: The railing added with the stair is simply a separate railing element that was automatically added with the stair.

FIGURE 11-4.4 Edit railing sketch lines

15. Select the **green check mark** on the *Design Bar* when finished.

16. Reset the 3D view so the roof and ceiling elements are visible.

Switching back to the **3D** view, you notice the railing lines in the walls are gone (Figure 11-4.5). Revit is consistent in the way many 3D components are defined and edited with 2D sketch linework; editing the stringer extensions is a similar process. This consistency helps reduce the learning curve.

FIGURE 11-4.5 Railing conflict resolved

The *Railing* tool has the ability to create fairly complex railings. The image below shows the interface for setting up the baluster placement (Figure 11-4.6). This kind of advanced control is beyond the scope of this textbook.

FIGURE 11-4.6 Dialog to control baluster and newel post placement

Make sure to examine the railing sample file available on Autodesk's online content library (seek.autodesk.com – search for "Revit samples" and select the railing option). You can download this file, open it, select a railing and view its properties to see how it works.

FIGURE 11-4.7
Railing sample file downloaded
from Revit's website

You can *Copy/Paste* a railing style from this drawing into one of your project files. Then you select your railing and pick the newly imported one from the *Type Selector*. This process was done to achieve the image below (Figure 11-4.8). Notice the traditional balusters and newel post.

FIGURE 11-4.8 Optional railing configuration

17. **Save** your project as **ex11-4.rvt**.

Self-Exam:

The following questions can be used as a way to check your knowledge of this lesson. The answers can be found at the bottom of the page.

1. The bathroom fixtures are preloaded in the template file. (T/F)

2. You do not need to be connected to the internet when you want to download content from Autodesk's content site SEEK. (T/F)

3. Revit content may not always be in compliance with local codes. (T/F)

4. You can use *Crop Region* to crop a portion of wall that is blank. (T/F)

5. Click the _____ tool to modify the path of a railing.

Review Questions:

The following questions may be assigned by your instructor as a way to assess your knowledge of this section. Your instructor has the answers to the review questions.

1. Revit provides several different styles of vanity cabinets for placement. (T/F)

2. Revit automatically adds a rail to every stair. (T/F)

3. It is not possible to draw dimensions on an interior elevation view. (T/F)

4. Cabinets typically come in 2" increments. (T/F)

5. Base cabinets automatically have a countertop on them. (T/F)

6. When you create a hole in a floor, Revit automatically adds a railing. (T/F)

7. You can use the _____ to control element visibility.

8. What is the current size of your Revit Project? _____

9. What should you use to assure accuracy when placing cabinets? _____

10. You use the _____ tool to make various components temporarily invisible.

Lesson 12
Residence: SCHEDULES:

You will continue to study the powerful features available in Autodesk® Revit®. The ability to create parametric schedules is very useful; for example, you can delete a door number on a schedule and Autodesk Revit will delete the corresponding door from the plan. Be sure to watch the video on creating schedules located on the disc.

Exercise 12-1:
Room and Door Tags

This exercise will look at adding room tags and door tags to your plans. As you insert doors, Autodesk Revit adds tags to them automatically. However, if you copy or mirror a door, or add one in elevation, you can lose the tag and have to add it.

Adding Rooms and Room Tags:

You will add a *Room* object, which will also add a *Room Tag* to the current view, to each room on your first floor plan. A *Room* object is not visible by default. It is an object which is used to calculate area, volume and store information about the room (i.e., the I in BIM… **B**uilding **I**nformation **M**odeling).

1. In the **First Floor** view, select **Architecture → Room & Area → Room**

Placing a *Room* is similar to placing a ceiling in the reflected ceiling plan; as you move your cursor over a room, the room perimeter highlights. When the room you want to place a *Room* element in is highlighted, you click to place it in that room. You are actually placing a *Room* and a *Room Tag*.

2. Place your cursor within the *Entry* area and place a *Room* (Figure 12-1.1). Make sure *"Tag on placement"* is highlighted on the *Ribbon*.

By default, Autodesk Revit will simply label the space 'Room' and number it '1.' You will change these to something different.

FIGURE 12-1.1 Room & Room Tag added to entry

FIGURE 12-1.2 Room tags – First Floor

3. Press **Esc** or select *Modify* to end the *Room* command.

4. Click on the **Room Tag** you just placed to select it.

5. Now click on the room name label to change it; enter **ENTRY**.

6. Now click on the room number to change it; enter **100**.

7. Add *Rooms/Room Tags* for each room on the first floor, incrementing each room number by 1 (Figure 12-1.2). Be sure to change the room names as well.

   TIP: During placement, pressing the spacebar will toggle the tag between horizontal and vertical orientation.

Second and Basement Floors:

8. Add *Rooms/Room Tags* to the *Second Floor*. The numbering should start with 200; place the first room and then change the number to 200. This will make the remaining rooms the correct number. Do **not** change the room names (Figure 12-1.3).

9. Add *Rooms/Tags* to the *Basement Floor Plan*. The numbering should start with 1; **do** change the room names (Figure 12-1.4). Don't worry about the "00" prefix shown for the room numbers.

   FYI: Room tags can also be added to your building sections, as the Room element will now be there! When the Room element already exists, in plan or section, you use the Room Tag tool, not the Room command.

FIGURE 12-1.3 Second Floor – Room tags

FIGURE 12-1.4 Basement – Room tags

Adding Door Tags:

Next you will add *Door Tags* to any doors that are missing them. Additionally, you will adjust the door numbers to correspond to the room numbers.

Revit numbers the doors in the order they are placed into the drawing. This would make it difficult to locate a door by its door number if door number 1 was on the first floor and door number 2 was on the second floor, etc. Typically, a door number is the same as the room number the door swings into. For example, if a door swings into a room numbered 104, the door number would also be 104. If the room had two doors into it, the doors would be numbered 104A and 104B.

10. Switch to **First Floor** plan view.

11. Select **Annotate → Tag → Tag By Category** from the *Ribbon* (Figure 12-1.5).

    TIP: This tool can also be selected from the Quick Access Toolbar or typing TG.

FIGURE 12-1.5 Annotate tab

Notice, as you move your cursor around the screen, Revit displays a tag for any element which can have a tag, when the cursor is over it. This includes walls, doors, windows, etc. When you click the mouse is when Revit actually places a tag.

12. **Uncheck** the *Leader* option on the *Options Bar*.

13. Place a *Door Tag* for each door that does not have a tag; do this for each level.

    TIP: Press the spacebar to Rotate before clicking to place the tag.

    TIP: These should mainly be the doors in the Basement and the one added in elevation in the Living Room.

14. **Renumber** all the *Door Tags* to correspond to the room they open into; do this for each level. Figure 12-1.6 is an example of the first floor and Figure 12-1.7 of the second floor. **FYI:** Revit add-in tools can automate renumber doors.

    REMEMBER: Click Modify, select the Tag and then click on the number to edit it.

TIP – TAG ALL (Figure 12-1.5): This tool allows you to quickly tag all the elements of a selected category (e.g., doors) at one time. After selecting the tool, you select the category from a list and specify whether or not you want a leader. When you click OK, Revit tags all the untagged doors in that view. This helps to avoid not tagging a door. However, all doors will show up in a schedule whether they are tagged or not.

FIGURE 12-1.6 First Floor; door tags (tags enlarged for printing)

FIGURE 12-1.7 Second Floor; door tags (tags enlarged for printing)

TIP: *The wall Instance Parameter, via the Properties Palette, must be set to "room bounding" for the Room tool to consider a wall as part of the perimeter within a particular room; this is the default setting. For example, you could set a closet wall so it was not "room bounding" so Revit would ignore it when creating the Room, thus adding the closet square footage to the room total.*

15. **Save** your project as **ex12-1.rvt**.

Exercise 12-2:
Generate a Door Schedule

This exercise will look at creating a door schedule based on the information currently available in the building model (i.e., the *Room* and *Door* elements). The tags only report information stored within the element being tagged, so it is possible to delete a tag at any time without losing information. The tag can then be added later if required; tags are view specific.

Create a Door Schedule View:

A door schedule is simply another view of the building model. However, this view displays numerical data rather than graphical data. Just like a graphical view, if you change the view it changes all the other related views. For example, if you delete a door number from the schedule, the door is deleted from the plans and elevations.

1. Open ex12-1.rvt and **Save As ex12-2.rvt**.

2. Select **View → Create → Schedules → Schedules/Quantities**.

3. Select *Doors* under *Category* and then click **OK** (Figure 12-2.1).

FYI: The template you started with already has a door schedule set up and ready to go, so the first door you added was already scheduled. However, you will go through the steps of setting up a schedule so you understand how a schedule is created.

FIGURE 12-2.1 New Schedule dialog

You should now be in the *Schedule Properties* dialog where you specify what information is displayed in the schedule, how it is sorted, and the text format.

4. On the **Fields** tab, *Add* the information you want displayed in the schedule. Select the following (Figure 12-2.2):
   a. Mark
   b. Width
   c. Height
   d. Frame Material
   e. Frame Type
   f. Fire Rating

As noted in the dialog, the fields added to the list on the right are in the order they will be in the schedule view. Use the *Move Up* and *Move Down* buttons to adjust the order.

5. Do **NOT** click OK. You need to adjust one more thing.

FIGURE 12-2.2 Schedule Properties; Fields tab

TIP: If you accidentally clicked OK, *click the* Edit *button next to the Fields parameter in the Properties Palette.*

6. On the **Sorting/Grouping** tab, set the schedule to be sorted by the **Mark** (i.e., door number) in *Ascending* order (Figure 12-2.3).

TIP: The Formatting *and* Appearance *tabs allow you to adjust how the schedule looks. The formatting is not displayed until the schedule is placed on a sheet.*

7. Click the **OK** button to generate the schedule view.

You should now have a schedule similar to Figure 12-2.4.

FIGURE 12-2.3 Schedule Properties; Sorting tab

FIGURE 12-2.4 Door schedule view

Next, you will see how deleting a door number from the schedule deletes the door from the plan.

8. Switch to the **Door Schedule 2** view, under *Schedules/Quantities* in the *Project Browser*, if you are not already there.

Next, you will delete door *102* from the **Door Schedule** view; this was the door you added in an interior elevation, the exterior door in the *Living Room*.

9. Click in the cell with the number **102**.

10. Now click the **Delete** [Rows] button from the *Ribbon* (Figure 12-2.5).

FIGURE 12-2.5 Ribbon panel for the door schedule view

You will get an alert. Revit is telling you that the actual door will be deleted from the project model (Figure 12-2.6).

11. Click **OK** to delete the door
(Figure 12-2.6).

12. Switch back to the *First Floor* view and
notice that door 102 has been deleted
from the project model (Figure 12-2.7).

Revit

This will delete 1 instance(s).

Please note that you are not just removing rows
from the schedule, but also deleting the
associated elements and geometry from the
project.

OK   Cancel

FIGURE 12-2.6 Revit alert message

FIGURE 12-2.7 First Floor plan view; door 102 has been removed

13. **Save** your project as **ex12-2.rvt**.

*TIP: You can also change the door number in the schedule and even the size; however, changing the size actually
changes the door's Type Property which affects all the door instances of that type.*

Exercise 12-3:
Generate a Room Finish Schedule

In this exercise you will create a room finish schedule. The process is similar to the previous exercise.

Create a Room Finish Schedule:

1. Open ex12-2.rvt and **Save As ex12-3.rvt**.

2. Select **View → Create → Schedules → Schedule/Quantities**.

3. Select **Rooms** under *Category* and then click **OK** (Figure 12-3.1).

4. In the **Fields** tab of the *Schedule Properties* dialog, add the following fields to be scheduled (Figure 12-3.2):
   a. Number
   b. Name
   c. Base Finish
   d. Floor Finish
   e. Wall Finish
   f. Ceiling Finish
   g. Area

FIGURE 12-3.1 New Schedule dialog

Area is not typically listed on a room finish schedule. However, you will add it to your schedule to see the various options Revit allows.

5. On the **Sorting/Grouping** tab, set the schedule to be sorted by the **Number** field.

6. On the **Appearance** tab, set the Title text to 1/8" Arial (Figure 12-3.3).

   TIP: You can create a new text style that is set to bold or with a different font and then use it here.

7. Select **OK** to generate the **Room Schedule** view.

FIGURE 12-3.2
Schedule Properties - Fields

FIGURE 12-3.3
Schedule Properties - Appearance

Place cursor here to resize the column

<Room Schedule>

A	B	C	D	E	F	G
Number	Name	Base Finish	Floor Finish	Wall Finish	Ceiling Finish	Area
001	HALLWAY					271 SF
02	Room					39 SF
003	FAMILY ROOM					754 SF
004	SHOP					271 SF
005	MECH					84 SF
006	Room					38 SF
007	CRAFT					304 SF
100	ENTRY					282 SF
101	COAT CLOSET					39 SF
102	LIVING ROOM					786 SF
103	KITCHEN					280 SF
104	MUD ROOM					87 SF
105	BATH					38 SF
106	DINING					312 SF
107	GARAGE					749 SF
200	Room					345 SF
201	Room					241 SF
202	Romm					343 SF
203	Room					44 SF
204	Room					41 SF
205	Room					80 SF
206	Room					207 SF
207	Room					272 SF

FIGURE 12-3.4 Room Schedule view

Your schedule should look similar to the one to the left (Figure 12-3.4).

8. Resize the **Name** column so all the room names are visible. Place the cursor between *Name* and *Base Finish* and drag to the right until all the names are visible.

FYI: If you right-click on a column, you can select to hide it. Why add a column if you are just going to hide it? Well, for Revit to do calculations on data, the required parameters must be "in" the schedule, not just the project.

Modifying and Populating a Room Schedule:

Like the door schedule, the room schedule is a tabular view of the building model, so you can change the room name or number on the schedule or in the plans.

9. In the **Room Schedule** view, change the name for room **201** (lower right corner of floor plan) to **OFFICE**.

    TIP: *Click on the current room name and then click on the down-arrow that appears. This gives you a list of all the existing names in the current schedule; otherwise you can type a new name.*

10. Switch to the **Second Floor** plan view to see the updated *Room Tag*.

You can quickly enter finish information to several rooms at one time. You will do this next.

11. In the **Second Floor** plan view, select the **Rooms** (not the *Room Tags*) for all bedrooms (three total); move the cursor near the *Room Tag* until you see the room highlight with an "X" (Figure 12-3.5).

    REMEMBER: *Hold the Ctrl key down to select multiple objects.*

FIGURE 12-3.5 Second Floor Plan – Rooms selected

The parameters listed here are the same as the *Fields* available for display in the *Room Schedule*. When more than one room is selected and a parameter is not the same (e.g., different names), that value field is left blank. Otherwise, the values are displayed for the selected room. Next, you will enter values for the finishes.

12. In the *Properties Palette*, change the *Name* field; enter **BEDROOM**.

13. Enter the following for the finishes (Figure 12-3.6):
    a. *Base Finish:*   **WOOD**
    b. *Ceiling Finish:*   **GB**   *(Gb = gypsum board)*
    c. *Wall Finish:*   **PAINT-1**
    d. *Floor Finish:*   **CARPET-1**

FIGURE 12-3.6 Properties for three selected rooms

14. Click **Apply**.

15. Switch back to the ***Room Schedule*** view to see the automatic updates (Figure 12-3.7).

You can also enter data directly into the *Room Schedule* view but only one room at a time.

Hopefully, in the near future, Revit will be able to enter the finishes based on the wall's *Material* settings, as well as floor and ceiling types previously created in the project!

TIP: For the schedule, you can add fields and adjust formatting anytime by clicking on one of the edit buttons in the Properties Palette. This gives you the same options that were available when you created the schedule.

<Room Schedule>						
A	**B**	**C**	**D**	**E**	**F**	**G**
Number	Name	Base Finish	Floor Finish	Wall Finish	Ceiling Finish	Area
001	HALLWAY					271 SF
02	Room					39 SF
003	FAMILY ROOM					754 SF
004	SHOP					271 SF
005	MECH					84 SF
006	Room					38 SF
007	CRAFT					304 SF
100	ENTRY					282 SF
101	COAT CLOSET					39 SF
102	LIVING ROOM					786 SF
103	KITCHEN					280 SF
104	MUD ROOM					87 SF
105	BATH					38 SF
106	DINING					312 SF
107	GARAGE					749 SF
200	Room					345 SF
201	OFFICE					241 SF
202	BEDROOM	WOOD	CARPET-1	PAINT-1	GB	343 SF
203	Room					44 SF
204	Room					41 SF
205	Room					80 SF
206	BEDROOM	WOOD	CARPET-1	PAINT-1	GB	207 SF
207	BEDROOM	WOOD	CARPET-1	PAINT-1	GB	272 SF

FIGURE 12-3.7 Room Schedule; new data added

If you have trouble finding a room in the *Floor Plan* view, you can click the room number in the *Schedule* view and then click the **Highlight in Model** button on the *Ribbon*.

16. **Save** your project as **ex12-3.rvt**.

FYI: When the Room Tag *is selected, not the* Room element, *you can change its type from the Type Selector. The other option available, by default, is one without the square footage listed below the room number. For the cubic footage to show up, the* Area and Volumes Computations *dialog must be set to calculate volumes – see image to right.*

GARAGE   GARAGE   GARAGE

107   107   107

749 SF   6739 CF

FIGURE 12-3.8 Room Tag options in current project

Self-Exam:

The following questions can be used as a way to check your knowledge of this lesson. The answers can be found at the bottom of the page.

1. Doors are automatically numbered based on the room number. (T/F)

2. The area for a room is calculated when a *Room*, and tag, is placed. (T/F)

3. Revit can tag all the doors not currently tagged on a given level with the *Tag All* tool. (T/F)

4. You can add or remove various fields in a door or room schedule. (T/F)

5. Click Delete on the *Ribbon* to delete a door from a schedule. (T/F)

Review Questions:

The following questions may be assigned by your instructor as a way to assess your knowledge of this section. Your instructor has the answers to the review questions.

1. You can add a door tag with a leader. (T/F)

2. You can add a fire rating by selecting a door, then *Properties Palette*. (T/F)

3. A door can be deleted from the door schedule. (T/F)

4. The schedule formatting only shows up when you place the schedule on a sheet. (T/F)

5. It is not possible to add the finish information (i.e., base finish, wall finish) to multiple rooms at one time. (T/F)

6. To modify the schedule view, click Edit in the *Properties Palette*. (T/F)

7. Use the _____ palette to adjust the various fields associated with each Room in a plan view.

8. Most door schedules are sorted by the _____ field.

9. You can select a different *Room Tag* via the *Type Selector*. (T/F)

10. A schedule is just another way of looking at the building information model, a tabular view of the project database. (T/F)

Notes:

Lesson 13
Residence: Photo-Realistic Rendering:

You will take a look at the site design tools and the photo-realistic rendering abilities of Autodesk® Revit®. Revit uses two rendering technologies: **NVIDIA mental ray®** and **Autodesk Raytracer®**. Revit also has a Cloud Rendering feature, which is free to students and can generate Stereo Panorama images to be used with Google® Cardboard®. The disc has a video on rendering in Autodesk Revit.

Exercise 13-1:
Site Tools

This exercise will give the reader a quick overview of the site tools available in Revit. The site tools are not intended to be an advanced site development package. Autodesk has other programs much more capable at developing complex sites such as AutoCAD Civil 3D 2016. These programs are used by professional Civil Engineers and Surveyors. The contours, or surface tin, generated from these advanced civil CAD programs can be used to generate a topography object in Revit.

In this lesson you will create a topography object from scratch rather than using imported CAD geometry; you will also add a driveway and sidewalk.

Once the topography object (the topography object, or element, is a 3D mass that represents part *or* all of the site) is created, the grade line will automatically show up in building and wall sections, exterior elevations and site plans. The sections even have the earth pattern filled in below the grade line.

As with other Revit elements, you can select the object after it is created and set various properties for it, such as surface material, phase, etc. One can also return to *Sketch* mode to refine or correct the surface; this is done in the same way most other sketched objects are edited: by selecting the item and clicking *Edit Sketch* on the *Ribbon*.

Autodesk Site Designer

Autodesk recently made a new Revit add-in available to Subscription customers. The add-in, called Site Designer (see image below), has several tools intended to allow the building designer to create a more realistic surface with curbs, sidewalks and more. These features are all intermediate to advanced and thus will not be covered here. However, the reader may want to explore these tools on their own.

Overview of Site Tools on the Ribbon:

Below is a brief description of what the site tools are used for. After this short review you will try a few of these tools on your residence project.

<u>Toposurface</u>: Creates a 3D surface by picking points, specifying the elevation of each point picked, or by using linework within a linked AutoCAD drawing that were created at the proper elevations.

<u>Subregion</u>: Allows an area to be defined within a previously drawn toposurface; the result is an area within the toposurface that can have a different material than the toposurface itself. The subregion is still part of the toposurface and will move with it when relocated. If a subregion is selected and deleted, the original surface and properties for that area are revealed.

<u>Split Surface</u>: This tool is similar to the *Subregion* tool in every way except that the result is separate surfaces that can intentionally, or accidentally, be moved apart from each other. If a split surface is selected and deleted, it results in a subtraction or a void relative to the original toposurface.

<u>Merge Surfaces</u>: After a surface has been split into one or more separate surfaces you can merge them back together. Only two surfaces can be merged together at one time. The two surfaces to be merged must share a common edge or overlap.

<u>Graded Region</u>: This tool is used to edit the grade of a toposurface that represents the existing site conditions and the designer wants to use Revit to design the new site conditions. This tool is generally only meant to be used once; when used it will copy the existing site conditions to a new phase and set the existing site to be demolished in the new construction phase. The newly copied site object can then be modified for the new site conditions.

<u>Property Line</u>: Creates property lines in plan views only.

<u>Building Pad</u>: Used to define a portion of site to be subtracted when created below grade, and added when created above grade. An example of how this might be used is to create a *pad* that coincides with a basement floor slab which would remove the ground in section above the basement floor slab; otherwise the basement would be filled with the earth fill pattern. Several pads can be imposed on the same toposurface element, but they cannot overlap.

<u>Parking Component</u>: This is a parking stall layout that can be copied around to quickly lay out parking lots. Several types can be loaded which specify both size and angle.

<u>Site Component</u>: Items like benches, dumpsters, etc., that are placed directly on the toposurface at the correct elevation at the point picked.

<u>Label Contours</u>: Adds an elevation label to the selected contours.
FYI: Contours are automatically created based on the toposurface.

Site Settings:

The *Site Settings* dialog controls a few key project-wide settings related to the site. Below are brief descriptions of these settings.

The **Site Settings** dialog is accessed from the *arrow* link in the lower-right corner of the *Model Site* panel.

<u>Contour Line Display</u>: This controls if the contours are displayed when the *toposurface* is visible, via the check box, and at what interval. If the *Interval* is set to 1'-0" you will see contour lines that follow the ground's surface and each line represents a vertical change of 1'-0" from the adjacent contour line. The contour lines alone do not tell you what direction the surface slopes in a plan view; this is where contour labels are important. The *Passing Through Elevation* setting allows control over where the contour intervals start from. This is useful because architects usually base the first floor of the building on elevation 0'-0" (or 100'-0"), and the surveyors and civil engineers will use the distance above sea level (e.g., 1009.2'). So this feature allows the contours to be reconciled between the two systems. The *Additional Contours* section allows for more contour detail to be added within a particular area (vertically); on a very large site you might want 1'-0" contours only at the building and 10'-0" contours everywhere else. However, this only works if the building is in a distinctive set of vertical elevations. If the site is relatively level or an adjacent area shares the same set of contours, you will have undesirable results.

<u>Section Graphics</u>: This area controls how the earth appears when it is shown in section, for example, exterior elevations, building sections, wall sections, etc. Here is where the pattern is selected that appears in section; the pattern is selected from the project *Materials* similar to the process for selecting the pattern to be displayed within a wall when viewed in section. The <u>*Elevation of poche base*</u> controls the depth of the pattern in section views relative to the grade line.

<u>Property Data</u>: This section controls how angles and lengths are displayed for information describing property lines.

Creating Topography in Revit

1. Open your Revit project ex12-3.rvt and **Save As ex13-1.rvt**.

2. Switch to the **Site Plan** view via the *Project Browser*.

Here you will basically see what appears to be a roof plan view of your project (Figure 13-1.1). This view has its visibility set such that you see the project from above and the various site categories are turned on so they are automatically visible once they are created. Next you will take a quick look at the *View Range* for this view so you understand how things are set up.

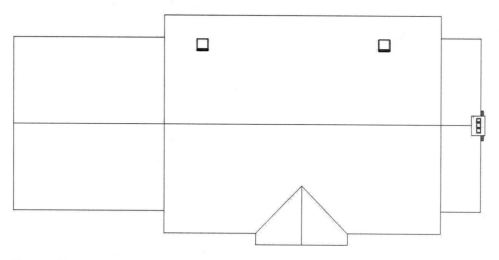

FIGURE 13-1.1 Initial Site Plan view

3. Make sure nothing is selected in the view so you have access to the view properties in the *Properties Palette*.

4. In the *Properties Palette*, scroll down if necessary, and select **Edit** next to *View Range*.

Here you can see the site is being viewed from 200′ above the first floor level, so your building or roof would have to be taller than that before it would be cut like a floor plan. The *View Depth* could be a problem here: on a steep site, the entire site will be seen if part of it passes through the specified *View Range*. However, items completely below the *View Range* will not be visible.

5. In the *View Depth* section, set the **Level** to **B.O. Footing**.

This change will ensure everything shows up on a steeper site, as you will now be looking deeper into the model.

6. Click **OK** to close the open dialog.

When creating the topography, you will want to be able to see the exterior walls so you can pick points on those walls to define the grade at the building. At the moment, the roof obscures the view of the exterior walls. Next, you will modify the view so the roof elements are transparent and dashed; this will reveal the perimeter of the building while still indicating where the roof overhangs are.

7. Select one of the roof objects in the *Site Plan* view.

8. Right-click and select **Override Graphics in View → By Category** (Figure 13-1.2).

   FYI: As the menu name implies, the graphics will only be modified in the current view. Also, by selecting "By Category" rather than "By Element" you will be modifying all roof elements, not just the selected one.

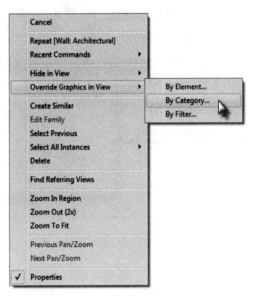

FIGURE 13-1.2 Graphics override by view

9. Click the **Open the Visibility Graphics dialog** and make the changes shown in Figure 13-1.3:

   a. Set the *Projection* lines for "Roofs" to **Dash 3/32″**.

   b. Check the box in the *Transparent* column for "Roofs."

FIGURE 13-1.3 Graphics override by view

Your *Site Plan* should now look similar to Figure 13-1.4.

FIGURE 13-1.4 Site plan with dashed roof

Next, you will make the floating skylights hidden in the *Site Plan* view as well. In addition to controlling the graphics by view, you can also control object visibility by view via the right-click menu. You will do this next to hide the skylights.

10. Select one of the skylights and then right-click (Figure 13-1.5).

11. From the pop-up menu, select **Hide in view → Category**.

> *TIP: This method is the only way to hide individual items (e.g., if you want to hide just one of the skylights) whereas the entire category can be hidden here or via the Visibility Graphics dialog for the current view.*

The skylights are now hidden; however, the hole in the roof is still visible.

> *TIP: You could use the Linework tool set to <Invisible Lines> to hide the opening if needed.*

FIGURE 13-1.5
Right-click with skylight selected

You are now ready to create the site object. The element in Revit which represents the site is called *toposurface*.

12. Select **Massing & Site → Model Site → Toposurface** from the *Ribbon*.

By default the *Place Point* tool is selected on the *Ribbon*; you are now in *Sketch* mode. This tool allows you to specify various points within the view at various elevations. Revit will generate a 3D surface based on those points, so the more points you provide, the more accurate the surface. Notice, on the *Options Bar* (Figure 13-1.6) that you can enter an elevation for each point as you pick them on the screen.

FIGURE 13-1.6 Options Bar for Toposurface tool

FIGURE 13-1.7 Partial South Elevation

What elevation should I enter on the Options Bar?

The elevation you enter for each point should relate to the *Level* datums set up in your project. For example, look at your *South Exterior* elevation (Figure 13-1.7). Recall that the first floor is set to 0'-0" and the top of foundation is set to -1'-3".

As you can see in the *South Elevation*, the only place you would want to add Points at an elevation of 0'-0" would be at the garage doors. Everywhere else should be at about -1'-6" so the grade does not rise higher than the top of the foundation wall and come into contact with any wood.

13. With the *Elevation* set to **0'-0"** pick the two points shown in Figure 13-1.8.

    TIP: *You should be able to Snap to the edge of the garage doors even though you cannot see them.*

14. Change the **Elevation** to **-1'-6"** (do not forget the minus sign) on the *Options Bar* and then pick the **points** as specified in Figure 13-1.9 on the next page.

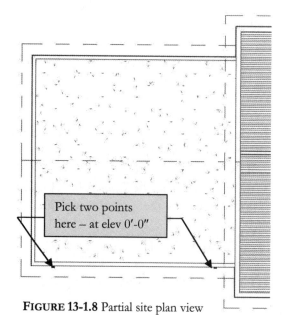

Pick two points here – at elev 0'-0"

FIGURE 13-1.8 Partial site plan view

FIGURE 13-1.9 Site plan view – 16 points to be selected (elev -1'-6")

15. Set the **Elevation** to **-2'-6"** and point the ten points shown in Figure 13-1.10 which will define the extents of the toposurface.

   FYI: The elevations selected will generally provide a positive slope away from the building; this will be visible in elevations and sections.

FIGURE 13-1.10 Site plan view – 10 points to be selected (elev – 2'-6")

16. Select the **green check mark** on the *Ribbon* to finish the surface.

Revit has now created the toposurface based on the points you specified. Again, the more points you add, the more refined and accurate the surface will be.

Ideally you would use the *Toposurface* tool to create a surface from a surveyors' points file or contour lines drawn in an AutoCAD file; Revit can automatically generate surfaces from these sources. This process is beyond the scope of this tutorial. See Revit's *Help System* for more information.

17. Switch to the **3D** view to see your new ground surface (Figure 13-1.11). **TIP:** Type **VV** and turn on the *Roof* category if needed.

Figure 13-1.11 3D view showing new ground surface

Unfortunately, the toposurface object cannot tell the difference between the inside and the outside of the building. So if you were to cut a section through the building, you would see the earth poche, or fill pattern, both inside and outside the building (Figure 13-1.12a). Therefore, you will need to create a *building pad* object that will "stamp" an area out of the ground (Figure 13-1.12b).

18. Switch to the **Basement Floor Plan** so you can see the foundation walls which will be used to define the perimeter of the pad.

19. Select **Massing & Site → Model Site → Building Pad**.

Building
Pad

FIGURE 13-1.12A Section BEFORE Building Pad is added

FIGURE 13-1.12B Section AFTER Building Pad is added

By default, the *Building Pad* object is created 12″ thick which is deeper than the basement floor slab and would show. Thus, you will edit the properties of the pad so it is only ½″ thick and does not interfere with any other model elements. The floor slab will hide the pad object.

20. Make sure nothing is selected and the *Properties Palette* is visible.

21. Click the **Edit Type** button on the *Properties Palette*.

22. Click **Edit** next to the *Structure* parameter.

23. Change the *pad* thickness from 1′-0″ to **1/2″**.

24. Close the open dialog box.

25. With **Pick Walls** selected on the *Ribbon*, select each of the foundation walls in the basement area (Figure 13-1.13).

FYI: Do not select the three exterior walls of the garage. There is no basement below the garage so the fill pattern should show up below the garage floor which is at elevation 0'-0".

FIGURE 13-1.13 Basement floor plan – walls selected to define the building pad

26. Click the **green check mark** to finish the pad.

You now have a *pad* object that "stamps" a portion of the ground surface down and out of the way for sections through the building.

If you had a basement with multiple levels, maybe a tuck-under garage at the basement level that dropped 8" lower than the rest of the basement, you would need to create multiple *pads* to "stamp" the ground down in different amounts.

Next, you will quickly create a driveway and sidewalk to wrap up this lesson.

You can use the *Subregion* tool or the *Split Surface* tool to create the driveway and sidewalks. The *Subregion* tool defines an area that is still part of the main site object; the *Split Surface* tool literally breaks the toposurface into separate elements. Splitting a surface can create problems when trying to move or edit the site, so you will use the *Subregion* tool.

27. Switch back to the **Site Plan** view.

Subregion

28. Select the **Subregion** tool and sketch the lines for the driveway (see Figure 13-1.14).

TIP: The sketch lines can extend out past the edge of the toposurface. The final subregion will actually still stop at the edge of the toposurface.

29. Click the **green check mark** on the *Ribbon* to finish the subregion.

FIGURE 13-1.14 Partial site plan – closed sketch lines for subregion

30. Switch to **3D** view to see your driveway (Figure 13-1.15). Notice the 2D lines sketched in the *Site Plan* view have been projected down onto the surface of the 3D site object!

FIGURE 13-1.15 Driveway added

Notice that the material is still the same as the main ground surface. You will learn how to change this in a moment.

Notice, also, how the grade slopes up at the garage doors because the two points that were placed on either side of the doors are at elevation 0′-0″.

When you select the toposurface and click *Edit Surface* on the *Ribbon*, you can select existing points and edit their elevations to refine the surface. You can also delete points or add new ones.

31. Use techniques previously covered to add a sidewalk as shown in Figure 13-1.16 below. You can also add a stair up to the front door (Figure 13-1.17).

Figure 13-1.16 3D view with driveway and sidewalk added; trees added later in this chapter

32. In the **Default 3D** view, select the *driveway* subregion.

33. Via the *Properties Palette*, Set the *Material* parameter to **Site – Asphalt**. Close open dialogs. **FYI:** *Be sure to select this from the* Materials *tab.*

34. Set the sidewalk *Material* to **Concrete – Case-in-place concrete**.

35. Set the main site element's *Material* to **Site – Grass**.

36. Make sure the *View Properties*, via the *Properties Palette* when nothing is selected, for your **3D** view is set to **Shaded, Consistent Colors or Realistic** so you can see a presentation version of the materials.

TIP: Set via the View Control Bar at the bottom of the Drawing Window.

Figure 13-1.17 Stair and railing added at front entry – railing shown from SEEK "sample railing" model

That concludes this overview of the site tools provided within Revit.

Exercise 13-2:
Creating an Exterior Rendering

The first thing you will do is set up a view. You will use the *Camera* tool to do this. This becomes a saved view that can be opened at any time from the *Project Browser*. Several cameras can be added to a project.

Creating a Camera View:

1. Open the **First Floor** plan view and **Zoom to Fit** so that you can see the entire plan (or type ZF).

2. On the *QAT*, select the down-arrow next to the 3D view and then select **Camera**. See image to the right.

3. Click the mouse in the lower right corner of the screen to indicate the camera eye location (Figure 13-2.1).

   NOTE: Before you click, Autodesk Revit tells you on the Status Bar it first wants the eye location, and you can set the eye level on the Options Bar.

4. Next, click near the entry doors (Figure 13-2.1).

Autodesk Revit will automatically open a view window for the new camera. Take a minute to look at the view and make a mental note of what you see and do not see in the view (Figure 13-2.2).

5. Switch back to the **First Floor** plan view.

6. Adjust the camera, using its grips, to look similar to Figure 13-2.3.

   TIP: If the camera is not visible in plan view, right click on the 3D view name in the Project Browser (3D View 1) and select Show Camera; do all this while still in the first floor plan view.

FIGURE 13-2.1 Placing a Camera in plan view

FIGURE 13-2.2 Initial Camera view

FIGURE 13-2.3 Revised camera – plan

7. Now switch to **3D View 1** and adjust the **Crop Region** to look similar to **Figure 13-2.4**.

> **FYI:** *You may need to adjust the Camera location back in the plan view as well.*

This will be the view you render later in this exercise.

FIGURE 13-2.4 Revised camera – 3d View 1

Assigning Materials to Elements:

Materials are high quality images which represent the materials your building will be made of.

Typically, materials are added while the project is being modeled. For example, when you create a material, using the *Materials* command on the *Manage tab*, you can assign it to elements in the model at that time. Of course, you can go back and add or change it later. Next, you will change the material assigned for the brick chimney.

8. Switch to **First Floor** plan view.

9. Select the fireplace, not the mantle.

10. Click **Edit Type** on the *Properties Palette*.

11. Click on the **Exterior Material** *value*; notice the material selected for the exterior finish is **Masonry – Brick** (Figure 13-2.5).

12. Click the icon to the right of the label **Masonry – Brick**.

Now you will take a look that the definition of the material *Masonry – Brick*.

FYI: From the Manage *tab you can also select* **Materials**.

You are now in the *Material Browser* dialog. You should notice that a material is already selected on the left. Next, you will select a different brick material.

FIGURE 13-2.5 Chimney properties

FIGURE 13-2.6 Materials Browser dialog

13. In the *Material Browser* dialog, select the *Appearance* tab and then click the **Replace this asset** link (Steps 1 and 2, Figure 13-2.6).

You can browse through the thumbnails and select any appearance in the list to be assigned to the *Masonry – Brick* material in Revit. The material does not have to be brick but would be confusing if something else were assigned to the *Masonry – Brick* material name.

14. Select the *Appearance Library* category and then *Masonry\Brick* (Steps 3 and 4), locate the **Non-Uniform Running – Red** and then click the Replace link (Step 5) (Figure 13-2.6).

Notice the material preview is now updated.

15. Click **OK** to close the *Material Browser* and *Properties* dialog boxes.

Now, when you render any object (wall, ceiling, etc.) that has the material "Masonry – Brick" associated with it, it will have the red brick on it.

If you need more than one brick color, you simply create a new material in the *Material Browser* dialog and assign that material to another element.

Project Location:

A first step in setting up a rendering is to specify the location of the project on the earth. This is important for accurate daylight studies.

Location

16. Select **Manage** → **Project Location** → **Location**.

17. In the *Project Address* field, enter **Minneapolis, MN**.

    a. You may also enter your location if you wish.

    b. It is even possible to enter the actual street address.

18. Press **Enter**.

FIGURE 13-2.7 Location Weather and Site dialog

You should now see an internet based map of your project location, complete with longitude and latitude (Figure 13-2.7).

19. Click **OK**.

Sun Settings:

Another step in preparing a rendering is to define the sun settings. You will explore the various options available.

20. Select **Manage** → **Settings** → **Additional Settings** (*drop-down list icon*) → **Sun Settings**.

21. Make the following changes (Figure 13-2.8):

    a. Solar Study: **Still**
    b. **Uncheck** *Ground Plane at Level.*
    c. Select **Summer Solstice** on the left.
    d. Change the year to **2015**.

FIGURE 13-2.8 Sun Settings dialog

22. Click **OK** to close the dialog

Setting Up the Environment:

You have limited options for setting up the building's environment. If you need more control than what is provided directly in Revit, you will need to use another program like Autodesk 3DS Max Design 2016, which is designed to work with Revit and can create extremely high quality renderings and animations; it even has daylighting functionality that helps to validate LEED® (Leadership in Environmental and Energy Design) requirements.

23. Switch to your camera view:
3D View 1.

24. Select the **Show Rendering Dialog** icon on the *View Control Bar*; it looks like a teapot (Figure 13-2.9).

FIGURE 13-2.9 Render dialog icon

FYI: This icon is only visible when you are in a 3D view, which is the same with the NavigationWheel and ViewCube.

The *Rendering* dialog box is now open (Figure 13-2.10). This dialog box allows you to control the environmental settings you are about to explore and actually create the rendering.

25. Select the **Autodesk Raytracer** rendering engine.

26. In the *Lighting* section, click the down-arrow next to *Scheme* to see the options; select **Exterior: Sun and Artificial** (Figure 13-2.11).

FIGURE 13-2.11 Lighting options

FIGURE 13-2.10 Rendering dialog

The lighting options are very simple choices; is the rendering an interior or exterior rendering and is the light source *Sun*, *Artificial*, or both? You may have artificial lights, that is, light fixtures like the ones you placed in the office but still only desire a rendering solely based on the light provided by the sun.

27. Also in the *Lighting* section, set the *Sun* to **Summer Solstice**.

FYI: In the Sun Settings dialog box, Revit lets you set up various "scenes" which control time of day. Two examples might be:
- *Daytime, summer*
- *Nighttime, winter*

Looking back at Figure 13-2.8; you would click *Duplicate* and provide a name. This name would then be available from the *Sun* drop-down list in the *Render* dialog box.

28. Click on the **Artificial Lighting** button.

You will now see a dialog similar to the one shown to the right (Figure 13-2.12). You will see several 2x4 light fixtures. The light fixtures relate to the fixtures you inserted in the reflected ceiling plans. It is very convenient that you can place lights in the ceiling plan and have them ready to render whenever you need to (i.e., render and cast light into the scene!). Here you can group lights together so you can control which ones are on (e.g., exterior and interior lights).

FIGURE 13-2.12 Scene Lighting dialog

29. Click **Cancel** to close the *Artificial Lighting* dialog.

30. Click the down-arrow next to *Style* in the *Background* area (Figure 13-2.13).

    a. Notice the options; click **Sky** to keep that option selected.

31. Click the "**X**" to close the Rendering dialog box for now. Your settings will be saved.

FIGURE 13-2.13 Background options

Notice that for the background, one option is Image. This allows you to specify a photograph of the site or one similar. It can prove difficult getting the perspective just right, but the end results can look as if you took a picture of the completed building.

Next, you will place a few trees into your rendering. You will adjust their exact location so they are near the edge of the framed rendering, so as not to cover too much of the building.

32. Switch to the **First Floor** plan view and select **Component** from the *Architecture* tab.

33. Pick **RPC Tree – Deciduous : Largetooth Aspen 25'** from the *Type Selector* on the *Properties Palette*.

    FYI: If the tree is not listed in the Type Selector, click Load Family and load the RPC Tree - Deciduous tree family from the Plantings folder.

34. Place four trees as shown in **Figure 13-2.14**; you will make one smaller in a moment.

FIGURE 13-2.14 First Floor – with trees added

35. Adjust the trees in plan view, reviewing the effects in the *3D View 1* view, so your 3D view is similar to Figure 13-2.15.

    TIP: Adjust the crop region if required.

36. In the **First Floor** plan view, select the tree that is shown smaller in **Figure 13-24**.

37. Click **Edit Type** on the *Properties Palette*.

38. Click **Duplicate** and enter the name **RPC Tree – Deciduous : Largetooth Aspen 18′**.

39. Change the *Height* to **18′** (it is currently 25′), and then click **OK** to close the open dialog boxes.

The previous three steps allow you to have a little more variety in the trees being placed. Otherwise they would all be the same height, which is not very natural.

FIGURE 13-2.15 3D View 1 – with trees

40. Open the **3D View 1** camera view.

41. Open the *Rendering* dialog.

42. Make sure the *Quality* is set to **Draft**.

> **FYI:** *The time to process the rendering increases significantly as the quality level and resolution are raised.*

43. Click **Render** from the *Rendering* dialog box.

You will see the following progress bar while Revit is processing the rendering (Figure 13-2.16).

FIGURE 13-2.16 Rendering progress

After a few minutes, depending on the speed of your computer, you should have a rendered image similar to Figure 13-2.17 on the next page. You can increase the quality of the image by adjusting the quality setting in the *Render* dialog. However, these higher settings require substantially more time to generate the rendering. The last step before saving the Revit project file is to save the rendered image to a file.

FYI: Each time you make changes to the model that are visible from that view, you will have to re-render the view to get an updated image. Depending on exactly how your view was set up, you may be able to see light from one of the light fixtures in the second floor office or see the stair and railing through the window. Revit can have the glazing in windows set to be transparent! Renderings with artificial lighting can take a lot longer to render.

FIGURE 13-2.17 Rendered view – low resolution draft setting

44. From the *Rendering* dialog select **Export**.

   FYI: The 'Save to Project' button saves the image within the Revit Project for placement on Sheets; this is convenient but does make the project size larger so you should delete the old ones when they are not needed anymore!

45. Select a *location* and provide a *file name*.

46. Set the *Save As* type to **JPEG**.

47. Click **Save**.

The image file you just saved can now be inserted into MS Word or Adobe Photoshop for editing or it can be emailed to your client.

Design Options can also be rendered:

You can render your design options in addition to the primary options. As mentioned before, you can copy a view and change its visibility settings to show specific design options or you can just change the settings for the current view. You will do that next.

48. In the **3D View 1** view, adjust the **View Properties** so the curved entry roof and taller entry windows are visible. Refer back to the *Design Options* section if necessary – page 9-25.

49. Switch to plan view and change the tree in front of the house to another option available from the *Type Selector* or the Library.

50. **Render** the image, adjusting these settings:

    a. Quality: **Medium**
    b. Output Settings: **Printer @ 300dpi**
    c. Lighting: **Exterior: Sun only**

51. **Save** your project as **ex13-2.rvt**.

FIGURE 13-2.18 Rendered view with design options adjusted

Notice the large tree casts shadows on the ground; you can also see reflections of the tree in the windows when the angle and lighting are right. Remember, the angle and location of the shadows are based on the time, date and location on the earth; if you change those settings, the shadows will change accordingly. You also need to set true North for the given site! This can be done via **Mange → Project Location → Rotate True North**.

As you can imagine, an image like this could really "sell" your design to the client. Revit makes the process to get to this point very easy compared to legacy CAD programs and techniques used prior to Revit.

Exercise 13-3:
Rendering an Isometric in Section

This exercise will introduce you to a 3D view tool called *Section Box*. This tool is not necessarily related to renderings, but the two features used together can produce some interesting results.

Setting up the 3D View:

1. Open file ex13-2.rvt and **Save As ex13-3.rvt**.

2. Switch to the **Default 3D** view via the icon on the *QAT (not the 3D View 1 from Exercise 13-2)*.

3. Make sure nothing is selected so the *Properties Palette* shows the current view's properties. If something is selected, you can still see the current view's properties by selecting **3D View: {3D}** from the drop-down list below the *Type Selector*.

4. Activate the **Section Box** parameter and then click **Apply**.

You should see a box appear around your building, similar to Figure 13-3.1. When selected, you can adjust the size of the box with its grips. Anything outside the box is not visible. This is a great way to study a particular area of your building while in an isometric view. You will experiment with this feature next.

Section Box (shown selected)

Six grips to manipulate the Section Box – only visible while the *Section Box* is selected

FIGURE 13-3.1 3D view with Section Box activated

5. To practice using the **Section Box**, drag the grips around until your view looks similar to Figure 13-3.2.

   TIP: This may require the ViewCube tool as well, or hold Shift + drag the Wheel button on the mouse.

   a. Click and drag the grip from the top downward.

   b. Click and drag the grip for the East (right) face toward the West (left).

FIGURE 13-3.2 3D view with adjusted Section Box

Did you notice the grips look different? One grip looks like two arrows rather than a small square. You can still click on any part of the grip and drag it, but you can also single-click on one of the arrows to slightly adjust the section box in the direction the arrow points. This is similar to the nudge feature, when an element is selected and you use the arrows keys to move it just a little bit.

This creates a very interesting view of the First Floor plan. What client would have trouble understanding this drawing?

6. Now readjust the **Section Box** to look similar to **Figure 13-3.3**.

FIGURE 13-3.3 3D view

7. From the *Manage* tab, select **Sun Settings** and change the following *Sun* settings (Figure 13-3.4): ***TIP:** Set* Solar Study *to* Still *first and then click any named preset.*

    a. New name: **28 February 8am** (via Duplicate)

    b. Month: **2** (February)

    c. Day: **28**

    d. Time: **8:00am**

FYI: Do not forget, without doing any rendering in Revit you can turn on the shadows in any view. You can even turn on shadows in your 2D exterior elevation view (see below) for a great effect with little effort!

FIGURE 13-3.4 Modified Sun Settings

8. Select the **Render** icon, select the *Scheme*: **Exterior: Sun only**, and then set *Sun* to **28 February 8am**.

9. Set the options as shown in the image to the left, including setting the *Background Style* to **Color**.

10. Select the **Region** option and then adjust the "render region crop" that appears in the view to indicate the area to be rendered.

TIP: This tool is nice for checking a material before rendering the entire building, which takes longer.

11. Click the **Render** button.

The image will take a few minutes to render, again depending on the speed of your computer. When finished it should look similar to **Figure 13-3.5**. The image looks much better on the screen or printed in color.

As mentioned previously, you can increase the rendering quality settings to get much better results, though it simply takes more time. Also, the higher quality images can be printed larger without pixilation. If you have time, try changing the Quality to High or Best and the Resolution to 300dpi. Note the difference in the time to complete.

Adjusting an Element's Material:

As previously mentioned, most elements already have a material assigned to them. This is great because it allows you to quickly render your project to get some preliminary images. However, they usually need to be adjusted. You will do this next.

FIGURE 13-3.5 Rendered isometric view - draft settings selected

12. In the *Render* dialog, click the *Show Model* button at the bottom; the rendered view disappears. Close the *Render* dialog.

13. Select one of the cabinets in the kitchen.

14. Click the **Edit Type** button in the *Properties Palette*.

Notice the Cabinet Material parameter is set to **<By Category>** (Figure 13-3.6). You could change the material here for just the selected cabinet type; however, by setting a material to be *By Category* you can quickly change the material for all the cabinets at one time, without having to select every cabinet.

Sun Path

It is possible to turn on the feature called Sun Path. This shows the path of the sun over a day and a year. This is accessed from the View Control Bar while in a 3D view.

Once on, you can click and drag the sun along its daily or yearly path!

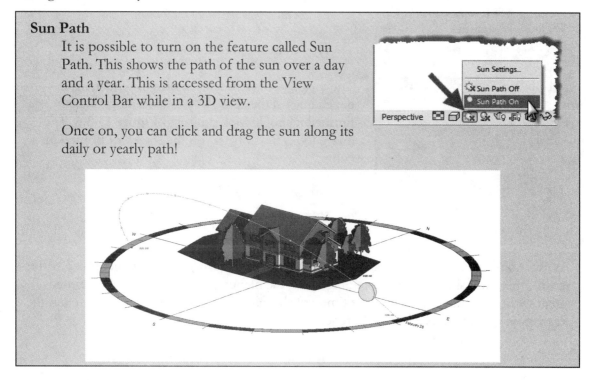

15. **Close** the *Type Properties* dialog.

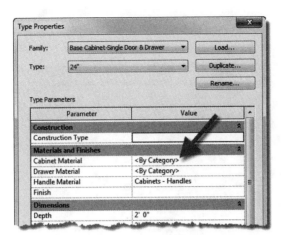

FIGURE 13-3.6 Cabinet properties

The next step will open the dialog box which controls color, line weight, line pattern and material, for both hatching and rendering representations. This is for the entire project, with the exception of any overrides added per view via VV.

16. Select **Manage → Settings → Object Styles**.

17. Expand the **Casework** category (Figure 13-3.7).

FIGURE 13-3.7 Object Styles dialog

The *Cabinet* subcategory has a material assigned to it called **Cabinets**.

18. Click on **Cabinets** in the *Material* column, and then click the "**...**" button that appears to the right.

You are now in the *Material Browser* dialog box, where you can create and edit *Materials*.

19. Open the *Asset Browser* by clicking the **Replace this asset** link on *Appearance* tab as previously covered (Figure 13-3.8).

20. Change the *Appearance* material to
    Cherry - Natural Low Gloss (Figure 13-3.8).

    TIP: Select the category label Wood *under Appearance Library first.*

FIGURE 13-3.8 Material dialog – with *Asset Browser* open

21. Click **OK** to close the open dialog boxes.

22. You can now re-render the 3D view and see the results.

23. **Save** your project as ex **13-3.rvt**.

    TIP: While in the 3D view with the Section Box active, you can zoom in to an area, just like you can in other views, and render that enlarged area (just check the "Region" option in the Render dialog). Similarly, you can change the material for the counter top, faucet, dishwasher, etc.

Exercise 13-4:
Creating an Interior Rendering

Creating an interior rendering is very similar to an exterior rendering.
This exercise will walk through the steps involved in creating a high quality interior rendering.

Setting Up the Camera View:

1. Open ex13-3.rvt and **Save As ex13-4.rvt**.

2. Open the **First Floor** plan view.

3. Select the **Camera** tool from the *QAT*.

4. Place the *Camera* as shown in **Figure 13-4.1**.

FIGURE 13-4.1 Camera placed – Kitchen

Revit uses default heights for the camera and the target. These heights are based on the current level's floor elevation plus the eye height of an average height person. These reference points can be edited via the camera properties.

Revit will automatically open the newly generated camera view. Your view should look similar to **Figure 13-4.2**.

FIGURE 13-4.2 Initial interior camera view

5. Using the **Crop Region** rectangle, modify the view to look like **Figure 13-4.3**; select it and then drag the grips.

6. Uncheck **Far Clip Active** in the *Properties Palette*. Copy the two trees in the back of the house into a position so they can be seen through the window over the sink.

    TIP: You will have to switch to plan view to adjust the camera's depth of view to see the trees. REMINDER: If the camera does not show in plan view, right-click on the camera view label in the Project Browser, while in plan view, and select Show Camera. You may need to switch between the plan and camera views several times to adjust the trees so they are visible through the windows.

7. Switch back to **First Floor** plan to see the revised *Camera* view settings.

Notice the field of view triangle is wider based on the changes to the **Crop Region** in the camera view (Figure 13-4.4).

FIGURE 13-4.3 Modified interior camera

FIGURE 13-4.4 Modified camera – First Floor

FIGURE 13-4.5 Camera properties

8. Select the *Camera*.

9. Make sure the **Eye Elevation** is **5'-6"** (Figure 13-4.5).

Notice the other settings for the camera; these are the properties for the 3D view itself. Changing the *Target Elevation* would cause the camera to look up at the ceiling or down at the floor depending on the value entered.

10. Click **Apply** if any changes were needed.

The vertical lines are distorted due to the wide field of view, crop region. This is similar to what a camera with a 10-15mm lens would get in the finished building.

Creating the Rendering:

Next you will render the interior kitchen view.

11. In the interior camera view, create a new item in *Sun Settings* dialog as shown below (Figure 13-4.6).

> *Name*: Kitchen
> *Azimuth*: 302.00
> *Altitude*: 34.00

You just created a "fake" sun angle to make the rendering look better for presentation purposes. This may be useful if the exact north is not known or the designer wants to leverage a little artistic freedom.

FIGURE 13-4.6 Sun Settings

12. Select **Show Rendering Dialog** from the *View Control Bar*.

13. Set the *Engine to* **Autodesk Raytracer, Medium** *quality and* **150 dpi**.

14. Set the *Scheme* to **Interior: Sun only**; be sure to select "interior:" as it makes a big difference.

15. Click **Render** to begin the rendering process.

This will take several minutes depending on the speed of your computer. When finished, the view should look similar to **Figure 13-4.7**.

16. Click **Export** from the *Rendering* dialog box to save the image to a file on your hard drive. Name the file **Kitchen.jpg** (jpeg file format).

You can now open the *Kitchen.jpg* file in Adobe Photoshop or insert it into a MS Word type program, or equivalent, to manipulate or print.

To toggle back to the normal hidden view, select **Show the Model** from the *Rendering* dialog box.

There are many things you can do to make the rendering look even better. You can add interior light fixtures and props (e.g., pictures on the wall, items on the counter top, and lawn furniture in the yard). Once you add interior lights, you can adjust the Sun Setting to nighttime and then render a night scene.

> *TIP: Setting the Output to Printer rather than Screen allows you to generate a higher resolution image. Thus, between the Quality setting and the Output setting you can create an extremely high quality rendering, but it might take hours if not days to process!*

Revit also gives you the ability to set a material to be self-illuminating. This will allow you to make a button on the dishwasher look like it is lit up or, if applied to the glass on the range door, like the light in the oven is on! You can also set a lamp shade to glow when a light source has been defined under it so it looks more realistic.

FIGURE 13-4.7 Rendered view

You can quickly add another camera view to look at the other half of the kitchen. The ability to stretch the *Crop Region* allows you to create interesting views like the one below, which is really more like a panoramic view than a traditional camera view (Figure 13-4.8).

FIGURE 13-4.8 Another rendered view

17. **Save** your project as **13-4.rvt**.

Realistic Display Setting:

In addition to *Shade* and *Hidden Line* display settings you can also select *Realistic*. This will show the *Render Appearance* materials on your building without the need to do a full rendering. However, the shades and shadows are not nearly as realistic as a full rendering.

This is a great way to get an idea on how the materials look but you will find it best to minimize the use of this setting as Revit will run much slower.

Duplicating a Material:

It is important to know how to properly duplicate a *Material* in your model so you do not unintentionally affect another *Material*. The information on this page is mainly for reference and does not need to be done in your model.

If you **Duplicate** a *Material* in your model, the **Appearance Asset** will be associated to the new *Material* AND the *Material* you copied it from! For example, in the image below, we will right-click on Carpet (1) and duplicate it. Before we duplicate it, notice the *Appearance Asset* named "RED" is not shared (arrow #3 in the image below).

Once you have duplicated a *Material*, notice the two carpet materials in this example; now indicate they both share the same *Appearance Asset*. Changing one will affect the other. Click the **Duplicate this asset** icon in the upper right (second image).

Once the *Appearance Asset* has been duplicated (third image), you can expand the information section and rename the asset. You can now make changes to this material without affecting other materials.

Exercise 13-5:
Adding People to the Rendering

Revit provides a few free RPC people to add to your renderings; RPC stands for Rich Photorealistic Content. These are files from a popular company that provides 3D photo content for use in renderings (http://www.archvision.com). You can buy additional content in groupings such as college students or per item. In addition to people, they offer items like cars, plants, trees, office equipment, etc.

Loading Content into the Current Project

1. Open ex13-4.rvt and **Save As 13-5.rvt**.

2. Switch to the **First Floor** plan view.

3. Select the **Component** tool from the *Architecture* tab.

4. Click the **Load Family** button on the *Ribbon*.

5. Browse to the **Entourage** folder and select both the **RPC Male** and **RPC Female** files, using the Ctrl key to select both at once, and click **Open** to load them.

6. Place one **Male** and one **Female**, specified via the *Type Selector*, as shown in **Figure 13-5.1**.

FIGURE 13-5.1 Kitchen – RPC people added

The line in the circle (Figure 13-5.1) represents the direction a person is looking. You simply *Rotate* the object to make adjustments. The image below shows the RPC people that can be placed in your project. **Notice the two families each have multiple types.**

FIGURE 13-5.2
Type Selector – Properties Palette

7. Switch to your interior kitchen camera view.

8. Set the *Quality* setting to **Medium**.

9. Set the *Scheme* to **Kitchen**.

10. Click **Render**.

Additional RPC content can be purchased from ArchVision via their website: www.archvision.com. They also have a yearly subscription option which provides hundreds of trees, cars and people to add to your renderings.

Your rendering should now have people in it and look similar to **Figure 13-5.4**. Notice how the people cast shadows; remember the only light source is the sunlight coming through the two windows and the glass door. If you want to change the people, simply select them and pick from the *Type Selector*.

Adding people and other "props" gives your model a sense of scale and makes it look a little more realistic. After all, architecture is for people. These elements can be viewed from any angle. Try a new camera view from another angle to see how the people adjust to match the view and perspective; see Figure 13-5.3, front of the female model versus the side view below.

FIGURE 13-5.3 Interior kitchen view with people added

FIGURE 13-5.4 Interior kitchen view with people added

11. **Save** your project as **ex13-5.rvt**.

The image below shows all the transportation content available through Archvision. When using their subscription option, you have access to all of their content (including people, trees and more). Using the Archvision Dashboard program, you simply drag and drop content into Revit. Students should contact Archvision about special student options. These elements work in Realistic views, renderings and A360 Cloud renderings.

Sketchy Lines

Be sure to Check out the **Sketchy Lines** options available via View Properties → **Graphic Display Options**. Tip: Also turn on **Smooth lines with anti-aliasing** when using the *Sketchy Lines* feature.

Self-Exam:

The following questions can be used as a way to check your knowledge of this lesson. The answers can be found at the bottom of the page.

1. Creating a camera adds a view to the *Project Browser* list. (T/F)

2. Rendering materials are defined in Revit's *Materials* dialog box. (T/F)

3. After inserting a light fixture, you need to adjust several settings before rendering to get light from the fixture. (T/F)

4. You can adjust the season, which affects how the trees are rendered. (T/F)

5. Use the _____ tool to hide a large portion of the model.

Review Questions:

The following questions may be assigned by your instructor as a way to assess your knowledge of this section. Your instructor has the answers to the review questions.

1. Draft renderings can be printed very large with no pixilation. (T/F)

2. You cannot get accurate lighting based on day/month/location. (T/F)

3. Adding components, i.e. families, to your project does not make the project file bigger. (T/F)

4. Creating photo-realistic renderings can take a significant amount of time for your computer to process. (T/F)

5. The RPC people can only be viewed from one angle. (T/F)

6. The RPC components do not cast shadows. (T/F)

7. Adjust the _____ to make more of a perspective view visible.

8. You use the _____ tool to load and insert RPC people.

9. You can adjust the Eye Elevation of the camera via the camera's _____.

10. What is the file size of (completed) Exercise 13-5? _____ MB

Lesson 14
Residence: Construction Documents Set:

This lesson will look at bringing everything you have drawn thus far together onto sheets. The sheets, once set up, are ready for plotting. Basically, you place the various views you have created on sheets. The scale for each view is based on the scale you set while drawing that view, which is important to have set correctly because it affects the text and symbol sizes. When finished setting up the sheets, you will have a set of drawings ready to print individually or all at once. The disc has a video on creating sheets and sheet lists.

Exercise 14-1:
Setting up a Sheet

Creating a Sheet View:

1. Open ex13-5.rvt and **Save As** 14-1.rvt.

2. Select **View → Sheet Composition → Sheet**.

Next Autodesk® Revit® will prompt you for a *Titleblock* to use. The template file you started with has two *titleblock families* from which to choose: 11 x 17 and 22 x 34 (Figure 14-1.1).

3. Select the **D 22x34 Horizontal** titleblock and click **OK**.

That's it; you have created a new sheet that is ready to have views and/or schedules placed on it!

NOTE: A new view shows up in the Project Browser under the heading Sheets. Once you get an entire CD set ready, this list can be very long.

Autodesk Revit also lets you create placeholder sheets which allow you to add sheets to the sheet index without the need to have a sheet show up in the *Project Browser*. This is helpful if a consultant, such as a food service designer, is not using Autodesk Revit. This feature allows you to add those sheets to the sheet index. Placeholder sheets can only be added in the sheet list schedule by using the *New Row* tool on the *Ribbon*. Once a placeholder sheet exists, it can be turned into a real sheet by selecting from the lower list in the dialog to the left.

FIGURE 14-1.1 Select a Titleblock

FIGURE 14-1.2 Initial Titleblock view

4. **Zoom in** to the sheet number area (lower right corner).

5. Adjust the text to look similar to **Figure 14-1.3**. Click on the text and edit it; make sure *Modify* is selected first.

John Brown

New Residence

Unnamed

Project number	2015-048
Date	March 3, 2015
Drawn by	Daniel J. Stine
Checked by	Bob T. Checker

A5.01

Scale	

3/5/2015 12:55:24 PM

TIP: Select the title block, hover the cursor over the text you wish to edit, and then click. Notice some of the fields are filled in based on the project set up you did earlier in the book (chapter 5); project name and number for example.

Notice the time and date stamp. This helps to remember when a sheet was plotted, especially if you forget to update the date before printing.

FIGURE 14-1.3 Revised Titleblock data

6. **Zoom out** so you can see the entire sheet (type ZF).

7. With the sheet fully visible, click and drag the **Living Room - East** label, under *Elevations (Interior elevations)*, from the *Project Browser* onto the sheet view. Let go of the mouse button once it is within the drawing window; do not click yet.

You will see a box that represents the extents of the view you are placing on the current sheet. If the box is larger than the sheet, this means the *View Scale* is to a scale that is too large. You would need to open the view and adjust the *View Scale*.

8. Move the *Viewport* around until the box is in the upper-right corner of the sheet (this can be repositioned later at any time) and click to place.

Your view should look similar to **Figure 14-1.4**.

FIGURE 14-1.4 Sheet with Living Room view placed on it

9. Click the mouse in a white area, not on any lines, to deselect the *Living Room - East* view. Notice the extents box goes away.

① **Living Room - East**
   1/2" = 1'-0"

FIGURE 14-1.5 Drawing title

10. **Zoom in** on the lower left corner to view the drawing identification symbol that Revit automatically added (Figure 14-1.5).

NOTE: Each drawing placed on a sheet automatically gets a number, starting with one. The next drawing you add will be number two.

The view name, from the *Project Browser*, is listed as the drawing title. This is another reason to rename the elevation and section views as you create them.

Also notice that the drawing scale is listed. Again, this comes from the *View Scale* setting for the *Living Room - East* view.

As you can see, if you added furniture to the living room, the furniture shows up; normally this would be turned off. You can turn these off using the same technique covered later in this chapter for the trees in the exterior elevations.

Setting up the Floor Plans:

Setting up floor plans is easy; actually, they are already set up from the template you started with.

11. From the *Sheets* section in the *Project Browser*, double-click on the sheet named **A1 – First Floor Plan** to open it.

As you can see, the floor plan is already set up on a sheet. Again, a few things can be turned off (i.e., trees, RPC People) per the techniques covered next. You would also want to move the exterior elevation tags closer to the building so they are within the title block if they are not already.

12. Adjust the location of the plan view on the sheet if needed. Click and drag to move it.

13. Change the sheet number to **A2.01**, and then close the First Floor Plan, *Sheet.*

Setting up the Exterior Elevations:

Next you will set up the exterior elevations. Again, the sheets are already set up but the views have not been placed on the sheets like the floor plans have.

14. Open Sheet **A6 – Elevations**, and drag the *South* elevation view onto the sheet. Place the drawing near the bottom and centered on the sheet.

Your drawing should look similar to Figure 14-1.6.

FIGURE 14-1.6 South exterior elevation

Next, you will turn off the trees in the *South* view. Normally you would turn them off in all views. However, you will only turn them off in the *South* view to show that you can control visibility per view on a sheet.

15. In the sheet view, click on the *South* exterior elevation view to select it; the outer extents rectangle is called the *viewport* (Figure 14-1.6).

16. Now **right-click** and select **Activate View** from the pop-up menu. *TIP: You can also double-click within the view to activate it.*

At this point you are in the viewport and can make changes to the project model to control visibility, which is what you will do next.

17. Turn on **View Cropping** and **Show Crop Region** on the *View Control Bar;* adjust the crop region to minimize the space needed by the view on the sheet. When finished, hide the crop region.

18. Make sure nothing is selected. With nothing selected in the view, the *Properties Palette* is displaying the activated view's properties, just as if you were in the view and not the sheet.

19. Click the **Edit** button next to *Visibility/Graphics Overrides. TIP:* Or type VV.

20. In the *Visibility* dialog **uncheck Planting**.

21. Close the open dialog box.

22. Right-click anywhere in the drawing area and select **Deactivate View** from the pop-up menu. *TIP: Double-clicking outside of view also will deactivate the view.*

Now the trees are turned off for the *South* elevation; if you would have had another elevation view on this same sheet, the trees would still be visible for that view.

23. Add the *North* elevation to the **A7 – Elevations** *Sheet*.

> *TIP: You may need to switch to the North view and turn on the Crop and Crop Display icons on the View Control Bar to make the area placed on the sheet smaller so it will fit; when finished, turn off Crop Display but leave Crop View turned on. Or use the Activate View option just covered.*

Now you will stop for a moment and notice that Revit is automatically referencing the drawings as you place them on sheets.

24. Switch to *First Floor* (Figure 14-1.7).

Notice in Figure 14-1.7 that the number A6 represents the sheet number that the drawing can be found on. The number one (1) is the drawing number to look for on sheet A6. The empty tag is the enlarged elevation view you set up earlier in the book; it has not been placed on a sheet yet so it is not filled in.

FIGURE 14-1.7 First Floor – elevation tag filled-in

Setting up Sections:

25. Open *Sheet* **A8 – Building Sections** and place *Cross Section 1*.

26. Open *Sheet* **A9 – Building Sections** and place the *Longitudinal Section* view on the *Sheet*.

27. Switch to *First Floor* plan view and zoom into the area shown in Figure 14-1.9.

FIGURE 14-1.8 A9 – Building Sections sheet

Notice, again, that the reference bubbles are automatically filled in when the referenced view is placed on a sheet. If the drawing is moved to another sheet, the reference bubbles are automatically updated.

You can also see in Figure 14-1.8 that the reference bubbles on the building sections are filled in.

FIGURE 14-1.9 First Floor – Section ref's filled in

Set up the Remaining Sheets:

Next you set up sheets for the remaining views that have yet to be placed on a sheet, except for the 3D views.

28. Add the remaining views to the appropriate sheets; if one does not exist you can create a new sheet.

Question: On a large project with hundreds of views, how do I know for sure if I have placed every view on a sheet?

Answer: Revit has a feature called *Browser Organization* that can hide all the views that have been placed on a sheet. You will try this next.

Take a general look at the *Project Browser* to see how many views are listed.

29. Select **View → Windows → User Interface** (*drop-down*) **→ Browser Organization.**

30. On the *Views* tab, click the checkbox next to **not on sheets** (Figure 14-1.10).

31. Click **OK.**

32. Notice the list in the *Project Browser* is now smaller (Figure 14-1.11).

FIGURE 14-1.10 Browser Organization dialog

The *Project Browser* now only shows drawing views that have not been placed onto a sheet. Of course, you could have a few views that do not need to be placed on a sheet, but this feature will help eliminate errors. Also notice the label at the top: *Views (not on sheets)*; this tells you what mode or filter the *Project Browser* is in.

Next you will reset the *Project Browser*.

33. Open *Browser Organization* again and check the box next to **all** and click **OK** to close the dialog box.

TIP: You can also select the title Views *at the top of the Project Browser and toggle between filter types via the Type Selector.*

FIGURE 14-1.11 Project Browser

Sheets with Design Options:

Finally, you will set up a sheet to show the two *Design Options*.

34. Create a *Sheet* named **Entry Options** and number it **A100**.

35. Place both *Entry – Option 2* 3D views on the new sheet and change the scale to **⅛″ = 1′-0″**.

   TIP: Select the placed view and change the scale in the Properties Palette.

36. **Save** your project as **ex14-1.rvt**.

Each 3D view has its *Visibility* modified to show the desired *Design Options*. When a view is placed on a sheet, those settings are preserved.

Figure 14-1.12 Entry Options Sheet; two views with Design Options added

Exercise 14-2:
Sheet Index

Revit has the ability to create a *Sheet List* (or sheet index) automatically. This feature uses the same schedule creation interface previously covered. Whenever a sheet is added or removed from the project, this *Sheet List* will automatically update. You can even use the *Sheet List* to make changes to the sheet. For example, if you noticed a few sheets were not all uppercase you could change them in the *Sheet List* and the sheet itself would update as it represents the same information. You will study this feature now.

Creating a Sheet List View

 Sheet List

1. Open ex14-1.rvt and **Save As** ex14-2.

2. Select **View → Create → Schedules** *(down-arrow)* **→ Sheet List**.

You are now in the *Sheet List Properties* dialog box. Here you specify which fields you want in the sheet index and how to sort the list (Figure 14-2.1).

3. Add **Sheet Number** and **Sheet Name** to the right (click *Add →*).

4. Click **OK**.

FIGURE 14-2.1 Sheet List Properties Dialog; sheet number and name added

Now you should notice that the *Sheet Names* are cut off because the column is not wide enough (Figure 14-2.2). You will adjust this next.

5. Move your cursor over the right edge of the *Sheet List* table and click-and-drag to the right until you can see the entire name (Figure 14-2.2).

A	B
Sheet Number	Sheet Name
A2.01	First Floor Plan
A2	Second Floor Pl
A3	First Floor Refl
A4	Second Floor R
A5	Roof Plan
A6	Elevations
A7	Elevations
A8	Building Sectio
A9	Building Sectio
A10	Wall Sections
A11	Wall Sections
A12	Details
A13	Interior Elevatio
A14	Interior Details
A15	Schedules
C1	Site Plan
S0	Foundation Pla
S1	First Floor Fram
S2	Second Floor F
S3	Roof Framing
A0	Basement Plan
E0	Basement Elect
E1	First Floor Elect
E2	Second Floor El
A5.01	Unnamed
A100	Entry Options

<Sheet List>

FIGURE 14-2.2 Sheet List view; notice sheet names are cut off in right column

A	B
Sheet Number	Sheet Name
A2.01	First Floor Plan
A2	Second Floor Plan
A3	First Floor Reflected Ceiling Plan
A4	Second Floor Reflected Ceiling Plan
A5	Roof Plan
A6	Elevations
A7	Elevations
A8	Building Sections
A9	Building Sections
A10	Wall Sections
A11	Wall Sections
A12	Details
A13	Interior Elevations
A14	Interior Details
A15	Schedules
C1	Site Plan
S0	Foundation Plan
S1	First Floor Framing Plan
S2	Second Floor Framing
S3	Roof Framing
A0	Basement Plan
E0	Basement Electrical Plan
E1	First Floor Electrical
E2	Second Floor Electrical
A5.01	Unnamed
A100	Entry Options

<Sheet List>

FIGURE 14-2.3 Sheet List view; sheet names are now visible

Adjusting Which Sheets Show Up in the List:

Looking at the *Sheet List* (Figure 14-2.3), you decide to remove the *Entry design options* sheet (i.e., sheet A100) from the list as it is not part of the construction document set.

As with other schedules, this is live data which is directly connected to the model. If you change a sheet number here, the number will change throughout the project. If you delete a number (i.e., a row), Revit will delete the sheet from the project.

You will look at the option that allows you to remove a sheet from the list without deleting the sheet.

6. Right-click on sheet **A100** in the sheet list and select **Delete Row(s)**. You will NOT actually delete this sheet, so do not click **OK**.

You will get a warning stating the sheet will be deleted and what you should do if you only want to remove the sheet from the *Sheet List*.

7. Click **Cancel**.

8. Select *Sheet* **A100 – Entry Options** in the *Project Browser* and click **Properties**.

9. Uncheck **Appears In Sheet List** (Figure 14-2.4) and then click **Apply**.

Notice the *Sheet* was removed from the *Sheet List* view but is still in the project.

10. In the *Sheet List*, right-click on sheet **A13 Interior Elevations** and select **Delete Row(s)** from the menu.

11. Click **OK**.

Not only was the sheet removed from the *Sheet List*, it was also deleted from the project. However, any views placed on a sheet are not deleted from the project. Next, you will renumber a sheet via the *Sheet List*.

12. Click in the cell with the sheet number **A5.01** and change the number to read **A13**.

Now an existing sheet has been renumbered and so has all the detail, elevation and section bubbles that point to this sheet.

13. In the *Properties Palette*, click the **Edit...** button next to **Sorting/Grouping**.

14. Set *Sort By* to **Sheet Number**.

15. Click **OK** to close the open dialog box.

Now the sheets should be sorted correctly, including the sheet you just renumbered.

FIGURE 14-2.4 Properties for sheet A100

TIP: It is possible to create a custom parameter and sort the sheets using the information entered there. This allows you to place the sheets in any order you wish. Usually the "C" (i.e., civil) sheets are before the "A" (i.e., architectural) sheets. So, for example, all the "C" sheets could have the value "02" entered in the custom parameter, and the "A" sheets could all have the value "03" entered. Then, in sorting and grouping, you would sort by your custom parameter and then by sheet number. You can create the custom parameter on the Fields tab in the Sheet List schedule (Figure 14-2.1) by clicking the Add Parameter button.

Setting up a Title Sheet:

Now you will create a title sheet to place your sheet index on.

16. Create a new sheet:
    a. *Number:* **T1**
    b. *Name:* **Title Sheet**

17. From the *Schedules/Quantities* category of the *Project Browser*, place the view named **Sheet List** on the *Title Sheet* via drag-and-drop.

18. With the schedule selected on the sheet, drag the column grips so each row is only one line. (Figure 14-2.5).

19. Create a new text style named **1″ Arial**, and adjust the settings accordingly.

    TIP: Select the Text *tool, click* Edit Type *and then* Duplicate.

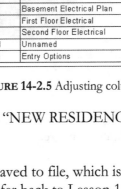

Sheet List	
Sheet Number	Sheet Name
A2.01	First Floor Plan
A2	Second Floor Plan
A3	First Floor Reflected Ceiling Plan
A4	Second Floor Reflected Ceiling Plan
A5	Roof Plan
A6	Elevations
A7	Elevations
A8	Building Sections
A9	Building Sections
A10	Wall Sections
A11	Wall Sections
A12	Details
A13	Interior Elevations
A14	Interior Details
A15	Schedules
C1	Site Plan
S0	Foundation Plan
S1	First Floor Framing Plan
S2	Second Floor Framing
S3	Roof Framing
A0	Basement Plan
E0	Basement Electrical Plan
E1	First Floor Electrical
E2	Second Floor Electrical
A5.01	Unnamed
A100	Entry Options

FIGURE 14-2.5 Adjusting column width

20. Add large text across the top of the sheet that reads "NEW RESIDENCE FOR JOHN BROWN" (Figure 14-2.6).

Next, you will place one of your rendered images that you saved to file, which is a raster image. If you have not created a raster image, you should refer back to Lesson 13 and create one now. Otherwise, you can use any PNG or JPG file on your hard drive if necessary.

If you used the *Save to Project* feature, you can simply drag one of the images listed under *Renderings* from the *Project Browser*. The interior kitchen rendering was added to the title sheet using this method. Here you can see Revit has added a *Drawing Title* tag beneath the image, which would allow you to reference this image from another location.

21. Select **Insert → Import → Image**.

Image

22. Browse to your JPG or PNG raster image file, select it and click **Open** to place the Image.

23. Click on your *Title Sheet* to locate the image; use the corner grips to resize the image.

Your sheet should look similar to Figure 14-2.6.

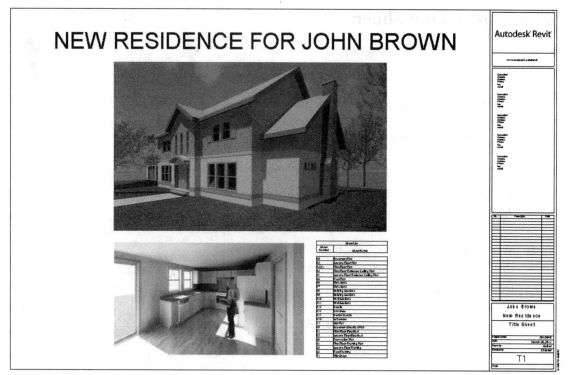

FIGURE 14-2.6 Sheet View: Title Sheet with drawing list, text and image added

24. Select **Insert → Import → Manage Images**.

You are now in the *Raster Image* dialog which gives you a little information about the image and allows you to delete it from the project (Figure 14-2.7).

FYI: You can delete a view from a Sheet without deleting the view from the project. Also, you can only place a view on one sheet; you would have to duplicate the view in order to have that view repeated.

TIP: You can use the standard modification tools on raster images (e.g., Move, Copy, Rotate and Resize). You can also control the draw order to make sure your leaders pointing at the image show up.

25. Click **OK** to close the *Manage Images* dialog.

FIGURE 14-2.7 Manage Images dialog

Exporting a 3D DWFx File:

The *3D DWFx* file is an easy way to share your project file with others without the need to give them your editable Revit file or the need for the recipient to have Revit installed.

> *NOTE: You can download Revit from Autodesk's website and run it in* viewer mode. *It's free – full Revit with no save functionality.*

The 3D DWFx file is much smaller in file size than the original Revit file. Also, *Autodesk Design Review* is a free DWF viewer which can be downloaded from www.autodesk.com.

26. Switch to your *Default 3D* view.

You must be in a 3D view for the 3D DWF feature to work. If you are not in a 3D view, you will get 2D DWF files:

27. Select **Application Menu** → **Export** → **DWF**.

DWF/DWFx
Creates DWF or DWFx files.

28. Click the **Next** button in the lower right (Figure 14-2.8); specify a file name and location for the DWF file and then click **Save**.

FIGURE 14-2.8 DWF export options

That's all you need to do to create the file. Now you can email it to the client or a product representative to get a cost estimate on windows, for example.

The 3D DWF file is about 2mb whereas the Revit project file is 13 MB. Your file sizes will vary slightly based on factors like the number of families loaded. In many cases, networks and servers are set up so they cannot receive large files via email, so the 3D DWF is very useful.

The DWF viewer is not installed with Revit 2016 (it was with the 2013 version of Revit). It can be downloaded from http://usa.autodesk.com/design-review/. Once installed, you can access it from *Start → All Programs → Autodesk → Autodesk Design Review 2013*. You can zoom, orbit and select objects. Notice the information displayed on the left when the front door is selected (see image below). Also notice, under the *Windows* heading the sizes and quantities are listed.

> *TIP: Autodesk Design Review 2013 is a free download from Autodesk. This is their full-featured DWF viewer and markup utility!*

This DWF file can also be used in conjunction with **Autodesk Quantity Takeoff** to develop cost estimates for your project. See Autodesk's website for more information.

FIGURE 14-2.9 3D DWF in Autodesk Design Review

29. **Save** your project as **ex14-2.rvt**.

Exercise 14-3:
Printing a Set of Drawings

Revit has the ability to print an entire set of drawings, in addition to printing individual sheets. You will study this now.

Printing a Set of Drawings:

1. **Open ex14-2.rvt.**

2. Select **Application Menu → Print → Print**.

3. In the *Print Range* area, click the option **Selected views/sheets** (Figure 14-3.1).

4. Click the **Select...** button within the *Print Range* area.

FIGURE 14-3.1 Print dialog box

You should now see a listing of all *Views* and *Sheets* (Figure 14-3.2).

Notice at the bottom you can show both *Sheets* and *Views*, or each separately. Because you are printing a set of drawing you will want to see only the sheets.

FIGURE 14-3.2 Set tool for printing

5. **Uncheck** the **Views** option.

The list is now limited to just *Sheets* that have been set up in your project.

6. Select all the drawing sheets except **A100**.

7. Click **OK** to close the *View/ Sheet Set* dialog.

8. IF YOU ACTUALLY WANT TO PRINT A FULL SET OF DRAWINGS, you can do so now by clicking OK. Otherwise click **Cancel**.

9. You do not need to save the file at this time.

> **FYI:** *Once you have selected the sheets to be plotted and click OK, you are prompted to save the list. This will save the list of selected drawings to a name you choose. Then, the next time you need to print those sheets you can select the name from the drop-down list at the top (Figure 14-3.2). On very large projects (e.g., 20 floor plan sheets) you could have a Plans list saved, a Laboratory Interior Elevations list saved, etc.*

If you have software on your computer to create PDF files, you can check the "combine sheets" option in the *Print* dialog (14-3.3). Many design firms create a multi-sheet PDF file to send to a print shop so they can produce the final printed sheets for the contractors to bid from. It is also possible to do the same thing with a multi-sheet DWF file, but fewer people have Autodesk's Design Review installed than Adobe's PDF Reader. However, both viewers are free; the PDF format is used by virtually everyone, not just the design industry. Another interesting option is 3D PDF files. Check out **Tetra4D.com** or **Bluebeam.com** for information on an add-in they sell for Revit. A 3D PDF can be viewed by anyone with the free Adobe Reader installed. **Check out the 3D PDF appendix on the disc.**

Good Luck!

You should now have a basic understanding of the Autodesk Revit software. **Good luck with your future Revit projects!** Be sure to visit *www.augi.com* to share knowledge with other Revit users.

Be sure to check out the Family creation and site design chapters located on the disc.

Self-Exam:

The following questions can be used as a way to check your knowledge of this lesson. The answers can be found at the bottom of the page.

1. You have to manually fill in the reference bubbles after setting up the sheets. (T/F)

2. You cannot control the visibility of objects per *viewport*. (T/F)

3. It is possible to see a listing of only the views that have not been placed on a sheet via the *Project Browser*. (T/F)

4. You only have to enter your name on one titleblock, not all. (T/F)

5. Use the _____ tool to create another drawing sheet.

Review Questions:

The following questions may be assigned by your instructor as a way to assess your knowledge of this section. Your instructor has the answers to the review questions.

1. You need to use a special tool from the *Ribbon* to edit text in the titleblock. (T/F)

2. The template you started with has two titleblocks to choose from. (T/F)

3. You only have to enter the project name on one sheet, not all. (T/F)

4. The scale of a drawing placed on a sheet is determined by the scale set in that view's *Properties*. (T/F)

5. You can save a list of drawing sheets to be plotted. (T/F)

6. Use the _____ tool to edit the model from a sheet view.

7. The reference bubbles will not automatically update if a drawing is moved to another sheet. (T/F)

8. On new sheets, the sheet number on the titleblock will increase by one from the previous sheet number. (T/F)

9. DWF files can consist of an entire set of drawings which a client/owner can view with a free download, similar to Adobe PDF files. (T/F)

10. It is not possible to remove a sheet from the *Sheet List* without deleting that sheet from the project. (T/F)

Notes:

Lesson 15
Introduction to Phasing and Worksharing

This chapter will start a small new exercise designed to explore two important features in Revit: Phasing and Worksharing. Unless a project is brand new, it will be using Revit's phasing feature. Additionally, if a project needs to be worked on by more than one person at a time, it will be utilizing Revit's Worksharing feature.

Note: This tutorial can be done at any time separate from the rest of the book.

Exercise 15-1:
Introduction to Phasing

Any project that involves remodeling or an addition should use the **Phases** feature in Revit. Revit is often referred to as three-dimensional modeling software. However, Revit's ability to manage elements over time is considered a fourth-dimension. This section will provide an introduction to Revit's phasing feature.

The **Phasing** dialog (Figure 15-1.1) is accessible from the Manage tab.

FIGURE 15-1.1 Project Phases tab; Phasing dialog

Most existing/remodel projects have two phases (Figure 15-1.1):
- Existing
- New Construction

Additional phases can be created, such as Phase 2 and Phase 3 (in this case, New Construction might be renamed to Phase 1). There should never be a phase called 'Demolition,' as Revit handles this automatically (more on this later).

Revit manages Phases with two simple sets of parameters:
- **Elements:**
  - Phase Created
  - Phase Demolished
- **Views**
  - Phase
  - Phase Filter

Among these four parameters, Revit is able to manage elements over time and control when to display them.

Element Phase Properties

As just mentioned, every model element in Revit has two phase-related parameters as shown for a selected wall in Figure 15-1.2.

The **Phase Created** parameter is automatically assigned when an element is created—the setting matches the phase setting of the view the element is created in. Put another way, in a floor plan view with the Phase set to *New Construction*, all model elements created in that view will have their Phase Created parameter set to *New Construction*.

The **Phase Demolished** parameter is never set automatically. Revit has no way of knowing if something should be demolished.

FIGURE 15-1.2 Element phase properties

View Phase Properties

Every view has two phase-related parameters, as shown for the floor plan view in Figure 15-1.3. Any elements added in this view would be designated as existing.

The **Phase** parameter can be set to any Phase that exists in the project. This setting can be changed at any time; however, it is best to have one floor plan view for each phase—thus, the Phase setting is not typically changed.

This setting represents the point in time the model is being viewed.

TIP: Create existing and demolition views in a company/personal template.

FIGURE 15-1.3 View phase properties

Phase Filters:

The **Phase Filter** setting controls which model elements appear in the view based on their phase settings.

To understand how the Phase Filter setting affects the view, look at **Manage → Phasing → Phase Filters** (See Figure 15-1.4).

Elements will appear in one of three ways:
- **By Category**   - Displayed as normal, no changes
- **Overridden**   - Modified based on Graphic Overrides tab settings
- **Not Displayed**   - These elements are hidden

Be careful not to confuse the *Phase Filter* column headings, New, Existing, Demolished and Temporary, as literal phases—they are not. Rather, they are a 'current condition' (a.k.a. **Phase Status**) based on a view's Phase setting and the element's Phase Created & Phase Demolished settings.

For example, the 'current condition' of an *Existing* wall in an *Existing* view is considered <u>New</u> because the phases are the same. Think of it as if you are standing in the year 1980, looking at a wall built in 1980—it is a new wall. Similarly, a *New Construction* wall in a *New Construction* view is also considered <u>New</u> in terms of how the Phase Filters work (now all *Existing* walls are considered <u>Existing</u>). You are now standing in the year 2015 looking at a wall built in 1980.

	Filter Name	New	Existing	Demolished	Temporary
1	Show All	By Category	Overridden	Overridden	Overridden
2	Show Complete	By Category	By Category	Not Displayed	Not Displayed
3	Show Demo + New	By Category	Not Displayed	Overridden	Overridden
4	Show New	By Category	Not Displayed	Not Displayed	Not Displayed
5	Show Previous + Demo	Not Displayed	Overridden	Overridden	Not Displayed
6	Show Previous + New	By Category	Overridden	Not Displayed	Not Displayed
7	Show Previous Phase	Not Displayed	Overridden	Not Displayed	Not Displayed

When Phase Status is Existing, then do this

FIGURE 15-1.4 Phase Filters; Phasing dialog

The three images below are of the same model as seen in three different views—each with a different combination of Phase and Phase Filter settings. Each condition will be explained in depth on the next pages.

View Settings:

Phase:	Existing	New Construction	New Construction
Phase Filter:	Show Complete	Show Previous + Demo	Show Previous + New

Existing Conditions:
When modeling existing building, create a **Level 1 – Existing** plan view; do this for each level in the building. This view will have the following phase-related settings:

- Phase: **Existing**
- Phase Filter: **Show Complete**

Any model element created in this view will automatically have Phase Created set to Existing.

Everything in the drawing to the right has the Phase Created set to Existing. FYI: One wall and both doors have their Phase Demolished set to New Construction—however, we cannot visually see that here.

The Phase Status is actually considered New in this view. The phase of the element matches the phase of the view. Thus, because the Show Complete Phase Filter has New set to By Category, there are no overrides applied to this view. We see the normal lineweights and fill patterns.

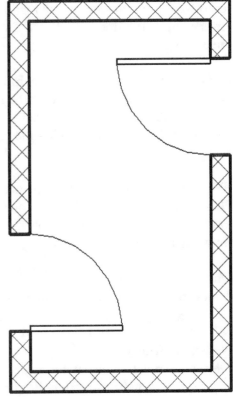

FIGURE 15-1.5 Existing view

Demolition Conditions:
When demolition is required, create a **Level 1 – Demo** plan view; do this for each level in the building. This view will have the following phase-related settings:

- Phase: **New Construction**
- Phase Filter: **Show Previous + Demo**

Often, new Revit users think it strange that the demo view needs to be set to New Construction—given no new elements appear in this view. However, looking at the existing view just covered—all existing elements (even ones set to be demolished) are considered "new." Therefore, the "time slider," if you will, needs to be moved past Existing to invoke the Phase Demolished setting. If this is still confusing, it should make more sense in the tutorial.

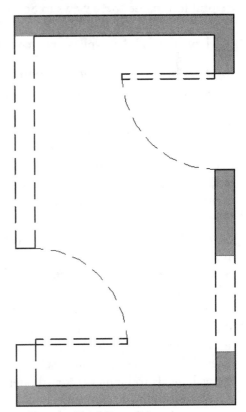

FIGURE 15-1.6 Demolition view

In Figure 15-1.6, the wall and two doors which appear dashed have their Phase Demolished set to New Construction. Recall that the view's phase is set to New Construction. In the lower right, a new door (i.e., Phase Created = New Construction) automatically demolishes the existing wall.

Notice the Phase Filter **Show Previous + Demo** has the <u>Demolished</u> *Phase Status* set to **Overridden**. So any element with the Phase Created setting set to a phase which occurs prior to the Phase setting of the current view, **and** the same element has a Phase Demolished setting that matches the current view's Phase setting, then it will show demolished.

FYI: If this project had a Phase named Phase 2, no existing elements set to be demolished in Phase 1 (i.e., New Construction in our example) could be shown in a view that's phase is set to Phase 2. Those elements simply do not exist anymore, and there is no reason to ever show them in this future context.

One final note on this demolition view: because Revit inherently understands the need to demolish elements, **it is never necessary to have a Demolition phase**.

New Conditions:

All Revit templates come with the default plan views set to New Construction. For projects with existing and demolition conditions, it might be helpful to rename these views to Something like **Level 1 – New** (similar for each level). This view will have the following phase-related settings:

- Phase: **New Construction**
- Phase Filter: **Show Previous + New**

The door and curtain wall shown in the Figure 15-1.7 have their Phase Created set to New Construction. The existing walls are shaded due to the Phase Filter having an override applied to existing elements (more on this later).

Demolished openings present a unique situation in Revit. When an opening, e.g. door or window, is demolished, Revit automatically infills the opening with a wall. By default, this wall is the same type as the host wall (this can be selected and changed to another type). This special wall does not have any phase settings and it cannot be deleted. If an opening in the wall is required, then

FIGURE 15-1.7 New construction view

the wall needs to be hidden or an opening family added. If the demolished door is deleted this special wall will also be deleted.

The Phase Filter used here has the Demolished items set to Not Displayed. Also, the Existing items are set to Overridden, which is why the existing walls are filled with a gray fill pattern. The overrides will be covered next.

TIP: Smaller projects might show the demo in the new construction plans, in which case the Show All Phase Filter might work better.

Phase Related Graphic Overrides

When the Phase Filter has a **Phase Status** set to **Overridden**, we need to look at the Graphic Overrides tab in the Phasing dialog to see what that means (Figure 15-1.8).

FIGURE 15-1.8 Graphic Overrides tab; Phasing dialog

In the context of a given view, if elements are considered Existing, and the selected Phase Filter has existing set to Overridden—then the settings for the Existing row shown above are applied.

All the walls being cut by the View Range in plan will have **black** lines with a lineweight of **3** (Figure 15-1.9). Simply click in the box below Cut/Lines to see these settings.

FIGURE 15-1.9 Line settings; Graphic Overrides

Existing walls, in this example, will also have a solid fill pattern set to gray (Figure 15-1.10). This convention is helpful to clearly delineate existing walls from new walls in printed bidding and construction documents.

FYI: Phase state overrides will override nearly all other graphic settings in the view (view Filter being an exception.)

FIGURE 15-1.10 Fill Pattern settings; Graphic Overrides

In Figure 15-1.8, Graphics Overrides tab, the **Hidden** setting for the Demolished row (Phase Status) means that the Visibility option has been unchecked (compare Figure 15-1.10). Any blank boxes have no overrides and Revit will still use the By Category equivalent.

Also in Figure 15-1.8, Graphics Overrides tab, notice there are several overrides applied to the New phase status. However, notice in Figure 15-1.4, Phase Filters tab, nothing in the New column is set to Overridden. Thus, the overrides for New do not apply to anything in the entire project currently.

Phasing and Rooms

The Room element has only one phase parameter: Phase. This parameter is set based on the Phase setting of the view it is placed in. However, this parameter is read-only and cannot be changed.

FIGURE 15-1.11 Phase setting for Room elements in existing view

In the image above, the view phase is set to Existing. If the view's phase is changed to anything other than existing, the Rooms and Room Tags will be hidden. Rooms are not really model elements that are built in the real world, so they are handled a little differently. As we will see in a moment, when walls are set to be demolished, Revit would not be able to maintain to existing Room elements in the new, larger area in the building. Thus, Rooms only exist per phase. The unfortunate side effect to this is that existing Rooms which have no changes need to have another Room element added for each Phase in the project. The room name and number are manually entered each time and are not connected in any way between phases.

> **TIP:** It is possible to Copy/Paste existing Rooms with no changes into a new view. This will save time retyping room names and numbers. However, there is still no connection between the two phases.

In the image below, we see the same model with a wall and door demolished. The Rooms and Room Tags shown are completely separate elements from those shown in the existing view.

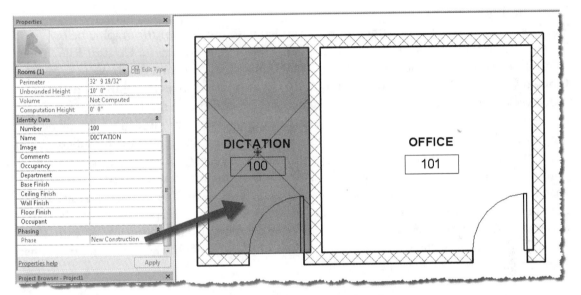

FIGURE 15-1.12 Phase setting for Room elements in new construction view

Phasing and Annotation

Most annotation elements are not affected by phasing; they are view specific and can tag an element whether it is New Construction or Existing. However, beware of a few exceptions.

View tags, such as Sections, Elevations and Callouts, all have Phase and Phase Filter settings. Actually, when these elements are selected, the properties presented in the Properties Palette are the same as the view properties seen when that item's view is active. The tag and view are connected—that is why the view is deleted when the section tag is deleted.

If a View's Phase setting is changed from New Construction to Existing, all the view tags will be hidden in that view (not deleted).

One more exception is that tags will disappear if the element they are tagging disappears due to phase-related view setting adjustments.

Exercise 15-2:
Introduction to Worksharing

When a Revit project requires more than one person to work on it, the Worksharing feature must be used. The feature is fairly simple, but everyone with access to the project must know a few basic rules to ensure things go smoothly.

Projects started from a template do not have Worksharing enabled. These projects can only have one person working in them at a time—just like most other files, e.g., a Word, Excel, AutoCAD, etc. file.

Worksharing Concept
The basic concept of Worksharing can be described with the help of the graphic below. When a regular Revit project file has Worksharing enabled, it becomes a **Central File**. The Central File is stored on the server where all staff have access (normal Read/Write access). **Once a Central File is created, it is typically never opened directly again.** Individual users work in what is called a **Local File**, which is a copy of the Central File, usually saved on the local C drive of the computer they are working on. When modifications are made to the Local File, the Central File is NOT automatically updated. However, the modified elements ARE checked out in that user's name—other users cannot modify those elements until they are checked back in. When a Local File is **Synchronized with Central**, the delta changes are saved; that is, only changes the user made are 'pushed' to the Central File, and then only changes found in the Central File, since the last Sync, and 'pulled' down (thus, the two way arrow). All elements checked out are typically relinquished during a Sync with Central. There is no technical limit to the number of users, though when there are more than 10 users the project can become sluggish.

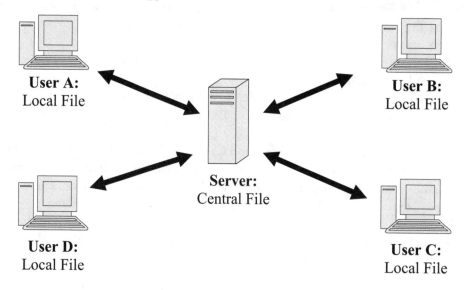

FIGURE 15-2.1 Revit project Worksharing concept

Overall, this system is very stable and has very few issues.

> **FYI:** Revit Worksharing does not work on cloud storage services such as Dropbox. There is too much latency in the network and several problems will be created including possible file corruption. There have been recent developments in using Revit Worksharing over the internet, but they involve Revit-specific software and/or hardware.

Enabling Worksharing

In just a few clicks of the mouse, Revit's Worksharing feature can be enabled; this section will describe how.

The main Worksharing tools are conveniently located on the Status Bar (Figure 15-2.2). These same tools plus a few others are located on the Collaboration tab in the Ribbon. The average user can get by with just the Status Bar tools, so that is all we will focus on in this introduction to Worksharing.

FIGURE 15-2.2 Worksharing tools on status bar

To enable Worksharing do this:

- Ensure project file is in a shared location on server
- Open the Revit project
- Click the **Worksets** button; far left in Fig. 15-2.2
- Click **OK** (Figure 15-2.3)
- Click **OK** (Figure 15-2.4)
- **Save** the project
- Click **Yes** (Figure 15-2.5)

FIGURE 15-2.3 Enabling Worksharing

The project file now has Worksharing enabled. **At this point the project file should be closed and all users will create a Local File** (covered in the next section). There is typically no reason to ever open this file again, even if only one person will be working on the project. It is not necessarily bad for someone to open the Central File, even with others working in Local Files, but following this rule will help minimize issues.

FIGURE 15-2.4 Worksets dialog shown after enabling Worksharing for the first time

Once Worksharing is enabled, two folders are created next to the Central File—one contains the same name as the project file (Figure 15-2.6). The "temp" folder only exists while the Central File is open.

The Central File cannot be moved and the folders defining the path to the file cannot be changed.

There is a special set of steps required if the Central File needs to be moved. This involves opening the Central File, or a Local File, **Detached From Central**—which is discussed more later on.

Save File as Central Model

This is the first time that the project has been saved since Worksharing was enabled. This project will therefore become the central model. Do you want to save this project as the central model?

If you want to save the file as the central model with a different name and/or different file location, click No and use the Save As command.

Yes   No

FIGURE 15-2.5 Worksharing related notice

Name	Date modified	Type	Size
Revit_temp	2/15/2015 7:51 AM	File folder	
Winston Towers Level 41 Remodel_backup	2/15/2015 7:51 AM	File folder	
Winston Towers Level 41 Remodel.rvt	2/15/2015 7:51 AM	Revit Project	4,192 KB

FIGURE 15-2.6 Folder created for Worksharing

Creating a Local File

Once a Central File has been created there is really no reason to ever open it directly again. Rather, each user creates a Local File to work in. This section describes how to do that.

The steps to create a Local File are simple:

- Open Revit
  - o Use the desktop icon or start menu
  - o <u>Do not</u> double-click on the Central File from Windows Explorer
- Click **Open**
- Browse to, and select, the Central File
- Ensure **Create New Local** is <u>checked</u> (Figure 15-2.7)
  - o This should be checked by default when a Central File is selected
- Click the **Open** button

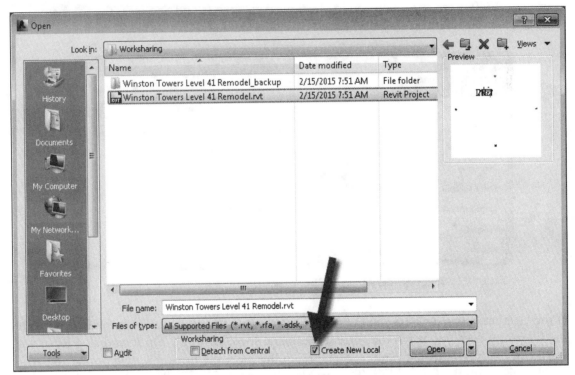

FIGURE 15-2.7 Create New Local check box; Revit Open dialog

The **Create New Local** option copies the Central File to the user's local hard drive (Figure 15-2.8). The file is located based on the "Default path for user files" setting in the **Options → File Locations** dialog. The local file has a slightly different name: **Central Filename + Username**. Once the open process is done, this user is in the newly copied Local File.

FIGURE 15-2.8 Local file created on user's hard drive

Each local file has one **Username** associated with it; the local filename includes the username on the end to help keep this straight. The Username is specified in the Options dialog (Figure 15-2.9). This is initially set to match the username of the Windows login/username. The username can be changed—in fact, Revit will change it to match your Autodesk A360 username when you log into the Autodesk Cloud Services (the username will not change if you are in a Local File).

FIGURE 15-2.9 Username setting in Options dialog

If the Username saved within the Local File (which does not really have anything to do with the filename) does not match the current username specified in the Options dialog Revit will warn you that this situation is not acceptable. In this case, the Local File will not be able to synchronize with the Central File. This problem can arise if/when Revit changes the username to match the Autodesk A360 account as just mentioned. In this case, the file should be closed and a new Local File created per the steps previously covered.

The Revit Username is the designator used to track who has what checked out. No two users may have the same username. Duplicate usernames, either at the same time or at different times, would cause corruption in the Revit database.

Saving; Local versus Central
Once Worksharing is enabled there are two ways in which each user working in their Local Files may save their work; **Local Save** and **Synchronize with Central**. These two options will be covered here.

While in a Local File, the user has two save options on the Quick Access Toolbar.

FIGURE 15-2.10 Save icons on QAT

- **Save Local**
  The first one is the normal **Save** icon (looks like a floppy disk). Every time this is selected, the Revit project is saved to the local hard drive. This ensures data will not be lost if Revit crashes or if the power goes out. A local save is fast as it does not involve the network and should be done often while working actively in the Local File.

- **Synchronize with Central**
  The second option is only available when Worksharing is active in the current project file. This command saves all the delta changes between the user's Local File and the Central File. This save takes more time as data is being saved across the network. This type is performed less frequently: once an hour, at the end of the day and when someone needs access to elements you have checked out.

The **Synchronize with Central** (SWC) command opens the dialog shown below (Figure 15-2.11). Avoid using the **Synchronize Now** option listed in the drop down as this option may not relinquish rights to items you have checked out.

While in the SWC dialog, **it is important to check all of the 'relinquish' boxes** which are not grayed out. If this is not done, elements will remain checked out in your name even when you are not working on the project. This can be a big problem for teammates working in the evenings or while you are on vacation!

FIGURE 15-2.11 Synchronize with Central dialog

Relinquish
In the image above, only one category has elements checked out for the current user: User-created Worksets. Checking this box will ensure all the checkout elements are available to others on the project team.

Save Before and After SWC
The Save local before and after SWC is checked by default. This is good practice, as Revit can sometimes crash during SWC (especially on large projects on 32bit computers). Saving local before SWC helps prevent data loss. Saving local after SWC ensures the new local file is up to date.

Compact Central
This option is often used once a week on large, complex projects. It only needs to be performed by one person. Doing this database management helps to keep the file optimized for performance and file size. When selected, the SWC takes significantly longer.

Comment
This allows the user to add a brief note about what changes they made. This is helpful if the central file needs to be rolled back to a previous version; the comments are listed in the related dialog.

> **TIP:** This author recommends users create a new Local File each day. The existing local file does not benefit from the Compact Central command, so creating a new Local File allows the user to work in the more optimized file. This also ensures the user is working on the latest version of the model, e.g., there are changes in the Central File which have not been downloaded yet—maybe another user worked all night on the project.

Detach from Central
Whenever a new Central File is needed or a user wants to look at a file without making changes, then **Detach from Central** should be used.

If a Central File becomes corrupt, any Local File can be used to replace the Central File. To do this:
- Open Revit (do not double-click on the project file)
- Click **Open**
- Browse to and select the Local File
- Check the **Detach from Central** option (Figure 15-2.12)
- Click **Open**
- Select **Detach and Preserve Worksets**

You are now in an unnamed, unsaved Central File. Simply save the file to the server and it will be a Central File. At this point, everyone will need to make new Local Files.

If someone wants to look at a Revit Project file without making changes they need to open the file Detached from Central. When this is done, there is no way to save any changes back to the original Central File as Revit does not know about it. It is important to understand that even copying a Central File to your desktop will automatically turn it in to a Local File when opened. Some make this mistake, thinking they will copy a file to see how others have created a Revit model—not realizing they are checking things out with their username! The consequence of this mistake is that staff working on the project can no longer edit parts of the model until the elements are checked back in.

FIGURE 15-2.12 Detach from Central checked; open dialog

<u>Know the Red Flags</u>

While in the Open dialog, if you select what you think is a Central File and the Create New Local is not checked, that is a red flag! There are two reasons why this would not be checked:

- The file is actually a Local File
  - o You may have accidently selected the Local File rather than the Central File
  - o Someone may have accidentally saved a local file over the Central File
    - ▪ In this case, they need to do a Save As; in Options check 'Make New Central' and save the file to the same location. Everyone needs to make a new Local File.
- The file is a different version of Revit
  - o A Revit project should not be upgraded unless everyone on the team is ready to do so
  - o If the file is saved in a newer version of Revit, that version must be used

Worksets

Once Worksharing has been enabled in a Revit project, every element, view and family is associated with a Workset. Here are a few things Worksets are used for:

- The underlying mechanism allowing multiple people to work in same file/model
- Opening specific Worksets limits geometry loaded, conserving computer resources
- Controlling visibility; project-wide or per view

Looking back at Figure 15-2.3, notice that modeled elements, if any exist, are divided up between two default Worksets when Worksharing is activated:

- **Shared Levels and Grids**
- **Workset1**

All the Levels and Grids in the model are associated with the same named Workset. FYI: when creating new Levels or Grids, the user needs to make sure they go on the correct workset.

All other elements in the model are placed on Workset1. Additionally, each view and family is associated with its own Workset—that is, one unique Workset per view and per Family.

This default setup is all that is ever needed on many projects. On large, complex projects additional Worksets are created. For Example:

- Core and Shell
- Level 1
- Level 1 Furniture
- Level 2
- Level 2 Furniture
- Etc.

Segregating model elements on separate Worksets is mainly done to conserve computer resources. For example, in the Open dialog, a user can choose to open only the <u>Level 1</u> and <u>Level 1 Furniture</u> worksets (Figure 15-2.13). For a 30 story building this can save a significant amount of RAM/Memory.

FIGURE 15-2.13 Specify worksets; Open dialog

The Worksets in the current Revit project are listed in the Worksets drop-down list on the status bar (Figure 15-2.15). The selected Workset is what all new elements will be placed on. In this example, all model elements would go only on Workset1.

FIGURE 15-2.14 Worksets drop-down on status bar

If elements are created on the wrong Workset, it is simple to change. Once Worksharing is enabled all elements have a Workset parameter (Figure 15-2.15). Simply select a different workset from the list in the Properties palette.

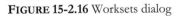

FIGURE 15-2.15 A selected elements workset; properties palette

Worksets Dialog

The Worksets dialog (Figure 15-2.16) can be accessed from the Worksets icon on the stats bar (Figure 15-2.2).

FIGURE 15-2.16 Worksets dialog

Clicking the **New** button allows additional Worksets to be created. Worksets can also be opened and closed when selected using the buttons on the right. The two default Worksets cannot be deleted. When deleting Worksets which contain elements, Revit prompts to select which Workset to move the elements to – deleting a Workset will not delete elements.

The **Editable** column should typically be set to **No**. This allows individual elements to be checked out by multiple people. When the Editable column is set to Yes, then only that person listed may edit anything on that Workset. This is sometimes done to limit who can change certain elements in the model. For example, if the structural model is in the same model as architectural and interior design, the structural engineer/designer might leave the structural Worksets checked so no one on the design team can accidentally move a column.

Unchecking the **Visible in all views** option will hide those elements in the entire project.

Workset visibility by View

Once Worksharing is enabled, each view's visibility/graphics override dialog has a Worksets tab (Figure 15-2.17). This allows elements to be hidden based on which Workset they are on. The default setting for visibility is to rely on the Worksets dialog (i.e., Use Global Setting). Two other options, Show and Hide, allow for a view specific setting independent of the global setting.

FIGURE 15-2.17 Workset options per view

Worksharing Display

One of the toggles on the View Control Bar provides a way to highlight a few Worksharing items (Figure 15-2.18). Revit is able to highlight, with different colors, which Workset elements are on, or who has what checked out at any given time. Clicking the **Worksharing Display Off** turns the highlights off.

FIGURE 15-2.18 Worksharing display visual toggles

Making Worksets Editable

It was already mentioned that an entire Workset should not be made editable, as no one else can edit any element on that Workset.

Most of the time, Revit will automatically check out elements when you begin to edit/modify them. However, some edits are more indirect and require the user to manually make the elements editable before changes may be made. When an element, or elements, is selected and a right-click is performed, there are two related options:

- Make Worksets Editable
- Make Elements Editable

Typically, only the second option is used—which checks out just the selected elements rather than the entire workset.

Worksets and linked models

If a linked model and the host model have the same named Workset, then Revit automatically connects the two. For example, if the structural

FIGURE 15-2.19 Making worksets editable

grids in the structural model are on a Workset called <u>Struct Grids</u>, and the architectural model also has a Workset called Struct Grids, then they will be connected. Turning off the global visibility of <u>Struct Grids</u> in the architectural model will turn off the structural grids, leaving the architectural grids visible. This would be done when the architects have used Copy/Monitor to create their own semi-independent copy of grids they can adjust lengthwise. Structural engineers might also want to do something similar for the architects' levels.

Each linked Revit model will also have a separate list of Worksets contained with the linked model itself. This provides granular control over Workset visibility per linked Revit model. For example, the structural model sometimes contains duplicate walls, compared to the architectural model, to highlight just the structural/bearing walls in their model. If those duplicate walls are placed on a separate Workset, then the other disciplines may turn them off.

To see the Worksets in linked models:
- In any view, type **VV**
- Click the **Revit Links** tab (Figure 15-2.19)
- Click the *Display Settings* button for the desired link
- Click the **Workset** tab

FIGURE 15-2.20 Worksets in linked models

While a Central file is being accessed others cannot access it – this includes Syncing with Central or opening the file. Sometimes prompts will appear during open that need to be closed before the file is finished opening. Ideally each user should not walk away from the computer while the file is opening.

Logging into A360
When logging into Autodesk A360, to access cloud services, Revit requires the A360 username and the Revit username match. If the Revit username is changed via Options, then the user needs to create a new Local File.

Conclusion
This concludes the introduction to Worksharing. It is important that everyone working on a Worksharing project understands this information to have a successful project without significant issues and/or downtime.

Exercise 15-3:
Phasing Exercise

This section will provide a hands-on tutorial of Revit's **Phasing** functionality. The exercise involves remodeling an existing building.

1. Open the Revit project file, located on the disc, called **Existing Widget Engineering Building.rvt** – this file is in the **Phasing and Worksharing** folder. There is another file with a similar name on the disc; be sure you have the correct file.

2. Ensure the **Level 1** floor plan view is open (Figure 15-3.1).

Notice the Phase setting for this view is set to Existing. Thus, any elements added in this view will be existing. In this tutorial, the boxed rooms will be converted to a conference room. Level 2 will also have some modifications, which will be discussed next.

FIGURE 15-3.1 Level 1 floor plan with Phase set to existing

3. Switch to the **Level 2** floor plan view (Figure 15-3.2).

On this level, the goal is to add offices, with walls and doors, in the boxed area.

FIGURE 15-3.2 Level 2 floor plan with Phase set to existing

The next step will be to set up separate views for the Existing and New Construction phases.

4. In the Project Browser, right-click on **Level 1** and select **Rename**.

     a. Change the view name to **Level 1 – Existing**

     b. Click **No** to rename the corresponding level and views.

5. Repeat the previous step for Level 2, creating a new plan named **Level 2 – Existing**

Next you will duplicate the two plan views and adjust their Phase setting for New Construction.

6. Right-click on *Level 1 – Existing* and select **Duplicate View → Duplicate**

7. Rename the newly created view to **Level 1 – New**; click **No** to rename the levels.

8. With nothing selected in the *Level 1 – New* plan view, change the following in the Properties Palette (15-3.3):

     a. Phase Filter: **Show Previous + New**
     b. Phase: **New Construction**

9. Repeat the previous three steps to create **Level 2 – New**

Due to the selected Phase Filter, the existing walls appear filled in the new views. Next, we will adjust the solid fill to be a shade of gray, rather than solid black.

FIGURE 15-3.3 Level 1 – New floor plan with Phase settings adjusted

10. Select **Manage → Phasing**

11. Select the **Phase Filter** tab (Figure 15-3.4)

Notice the Phase Filter we set for <u>Level 1 – New</u>, which is **Show Previous + New**. The existing items will be **Overridden**. This is what is causing the walls to be filled in black. Next we will adjust the overrides on the next tab.

FIGURE 15-3.4 Phase Filters tab; Phasing dialog

12. Select the **Graphic Override** tab

13. Follow the steps shown in Figure 15-3.5 to change the fill color to gray.

FIGURE 15-3.5 Graphic Overrides tab; Phasing dialog

You should notice, in ALL of the 'new' views, that the walls are now filled in gray rather than black. However, the wall lines are also gray and would be better black. You will also make that change.

14. Make the following change in the Phases dialog to adjust the lines to black for existing elements (Figure 15-3.6).

FIGURE 15-3.6 Graphic Overrides tab; Phasing dialog

Notice the existing walls are now filled with a solid gray pattern but the lines are solid black (Figure 15-3.7). This will make the existing elements contrast well next to new elements.

Now that the views are set up the original existing conditions can always be viewed in the 'existing' views and the new work in the 'new' views.

FIGURE 15-3.7 Existing walls shaded with black lines

Demolition

Next, some elements will be set to be demolished, and a third set of views will be created to see the demolition work.

15. Switch to the **Level 1 – Existing** floor plan view.

16. Zoom into offices 104 and 105 as shown in Figure 15-3.8.

FIGURE 15-3.8 Level 1 – Existing floor plan view – wall and two doors to be demolished

17. Holding the Ctrl key, select the wall and two doors pointed out in Figure 15-3.8.

18. With the three elements selected, set the Phase Demolished to **New Construction** (Figure 15-3.9).

Notice, with the wall and two doors selected, that the Type Selector says 'Multiple Categories Selected' and the drop-down list below (a.k.a. Properties Filter) indicated three elements are currently selected. When multiple items are selected, only the Common properties between those elements are displayed. In this case there are only five common parameters, two of which are related to phasing.

FIGURE 15-3.9
Phased Demolished set to New Construction

19. Move your cursor back into the drawing area and press **Esc**, or the Modify button, to unselect the elements.

Because you are in the existing view, nothing has changed graphically in the view.

20. Switch to **Level 1 – New** floor plan view (Figure 15-3.10).

Notice, due to the phase settings of the New view, the wall and two doors are hidden in this view. The Phase Filter **Show Previous + New** is set to hide demolished elements. One interesting thing that happened is Revit automatically infills demolished openings, both doors and windows, with a wall that matches the host wall type. This wall can be selected and adjusted to another wall type, but it cannot be deleted. If a "plain" opening is needed, with no door or frame, the infill wall needs to be manually hidden via right-click → hide element or using a view filter.

FIGURE 15-3.10 Level 1 – New floor plan view – wall and two doors hidden

21. Select one of the infill walls pointed out in Figure 15-3.10.

22. Notice the following in the Properties Palette:

    a.   The default wall Type matches the demolished door's host

    b.   The Type Selector allows different types to be selected

    c.   There are no phase parameters

    d.   This wall may not be deleted without deleting door

Next you will demolish the furniture. First, we will see that existing items may be set to be demolished in the New Construction views. Second, a problem related to demolishing elements within Groups will be reviewed.

23. While still in the **Level 1 – New** floor plan view, select one of the chairs at the desk in Office 105.

24. Set the Phase Demolished to **New Construction**.

The chair instantly disappears in the 'new' floor plan view.

25. Switch back to the Level 1 – Existing view to see the chair is still there.

26. In either Level 1 floor plan view, select one of the round tables with chairs in Office 105.

Notice the selected element is a Group and no phase properties are listed. The group can be edited and elements within the group changed to be demolished, but that would affect all instances of the Groups—which is not what we want. Thus, there are two options: create another Group for demolition or just un-group the elements to be demolished. For this smaller project we will do the latter.

27. With the Group still selected, click **Ungroup** on the Ribbon.

28. With the table and four chairs selected, set the Phase Demolished parameter to **New Construction**.

29. Repeat these steps to demolish all furniture in Offices 104 and 105. Do not delete the furniture tags in the existing views.

   FYI: Sometimes it is easier to demolish elements in a 'new' view as things will disappear as they are set to be demolished. This way you know you have everything once all elements are hidden in the view. This is especially helpful with things like system furniture which has smaller elements hidden under larger elements.

Adding New Elements

The next step in converting the two offices to a larger conference room is to add a door.

30. In the Level 1 – New floor plan view, add a **Door** as shown in Figure 15-3.11.

31. Press **Esc** to end the door command, and then **select** the door.

FIGURE 15-3.11 Door added in Level 1 – New floor plan view

Notice, in properties for the selected door, that its Phase Created is New Construction, which matches the Phase setting of the current view. Also, the Phase Demolished is set to none.

32. Looking at the **Level 1 – Existing** view, nothing has changed graphically at the new door location.

Next a view will be created to document the demolition work. This is a view, placed on a sheet, which indicates the elements to be demolished. Contractors need to know this for bidding and during construction.

33. Right-click on the **Level 1 – New** view and select **Duplicate View → Duplicate**.

34. **Rename** the newly created view to **Level 1 – Demolition**.

35. Change the Phase Filter to **Show Previous + Demo** for Level 1 – Demolition; the Phase setting should already be set to New Construction.

FIGURE 15-3.12 Level 1 – Demolition floor plan view

This new view shows all the elements to be demolished with dashed lines—this is an industry standard convention (Figure 15-3.12). Often, movable items such as furniture are not shown. Notice the opening for the new door is also identified. This tells the contractor that a portion of the existing wall needs to be removed; dimensions should be added to the demolition view so the new door is accurately positioned.

In the demolition view, notice the Phase is set to New Construction. The view phase must be past Existing in order for the demolish setting to kick in. Also, due to the Phase Filter (Show Previous + Demo), only Existing and Demo elements appear. All new elements are hidden, even though the view's phase is set to New Construction.

36. Using the information just covered, create a **Level 2 – Demolition** plan view.

37. In the **Level 2 – New** floor plan view, demolish the eight desks shown dashed in Figure 15-3.13.

Next, new walls and doors will be added.

FIGURE 15-3.13
Level 2 – Demolition floor plan view

38. In the **Level 2 – New** floor plan view, add the walls and doors shown in Figure 15-3.14; center the two walls on the exterior curtain wall mullions.

All the walls and doors just created in the 'new' view are set to New Construction for Phase Created. These elements do not appear in the existing view or the demolition views.

Room Elements
The final thing to consider for this introduction to phasing is the Room elements.

39. In the **Level 1 – Existing** view, select the **Room** element for Office 105.

FIGURE 15-3.14
Level 2 – New floor plan view

In the Properties Palette, notice the Phase is set to Existing and that it cannot be changed. Existing Rooms only appear in existing views and new Rooms only appear in new views. The phase is set based on the view the Room was placed in.

40. Switch to **Level 1 – New** and zoom in on the new conference room.

Notice there are no Room elements in this entire view. Given our specific remodel project, this logic starts to make sense. When two rooms become one larger room, Revit cannot automatically make the two existing rooms become one – especially without affecting the fidelity of the existing view.

Thus, Room elements must be added separately in the 'new' floor plan view.

41. In the **Level 1 – New** view, add a **Room** to the new conference room.

42. Edit the name to **CONFERENCE ROOM** and the number to **105**.

43. In the **Level 1 – New** view, add **Rooms** as shown in Figure 15-3.15; name and number as shown.

FIGURE 15-3.15 Rooms added; Level 1 – New floor plan view

The four Rooms just added have their Phase set to New Construction. These Rooms do not appear in the 'existing' views. Given these steps, it should be noted that the existing rooms have no connection to the new rooms in the same location. Thus, any changes to existing room names and/or numbers must be carefully coordinated.

> **TIP:** For existing room elements that don't change, i.e. the room name and number are the same in in both 'existing' and 'new' views, they can be copied and then pasted from one view/phase to another. This is a quick way to transfer the name and number data.

44. Add three **Rooms** to the **Level 2 – New** floor plan as shown in Figure 15-3.16.

FIGURE 15-3.16 Rooms added, Level 2 – New floor plan view

Room Tags in Demolition Views

The demolition views will only be able to show the 'new' Rooms because the view's phase is set to New Construction. This is a challenge as we want to show the existing rooms to make sure the contractor enters the correct area and removes the right stuff!

One trick, or workaround, is to create another 'existing' view and hide everything in the view except the Room and Room Tag categories. This new special view can be placed on top of the demolition view on the sheet. In fact, Revit will allow you to snap the two models together when placing one on top of another (you will see an alignment snap for both the X and the Y axis).

No Demolition Phase

It is important to reiterate that Revit handles the demolition phase automatically. There should never be an actual demolition phase in the Phases dialog.

Conclusion

This concludes the introduction to Phasing. There is more that can be covered on this topic, but the material presented should be enough to get started with Phasing in any project.

Exercise 15-4:
Worksharing Exercise

This section will provide a hands on application to worksharing, more than one person working in the project at one time. The tricky thing about this tutorial is that it is best followed with two people, at the same time, with access to the same network.

FYI: Worksharing does not work over the internet, using file sharing tools such as Dropbox, A360, Google Drive or Microsoft One Drive.

If this tutorial cannot be performed by two people, <u>at the same time</u>, on the same network there is a way to simulate this on one computer, by one person. As mentioned at the beginning of this chapter, Revit tracks each user based on their Username set in Options. Thus, opening two sessions of Revit on one computer and changing the Username for each allows Revit to 'see' two different users accessing the Central file.

Steps to simulate two users:

User A:
- Open Revit
- Application Menu → Options
  - Change Username to **User A**
- Open project; starting at step #1 below
- Continue following steps as User A

User B
Important: don't follow these steps until second user instructions begin – starting on page 15-40:
- Open a second session of Revit
  - This does not mean open another Revit project file
  - Double-click the desktop icon
  - This starts a second session of Revit on your computer
- Application Menu → Options
  - Change Username to **User B**
- Open the project file as instructed for User B
- Follow steps for User B using with this session of Revit
  - Notice the Local File name, seen on the Title Bar, contains 'User B' as a suffix

Before Closing The Revit Sessions
- Application Menu → Options
  - Restore your original Username

FYI: Do not log into A360 as that will change your username.

The steps just listed, allowing Revit to 'see' two users on the same computer, must be performed each time Revit is used. So, if this entire tutorial cannot be completed in one sitting, these steps must be followed each time. The reason has to do with how Revit stores the username. When the username is changed, a text file (Revit.ini) is adjusted. Each time Revit is opened, it reads this file to determine what the username is. Obviously there can only be one username, and it is based on the last session of Revit to change it.

Warning: Be Patient and Take Turns

The steps MUST be followed in the order listed by BOTH users or this tutorial will not work. When User A has a step, User B should be idle—not doing anything. There are no steps where both users are working at the same time. Once the basics are understood, students are encouraged to "go at it" with multiple users working at the same time. However, to highlight the way Worksharing actually works, we need to have one user make a change and then, after that, have another user do something so the sequence of events can be clearly seen.

Enabling Worksharing

The first step is to enable Worksharing. This is only done by only one person. If a second person is involved in this tutorial, that person is encouraged to watch User A perform these steps.

> **TIP:** It might be best to work through this tutorial twice—switching roles the second time.

1. <u>**USER A**</u>: Open the completed phasing project **Existing Widget Engineering Building.rvt** from the previous exercise.

    a. Make sure the file is on the network first, if two people will be following this tutorial.

    b. While in the **Open** dialog, notice the Worksharing options at the bottom—they are grayed out because the selected file does not have Worksharing enabled (Figure 15-4.1).

FIGURE 15-4.1 Worksharing options in the Open dialog

The process to enable Worksharing starts by simply opening the Worksets dialog.

2. **USER A**: Click the **Worksets** icon on the status bar (Figure 15-4.2).

FIGURE 15-4.2 Worksets icon on status bar

3. **USER A**: Click **OK** to accept the default Workset names (Figure 15-4.3).

This process can take a minute or two, depending on the speed of your computer (and the size of the project).

The Worksets dialog is now open (Figure 15-4.4).

At this point the Worksharing file has not been saved yet, so no one else can work in it.

FIGURE 15-4.3
Worksharing about to be enabled prompt

4. **USER A**: Click **OK** to close the Worksets dialog.

FIGURE 15-4.4 Worksets dialog

5. **USER A**: Click the **Save** icon on the Quick Access Toolbar.

   a. Notice the icon just to the right of the Save icon… this is currently grayed out.

6. **USER A**: Click Yes to the final worksharing related prompt (Figure 15-4.6).

FIGURE 15-4.5 Save icon

The file, in the location you opened it from, is now a Central File. Be careful not to edit, move or rename the folders created next to the central file.

On the Quick Access Toolbar, notice the regular Save icon is now grayed out and the icon to the right, Synchronize with Central is active. In the future, keep in mind that this is a clue that you are in the Central File— which you should not be in. **In fact, once this file is closed, you typically never need to open it directly again.**

FIGURE 15-4.6 Final prompt for worksharing

7. **USER A**: Close the project <u>and</u> close Revit.

The Revit project has officially been converted into a Worksharing file. User A did not really have to completely close Revit to continue with the next step. However, to clearly delineate the Central File set up steps from the multiple workers in the Central File, the application was closed.

FIGURE 15-4.7 Sync with Central

8. **USER A**: Open Revit – do not open the project file yet.

9. **USER A**: Select the **Open** icon on the Quick Access Toolbar.

10. **USER A**: Browse to and select the Central File, which is the same file and location from which this section was started with (See Figure 15-4.5). **Do not double-click or open the file yet.**

FIGURE 15-4.8 Central file selected; Open dialog

In the Open dialog (Figure 15-4.8) Revit can detect that the selected file is a Central File. When a Central File is selected, and the file version matches the version of Revit you are using, the **Create New Local** option is automatically checked. This is good—each user will always work in a Local File.

> 11. **USER A**: With the Central File selected and **Create New Local** checked, click **Open**.

User A is now in a Local File, which has a special connection back to the Central File. In the background, the Central File was copied to the local Documents folder and renamed to include the username as a suffix (Figure 15-4.8).

FIGURE 15-4.9 Windows Explorer; Local File

Warning: If the Central File is copied manually using Windows Explorer and then opened, it will also become a Local File with a connection to the Central File.

FIGURE 15-4.10
Save Local and Sync w/ Central

Notice while in a Local File, that both save icons are active on the Quick Access Toolbar (Figure 15-4.10). Click on the one on the left for a quick save to the Local File on your hard drive (save once every 15 minutes). Click the Sync with Central (maybe once an hour) when someone needs access to elements you have checked out and for sure before closing Revit.

Now User B will also open a Local File.

12. <u>**USER B**</u>: Open Revit – do not open the project file yet.

    a. Important: If the same person is simulating a second user, refer to the steps at the beginning of this section on opening a second session of Revit and adjusting the username in Options.

    b. If a second user will be following these steps on a second computer there is nothing extra to do.

13. <u>**USER B**</u>: Select the **Open** icon on the Quick Access Toolbar.

14. <u>**USER B**</u>: Browse to the Central File and select it; **Do not double-click or open the file yet.**

15. <u>**USER B**</u>: With the Central File selected and **Create New Local** checked, click **Open**.

User B is now in a Local File. Similar to User A, the Local File has a connection to the Central File on the server. Changes made to the Local File do not automatically change the Central File—however, modified elements are marked as checked out in the Central File. This prevents more than one person from making changes at the same time. We will see an example of this next.

16. <u>**USER B**</u>: Switch to the **Level 2 – New** floor plan view.

17. <u>**USER B**</u>: Zoom into the new offices in the Southwest corner of the building.

18. Adjust the wall shown in Figure 15-4.8 from 18' – 0" to **14' – 0"**.

FIGURE 15-4.11 Wall adjusted by user B

The adjusted wall has been checked out in the Central File, but the wall has not changed in the Central File yet. In fact, the wall has not changed in the Local File either. The modification only exists in your computer's memory (i.e., RAM). Next User B will do a Save Local so their work is committed to the hard drive.

19. **USER B**: Click the **Save** icon on the Quick Access Toolbar; see image to right.

The change is now saved to User B's hard drive. However, the Central File is still out of date and User A does not have access to the modification to the model.

20. **USER B**: Click the **Synchronize and Modify Settings** icon to the right of the Save icon.

> **TIP**: <u>Never</u> click the sub-option 'Synchronize Now' as elements may remain checked out.

21. **USER B**: Make sure all checkable boxes **are checked** except 'Compact Central Model' (Figure 15-4.12).

22. **USER B**: Click **OK**.

The Central File now has the updated wall; however, User A still cannot see the change as their Local File is still based on the original Central File and any changes they have made. (User A should not have made any changes yet in this tutorial.)

Synchronize with Central

Central Model Location:
...al Worksharing Model\Existing Widget Engineering Office Building.rvt   Browse...

☐ Compact Central Model (slow)

After synchronizing, relinquish the following worksets and elements:

☐ Project Standard Worksets   ☐ View Worksets
☐ Family Worksets   ☐ User-created Worksets
☑ Borrowed Elements

Comment:

☑ Save Local File before and after synchronizing with central

OK   Cancel   Help

FIGURE 15-4.12 Synchronize with Central dialog

23. **USER A**: Click the **Synchronize and Modify Settings** icon to the right of the Save icon.

24. **USER A**: Make sure all checkable boxes **are checked** except 'Compact Central Model.'

User A can now see the changes User B made. Every time a Sync with Central (SWC) is done, the delta changes are saved between the Local and Central models. Designers are often working on different parts of the building so it is not necessary to see each other's changes in real-time (plus the computers are not really that powerful, yet!).

Next we will look at what happens when users "step on each other's toes" and try to edit the same elements. There are really only two warnings anyone will ever see.

Two Worksharing-related warnings (paraphrased):
- Another user has this element checked out
- The element you are trying to change is outdated in your Local File

The first warning requires BOTH users to SWC—the user who changed the element(s) must SWC first. The second only requires the person who received the warning to SWC.

25. **USER A**: In the **Level 2 – New** floor plan, <u>change the door</u> swing in Office 203 as shown in Figure 15-4.13.

    a. **Do not save**

26. **USER B**: In the **Level 2 – New** floor plan, <u>try moving the door to the center</u> in Office 203.

The warning in Figure 15-4.14 immediately appears. This warning indicates that User A has this elements checked out. User B must ask User A to SWC, which can be done manually (by calling or talking to them) or clicking the Place Request button.

The next steps will walk through the resolution to this issue.

27. **USER B**: Click **Cancel** and ask USER A to SWC.

FIGURE 15-4.13 User A changed door swing

FIGURE 15-4.14 Worksharing warning

28. **USER A**: Perform a **Synchronize with Central**.

29. **USER B**: DO NOT do an SWC yet!!!

The Central File is up to date; however, User B's Local File still has the door shown with the wrong swing. Next, you will see the second and last Worksharing-related warning.

30. **USER B**: Try moving the door in Office 203 to the center of the room again.

The warning, shown in Figure 15-4.15, indicates User B now has the element checked out. However, Revit will not let the element(s) be changed until User B is seeing the elements in the correct location, the correct location being the most recent change to the element among all users.

Autodesk Revit 2016

Error - cannot be ignored

You now own the element, but your file is out of date. You must Reload Latest before editing the element.

[Show] [More Info] [Expand >>]

[OK] [Cancel]

FIGURE 15-4.15 Worksharing warning

31. **USER B**: Click **Cancel** and then perform an **SWC**.

User B's Local File has now been updated and they can now freely edit the door.

32. **USER B**: Try moving the door to the center of the room (Figure 15-4.16).

That is all there is to know about Worksharing! These same steps work for any number of users; however, project performance can suffer when more than about 8-10 users are in the model at one time.

The only thing left to discuss is what to do at the end of the day and what to do the next day.

FIGURE 15-4.16 User B moved door

We will assume the end of day has come and the design team is ready to go home.

33. **USER B**: Perform an SWC and then close Revit.

   a. For a single user simulating two users, change the Username, in Options, to User A before closing Revit.

34. **USER A**: Perform an SWC and then close Revit.

Now we will assume it is the next day and User A is ready to start working on the project. This author recommends creating a new Local File each day.

35. **USER A**: Open Revit.

   a. Ensure the Username is set to User A via Options.

36. **USER A**: Click the **Open** icon.

37. **USER A**: Browse to the **Central File** (not the Local File).

38. **USER A**: Select the file, and with **Create New Local** checked, click **Open**.

User A is prompted to either overwrite yesterday's file or copy the old file and add a 'timestamp' to the file name—and then create a new Local File. If you are sure you synced your changes at the end of the day yesterday, then use the first option. If you want to be safe, you can use the second option. However, the second option can fill your hard drive up pretty quickly.

39. **USER A**: Click **Append timestamp to existing filename** (Figure 15-4.17).

User A is now in a 'fresh' Local File which will have any changes which may have been made by others working last night. This new Local File will also benefit from **Compact Central** having been run by another user.

The old Local File has now been renamed and is accessible if needed (Figure 15-4.18).

FIGURE 15-4.17 Cannot Create Local File dialog

As mentioned previously in this chapter, any Local File can replace the Central File if needed. Also, if you want to just 'look' at a Revit model, be sure to open it with Detach from Central checked in the open dialog. This will open an unnamed file with no connection to the original central file – keep in mind no changes can ever be saved from the detached file to the original central.

FIGURE 15-4.18 Time stamped local file in Documents folder

40. **USER A**: SWC and then close Revit.

This concludes the brief introduction to Worksharing in Revit. Students are encouraged to continue experimenting in the sample project, making several changes by all users at the same time.

Autodesk Collaboration for Revit

A new development in Revit Worksharing is Autodesk Collaboration for Revit. This technology allows multiple users or companies to work in the same Revit model over the internet. This is not available for students yet; however, it may be in the future so be sure to visit the Autodesk student portal for more information.

See this location for commercial access: http://www.autodesk.com/products/collaboration-for-revit/overview

Self-Exam:

The following questions can be used as a way to check your knowledge of this lesson. The answers can be found at the bottom of the page.

1. Phasing makes Revit a 4D modeling program. (T/F)

2. More than one person can work in any Revit project file. (T/F)

3. For a Worksharing project, users work in their Local File. (T/F)

4. A Demolition phase should be created for remodel projects. (T/F)

5. The author recommends creating a new Local File each day. (T/F)

Review Questions:

The following questions may be assigned by your instructor as a way to assess your knowledge of this section. Your instructor has the answers to the review questions.

1. Elements to be demolished can just be deleted. (T/F)

2. Worksets can be used to optimize computer resources. (T/F)

3. Additional Worksets can be created. (T/F)

4. A Revit project can only have two phases: Existing and New Construction. (T/F)

5. To casually look at a Revit project set up for Worksharing, simply copy it to the Desktop using Windows Explorer. (T/F)

6. The Phase setting for a demolition view is New Construction. (T/F)

7. For a Worksharing project, everyone will see all changes in real-time. (T/F)

8. Compact Central should be run once a day. (T/F)

9. Every element in Revit has a Phase Filter parameter. (T/F)

10. Revit requires the A360 username and the Revit username match. (T/F)

Lesson 16
Introduction to Revit Content Creation:

This chapter will introduce you to many of the basic concepts which relate to using and creating families. The reader will benefit from learning to create custom content as the need often arises. An entire book could be written just on creating *Families*. This chapter is intended to provide a very basic introduction to help get you started.

Exercise 16-1:
Basic Family Concepts

Kinds of Families:

Autodesk Revit has three primary types of *Families*; they are

- *System Families*
- *Loadable Families*
- *In-Place Families*.

This book will mainly focus on the first, that being loadable families. Below is a brief explanation of each, followed by a graphic to help tell the story.

<u>System Families:</u>
Autodesk describes *System Families* generally as the portion of the building that is **constructed on site**. Things like walls, floors, ceilings, roofs, stairs, wiring, ductwork and piping are system families. These families can only be defined and exist within the *Project Environment*.

Unlike loadable families (doors, windows, furniture), System families cannot exist separately outside the project environment. This image shows a wall in plan with its various layers of material.

System Families have the ability to **host** *Loadable Families*. The concept of *Hosted Families* will be covered in more detail later in this section, but here is a simplified explanation: a wall hosted *Family*, such as a window, can only exist within a wall; it automatically moves with the wall and is deleted when the wall is deleted.

It is too bad that *System Families* cannot exist outside the project in individual files as it would be helpful to have several construction types predefined and load them when needed, as opposed to having them predefined within the Revit project template. Therefore, your options are to have the *System Family* predefined in a template file or Copy/Paste them between projects. This author prefers to load relevant content and not have extraneous items cluttering the selection lists. There are always tricks and workarounds to facilitating this concept but it is not as simple as *Loadable Families* which are described next.

Loadable Families:

Building components which are **constructed in a factory** and shipped to the project site are what mainly make up *Loadable Families*. These are typically just referred to as *Families* rather than "Loadable" Families; this book will mainly use the term *Family* and mean "*Loadable*" *Family*. Building elements such as doors, windows, furniture, casework, columns, beams, appliances, electrical devices (i.e., outlets and switches), electrical panels, mechanical equipment (i.e., VAV boxes, air handling units and water heaters), duct fittings and plumbing fixtures (i.e., toilets and sinks) constitute *Loadable Families*.

Plumbing fixtures, such as this toilet, are "loadable," that is, they can exist in a file outside of the project environment.

Image credit: Stabs, Wingate

As the name implies, these *Families* can be stored outside of the *Project Environment* within individual files (*.rfa is the family extension versus *rvt which is the project file extension). Using a "Load Family" command (found on the Insert tab), one is able to bring one or more Families into the Project Environment for placement.

In-Place Families:

Using a special command (*Architecture* → *Build* → *Component* → *Model In-Place*) within the *Project Environment* it is possible to create what is called an *In-Place Family*. This feature allows you to create a *Family* within the context of your project.

The *In-Place Family* has a couple of rather significant warnings that go along with it. First, it is meant for one-off items like a reception desk or a unique built in cabinet. If you copy an *In-Place Family* it is really just making another independent instance of the family – which makes the Revit project file grow in size. If you know something will occur more than once it should be created as a *Loadable Family*, not

Stone trimmed opening created as an in-place family to interface with project conditions.
Image courtesy of LHB, Inc.

an *In-Place Family*. Second, *In-Place* families cannot ever exist outside the *Project Environment*, similar to System Families, so the item may not be added to your firm's library for use on another project. One last point is from Autodesk's "Revit Platform Performance Document": *In-Place Families* tend to reduce system performance within the Project Environment, especially on larger projects.

So with these points in mind it is best to use *Loadable Families* whenever possible. However, they are still acceptable in some situations.

Creating *In-Place Families* will not specifically be covered in this book. However, the process is almost identical in several ways to creating *Loadable Families* so you should be able to create them without too much trouble when needed.

FIGURE 16-1.1 Types of Families; System, Loadable and In-Place

Nested Families:

It is possible to insert one or more *Families* into another *Family*; this is called nesting a family. One way in which this is useful might be two double-hung windows, as shown in the image above. Although it is possible to simply place the two windows close to each other in the project, this does not represent the reality of how the window will need to be documented in the project and how it will be delivered to the job site. The two windows would typically be mulled together by the window manufacturer and shipped and installed as one unit. By nesting one family into another and then copying it, you can quickly create a two window unit, which can also be tagged as one window. Lastly, nested families can typically have their position controlled more easily by parameters because it acts as one element rather than several or even hundreds.

Hosted Families:

Loadable Families can be created to be Hosted or Non-hosted. As briefly mentioned above, the host is a *System Family* (e.g., a wall, floor, ceiling or roof) and when the host is moved, copied or deleted the Hosted Family is moved, copied or deleted.

Wall hosted family - Window.
Image credit: Stabs, Wingate

This feature helps solve some coordination problems but also creates a few new problems.

Problems solved:
When a wall is moved, things like cabinets, toilet fixtures, windows, specialty equipment (e.g., paper towel dispensers, grab bars, mirrors, etc.), doors and electrical devices (e.g., light switches and outlets) all move with the wall. This significantly helps with last minute coordination.

Roof hosted family – Solar
Conforms to slope of roof.
Image credit: Stabs, Wingate

Problems created:
A few problems have surfaced when using hosted content. For example, when designing a kitchen the wall cabinets are hosted. It is difficult to quickly mirror one's kitchen design. Also, when a supply air diffuser is hosted by a ceiling there is occasionally a problem with the ductwork when the ceiling is moved vertically.

Ceiling hosted family – Light Fixture
Image credit: Stabs, Wingate

Oftentimes the benefits outweigh the problems created.

> **TIP:** *One technique is creating your content initially as non-hosted and then nest that family into a hosted family, giving you access to both types, which is convenient as it is not possible to convert from one type to the other. Quick examples of why you would want to do this: wall cabinets in a kitchen are sometimes hung from rods above a peninsula countertop. Also, light fixtures which are attached to a ceiling are sometimes suspended within mechanical rooms or basements which do not have ceilings.*

Face based family – FE Cabinet
Image courtesy of LHB, Inc.

Family Types:

Revit *Families* have the ability to hold information in placeholders called parameters. These parameters are defined, when created, to hold a specific kind of information; for example, text, integer, number, length, currency, yes/no, etc. This helps to validate data when it is entered. You cannot type text into a parameter that is set to currency. Finally, some of the parameters, such as lengths, can be associated with actual dimensions in the *Family*. Adjusting a length parameter value actually changes the size of the *Family*.

Wall Cabinet:
With the information from the previous paragraph in mind, it is time to discuss how slight variations are dealt with for content that is geometrically the same; that is for example, a wall cabinet is a rectangular box that has four different heights, two different depths and several widths.

It is possible to create 100 individual *Families*, each of which represents one wall cabinet. However, this would be very cumbersome to manage; if one change was required you would have to open 100 files and make the same change 100 times. This is where *Family Types* are employed.

A single *Family* can have several *Types* defined. A *Type* is simply a saved state of all the parameter settings. For example, the wall cabinet may have two *Types* defined as follows:

Type A

Parameter	Value
Width	**24"**
Depth	14"
Height	24"
Model	**W241424**
Manufacturer	Merillat
LEED – 500mi	Yes/No

Type B

Parameter	Value
Width	**27"**
Depth	14"
Height	24"
Model	**W271424**
Manufacturer	Merillat
LEED – 500mi	Yes/No

Normally the *Type* name would be more meaningful than Type A and Type B. As you can see, the various parameters can be edited within each type. Therefore, one wall cabinet Family can represent 100 different sizes.

Some of the information in the table above has a direct impact on the 3D geometry; the Width, Depth and Height parameters can be associated with dimensions in the *Family*. When the parameter is changed the size of the *Family* actually changes. So one only has to change the *Family* type in a *Project Environment* to change the size of the placed *Family*. And, of course, some of the information has no effect on the 3D geometry. Rather it is used to track design decisions and for scheduling purposes. Shared parameters can show up in schedules.

There are always exceptions to the rule, but generally speaking, anytime the geometry changes you need to create a new *Family*. For instance, one Family can represent all the wall cabinets with a single door. But when the cabinet width dictates two doors a new *Family* is required. This change in geometry cannot easily be managed within a single *Family*.

When the geometry changes a new Family is typically required.
The example above has different handle, door and drawer locations.

Family Types within the Project Environment:

When utilizing content within the *Project Environment* the *Family* and *Types* are presented as shown in the image below (Figure 16-1.2). Notice *Chair-Desk* only has one *Type* defined within that *Family* whereas *Cook Top-2 Unit* has three. Within the project anyone on the design team can manually add or delete *Types* associated with any *Family*.

FIGURE 16-1.2 Family Types within the Project Environment

Type Catalog:

There is one last concept to point out about *Family Types* before moving on. When a *Family* is loaded into a project all of its *Types* are automatically loaded. Sometimes this is good and other times it is not. The image on the previous page (Figure 16-1.2) shows manageable lists of *Families*. However, you can imagine how this list would get rather long if you loaded the wall cabinet *Family*, described on the previous pages, that had 100 types. Not only would the list be long, but you are likely only using one depth and two heights.

To better manage this situation Revit has a feature for *Families* called a *Type Catalog*. Rather than loading all of the *Types* into the project with the *Family*, the user is prompted to select the *Types* desired. This process could be repeated until all of the *Types* are ultimately loaded for a specific *Family*.

The image below (Figure 16-1.3) shows the dialog box the user is presented with when loading the steel wide flange beam *Family*.

Type	W	A	d	bf	tw	tf	
	(all)	(all)	(all)	(all)	(all)	(all)	
W44X335	335	0.68 SF	3' 8"	1' 3 115/128"	0' 1 1/32"	0' 1 197/256"	0'
W44X290	290	0.59 SF	3' 7 77/128"	1' 3 205/256"	0' 0 221/256"	0' 1 37/64"	0'
W44X262	262	0.53 SF	3' 7 77/256"	1' 3 205/256"	0' 0 201/256"	0' 1 27/64"	0'
W44X230	230	0.47 SF	3' 6 115/128"	1' 3 205/256"	0' 0 91/128"	0' 1 7/32"	0'
W40X593	593	1.21 SF	3' 7"	1' 4 179/256"	0' 1 101/128"	0' 3 59/256"	0'
W40X503	503	1.03 SF	3' 6 13/128"	1' 4 51/128"	0' 1 69/128"	0' 2 195/256"	0'
W40X431	431	0.88 SF	3' 5 77/256"	1' 4 51/256"	0' 1 87/256"	0' 2 23/64"	0'
W40X397	397	0.81 SF	3' 5"	1' 4 13/128"	0' 1 7/32"	0' 2 51/256"	0'
W40X372	372	0.76 SF	3' 4 77/128"	1' 4 13/128"	0' 1 41/256"	0' 2 13/256"	0'
W40X362	362	0.74 SF	3' 4 77/128"	1' 4"	0' 1 31/256"	0' 2 3/256"	0'
W40X324	324	0.66 SF	3' 4 51/256"	1' 3 115/128"	0' 1"	0' 1 207/256"	0'

FIGURE 16-1.3 Selecting specific *Types* when loading a *Family* via the *Type Catalog*

The implementation and use of *Type Catalogs* will be covered later in the book.

The first *Family* you create, in the next lesson, will not even have a *Type* as they are optional.

Instance and Type Parameters:

When creating *Parameters* for use in a *Family* you need to decide if it is an *Instance* or a *Type* parameter. Remember, parameters are placeholders for information in which some of them can be linked to geometry size and visibility.

An **Instance Parameter** only impacts the one or more *Families* that are selected or about to be created within the *Project Environment*, whereas the **Type** parameter affects all instances of the *Family* within the project.

A good example to describe how Instance/Type parameters are used in a project is to consider a window. Looking at the image below you can see this window *Family* has been set up so that the width and height parameters are *Type* and the <u>Sill Height</u> is an *Instance* parameter. *FYI: You only know this here by the labels and arrows provided in the image (Figure 16-1.4).*

This works with the standard industry convention where all windows that are the same size (i.e., width and height) are labeled with a common mark or tag. For example, the 2′x4′ window below might be referred to as "W1" in a project. Thus, if it was determined that all W1 window types need to increase in size to let in more natural light, changing one window's *Type Properties* would change the size of all "W1" windows in the project. On the other hand, the <u>Sill Height</u> dimension needs to be an *Instance* parameter. The "W1" windows might be 2′-4″ above the first floor and 2′-8″ above the second.

It is possible to edit a family and change a parameter from a *Type* to an *Instance*, with one exception: some parameters that are predefined in the template files are not editable. You cannot even change the name.

Final thought: a table *Family* might have its width and depth parameters set as *Type* or as *Instance* depending on how the design team wanted to use it in the project.

FIGURE 16-1.4 Exterior view of a window in the Family Editor

Family Templates:

When starting a new *Family* you need to know what it is and how it will be used in a project. With this information you can then select a *Family Template* from which to begin the content creation process.

Selecting the correct template saves time setting up the most basic parameters and in some cases is critical to the *Family* working. For example, the door and the window templates have the following parameters set up:

Door Template		Window Template	
Parameter	*Value*	*Parameter*	*Value*
Width	3'-0"	Width	3'-0"
Height	7'-0"	Height	4'-0"
Frame Width	3"	**Sill Height**	3'-0"
Model	*blank*	Model	*blank*
Manufacturer	*blank*	Manufacturer	*blank*

Other templates, such as **Generic Model**, do not have a <u>Width</u> and <u>Height</u> parameter predefined. Additionally, the door and window templates are wall hosted whereas the *Generic Model* is not.

Revit Architecture comes with over 70 template files. This book will only provide a discussion on a handful of them, but many are self-explanatory and it should be possible to discern what most of them are for after completing this book.

Family Categories:

Another item that needs to be covered at an overview level is the concept of a *Family Category*. Each *Revit Family* needs to be assigned to a specific category. This is done automatically by way of the template files for most *Families*. For example, starting a new *Family* from the window template file, the category has been set to window as shown in Figure 16-1.5.

The category setting does two basic things: it controls which command is used to place the *Family* and it relates directly to manipulating visibility within the project; turning off the window category for a specific view makes all the windows disappear in that view.

FIGURE 16-1.5 Family categories

Custom Family Libraries:

Whether you are creating content for personal use or for a large firm, you should have a plan on how and where to store your custom content. There are probably an infinite number of solutions to this problem, but a relativly simple one will be suggested here.

It is best to store your custom Revit content in a separate folder and not in the folders that contain the Revit OOTB content (OOTB = out of the box, meaning the content that comes with the software). It is best to segregate the content that has been created or edited to comply with your firm's graphic or design standards. Additionally, each year when a new version of Revit is released you would need to sift through all the OOTB content folders to find your custom content.

Revit has a specific set of folders created to house the OOTB content (see Figure 16-1.6). One suggestion is to create those same folders in a parallel folder and place your content there. Then, when content is needed, a user might first look through the OOTB location and then the firm location. At some point your custom content may be sufficient enough to reverse the order in which you look for content (i.e., Firm folder and then OOTB folder).

Of course, in a firm setting, the content should be located on a server so everyone has access to the same content, and so it gets backed up!

Naming Families:

The name of the *Family* file (.rfa files) on your hard drive, or server, is also the name the users see in Revit. The following information is offered as a suggestion, as there is no hard and fast rule on *Family* naming.

The *Family* name should be concise and as short as possible, and it should not contain information that will appear in the *Type* name, or vice versa. For example:

Family name	*Type name*
Metal Locker – **Tall**	**Tall** 18″ x 18″

- Annotations
- Boundary Conditions
- Cable Tray
- Casework
- Columns
- Conduit
- Curtain Panel By Pattern
- Curtain Wall Panels
- Detail Items
- Doors
- Duct
- Electrical
- Entourage
- Fire Protection
- Furniture
- Furniture System
- Lighting
- Mass
- Mechanical
- Openings
- Pipe
- Planting
- Plumbing
- Profiles
- Railings
- Site
- Specialty Equipment
- Structural Columns
- Structural Connections
- Structural Foundations
- Structural Framing
- Structural Rebar Shapes
- Structural Retaining Walls
- Structural Stiffeners
- Structural Trusses
- Sustainable Design
- Titleblocks

FIGURE 16-1.6
OOTB Family Folders

The *Family* name should be as generic as possible so others on the design team, or in the firm, can quickly ascertain what the various *Families* are. If only one type of locker is used then the *Family* name can be more generic. Similarly, the *Type* name within the *Family* should be easy to understand if possible; show the size of the locker rather than the model number. For example:

Generic naming convention:

Family name	*Type name*
Metal Locker – Tall	18″ x 18″

Detailed naming convention:

Family name	*Type name*
Arrow Locker – Tall	ALT181860

Locker family shown
in perspective.

Remember, a *Family* often has several types defined within it. Thus, the example above would have several similarly named types which define several locker sizes.

The detailed naming convention above would be appropriate if a design firm used several locker manufacturers depending on the project type; maybe they specialize in sports facilities and design various types of locker rooms.

Another option, based on the example above, is to have a detailed *Family* name and a generic *Type* name:

Family name	*Type name*
Arrow Locker – Tall	18″ x 18″

A good naming convention will help promote efficiency in the project environment. Many of the *Families* are added to the Revit model via the catch-all tool: **Component: Place a Component** (on the *Architecture* tab). When the *Component* tool is active, the *Element Type Selector* lists all the *Families* that are loaded into the project; that is, all the *Families* that do not have their own insertion tool as windows and doors do.

These *Families* are listed in alphabetical order in the *Element Type Selector* within the project environment. Therefore, if the *Families* are not named properly, you might have a toilet at the bottom of the list, a bathtub near the top and many other types of content sprinkled in between.

One solution to this problem would be to implement some sort of abbreviation or prefix naming system.

- Families
  - Annotation Symbols
  - Casework
  - Ceilings
  - Columns
  - Curtain Panels
  - Curtain Systems
  - Curtain Wall Mullions
  - Detail Items
  - Doors
  - Floors
  - Furniture
  - Lighting Fixtures
  - Parking
  - Pattern
  - Planting
  - Plumbing Fixtures
  - Profiles
  - Railings
  - Ramps
  - Roofs
  - Site
  - Specialty Equipment
  - Stairs
  - Structural Beam Systems
  - Structural Columns
  - Structural Foundations
  - Structural Framing
  - Walls
  - Windows

FIGURE 16-1.7 Project Browser within the Project Environment showing Family Categories

Each *Family* falls within a *Family Category* as previously discussed. These categories are listed within the *Project Browser*; note the list varies depending on the content currently loaded into the project. Creating a two letter prefix would sort the content by category within the *Element Type Selector*. For example:

CW	= Casework
FN	= Furniture
PF	= Plumbing Fixtures
SE	= Specialty Equipment

This naming convention would cause all the related content to be grouped together within the *Element Type Selector*.

FIGURE 16-1.8 Element Type Selector within the Project Environment showing loaded Families available for placement via the Component tool. **Left**, default naming; **right**, prefix added to control sort order.

Utilizing a naming convention like this means a firm's name or initials cannot appear at the beginning of the name.

Family and Type naming is highly subjective so one firm's solution may be completely different from another's. But, in any case, some sort of standard should be developed and agreed upon within each design firm.

Exercise 16-2:
The Box: Creating the Geometry

The emphasis will be placed on Revit features and techniques related to *Families* and not so much on geometry. A simple box will be created and then utilized to show many of the things that can be done with, and within, a *Family*. So, to keep things simple early on, a basic box will be used.

This exercise demonstrates how to start a *Family* and develop a 3D box that can be adjusted in size, i.e., a **parametric box**. Note that more detailed steps and graphics will be provided the first time a subject is covered. The subsequent steps for the same subject will be less detailed and may not contain graphics. It is therefore beneficial to work through the lessons in order.

Creating a New Family:

1. Open Revit Architecture 2016.

    a. Revit, Revit Structure or Revit MEP may also be used.

    b. There is no difference to the user between 32bit and 64bit versions of the software. Therefore it does not matter which one is used with this book.

2. **Application Menu → New → Family** (Figure 16-2.1)

Assuming Revit was installed properly you should see a large list of files from which to choose. If not, you may download the *Family* template files from Autodesk's website.

The template names make it rather obvious as to what each template file is intended to be used for. When a template is selected, Revit makes a copy of the file and then opens it as an unnamed *Family* called **Famly1** until saved.

FIGURE 16-2.1 Starting a new Family

3. Select **Generic Model.rft** and then click **OK** (Figure 16-2.2).

FIGURE 16-2.2 Selecting a Family template file

The initial view is a plan view from the top (Figure 16-2.3). As seen in the *Project Browser*, the following views have been established via the template file:

- Floor Plan
- Ceiling Plan
- 3D View
- Elevations
    - o Back
    - o Front
    - o Left
    - o Right

FIGURE 16-2.3 Initial view shown reference planes

In the initial plan view, Figure 16-2.3, are two *Reference Planes*: one horizontal and one vertical. These two *Reference Planes* define the center of the content about to be created, in each direction. The intersection of the two also defines the origin. The origin is the insertion point, relative to your cursor, when placing the *Family* in a project. Ultimately the box to be created needs to be centered on the intersection of the reference planes.

The *Reference Planes* do not appear in the *Project Environment*. However, Revit is aware of them and can use them when dimensioning and aligning to other elements; this depends on how a few properties for the *Reference Planes* are set, but in any case the *Reference Planes* are never visible.

Creating the Framework for a New Family:

A common method used when creating Revit content is to first add *Reference Planes*, make them parametric and then create the 3D geometry and lock its edges to the *Reference Planes*. This allows complex *Families* to be broken down into more manageable elements and makes controlling multiple 3D objects easier (i.e., moving one reference plane moves several 3D objects).

In the next few steps you will create *Reference Planes* that ultimately will control the size and location of a 3D box.

4. Select **Create → Datum → Reference Plane**.

To add a *Reference Plane* one simply picks two points in a view. A *Reference Plane* is a 3D plane that will appear in all views which cut through it, on end (or perpendicular to), or are within the Select/Elevation/Plan "view range." The edges of the *Reference Planes* are typically only visible unless "show" is toggled on under the *Create* tab on the *Ribbon*, and then only the current *Work Plane* is shown.

5. Add a horizontal *Reference Plane* as shown in Figure 16-2.4.

    a. The exact location and length does not matter at this time; it will be adjusted later.
    b. Make sure the *Reference Plane* is snapped to the horizontal plane before picking the second point. Watch for the cyan-colored dashed line and a *tooltip* which displays the word horizontal.

    FYI: The use of the word "horizontal" above is in reference to the computer screen.

The first *Reference Plane* has now been added to the new *Family*. Later in the book, a dimension will be added between the two parallel *Reference Planes* shown in Figure 16-2.4. This dimension can be locked so it does not move or made to be parametric in which case the end user in the project environment can edit a value in the properties of a selected element, causing the *Reference Plane* to move accordingly.

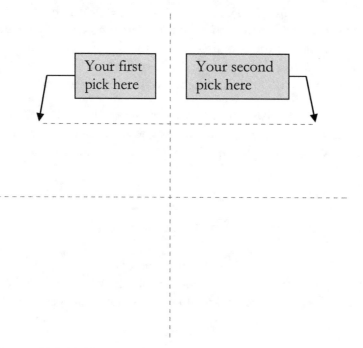

FIGURE 16-2.4 Adding a "horizontal" reference plane

6. Switch to the **Right** elevation view by double-clicking on it in the *Project Browser*.

Notice that the newly added *Reference Plane* is visible in this view, as well as the <u>Left</u> view. Again, this is because the *Reference Plane* is a 3D element.

FIGURE 16-2.5 Newly created *Reference Plane* visible in the "side" views

7. Close the **Right** elevation view and switch back to the **Plan** view.

8. Draw three more *Reference Planes* approximately as shown in Figure 16-2.6.

9. Select **Modify**, on the *Ribbon*, to finish the *Reference Plane* command.

FIGURE 16-2.6 Three more reference planes added

The four *Reference Planes* just drawn will ultimately serve as the guides for the edge of the 3D box. The top and bottom edges of the box will be controlled by *Reference Planes* not visible in the current view.

Next, the newly added *Reference Planes* position will be adjusted relative to the center or origin *Reference Planes* that came with the template file. This can be done simply by selecting one *Reference Plane* at a time and editing the on-screen temporary dimension which appears.

10. Select the top horizontal *Reference Plane* (Figure 16-2.7).

11. Edit the *Temporary Dimension* to be **2'-0"** (Figure 16-2.7).

    a. If needed, adjust the ends of the *Reference Planes* so they cross each other and form a corner as shown below. Procedure: select a *Reference Plane* and then click and drag on the visible endpoint grip.

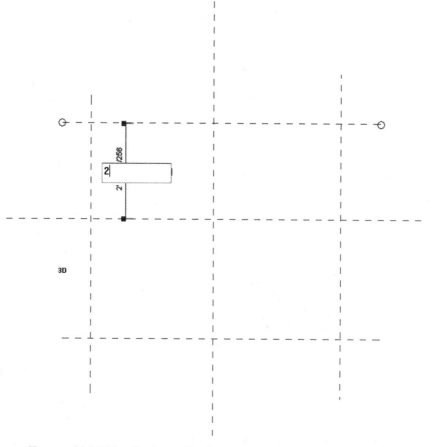

FIGURE 16-2.7 Top "horizontal" reference plane selected

12. Modify the remaining three *Reference Planes* to have the same **2'-0"** dimension off of the original centerline/origin *Reference Planes* that came with the template.

The four *Reference Planes* now define the extents of a 4'-0" x 4'-0" box. This only defines the sides of the box. Next the top and bottom of the box will be defined.

FIGURE 16-2.8 Four reference planes with position adjusted

13. In the *Project Browser*, double-click **Front** under *Elevations*.

The Front (or South elevation) shows two of the four *Reference Planes* created in this exercise. All *Reference Planes* that are perpendicular to the view are visible, as long as they are within view range. Additionally, the center (left/right) *Reference Plane* and one in line with the **Ref. Level** is visible, both of which came from the template.

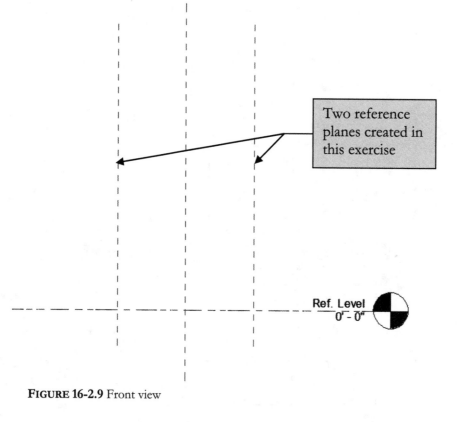

FIGURE 16-2.9 Front view

Next, a *Reference Plane* will be drawn as a guideline for the top of the 3D box. A *Reference Plane* is always drawn perpendicular to the "plane" that is being defined.

14. Draw a *Reference Plane* **2'-0"** above the Ref. Level (Figure 16-2.10).

FIGURE 16-2.10 Front view; relocated ref. level

15. Switch back to the plan view, double-click **Ref. Level** under *Floor Plans* in the *Project Browser*, or Double-click the blue target; see Figure 16-2.10.

Creating the 3D Geometry:

Now that the framework, or guidelines, have been established using Reference Planes, the 3D geometry can be created. A simple box will be created.

16. Select **Create → Forms → Extrusion** from the *Ribbon*.

17. Draw a square within the outer *Reference Planes*, Figure 16-2.11.

    a. Select "rectangle" on the *Ribbon* in the *Draw* panel.

    b. Notice the depth is set to 1'-0" on the *Options Bar*; this is fine.

    c. The exact size does not matter here.

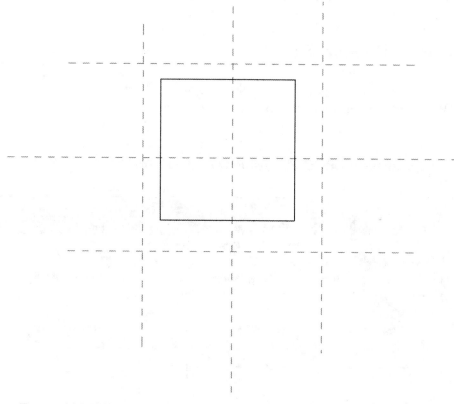

FIGURE 16-2.11 Sketch lines for 3D extrusion

When creating a *Solid Extrusion*, a simple 2D outline is sketched as in Figure 16-2.11. This defines the perimeter of the extrusion. When "finish extrusion" is selected, the 2D outline is extruded perpendicular to the sketch lines to a thickness (or depth) specified on the *Options Bar*.

The 2D sketch must be "clean" meaning no gaps or overlaps occur at the corners. Because the rectangle option was selected the outline will automatically be "clean."

18. Select the **green check mark** on the *Ribbon*.

With the previous three simple steps a 3D box was created. This box will now serve as our "test subject" for an introduction on many of the basic options and settings that can be done with a *Family*.

The last step, in this exercise, is to align and lock the 3D geometry to the *Reference Planes*. Thus, whenever the *Reference Planes* move so will the geometry. Revit provides a tool to easily do this; it is called **Align**. The tool brings two lines and/or surfaces into alignment. Once the *Align* tool has been employed, the opportunity to "lock" the relationship is available. This lock creates a parametric relationship within the *Family*. This is just one of the tools in which a *Family* can be made parametric.

19. Select **Modify → Align** on the *Ribbon*.

20. Select the vertical *Reference Plane* on the right (Figure 16-2.12).

21. Select the right-hand side of the box.

The right side of the box should now be aligned with the *Reference Plane* (Figure 16-2.12). If the *Reference Plane* moved rather than the edge of the box, click **Undo**. When using the *Align* tool, the element that does not move is selected first.

22. Click the **Padlock** icon that appears to lock the relationship between the edge of the box and the *Reference Plane*.

    a. Figure 16-2.12 shows the icon in its initial position, unlocked.

    b. Clicking the "unlocked" icon will change it to a "locked" icon.

    c. When a *Reference Plane* is selected the "locked" icon will appear.

        i. This lets the users know a "lock" exists.

        ii. Clicking the "locked" icon will unlock the relationship.

    d. Selecting the 3D box does not reveal the locked icon (except when in "edit sketch" mode).

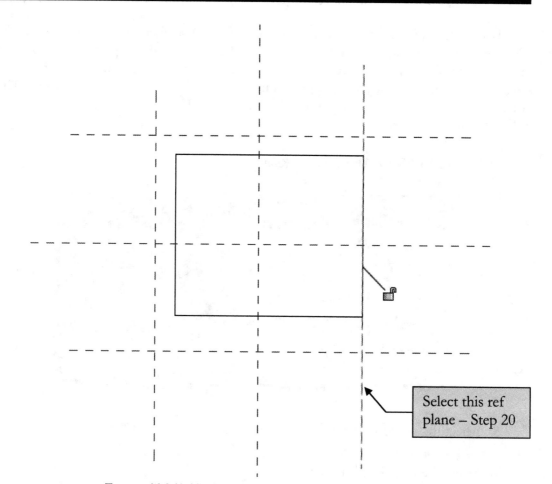

Select this ref
plane – Step 20

FIGURE 16-2.12 Aligning 3D geometry to reference planes

23. **Align** and **Lock** the other three sides of the box (Figure 16-2.13).

    a.   Remember to select the *Reference Plane* first.

    b.   Select *Undo* on the *Quick Access Toolbar* if you select things in the wrong order.

The four sides of the 3D box now have a parametric relationship to the four *Reference Planes* created in the plan view.

Next, the top and bottom of the 3D box will be *Aligned* and *Locked* to *Reference Planes.*

24. Switch to the **Front view** via the *Project Browser.*

FIGURE 16-2.13 Side of 3D box aligned with *Reference Planes*

25. **Align** and **Lock** the top of the box, which is 1'-0" high, to the top *Reference Plane* (Figure 16-2.14).

FIGURE 16-2.14 Aligning 3D geometry to reference planes

26. **Select the 3D box** to reveal the edit grips (Figure 16-2.15).

Notice the four triangle shaped grips on each side of the box. These grips can be dragged, which repositions the selected side. The one limitation with editing geometry with these grips is that there is no way to control the distance in which the edge is moved.

FIGURE 16-2.15 3D geometry selected, edit grips revealed

In the next step, the bottom of the box will be raised to make it easier to *Align* and *Lock* it to the bottom *Reference Plane*. It is not required that this be done. However, it is easier to select things in the correct order and assure the desired things are selected, which can be challenging when several things overlap.

27. Click and drag the bottom grip up as show in Figure 16-2.16; the exact position does not matter.

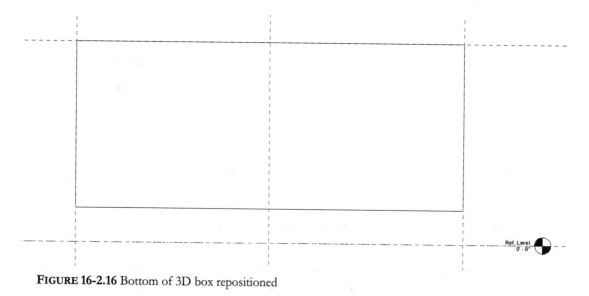

FIGURE 16-2.16 Bottom of 3D box repositioned

28. *Align* and *Lock* the bottom edge of the 3D box with the bottom *Reference Plane*.

29. Switch back to the **Plan View**.

Flexing the Family:

Now that the 3D box has been tied to the *Reference Planes*, anytime the *Reference Planes* are moved the 3D box will move with it. This will be tested next.

30. Select the *Reference Plane* on the right and use the **Move** tool to move it **1'-0"** more to the right (Figure 16-2.17).

   a. The *Move* tool is only visible when something is selected.
   b. The exact distance here does not matter.

31. Notice the 3D box moves with the *Reference Plane* (Figure 16-2.17).

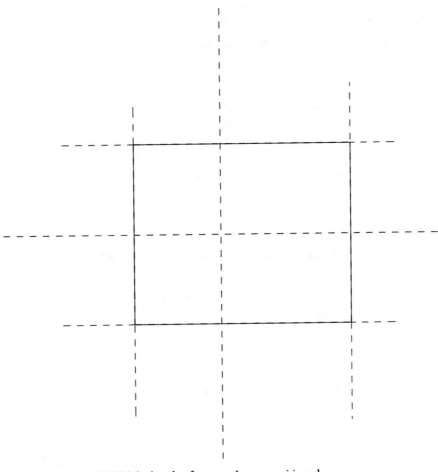

FIGURE 16-2.17 Right-hand reference plane repositioned

32. Click **Undo** on the *Quick Access Toolbar* to undo the previous step.

Now the *Family* will be loaded into a project to show how that process works. Once in the project, the content does not have any direct connection to the external *Family* created in this lesson.

33. Open a **new project**; see chapter one if needed.

    a.   Use the default template.

34. Switch back to the **Family Editor** by pressing **Ctrl + Tab**.

    a.   Ctrl+Tab cycles through open projects and views.

Before loading the *Family* into a project it should first be saved to a file. The main reason is to establish the *Family's* name. The *Family's* file name becomes the name of the content within a Revit project.

35. Save the *Family* to your hard drive as **Box.rfa**.

    a. The location where the file is saved does not matter, however it would be a good idea to create a folder in which all the files created in this text are stored.

    b. It is highly recommended that all data files be backed up regularly. If a Revit file becomes corrupt a backup may be the only solution; another option would be to send the file to Autodesk support and they may be able to salvage it.

36. Click the **Load into Project** button on the *Ribbon*.

Revit automatically switched back to the Revit Project.

Load into
Project

37. *In the project:* Select **Architecture → Build → Component**.

38. With the *Box* family current in the *Element Type Selector*, click somewhere within the floor plan view to place an instance of the box.

39. Click the **3D** icon on the *Quick Access Toolbar* to see the 3D box.

40. **Save** the *Family* as **Box** and the *Project* as **Box Project**.

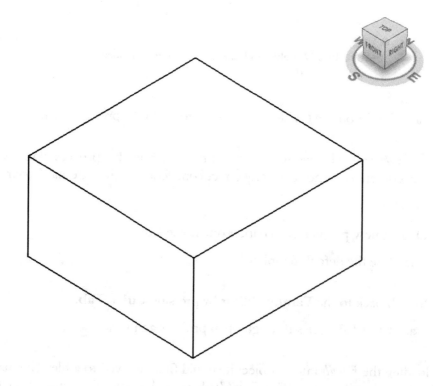

Exercise 16-3:
The Box: Adding Parameters

In this exercise the steps required to make the box parametric will be covered. Parametric, in this case, means that certain parameters control the size of the box. Thus, in the project environment it is possible to select the box, go to its properties, edit a few parameters (e.g., width and height) and then the box will change size accordingly. This is a very powerful feature and can save time creating content, as a *Family* is not required for every size.

All parameters are either a ***Type*** parameter or an ***Instance*** parameter. An introduction to this concept was presented on page 16-8 of this chapter. This exercise will help to better explain the differences and how to implement them.

1. Open the ***Box*** *Family* created in the previous exercise.

   a. It is recommended that a copy of the "Box" *Family* be saved for each exercise in case problems arise and an older file is needed to revert back to. Maybe copy the "Box" *Family* file and rename it to Box 16-2 to save a copy of the *Family* from the previous exercise.

Adding Dimensions:

The first step in making 3D geometry parametric is to add dimensions in a view. Two dimensions will be added in plan view, which will eventually be tied to parameters to control the width and depth of the 3D box.

2. In the *Ref. Level* plan view, select **Annotate → Dimension → Aligned**.

Aligned

3. Click the vertical left and right *Reference Planes*, and then click a third point to position the dimension line (Figure 16-3.1).

   TIP: The third click needs to be in a blank area, as clicking on something will add another segment to the dimension string.

   TIP: Be careful to select the reference plane and not the 3D box.

4. Similar to the two previous steps, add another dimension for the other side of the box (Figure 16-3.2).

FIGURE 16-3.1 Dimension added to reference planes

FIGURE 16-3.2 Second dimension added

Creating Parameters:

Now that the dimensions are placed, they can be tied to parameters. The dimensions can be tied to previously created parameters or a new parameter can be created based on the selected dimension. The latter will be employed, that is, selecting a dimension and then creating a parameter for it.

When defining a parameter, the user must specify the following:

- Name
- Parameter Type
  - Family Parameter
  - Shared Parameter
- Group parameter under
- Instance or Type
- Discipline
- Type of Parameter

You will gain a better understanding of how these various settings work once you start using them, but the following descriptions are offered as a primer for what is about to be covered in the next few steps.

Name: The *Parameter Name* should be descriptive. It can have spaces and symbols. However, dashes and other mathematical formula symbols should be avoided as they will confuse Revit when using them to do calculations. The name IS case sensitive. One common naming convention is to name all custom parameters with all uppercase letters to distinguish the Revit default parameters from the custom ones. The name can be changed at any time.

Parameter Type: The *Parameter Type* concept takes a little time to fully understand. A simple explanation will be provided here so as not to get too bogged down in the details early on.

Family parameters: cannot appear in schedules (e.g., a door schedule or a furniture schedule) or be used in tags (e.g., a door tag or a furniture tag). Thus, if one were to create a *Family Parameter* to keep track of the recycled content, that value (e.g., 80%) could not appear in a schedule, nor could it appear in a tag (e.g., a tag that listed the item number and directly below it the 80% value). This is the option that will be used initially in this book.

Shared parameters: can be shared by multiple projects and families and appear in schedules and tags. This method requires the use of an external text file to manage the parameters.

Group parameter under: The *Group parameter under* setting simply specifies which section to place the parameter in when displayed in the properties dialogs in the project (see Figure 16-3.3). This setting can be changed at any time after the parameter has been created.

Instance vs. Type: The *Instance* vs. *Type* parameter has already been discussed; see page 16-8. This setting can be changed at any time after the parameter has been created.

Discipline: This setting is simply a way to manage the large number of value types as can be seen in the information below.

FIGURE 16-3.3 Instance Propertied dialog for box family (in a project environment)

Type of Parameter: The *Type of Parameter* is how Revit knows what type of information will be stored in a specific placeholder or parameter.

Looking at the images to the left, one can see the various disciplines and parameter types that can be used.

Setting this properly has the following benefits:

- *Input validation*: when a *Parameter* is set to the type *Integer*, a user working with the family in a project cannot enter a decimal number.

- *Proper formatting*:
  - Common, Currency = 1.50
  - Electrical, Wattage = 60 W
  - Structural, Force = 2.45 kip

FYI: Additional formatting can be done in the project via Project Units and also within the scheduling functionally.

This setting cannot be changed once the parameter has been created; it would have to be deleted and recreated.

Revit MEP and Revit Structure both have additional parameter types.

5. Select the horizontal dimension (see Figure 16-3.4).

Notice one of the options, on the *Option Bar*, is **Label**, and it has a drop-down list next to it. This might better be titled "Parameter" because the drop-down list presents *Parameters* that can be tied into the selected dimension and is ultimately used to drive the dimensions from the *Properties* dialog from within a project. However, once a parameter has been tied into a dimension a *Label* does show up next to the dimension text as will be seen in a moment, so the *Label* title is not totally inappropriate.

6. From the **Label** drop-down list, on the *Options Bar*, select **<Add parameter>** (see Figure 16-3.4).

FIGURE 16-3.4 Adding a parameter to a previously drawn dimension

The information on creating parameters, covered on the previous two pages, can now be put to use. Notice, in Figure 16-3.5, that the *Discipline* and *Type* of *Parameter* have been automatically selected because there are no other options when tying a parameter into a dimension. Therefore, creating a parameter for a dimension using this method saves a little time.

7. Enter the following in the *Parameter Properties* dialog (Figure 16-3.5):

   a. *Parameter Type:*   **Family parameter**
   b. *Name:*   **Width**
   c. *Group under:*   **Dimensions**
   d. *Instance vs. Type:*   **Type**

FIGURE 16-3.5 Creating the *Width* parameter

8. Repeat the previous steps to add a **Depth** parameter or label to the vertical dimension in the *Ref. Level* view.

Notice, on the *Options Bar*, that previously created parameters are listed in the *Label* drop-down list. If the Width parameter were selected for the vertical dimension, one parameter would drive both the width and height of the box.

Looking at Figure 16-3.6, notice both dimensions have a *Label* associated with the dimension. This *Label* helps keep track of which dimensions are parametric. Another use for dimensions in a family is to "lock" it in order to maintain a relationship or spacing.

Even though the *Reference Planes* show up in the elevation views (front, left, etc.), the dimensions do not. So it is not visually obvious in the Left view that the *Depth* parameter has been created.

FIGURE 16-3.6 *Depth* parameter added

Next, an *Instance Parameter* will be created for the height of the box. Once the box family is loaded into a project, the height can vary from box to box (i.e., per instance). However, if the width (or depth) is changed, all boxes in the project will change. You will test this in a project momentarily.

9. Switch to the **Front** view.

Notice the *Width* dimension is not visible in this view.

10. Add a **dimension** from the *Reference Level* to the *Reference Plane* at the top of the box.

11. Add a **Height** parameter to the dimension (see Figure 16-3.7 and 16-3.8).

    a. Be sure to select the **Instance** option.

FIGURE 16-3.7 Creating the *Height* parameter

As can be seen in Figure 16-3.8, the Height parameter has been successfully added. This dimension can be seen in opposite views, the <u>Back</u> view in this case, but it cannot be seen in the side views, Left and Right in this case.

FIGURE 16-3.8 Front view; *Height* parameter added

Flexing the Family:

Now that parametric dimensions have been added to the *Family* it is necessary to flex them and make sure they work as intended before loading into a project.

12. Switch to the **3D view** via the *Quick Access Toolbar*.

13. Click the **Types** tool on the *Ribbon*.

> **FYI:** *Notice the last three tools on the* Ribbon *are repeated for each tab; this is for convenience within the Family Editor.*

The *Family Types* dialog is now open (Figure 16-3.9). Notice the three parameters created are showing up, and under the specified *Dimensions* heading. The easiest way to "flex" the *Family* is to move this dialog off to one side, adjust the dimension(s) and then press *Apply*. When *Apply* is selected, the changes are applied to the *Family* without the need to close the dialog box.

Also, notice the Height parameter has "(default)" next to its name. This is because it is an Instance parameter. The Height can vary, but when the Family is initially placed, the "default" value will be used.

Parameter	Value	Formula	Lock
Dimensions			
Width	4' 0"	=	
Height (default)	2' 0"	=	
Depth	4' 0"	=	
Identity Data			
Type Image		=	
Keynote		=	
Model		=	
Manufacturer		=	
Type Comments		=	
URL		=	
Description		=	
Assembly Code		=	
Cost		=	

Family Types: New... / Rename... / Delete

Parameters: Add... / Modify... / Remove / Move Up / Move Down

Sorting Order: Ascending / Descending

Lookup Tables: Manage...

OK / Cancel / Apply / Help

FIGURE 16-3.9 Family Types dialog

14. In the *Family Types* dialog, make the following adjustments:

   a. Height: **6"**

   b. Width: **1'-0"**

   c. See Figure 16-3.10.

FIGURE 16-3.10 Family Types dialog - Modified

15. Move the dialog box off to one side so the 3D view of the box can be seen, and drag on the dialog title bar; this will allow the changes to the box to be seen.

16. Click **Apply**.

TIP: Clicking Apply *within a dialog box commits the changes to the model. This allows the user to see if the modification looks correct before closing the dialog box and possibly needing to reopen it. If the changes do not need to be visually inspected first, the* OK *button can simply be selected – it is not necessary to click* Apply *first.*

The size of the box should now be modified as shown in Figure 16-3.11 below. When flexing the family, the size was changed by a large enough amount to make it unmistakable that a change occurred. Just changing the numbers by an inch or two might make it hard to notice the adjustment visually.

Next the box will be loaded into the Project environment; there it will be shown how the family can be adjusted via the properties.

Because the *Width* and *Depth* are **Type Parameters**, any change will affect all instances of the box. On the other hand, with the *Height* being an **Instance Parameter** – one change will only affect the selected objects.

FIGURE 16-3.11 3D Box - Modified

17. Open the *Project* from the previous exercise **Box Project**. Do <u>not</u> close the **Box** *Family*.

18. Press **Ctrl + Tab** until the **Box** *Family* is current (Ctrl + Tab switches between the currently open views).

19. Click the **Load into Project** button on the *Ribbon*.

Load into Project

The **Box Project** is a Revit *Project* that already contains a *Family* named **Box**, which was loaded at the end of the previous exercise. When Revit notices that a *Family* is being loaded with the same name as one previously loaded, it will present the user with the **Family Already Loaded** dialog, see Figure 16-3.12, which provides a few options in which to choose from. Revit will not assume that the file being loaded is a replacement for the previously loaded *Family*. Rather, the user must decide by selecting one of two overwrite options or clicking *Cancel* to not load the *Family* at all. It could be that a totally different box was created or downloaded and should not replace the currently loaded box; in this case you would click *Cancel* and rename the *Family* so it does not conflict with the previously loaded one.

Most of the time the first overwrite option should be selected, as the second may overwrite project specific changes to the *Family* such as the **Cost** parameter.

20. Click **Overwrite the existing version.**

FIGURE 16-3.12 Family Already Exists prompt

TIP: Revit will only display the "Family Already Exists" prompt if the Family file being loaded has been modified as compared to the version already in the Project file.

If the user has more than one Revit project open, a dialog displays in which the user selects which project(s) to load the *Family* into.

The **Box Project** file becomes the current view on the computer screen and the **Box** *Family* changes size to match the values of the newly added *Parameters*.

21. In any view (i.e., Level 1, Elevations, 3D), **select** the previously placed **Box** within the *Drawing Window*.

Notice the selected element temporarily turns blue and the *Modify Generic Models* contextual tab is displayed on the Ribbon.

22. With the Box selected, notice the *Properties Palette*.

Of the three parameters created in this exercise, only one shows up under the *Instance Parameters* (see Figure 16-3.13). The other two parameters, <u>Width</u> and <u>Depth</u>, will be visible in the *Type Parameters* dialog which will be explored next.

FIGURE 16-3.13 Instance Properties for updated Box family

23. In the *Properties Palette* dialog box, click **Edit Type**.

The two *Type Parameters* show up here in the *Type Properties* dialog; see Figure 16-3.14. An example will be shown next on exactly what the difference is between an *Instance Parameter* and a *Type Parameter*. However, it may be helpful to go back, at this time, and review the **Instance and Type Parameters** discussion earlier in this chapter (see page 16-8) before proceeding.

FIGURE 16-3.14 Type Properties for updated Box family

24. Close the dialog box by selecting **Cancel**.

Next, two additional boxes will be placed to show the difference between *Instance and Type Parameters*. This can be accomplished by clicking the *Place a Component* button on the *Architecture* tab, as was done to place the first box, or by simply copying the existing box.

25. Select the box, if not already selected, and then click **Copy** on the *Ribbon*.

> *WARNING: Do not click the* Copy *command in the* Clipboard *panel, this is for copies between views or projects! Rather, use the* Copy *command on the* Modify *panel.*

26. Make two copies of the *Box Family*, **6'-0"** towards the **right** as shown in Figure 16-3.15 below.

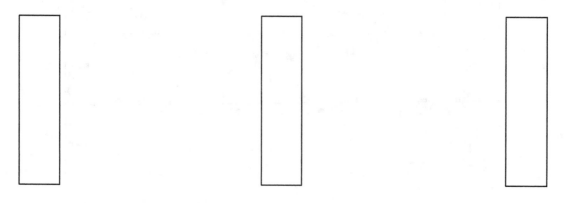

FIGURE 16-3.15 Box family copied for *Type* versus *Instant* study

27. Select the *Box* instance on the far left, and then view its *Type Parameters*; click **Edit Type** on the *Properties Palette*.

28. Change the **Width** *Parameter* from 1'-0" to **4'-0"**.

29. Click **OK** to close the *Type Parameter* dialog.

Because the <u>Width</u> *Parameter* is a *Type Parameter*, all instances of the type <u>Box</u> are updated instantly; see Figure 16-3.16 below. The <u>Depth</u> and <u>Height</u> for each remain unchanged. It makes no difference which box is selected anywhere in the *Project*. If this box existed on 20 different floors and in multiple phases, they would all have been updated. This is an important concept to understand because, just as it is easy to make several corrections or revisions with this technique, it is just as easy to make several errors in the design.

If additional widths are needed, either an additional *Type* would need to be added to the *Family* or a totally new *Family* would need to be created. *FYI: If the geometry is the same, and just the dimensions need to change, one would typically make a new* Type *within an existing* Family, *rather than a new* Family.

FIGURE 16-3.16 Type parameter <u>Width</u> changed

Next, the *Instant Parameter* <u>Height</u> will be studied. To see this change a vertical (i.e., elevation) or 3D view needs to be opened.

   30. Switch to the **South** exterior elevation via the *Project Browser*.

FIGURE 16-3.17 South exterior elevation

Notice the Boxes are all **6″** tall (Figure 16-3.17) which was set previously in the *Family Editor*, prior to being loaded into the current *Project*.

31. Select the box in the middle and view its *Instance Properties* via the *Properties Palette*.

32. Change the **Height** from 6″ to **2′-3½″**.

Notice that just the selected instance was changed.

FIGURE 16-3.18 South exterior elevation middle box modified

TIP: It is possible to change multiple instances at once if they are all selected prior to editing the Properties Palette *dialog. Additionally, if EVERY instance in the entire Project needs to be modified, simply select one and then right-click and pick the "Select all instances" option. Caution should be used when employing the second tip as things change in ALL views and on ALL levels, and in ALL phases of the current Project, when the "entire Project" options is selected.*

33. **Save** both the *Project* and the *Family* as they will be further developed in the next exercise.

Revit Model Content Style Guide

Autodesk has recently released a document intended to help standardize how Revit content is made. This will help when sharing projects between offices and when downloading content from manufacturer's websites. Specifically, adding tags and scheduling will be greatly streamlined. This new document may be viewed and downloaded from the following location:

http://seek.autodesk.com/manufacturer.htm

Look for a link on the right-hand side called *Revit Model Content Style Guide*.

Exercise 16-4:
The Box: Formulas and Materials

The ability to add formulas and materials will be covered in this exercise.

The ability to add **formulas** means that the <u>Width</u> *Parameter* could be "programmed" such that it is always half the size of the depth *Parameter*; this is the example that will be explored in this exercise. Additionally, one could control the spacing of shelving brackets based on the length of the shelf, or the size of a lintel based on the width of the window below it, the lintel would need to be in the window family in this case. As should be obvious, the possibilities are many.

Defining **materials** in the *Family Editor* means that the component is ready to be rendered the moment it is placed in the project. It may not always be possible to anticipate what the material should be, but it is often more convenient to have something selected rather than nothing, which renders a flat gray color.

Cabinets with different materials applied (same family)

Adding a formula:

The following steps show how to add a formula to a parameter.

1. Open the **Box** *Family* created in the previous exercise.

    a. It is recommended that a copy of the **Box** *Family* be saved for each exercise in case problems arise and an older file is needed to revert back to. Maybe copy the **Box** *Family* file and rename it to **Box 16-3** to save a copy of the *Family* from the previous exercise.

2. Click the **Types** button on the *Ribbon* (see image to right).

Notice in the *Family Types* dialog below that a column named *"Formula"* exists. *Whenever* something is entered in this column the *Value* is grayed out for that *Parameter* (i.e., row); the result of the formula becomes the *Value* for that *Parameter*. A preliminary example is shown below.

FIGURE 16-4.1 Family Types dialog

It is often helpful to open and explore the various *Families* that come with Revit; this can provide much insight on how to do certain things. The image below shows several formulas used to define a pipe elbow *Family* that comes with Revit MEP. The values next to the formulas are the result of the adjacent formula; it is not possible to manually enter a value in this case when a formula is present. Notice how other parameters can be used in formulas; this is case sensitive.

Parameter	Value	Formula
Dimensions		
Tick Size (default)	115/256"	= Fitting Outside Diameter * 0.4 * tan(Angle / 2)
Nominal Radius (default)	1/2"	=
Nominal Diameter (default)	1"	= Nominal Radius * 2
Insulation Radius (default)	9/16"	= Fitting Outside Radius + Insulation Thickness
Fitting Outside Diameter (default)	1 1/8"	= text_file_lookup(Lookup Table Name, "FOD", Nominal Dia
Center to End (default)	13/16"	= Center Radius * tan(Angle / 2)
Angle (default)	90.000°	=

FIGURE 16-4.2 Sample Family showing complex formulas

3. For the *Width* parameter, in the *Formula* column, enter the following: **Depth/2** (see Figure 16-4.3).

4. Click into a different cell within the *Family Types* dialog to see the *Value* update.

Notice the <u>Width</u> Value is now half of the <u>Depth</u>, i.e., 2'-0" (see Figure 16-4.3).

FIGURE 16-4.3 Adding formula to control the width

TIP: When using parameters in a formula, keep the following in mind:

- *Parameters in formulas must match the case (i.e., uppercase, lowercase, mixed) of the Parameters being referenced. Typing "depth" rather than "Depth" in the example above would not work – Revit would show an error message.*
- *A Parameter used in a formula must exist in the Family before it can be used.*
- *If a Parameter is deleted, any formulas that use that Parameter will also be deleted. Revit will present a warning first.*
- *If a Parameter is renamed, Revit will automatically rename the Parameter in all formulas in which it is used.*

Below are a few of the basic symbols Revit can use in formulas. See Revit's *Help System* for a full list:

- *Addition*: **+**

- *Subtraction*: **-**

- *Multiplication*: *****

- *Division*: **/**

- *Tangent*: **Tan**

- *Cosine*: **Cos**

- *Sine*: **Sin**

> Conditional Formatting
>
> It is also possible to use conditional statements in a formula such as IF, AND, OR, <, >, =
>
> Here are a few examples:
>
> - if(Depth > 3', 2', 1')
>
> - if(and(Depth > 3', Height = 1'), 2', 1')
>
> - See Revit's *Help* for more info.

Next the *Family* will be loaded into the *Project Environment* to see the formula in action.

5. Open the project file **Box Project**, and then switch to the **3D view**.

6. Press **Ctrl + Tab** until the **Box Family** file is current.

7. Click the **Load into Project** button on the *Ribbon*.

Notice the size of the box changes. When the <u>Depth</u> is now changed, the <u>Width</u> will automatically be updated. This will be tested next.

8. Select one of the boxes and, via its *Type Properties*, change the **Depth** to **6′-0″** and then

    a. Click in an adjacent cell.

    b. Notice the <u>Width</u> instantly updates.

9. Click **OK** to close the dialog and accept the changes.

All three boxes change size: 6′-0″ depth and 3′-0″ width. The height is still an *Instance Parameter* so it remained unchanged.

10. Switch back to the box family.

Next, a brief look at a few variations.

The following revisions will not be saved; the Cancel button will be selected to discard the next two steps.

11. Change the formula for *Width* to simply read **Depth** (see Figure 16-4.4).

FIGURE 16-4.4 Modifying formula to control the width

Thus, it is possible to have one *Parameter* simply equal another one.

12. Click **Cancel** to discard the formula change.

Another way to achieve the results shown in the previous image and steps is to have one *Parameter* control two dimensions. This would reduce the number of *Parameters* from three to two as the *Family* currently stands. The image on the next page (see Figure 16-4.5) shows an example of this. Simply select a previously drawn dimension and then select the desired *Parameter* from the *Label* drop-down list on the *Options Bar*. This is only visible when a dimension is selected.

One *Parameter* could control several dimensions. A *Parameter* has to be of type *Length* (versus *Text, Currency, Volume, Yes/No*, Etc.) to work with a *Dimension*. The *Label* drop-down list will automatically filter the list.

It is best if the dimensions reference the *Reference Planes* rather than the 3D geometry.

FIGURE 16-4.5 One Parameter controlling multiple dimensions

This concludes the brief introduction to adding formulas to a *Family*. The remainder of this exercise will shift gears a bit and look at adding materials to the box family.

Adding a Material:

Adding a *Material* in the *Family* can save time for the design teams using the content when it comes to creating renderings.

    13. Select the 3D extrusion that represents the box in the *Family Editor*.

    14. View the *Properties Palette* dialog box.

Notice, in Figure 16-4.6, that the *Material* is set to *By Category*. This will be changed to something specific to this *Family*.

FIGURE 16-4.6 Instance Parameters for 3D geometry

15. Click in the cell with *<By Category>* to reveal the small link button to the right; see Figure 16-4.6.

16. Click the **link-button** to open the *Materials* dialog.

Notice the *Family* has a limited number of *Materials* loaded; see Figure 16-4.7. The following sequence of steps will show how to create a new *Material* and define it.

FIGURE 16-4.7 Materials for the Box Family, not the Box Project

17. Click the **Create New Material** icon in the lower left corner; see arrow in Figure 16-4.7.

18. Right-click the new *Material* and **Rename** it to **Box Material**; see Figure 16-4.8.

19. Click the **Surface Pattern** preview area (currently set to "none"); see Figure 16-4.9.

TIP: Make sure the Graphics tab *is selected to see the* Surface Pattern *area.*

FIGURE 16-4.8 Naming new material

FIGURE 16-4.9 Setting surface pattern

A new "Model" *Surface Pattern* will be created. A "Model" pattern will not change scale with the *View Scale* in the *Project Environment*; this is meant for real-world items like siding, title, CMU, etc. as seen in elevation. Conversely, the "Drafting" patterns do change scale with the *View Scale* and is meant for representative patterns typically used in sections to imply a certain material.

20. Select **Model** for *Pattern Type* and then follow the steps shown in Figure 16-4.10 to create a new "Model" based *Fill Pattern* named **3″ Tile**.

FIGURE 16-4.10 Creating a new model based surface pattern

21. Click **OK** to close the *Fill Patterns* dialog but not the *Materials* dialogs!

Next you will add an *Appearance* asset so you can control how the material will appear in a rendering.

22. Click to add an **Appearance** asset (Figure 16-4.11).

23. Set the *Render Appearance* to **3in Square - Terra Cotta** (from the *Appearance Library*).

FIGURE 16-4.11 Selecting rendering appearance

24. Click **OK** to close the *Materials* dialog box.

The fill pattern is now visible; see Figure 16-4.12. However, the render appearance is not visible until loaded and rendered in a project. Per steps previously covered in the textbook, load the family into the project and do a rendering in a 3D view.

TIP: When loading a Family, if the project already has a material named "box material" per the above example, the material definition in the project will take precedence if the two are not identical.

25. **Save** the Box *Family*.

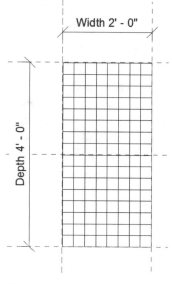

FIGURE 16-4.12 Family Editor

26. Load the updated *Family* into the **Box Project** (*Project* file).

When the newly updated *Family* is loaded into the project, the **Fill Pattern** shows up right away (Figure 16-4.13). The fill pattern can be selected on each face of each box and be rotated and reposition as desired in the *Project Environment*.

FIGURE 16-4.13 Box family in project environment

27. Switch to a 3D or Camera view and create a **rendering** to see the *Render Appearance* material.

    a. Adding a floor below the boxes will allow the shadows to show up as in the image to the right.

28. **Save** the *Project*.

FIGURE 16-4.14 Rendered in project environment

Changing the Material in the Project Environment:

So far, the *Material* for the Box has been "hard wired" within the *Family* and cannot be changed once in the *Project Environment*. In this last set of steps, the techniques required to achieve this goal will be covered.

Just to make things more clear: it is possible to create several 2D shapes in a single *Family*. For example, a door has a solid for the frame, the door panel and a vision panel; see the image to the right (Figure 16-4.15).

Therefore, it would not make sense for Revit to provide one built-in parameter that controls the *Material* for everything in the *Family*.

FIGURE 16-4.15 Door family with multiple materials defined

In the door example, a parameter is created for each *Material* needed in the *Family*. Next, each solid in the *Family* is mapped to one of the three *Parameters*. It is possible for one *Parameter* to control the *Material* of several 3D elements, e.g., a "glass material" *Parameter* controls the *Material* for all seven pieces of glass in Figure 16-4.15.

29. In the Box *Family* click the **Types** button.

30. Click the **Add...** button to make a new *Parameter*.

31. Modify the *Parameter Properties* dialog as shown in Figure 16-4.16.

    a. *Name*: **Finish Material**

    b. *Group*: **Graphics**

    c. *Type*: **Material**

32. Click **OK**.

FIGURE 16-4.16 Creating a new parameter

33. In the *Family Types* dialog, change the "value" for **Finish Material** to **Box Material**. (See Figure 16-4.17.)

FIGURE 16-4.17 Setting material for new parameter

At this point, a new *Parameter* has been created but does not control anything yet. In the next few steps you will map the *Material* for the 3D box to the *Material* parameter just created in the previous steps. After this, the *Family Types* parameter will be the only way to change the *Material* for the box.

34. Click **OK** to close the *Family Types* dialog box.

35. Select the box and then look at the **Properties Palette**.

36. Click the small mapping icon to the far right of the **Material** *Parameter* (see Figure 16-4.18).

FIGURE 16-4.18 Mapping material to parameter

FIGURE 16-4.19 Mapping material to parameter

The *Associate Family Parameter* dialog is now displayed. Revit presents the user with a list of *Parameters* that are of the *Type* "material" (versus text, currency, etc.). At this point, the only option is the *Parameter* just created.

37. Select **Finish Material** from the list and then click **OK** (see Figure 16-4.19).

Now that the *Material* is mapped to a *Parameter*, notice that the mapping icon now has an **equal** sign in it and the rest of the row is grayed out; see Figure 16-4.20. The grayed out *Material* means that the *Family Type Parameter* is now controlling this *Instance Parameter*.

FIGURE 16-4.20 Mapped material

38. **Save** the **Box** *Family* again.

39. **Load** the *Family* into the box Project.

40. Select one of the boxes and view its **Type Parameters**.

41. Notice **Finish Material** is now an option.

42. **Save** the **Box Project** file.

Exercise 16-5:
The Box: Family Types and Categories

This exercise will study *Family Types*. A *Type* is simply the ability to save various parameter settings in a *Family* so they do not need to be entered manually within each Project.

Thus far, in this chapter, a *Family* with just a single *Type* has been created. Any new *Family* automatically has one *Type* if none are specifically created; the *Type* name is the same as the *Family* name once loaded into the *Project Environment*. This exercise will look at how to create several predefined *Types* within the *Family Editor* and how to create additional *Types* on the fly within the *Project Environment*.

Why use Types? Let us say a "Box" manufacturer offers several standard sizes. When creating the *Family* for the "Box," it would be most expedient to create a *Type* for each standard option. This would save the end-user(s) time in more ways than one. If a design firm had trusted custom Revit content, an end-user could load the "Box" *Family* and pick a size from the predefined *Types* knowing that they are real options. Maybe some rarely used or over priced options are intentionally omitted. However, just not having to enter the data manually can be a great benefit.

The reader may wish to turn back to the first exercise in this chapter and review the information initially presented on this topic; see page 16-5.

Finally, the use of **Categories** will be studied. Revit uses *Categories* to control visibility and to determine which command will be used to place a *Family* (e.g., Door tool, Window tool, Mechanical Equipment tool, Component tool).

1. **Open** the *Family* named **Box**.

2. Click the **Types** button on the *Ribbon*.

Notice, in Figure 16-5.1, that the *Name* drop-down at the top is blank. Clicking the *New* button on the right allows one or more named *Types* to be created.

Once *Types* exist, all the *Parameter* **Values** below relate specifically to the selected named *Type*.

FIGURE 16-5.1 Family Types – no types created yet

Next, four *Types* will be created in the <u>Box</u> *Family*. Each *Type* will have a different <u>Depth</u> assigned to it.

3. In the *Family Types* dialog, click the **New...** button.

4. Enter **2'-0" x 4'-0"** for the name of the first *Type* (Figure 16-5.2).

FIGURE 16-5.2 Naming the family type

Type names should be descriptive and not duplicate any part of the *Family* name (i.e., the name of the file on the hard drive). In this example the exact size will be used as the *Type* name. In other cases it might be more useful to list the model number or some other descriptive wording.

5. Click **OK**.

Now one *Type* exists in the *Name* drop-down list. Note that the *Type* name matches the values below; this was intentional. However, it should be stated that the name and values could be inconsistent. The name has no direct control over any of the *Parameter* values, i.e., the

FIGURE 16-5.3 Named family type

name 2'-0" x 4'-0" does not automatically make the <u>Depth</u> and <u>Width</u> *Values* match. Thus, the person creating the *Family* needs to do some QA (quality assurance) checking. This will be made clear in the next few steps.

6. Click the **New...** button again.

7. Enter the name **3'-0" x 6'-0"**.

   a. Remember, because of the formula added in the previous exercise, the <u>Width</u> is always half the <u>Depth</u>.

The **Box** *Family* now has two *Types* created; each can be easily selected within the *Project Environment*.

Revit is now managing two complete lists of *Parameters*: one for each *Type*. As will be proven momentarily, the *Values* (i.e., Width and Depth) can vary from one list to the other.

As seen in Figure 16-5.4, the new *Type* did not change the *Parameter Values* below. Next this will be changed.

FIGURE 16-5.4 Second named family type

8. With the *Type* 3'-0" x 6'-0" current, change the Depth to **6'-0"**.

FIGURE 16-5.5A First type settings

FIGURE 16-5.5B Second type settings

9. Using the *Name* drop-down list, switch back and forth between the two options; notice the *Parameter Values* change (Figures 16-5.5A and B).

10. Create two more *Types* per the information below:
    a. *Name*: **4'-0" x 8'-0"**   **5'-6" x 11'-0"**
    b. *Depth*: **8'-0"**   **11'-0"**

Now that several *Types* have been defined in the **Box** *Family* it will be loaded into the *Project Environment* to see how they work.

11. **Open** the **Box Project** file, if not already open.

12. In the <u>Box</u> *Family* file, click the **Load into Project** button.

13. Select **Overwrite the existing version**.

14. Select the **Component** tool from the *Architecture* tab on the *Ribbon*.

15. Select the **Type Selector** (Figure 16-5.6).

FIGURE 16-5.6 *Type Selector* in the project environment

Looking at Figure 16-5.6, notice all the *Types* created in the *Family Editor* are now available under the *Family* name **Box**. A *Type* named **Box** is also listed because the *Family* was previously loaded without any specific *Types* created; and as mentioned previously, when no *Types* exist Revit will create one with the same name as the *Family*. This can be deleted for renamed in the *Project Browser*, within the *Families* section.

Selecting a Category

Selecting a *Category* is actually one of the first things typically done when starting a new *Family*. However, this change was left until now to make it perfectly clear what this setting does.

NOTE: Some Family *templates will already have the correct* Category *selected (e.g., door, window, casework templates). However, the* **Box** Family *was started with the* **Generic Model** *template, so the* Category *needs to be set manually as this template can be used for many things.*

16. **Open** the **Box** *Family* (if not already open).

17. On the *Create* tab, click **Category and Parameters**.

This list represents all the *Categories* used by Revit to control visibility and determine which tool inserts any given *Family*. *Categories* are also used by *Filters* and for scheduling. This list is "hard wired" and cannot be modified in any way.

This list is for Revit Architecture; the initial list is different for each flavor of Revit. However, clicking the "Show categories from all disciplines" option will show the same list in all three flavors of Revit.

At this point we will pretend that our **Box** *Family* is *Furniture*. Once set to be "furniture," the **Box** will show up in the *Furniture* schedule(s) and be visible (or not visible) based on the visibility and filter settings for any given view.

18. Click **Furniture** and then click **OK**.

FIGURE 16-5.7 Family Category and Parameters dialog

TIP:

The **Furniture** *category is generally for freestanding items that are not fastened to the building. Examples might be chairs, tables, desks, beds, etc.*

*The **Furniture Systems** category is for modular desks, often called cubicles. These can be fastened to the wall and/or have power and data hardwired to them. Thus they are different enough from regular furniture to warrant a separate section.*

19. **Save** the **Box** *Family*.

Next the modified *Family* will be loaded into the project and tested.

20. Load the *Family* into the **Box Project** file per steps previously covered.

21. In the **Box Project**, switch to the default **3D view**.

The next few steps will show how the visibility of the furniture category now affects the <u>Box</u> family.

22. Type **VV** to control visibility settings for the current view.

23. Uncheck *Furniture* on the *Model Categories* tab (Figure 16-5.8).

Notice there is a category for "Generic Models" as well. This would have allowed control of the **Box** *Family* previously. However, this category should be used sparingly due to its ambiguity.

24. Click **OK**.

The three boxes should have been hidden from the 3D view. They should still be visible in other views as long as the view's *Visibility Graphics Override* dialog did not have the *Furniture Category* turned off.

25. Per the previous steps, **turn the Furniture Category back on** in the *3D view*.

26. **Save** the **Box Project** file.

FIGURE 16-5.8 VISIBILITY control in the project

Revit does not have a specific *Furniture* tool on the *Ribbon* so new instances of the **Box** *Family* would still be placed using the *Component* tool.

Care should be taken to select the correct *Category* for Revit *Families*. If someone is in a hurry they may hastily select a wrong *Category* which could have a huge negative impact on a project in terms of budget and completion time.

For example, a "smart board" for a classroom might be placed on the *Furniture Category* when it should have been placed on *Electrical Equipment*. Near the end of the project the design team decides to turn off all the *Furniture* for the construction documents set, as it was laid out for design only and is not part of the bid set. Now, the final set is missing all of the "smart boards" in the floor plans, ceiling plans and interior elevations.

Much more could be said and taught about *Family* creation but is beyond the introductory scope of this text.

Smart board family with materials

Self-Exam:

The following questions can be used as a way to check your knowledge of this lesson. The answers can be found at the bottom of this page.

1. *Loadable Families* can be imported into a project as needed. (T/F)

2. How a *Family* is named is not important. (T/F)

3. The <u>sill height</u> of a window is usually an *Instance* parameter. (T/F)

4. Use the _____ tool to create the framework for a new *Family*.

5. The solid tool, used in this chapter, to create the 3D box: _____.

Review Questions:

The following questions may be assigned by your instructor as a way to assess your knowledge of this section. Your instructor has the answers to the review questions.

1. The 3D box, drawn in this chapter, was aligned and then locked to the reference planes as part of the process of creating parametric content. (T/F)

2. *Loadable Families* are typically preferred over in-place *Families*. (T/F)

3. A <u>family name</u> and a *Family's* <u>type name(s)</u> should not have redundant information. (T/F)

4. It is possible to specify if a parameter is an <u>instance</u> or <u>type</u> while in the process of creating it. (T/F)

5. When the geometry changes, a new *Family* is typically required, rather than being able to use named *Types*. (T/F)

6. The tool used to get a completed family into a project (while in the family editor environment): _____.

7. Of the two types of *Fill Patterns*, only the _____ type patterns do not change size when the view scale changes.

8. A *Family's* _____ setting controls/determines its visibility and which tool is used to place the item in the project environment.

9. When a *Parameter* is associated to one or more dimensions, the *Parameter's* value controls the length of the dimension (and object being dimensioned). (T/F)

10. It is not possible to make one parameter to always be one half the size of another. (T/F)

INDEX

A

Activate View — 14-5
Align — 5-11, 5-26, 10-7, 16-23
Annotation — 2-11, 8-36
Appears in Drawing List (sheet index) — 14-12
Application Menu — 1-12
Arc, Detail Lines — 4-18, 4-25
Array — 4-27, 5-53
Attach — 7-15

B

Bath Room — 11-1
Browser Organization — 14-8
Bulkhead — 8-24

C

Cabinets — 11-2, 11-7
Callout — 10-15
Camera — 13-15, 13-35
Camera; Eye Elevation — 13-38
Ceiling height — 8-17
Ceiling Properties — 8-23
Ceiling tool — 8-17
Ceiling; Bulkhead — 8-24
Ceiling; Deleting — 8-21
Chain (option) — 5-9
Circle (detail line) — 3-13
Close Revit project — 1-29
Component — 8-31, 9-13, 11-20
Component, Load — 10-29
Conditional Formatting — 16-48
Context Menu — 1-21
Contextual Tab — 1-15
Control Arrows — 7-7
Copy — 3-26
Copy to Clipboard — 4-23, 6-7, 6-20, 8-11
Counter Top — 11-3, 11-8
Crop Region — 9-5, 11-18, 13-17, 13-36
Crossing Window — 3-21

D

Deactivate View — 14-5
Default 3D View — 1-35, 5-21
Delete — 3-20

Design Options — 9-25, 14-9
Detach from Central — 15-16
Detail Components — 10-29
Detail Level (view) — 5-19, 7-1, 10-3
Detail Lines — 3-3, 3-10, 3-11, 3-18, 4-13
Dimension tool — 2-14, 3-6, 6-35, 6-38
Dimensions; Activate — 7-31
Dimensions; Locking — 3-8, 5-13
Dimensions; Masonry — 5-11, 5-24, 5-36
Dimensions; Suffix — 10-25
Dimensions; Witness Line — 5-27
Dimension Snaps — 3-16
Door Tag — 5-41, 12-4
Door tool — 2-5, 5-35, 6-10
Door; Load Family — 5-37
Door; Properties — 5-42
Door Schedule — 12-6
Drafting View — 3-3, 4-2, 4-4
Drop-down Button — 1-12
3D DWF — 14-15

E

Element Properties — 5-48
Elevation — 1-7, 9-1, 9-16, 11-4, 11-13
Ellipse — 4-21
Export Image — 13-36, 13-39
Extrusion — 16-21

F

Families — 16-1
Family Types — 16-5, 16-59
Far Clip Plane — 9-5, 10-2
Fillet Arc — 4-14
Fill Pattern, New — 16-53
Filter — 5-19, 6-19
Fireplace — 5-54
Flip Symbol (element control) — 5-20, 5-42
Floor tool — 8-1
Furniture — 11-20
Footing, Continuous — 10-10
Formula — 16-45

H

Hide / Isolate   6-13, 11-22

J

Join Geometry   6-9
Join/Unjoin Roof   7-27, 7-28

K

Kitchen Layout   11-7

L

Length (entering)   4-3, 9-15
Level   1-5, 6-34, 7-19
Light Fixture   8-31, 8-35
Linework   10-13, 11-16
Load Family   5-36
Local File   15-13, 15-39

M

Materials   8-15, 8-22, 16-50
Measure   2-4
Mirror   4-26
Modify   3-5
Move   3-26, 4-5, 4-9, 4-23,
                        5-20

N

New (project)   1-30, 5-2

O

Offset   4-15
Open   1-25
Open Documents   1-28
Openings   5-45, 10-8
Options bar   1-11, 1-19

P

Parameter, Material   16-56
Parameter, New   16-31
Paste Aligned   6-7, 6-20
Phase Created/Demo   25-2, 15-28
Phasing Dialog   15-1, 15-26
Phase Filter   15-3
Print   2-15, 14-17
Project Browser   1-20, 5-4, 5-38
Project Browser   5-52, 14-8
   Organization
Project Information   5-5

Q

Quick Access Toolbar   1-11, 1-13

R

Railing (guardrail)   11-25, 11-29
Raster Images   14-14
Rectangle (dtl. line)   3-12
Redo   3-5
Reference Plane   1-5, 16-15
Rendering   13-25
Rendering material   13-18, 13-32
Rendering;   13-42
   RPC People
Repeating Detail   10-34
Ribbon   1-11, 1-13 ~ 1-18
Roof tool   2-9, 7-1
Roof; Flat   7-9
Roof; Gable   7-4, 7-11, 7-21
Roof; Hip   7-3, 7-28
Roof; Join/Unjoin   7-27, 7-28
Roof; Shed   7-6
Room Schedule   12-10
Room Tag   12-1
Room Tag; Properties   12-13
Rotate   3-26, 8-20

S

Save   1-29
Schedule/Quantities   1-9, 12-6, 12-10
Scale   3-30, 4-22
Scroll Wheel   1-36
Section   10-1
Section Box   13-28
Section; Far Clip Plane 9-4
Selection Window   3-22
Shadows   13-30
Sheet   5-6, 14-1
Sheet Index   14-10
Show the Model   13-39
Skylight   7-30
Sketchy Lines   13-45
Snap   2-8, 3-15
Solid Form   9-35
Split (wall)   5-29
Split Button (UI)   1-12
Stair   6-22
Stair Width   6-26
Status bar   1-11, 1-20, 5-11
Sun Path   13-42
Sun Settings   13-20, 13-30
Surface Pattern   8-22

Sweeps   5-32
Synchronize with   15-15
  Central

T
TAB key   2-8, 8-12
Tag all   12-4
Template   1-31, 5-2
Text Properties   8-38
Text Tool   2-11, 3-34, 8-36,
                                   8-37, 10-25
Titleblock   14-1
Trim   5-29
Type Catalog   16-7
Type Parameters   5-42
Type Selector   1-11, 1-19, 5-3

U
Underlay   6-1, 6-15
Undo   3-5
User Interface   1-11
Username   15-14, 15-35

V
View Control Bar   1-11, 1-21
View Range   5-51
View Scale   2-12, 6-9, 9-7, 9-21,
                                   10-16
Viewport   14-3
Visibility Graphics   8-5, 11-22, 15-20
  Overrides

W
Wall; Footing   10-10
Wall Height   5-22, 6-3
Wall tool   2-2, 5-4, 5-8, 5-14,
                                   5-23, 6-15
Wall tool; Base   8-25
  Offset
Wall tool; Chain   5-9
Wall tool; Edit   5-16, 5-31
  Assembly
Web Library   5-38, 5-54
Window; Duplicate   5-50
Window tool   5-46, 6-12
Window; Properties   5-49
Window; Sill Height   5-48
Worksets   15-17
Worksets Dialog   15-12, 15-19
Worksharing   15-10, 15-36

Z
Zoom   1-33

Sections *Sample image from page 14-7*

Renderings *Sample image from page 13-43*

3D Views *Sample image from page 13-29*

Interior Elevations *Sample image from page 9-23*